IMPERIALISM REVISITED

STUDIES IN MILITARY AND STRATEGIC HISTORY

General Editor: Michael Dockrill, Reader in War Studies, King's College, London

Published titles include:

Nigel John Ashton
EISENHOWER, MACMILLAN AND THE PROBLEM OF NASSER:
Anglo-American Relations and Arab Nationalism, 1955–59

G. H. Bennett
BRITISH FOREIGN POLICY DURING THE CURZON PERIOD,
1919–24

David A. Charters
THE BRITISH ARMY AND JEWISH INSURGENCY IN PALESTINE,
1945–47

Paul Cornish
BRITISH MILITARY PLANNING FOR THE DEFENCE OF
GERMANY, 1945–50

Robert Frazier
ANGLO-AMERICAN RELATIONS WITH GREECE: The Coming of
the Cold War, 1942–47

Brian Holden Reid
J. F. C. FULLER: Military Thinker

Stewart Lone
JAPAN'S FIRST MODERN WAR: Army and Society in the Conflict
with China, 1894–95

Thomas R. Mockaitis
BRITISH COUNTERINSURGENCY, 1919–60

Roger Woodhouse
BRITISH POLICY TOWARDS FRANCE, 1945–51

Studies in Military and Strategic History
Series Standing Order ISBN 0–333–71046–0
(outside North America only)

You can receive future titles in this series as they are published by placing a standing order. Please contact your bookseller or, in case of difficulty, write to us at the address below with your name and address, the title of the series and the ISBN quoted above.

Customer Services Department, Macmillan Distribution Ltd
Houndmills, Basingstoke, Hampshire RG21 6XS, England

Imperialism Revisited

Political and Economic Relations between Britain and China, 1950–54

David Clayton
Lecturer in Economic History
University of York

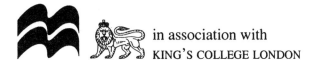

in association with
KING'S COLLEGE LONDON

First published in Great Britain 1997 by
MACMILLAN PRESS LTD
Houndmills, Basingstoke, Hampshire RG21 6XS and London
Companies and representatives throughout the world

A catalogue record for this book is available from the British Library.

ISBN 0–333–64344–5

First published in the United States of America 1997 by
ST. MARTIN'S PRESS, INC.,
Scholarly and Reference Division,
175 Fifth Avenue, New York, N.Y. 10010

ISBN 0–312–17320–2

Library of Congress Cataloging-in-Publication Data
Clayton, David, 1969–
Imperialism revisited: political and economic relations between
Britain and China, 1950–54 / David Clayton.
p.   cm.   (Studies in military and strategic history)
Includes bibliographical references.
ISBN 0–312–17320–2 (cloth)
1. China—Foreign relations—Great Britain.   2. Great Britain–
–Foreign relations—China.   3. China—Foreign relations—1949–1976.
4. Great Britain—Foreign relations—1945–   5. China—Foreign
economic relations—Great Britain.   6. Great Britain—Foreign
economic relations—China.   I. Title.   II. Series.
DS740.5.G7C53 1997   96–49262
                                                                CIP

This book is printed on paper suitable for recycling and made from fully managed and
sustained forest sources.

10   9   8   7   6   5   4   3   2   1
06   05   04   03   02   01   00   99   98   97

Printed in Great Britain by
The Ipswich Book Company Ltd
Ipswich, Suffolk

Contents

List of Tables

Acknowledgements

The bulk of the research for this book was undertaken for a PhD thesis at the University of Manchester, which was funded by the British Academy. I would like to thank Dr Peter Lowe for his guidance, advice and encouragement. A special word of thanks to Peter for striking the perfect balance, being both enthusiastic and patient. I would also like to thank colleagues and peers with whom I have discussed my research in the Department of History at the University of Manchester, and in the Department of Economics and Related Studies at the University of York. The environments they have created and questions they have posed were and continue to be of great stimulation. I should also like to acknowledge the help offered by librarians and archivists in the various libraries, archives and research centres visited. My special appreciation to the staff of the Public Record Office, Kew and John Rylands University Library, Manchester. Further thanks to those who have aided my research at the School of African and Oriental Studies, the London School of Economics, the Institute of Historical Research, the Labour Party Archives, the Central Reference Library, Manchester and the J.B. Morrell University Library, York.

The assistance, advice and release provided by family and friends has been essential throughout. I am indebted to numerous people for their comments on various chapters, most notably Jenny Clayton, Mick Nevin, Norris Nash and Lauren. In the end, I am responsible for all errors and omissions in this work.

Throughout my life, my parents have offered encouragement and never questioned the path I have taken; I thus dedicate the book to them.

List of Abbreviations

ABBREVIATIONS USED IN TEXT

BAT	British-American Tobacco Company
CAAC	Civil Aviation Administration of China
CAT	Civil Air Transport
CATC	Central Air Transportation Corporation
CCP	Chinese Communist Party
CHINCOM	China Co-ordinating Committee
CNAC	Chinese Nationalist Aviation Corporation
COCOM	Co-ordinating Committee of the Paris Consultative Group of nations working to control export of strategic goods to communist countries.
CPG	Chinese People's Government
DPRK	Democratic People's Republic of Korea (North)
ECAFE	Economic Commission for Asia and the Far East (UN)
ECOSOC	Economic and Social Council (UN)
FBI	Federation of British Industries
FTU	Federation of Trade Unions (Hong Kong)
GATT	General Agreement on Tariffs and Trade
ICI	Imperial Chemical Industries
IMF	International Monetary Fund
KMT	Kuomintang (Chinese Nationalists)
MAAG	Military Assistance Advisory Group (US)
NSC	National Security Council
PLA	People's Liberation Army
PRC	People's Republic of China
ROK	Republic of Korea
SCAP	Supreme Commander for Allied Powers in Japan
TUC	Trade Union Congress
UNICEF	United Nations International Children's Emergency Fund

ABBREVIATIONS USED IN SOURCES

BDCC	British Defence Co-ordination Committee
BT	Board of Trade Records

CAB	Cabinet Office Records
CCFELF	Commander in Chief Far East Land Forces (British)
CHAS	China Association Papers
CO	Colonial Office Records
CPGB	Communist Party of Great Britain
DBPO	*Documents of British Policy Overseas*
DDRS	Declassified Documents Series (US)
Defe	British Chiefs of Staff/Joint Planning Staff Records
DO	Defence Committee of the Cabinet Records
FO	Foreign Office Records
FRUS	*Foreign Relations of the US*
IRD	Information Research Department, Foreign Office
JCS	Joint Chiefs of Staff
LPA	Labour Party Archives
LPPCC	Labour Party Press Cuttings Collection
MoD	Ministry of Defence
MoT	Ministry of Transport (& Civil Aviation)
NEC	National Executive Committee, Labour Party
NIE	National Intelligence Estimate
PREM	British Prime Minister's Office Records
UKHC	United Kingdom High Commissioner

Introduction

The worst sin towards our fellow creatures is not to hate them, but to be indifferent to them; that's the essence of inhumanity.

George Bernard Shaw, *The Devil's Disciple*, II

ORIENTATION

In the early 1950s China's relationship with the West changed profoundly. China became 'divided' between the Chinese communist-controlled mainland and the Chinese Nationalist-controlled Taiwan. China adopted a communist economic system which altered the relationship between China and the world economy. Between November 1950 and July 1953, China and the West were at war in Korea. At the bilateral level of Sino-British relations, changes were dramatic but also full of interesting contradictions and paradoxes: Britain and China did not enter into full, formal political relations during this period; Sino-British trade rose, collapsed and then rose again; British foreign direct investments in China were not nationalised or expropriated but their position became commercially untenable; Hong Kong survived as a British imperial enclave in a communist country. The aim of this book is straightforward: to explain these changes in international relations.

The orientation of the book will be Anglocentric and will thus have two main threads: to explore the nature of British government policy towards China and to assess why the British state adopted such a policy. But the book will also have a multinational dimension. As we shall see, in order fully to explain developments in the period, the dynamics of Sino-British-American-Russian relations have to be explored. The study will treat the nation-state as the dominant agent shaping international relations in the period, but will also attempt to discover the social, economic and political roots of British, Chinese and American government policy.

The book is primarily based on material in British government and business archives; but also uses translated and published Chinese government records, Chinese press articles, and published American government material. I am also heavily indebted to the work of other scholars in the field.

HISTORIOGRAPHICAL FRAMEWORK

This work fits into the wider historiography in three main ways.

Firstly, it is part of a body of work that places imperialism back in a central position in history.[1] As we shall see, the British government pursued a liberal policy towards China. Both Labour and Conservative governments wanted to establish diplomatic relations with China, to integrate China into the world community and secure China's admission to the UN. This policy sprang from a desire to maintain British imperial interests in Asia. The key propositions that the book will explore are thus: why did Britain want to hold on to empire and what impact did this have on British policy towards China? Did the British state want an empire because territory abroad meant a global role for Britain and thus 'influence' for British policy-makers? Or was it because an empire was perceived as important for commercial and industrial classes and hence for the British economy?

The book draws on the recent work by P.J. Cain and A.G. Hopkins, which argues that the British empire was brought about and maintained by a complex, symbiotic relationship between the British state and commercial rather than industrial elites, a relationship which operated at social, economic and political levels. Cain and Hopkins argue that financial not industrial capital came to define the national interest, and that by the post-war period the mercantile part of the national economy, epitomised by and based in the City of London, was perceived to be economically important because it generated invisible earnings on foreign investments.[2] It is argued that this part of the economy could not survive without British overseas empire and hence underpinned its retention in the post-1945 period. There is not the room to develop the interconnections between the City, the establishment, merchants and the state within the confines of this work, nor fully to speculate whether this was a rational economic strategy for the British economy to follow.[3] However, Sino-British relations are interesting because they allow us to study how this relationship between British mercantile interests and British Labour and Conservative governments worked; and to assess to what extent it shaped government policy towards China. Individual business archives have not been examined due to the problems accessing such disparate, vast and private records, but the records of the China Association provide a very useful source for this study. The organisation, founded in 1889, represented British industrial concerns including Shell Petroleum Co., British and American Tobacco Co. Ltd, Imperial Chemical Industries, and commercial concerns such as Jardine Matheson and Co. Ltd, Butterfield and Swire, Wheelock Marden and Co. Ltd, Alfred Holt and Co., the Hong Kong and Shanghai Banking Corporation and the Chartered Bank of India, Australia and China.

Secondly, the book takes inspiration from, and at times issue with, a vast literature exploring how Britain adapted its global role to an increasingly powerful and, some would argue, economically and politically hegemonic American state. In this sense, British policy towards China in the early 1950s is an extremely interesting case study because British and American policies differed on this issue more than on any other. In comparison to a British policy which sought to integrate China economically and politically into the world community of trading nations, American policy towards China increasingly sought to prevent China's admission to the UN, to encircle China militarily, and to curtail world trade with the People's Republic of China (PRC). This study will examine how and why British governments adjusted policy in the face of American pressure. By using this case study it will be possible to assess what degree of autonomy the British government really enjoyed over foreign policy and what influence it was able to enact on the American foreign policy decision-making process. In addition, a comparison of these different British and American policies towards China will allow more forthright conclusions to be drawn on what factors influenced the policy-making process in Britain. It will become increasingly clear that to explain why Britain and America adopted and stood by these different policies towards China, we must come back to two related influences: to the issue of imperialism and to the different social and political forces in the US and in Britain influencing the policy-making process.

Thirdly, this book fits into a vast literature on the complex relationship between capitalist and communist states, and on the origins of the cold war. It will draw heavily on the works of authors on American-Chinese relations, including Nancy Bernkopf Tucker, Gordan Chang, Warren Cohen and John Gaddis. It will also embrace the extensive range of opinions on the origins of the Korean War held by Bruce Cumings, Rosemary Foot, Chen Jian, Sergei Goncharov, John Lewis, Xue Litai, William Stueck, Peter Lowe and Michael Dockrill. The work takes a lead from the books by Robert Boardman and Brian Porter, who studied Sino-British relations without access to official government records. It responds to recent studies by James Tang, Wenguang Shao and Qiang Zhai, who used British, American and Chinese government and business records to explore the state of economic and political relations between Britain and China in the period 1950–54.[4] It also draws on the articles and books by Ritchie Ovendale, David Wolf and Zhong-ping Feng, which assessed British recognition of the PRC.[5] It is here we begin this study.

A LIBERAL POLICY FORMULATED

Initiated in December 1948 as an attempt to maintain an economic and diplomatic 'foot in the door', British policy towards China was discussed during 1949 and culminated in October with a decision to recognise the PRC.[6] This British policy was a break from a previous one which, during the early years of the Chinese Civil War, espoused the values of non-intervention.[7] British recognition of Communist China was based on legal principles; the Chinese communists had established the PRC in October 1949 and controlled the majority of the Chinese mainland. Nevertheless, the decision cannot be seen simply as a legal nuance 'to secure a convenience', but instead must be viewed as the outward expression of a coherent British government policy, which sought political and economic relations with China.[8] It was underpinned by two ultimately mistaken assumptions: that the Truman administration in the US would follow a similar policy to deal with the threat posed by the emergence of a unified and communist Chinese state; and that the Chinese People's Government (CPG) would reciprocate on Britain's offer of relations. We will turn to both of these key notions during Chapter 1.

The British government justified its thinking on China in geo-strategic terms. The government believed diplomatic and economic relations with the West and membership of the UN would integrate China into the world system, undermining its inclination towards isolationism and reducing the PRC's reliance on diplomatic and economic contact with the Soviet Union.[9] The Foreign Office argued that the Soviets would not be able to resist extending their influence in China, especially in territories where they shared a common border such as Manchuria, Outer Mongolia and Sinkiang. Moreover, it was argued that the Soviet Union could not provide sufficient economic support to underpin Chinese economic reconstruction. A moderate internationalist approach, therefore, might preclude China's complete reliance on the Soviet Union and, in the event of a Sino-Soviet schism, allow the Chinese communists to turn to the West. Ernest Bevin, the British Foreign Secretary, wanted recognition because otherwise 'the existing tendency of the

Communist government to look to the Soviet Union' might have increased.[10] If Sino-Soviet tensions could be increased, the Foreign Office believed that Soviet political and military resources would be diverted from Europe. However, this geo-strategic reasoning was more a way of legitimising British policy – both externally to the Americans and internally in Whitehall – than an explanation of why Britain adopted the policy in the first place. As will become clear over the course of this book, the US had a radically different approach for achieving a similar geo-strategic end: it attempted to isolate China economically and politically in order to increase tensions between China and the Soviet Union. These radically different policies did not emerge because Britain and the US came to different conclusions on the nature of the Sino-Soviet alliance, but arose instead because Britain and America had different imperial concerns and different domestic political environments. We shall study the formation of US policy towards China in more depth in Chapter 1.

An interesting influence on the British decision to recognise the PRC was Britain's relationship with the Asian Commonwealth. Asian opinion, and especially the Indian Prime Minister Jawaharlal Nehru, pressed strongly for the early recognition of Communist China, arguing that the Chinese revolution embodied the resurgence of Asian nationalism. The Labour government did not want to be out of step with the Indians or bring into doubt its claim, heart felt by many in the Labour Party, that it was in touch with and sympathetic to the forces of nationalism in Asia. Clement Attlee, the Labour Prime Minister, was conscious of the need for close bonds with India. The cultivation of these ties, however, was not only a humanitarian gesture, but rather a way of maintaining British political and economic influence in the Far East.[11] The Asian Commonwealth was thought to be a stable bridge between the West and Asia, a bulwark against communism in the Far East and a way of legitimising and maintaining Britain's economic interests in the area.

British policy towards China was also influenced by a political consensus within the country. The left-wing of the Labour Party wanted a progressive foreign policy in the Far East, which did not intensify the cold war by polarising differences between the Chinese communists and the West. There were some on the right of the Conservative Party, notably Lord Salisbury, who opposed recognition, but the Conservative leadership, including Anthony Eden and Winston Churchill, argued that it was legally justifiable. Neither left nor right wanted Britain to retreat from the Far East; nor did they wish to relinquish trading possibilities with China by refusing to recognise the communists. The British press, divided over the nature of Chinese communism, generally supported accommodation with the PRC and was hopeful about prospects for trade with the new regime.[12]

It was economic considerations, however, which determined British policy-making on recognition. China had long been perceived by British governments and by British businessmen as a vast market for British exporters, and the potential of the China market continued to influence the decision-making process.[13] In 1949 Bevin informed the cabinet that if Britain did not recognise the PRC it might force the Chinese communists to 'tighten their belts and do without Western economic assistance'.[14] This line originated from and was supported by the Board of Trade. In 1947 the Board of Trade argued that 'since it is perfectly obvious that the developed markets of America, Western Europe, etc., cannot absorb a large increase in imports from the US as well as from our competitors, we must look seriously at the large underdeveloped markets, of which China is an obvious example'. It argued that British trade with China, estimated at 0.8 per cent of total British trade in 1946, was 'not an adequate amount of business for us to be transacting with one quarter of the earth's inhabitants'.[15] It is worth noting that the corresponding figures for 1913, 1922 and 1936 were 2.36 per cent, 2.8 per cent and 1.27 per cent. Moreover, in the 1940s the Board of Trade argued that China remained a useful source of imports because it lay outside the dollar area, and hence would help to alleviate one of the key structural problems facing the British economy in the post-war period: its shortage of dollars. But, as Chapter 7 will explore, the economic rationale for developing trade with China in the 1950s was not strong. There were other non-dollar areas of supply for most of the goods which China produced, such as tea, soya beans, rice, eggs and bristles, and these were more fully integrated into multilateral world payments systems. The Sterling Area, which included most British colonies including Malaya and Hong Kong, dominion territories such as Australia, Canada and South Africa, and parts of the Commonwealth including India, was Britain's most important source of such imports. Moreover, China was not an attractive market in terms of Britain's external balance of payments. In reality, British manufacturing goods had to go to the US to earn dollars, and then to the Sterling Area, both to alleviate the huge deficits that Britain had run up during the war and to ensure that Britain had a reliable and convenient source of raw materials.

Doubts about the macro-economic worth of trade with China were not articulated by the government in the late 1940s for two reasons: because British business interests wanted to trade with China and maintain overseas investments in China and Hong Kong; and because the British government wanted to retain imperial possessions in the Far East.[16]

Business pressure came from a diverse range of sources. Firstly from British manufacturing firms with markets in China and the Far East. They still believed that China would be a vast potential market and that Britain had to exploit any possible opportunities for trade, especially as the Chinese would hardly welcome Japanese goods after the barbarous nature of Japanese rule in China in 1937–45. In 1950, for example, the Manchester Chamber of Commerce advocated a positive policy towards Britain's investment in China:

> If they are to survive, no time should be lost in giving at least *de facto* recognition to the new regime in China. It is there to stay and reports indicate that there is a welcome freedom from corruption which its predecessor could not claim. If we free the channels of trade and commerce with the Western democracies, we may prevent the lowering of another iron curtain in the Far East.[17]

Secondly, and more significantly, it came from the China Association. In 1949 the China Association was uncertain about the exact nature of Chinese communist policy towards foreign investments in China. It accepted that the CPG would determine how trade was conducted and that it would want to submit businesses to government control; it was acknowledged that 'if the Communists think foreign trade and intercourse will endanger the control of their powers they will do without it'. Nevertheless, the Association believed that the needs of economic reconstruction and development would persuade the Chinese communists to adopt a moderate stand on foreign business. It also argued that Chinese businessmen would resist government control because 'the profit motive and the family system are practically the only forces which count in the economy of the country'.[18] British businessmen in China viewed communist economic policy as an extension of Kuomintang attempts to control the Chinese economy and not as an attempt to introduce a new economic system where there would be no place for British foreign direct investment.

What will also become evident during the course of this study is that the British government was more responsive to certain sectors of the business lobby. Firms based in Britain articulated their demands through Chambers of Commerce and via their local MPs in Parliament, while the China Association, based in London and with close social ties to the establishment, had the direct ear of ministers. Consequently, business pressure influenced government in a number of ways. Firstly it had a political dimension. Had Britain not recognised China, business concerns would have criticised the government for abandoning British interests. The loss of such economic assets may also have been exploited by opposition parties in Parliament and may have been poorly received by the British public. Anthony Eden, the shadow Foreign Secretary, argued in the House of Commons that:

> Our commercial interests in China are of immense importance, not only to this country, but let it be recalled in China too. They exceed those of any other foreign country and we are frankly concerned about them ... it will advantage no one – not these firms, not anyone else – to embark on a policy of appeasement which, as our own bitter experience has shown in so many parts of the world, can be so ruthlessly exploited at our expense.[19]

Secondly, however, it had an economic dimension. In 1949 British investments in China were estimated at £110–300 million and those in Hong Kong at £150 million.[20] The government did not want British businesses to lose their vast investments in China and Hong Kong. By the late 1940s, the Foreign Office doubted whether British businessmen could hold on to financial assets in a communist state; it did not believe the PRC could reconcile the existence of a resident foreign business community with communist ideology.[21] However, the government did not want such assets automatically relinquished because it would set a bad precedent for other vulnerable British interests across the globe, notably in the Middle East, and might also be a warning sign to future investors. But more importantly, the government argued that British businessmen might be able to continue in the short to medium term because the Chinese economy required trade with the West and hence would have to rely initially on the resident foreign merchants operating in China and Hong Kong. This might give British merchants a foothold in the market, which might have outlasted any expropriation of British assets on the mainland. In October 1949 Bevin informed his cabinet colleagues that: They have trade to offer and we have an immovable stake in their territory which can only be maintained by trade.'[22]

Most significantly, the formulation of British policy towards China had an imperial dimension. The decision by the British government to retain imperial possessions in Singapore, Malaya, and more especially in Hong Kong, lay at the heart of British policy towards China. The British government wanted an empire in the Far East because it was perceived to be important for maintaining Britain's Great Power status and was thought to be valuable for the British economy; these territories generated invisible earnings, were markets for British exporters, a source of raw materials, and, as part of the Sterling Area, supported the pound.[23] British trade with Hong Kong was increasing in the 1940s; in 1949 exports to the colony had reached 1.5 per cent of total British exports, while imports from Hong Kong were 0.5 per cent of total British imports.[24] As Britain did not want to withdraw from the Far East and did not have the resources to resist a resurgent and expansionist China, it had to adopt a moderate line with the Chinese communist regime. A strategy which tried to isolate and encircle China militarily would antagonise the PRC, causing it to undermine Britain's position in Asia. Equally, trade with China was important for the Malayan economy, and, by indicating that Britain was willing to accept Chinese nationalism, recognition would help the colonial authorities improve their relationship with the large Chinese communities in Malaya and Singapore.[25] Ultimately, however, it was the retention of Hong Kong which shaped British government thinking on policy towards China. The British government's determination to retain Hong Kong necessitated political contact with China; a crown colony on the Chinese mainland was not defensible against a Chinese communist assault and hence Britain needed to pacify China by establishing political relations.[26] Moreover, Hong Kong made British trade with China viable in the longer term; Hong Kong gave British business a more secure base in the Far East and, because Hong Kong ran a budget deficit with China, gave the Chinese communists the foreign exchange to buy British exports.[27] It was thus over the issue of Hong Kong that the interests of British mercantile firms and the British government coincided.

We shall explore the retention of Hong Kong in more detail in Chapter 5, but first we shall examine how the British government reconciled policy towards China with a number of dramatic developments. These are the Chinese refusal to establish political relations with Britain, growing Sino-American antagonism, the emergence of 'Two Chinas' and the outbreak of war in Korea.

1 History Revisited: Sino-British Political Relations, January–June 1950

Face to Face
In silence I sat facing my guest;
To the end I sat and said not a word.
I desired to make a show of friendship:
I sought in my mind but found nothing.
If good words are not joined to affection,
I trow that you, sir, would not desire such.
Our minds were open, and we both forgot each other;
What harm in this where you and I are concerned?
                                    Kuei Tzu-mou (1563–1606)

In 1793 the Macartney mission tried to open up the whole of China to trade and political contact with Britain. In 1950 the British Labour government once again attempted to establish political and economic relations with China when, on 6 January, it recognised the Chinese People's Government. On both occasions the British failed. Between January and June 1950, diplomatic relations between Britain and China remained ambiguous in form and ineffective in operation; Sino-British trade was on the increase but its institutional framework was haphazard and fluid; British investments in China lost a lot of money rapidly. (See Chapters 6 and 7 on Sino-British trade and the collapse of business in China.) This chapter will explore why the Chinese responded in an intransigent manner, what this meant for the British government's liberal policy, and how and why the American government's policy towards the CPG began to diverge from that of the British.

NATIONALISM BEFORE INTERNATIONALISM: CPG POLICY TOWARDS BRITAIN

The CPG did not reciprocate on Britain's offer to establish formal political relations.[1] It accepted that John C. Hutchison, Britain's chargé d'affaires, was in China to work out a procedure for establishing relations, but in

practice no formal Sino-British negotiations took place. China's attitude appears to have been misconceived. Full diplomatic relations would
have allowed the PRC to establish an embassy in London and would
have enabled the PRC to establish consuls in Malaya and Singapore,
allowing the Chinese Communist Party (CCP) to represent Chinese
residents overseas and to establish close contacts with the Malayan
Communist Party. If the Chinese communists had established relations
with Britain, other states may have been encouraged to recognise the
regime.[2] Moreover, formal relations would certainly have facilitated
trade with the West, which the Chinese communists thought would be
useful for economic development.

The CPG stated that it was 'willing to establish diplomatic relations
with any foreign government that is willing to observe the principles of
equality, mutual benefit, and mutual respect of territorial integrity and
sovereignty'.[3] The Chinese government argued that the British government's position on these three issues meant their prerequisites had not
been met. Firstly, they believed a court case in Hong Kong, adjudicat-
ing on a dispute over the ownership of aircraft claimed by the CPG
and by an American company (with close connections with the Chinese
Nationalists – the KMT), was a government ploy to stop the aircraft
returning to China. Secondly, Britain had retained diplomatic representation with Taiwan. Thirdly, rather than voting positively for Communist China's admission to the UN, Britain abstained.[4] These were
matters of principle to the PRC. Article 56 of the Common Outline of
Chinese Policy stipulated: if a nation 'severed relations with the KMT
reactionaries and adopted a friendly attitude towards the CPG, then
the CPG shall negotiate and establish diplomatic relations with them'.[5]
Though the KMT had been decisively defeated on the mainland and
exiled to Taiwan, it was still a political threat to the new communist
state. From a Chinese communist perspective, the British attitude was
pedantic and legalistic, hypocritical and 'double faced'.[6] China feared
that America, tacitly supported by Britain, would aid the Chinese
Nationalist regime in Taiwan and use the island as a springboard to
oppose Chinese communist rule on the mainland. Britain's voting policy
in the UN aggrieved China because representation in the UN would
legitimise the PRC and discredit the Chinese Nationalists. Chou En-lai,
the Chinese Minister for Foreign Affairs, considered 'the continued presence
to this day of the illegitimate delegates of such a reactionary remnant
clique in the UN and the Security Council as completely unjustified'.[7]

At the same time, Britain's position on these issues does not fully explain
the Chinese reaction. It is clear that Mao's attitude was predetermined

well before January 1950. He stated: 'As for the question of recognition of our country by the imperialists, we should not be in a hurry to solve it now and need not be in a hurry to solve it even for a fairly long period after countrywide victory.'[8] As Michael Sheng and Chen Jian have shown, Chinese archival records prove that Mao had ruled out a rapprochement with the US in the late 1940s.[9] Britain's attitude merely confirmed China's perception of the West. There were more urgent geo-strategic and political considerations precluding a positive response and deeper intellectual currents working against political contact between China and the West. First and foremost, for ideological, geo-political, strategic and economic reasons, the PRC required a close relationship with the Soviet bloc. In 1949 Mao had affirmed that the regime would 'lean to one side' and in February 1950 China and the Soviet Union signed the Treaty of Friendship, Alliance and Mutual Assistance. The treaty provided the PRC with a strategic alliance and military and economic aid for China's post-war reconstruction.[10] China gained $300 million to finance reconstruction and rehabilitation and the treaty guaranteed Soviet support in the event of aggression by Japan or a country allied to her. Britain's decision to recognise the PRC coincided with the negotiations leading up to the signing of the Sino-Soviet Treaty and British recognition reinforced Soviet doubts about China's relationship with the West and about the depth of her ideological commitment to cold war politics. As Sergei Goncharov, Xue Litai and John Lewis have shown in their authoritative work, negotiations between Mao and Joseph Stalin in Moscow were protracted and riven by personal jealousies, power politics and ideological differences. Consequently, a favourable Chinese response to British recognition was politically difficult.[11]

However China's attitude towards contact with the West can only really be explained at an ideological rather than a diplomatic level This ideology was nationalist rather than internationalist. As Steven Levine notes, Chinese foreign policy was driven by a desire to further national interest. He argues Marxist-Leninism only provided the communists with a framework for analysing world affairs and a dogmatic vocabulary with which to respond to world events.[12] Significantly, imperialism's historical legacy had shaped Chinese nationalism into an ideology making relations with the West problematic. Imperialism in China had diverse forms. It had operated at an informal level: western and Japanese capital had dominated modern industrial and commercial enterprise in China and had underpinned the financial position of various imperial and republican Chinese states. This form of imperialism was epitomised by western foreign direct investments in China. Imperialism also operated at a formal level: Hong Kong was ceded to Britain in 1842; Taiwan to Japan in 1895; and in the 1930s and 1940s Japanese military might secured Manchuria and then half of China. Imperialism's impact on Chinese economic, social and political life was spatially and temporally complex. In some ways it divided China: socially some classes established close intellectual, political or business links with imperial forces, while others remained isolated from, ignorant of, or frustrated by outside influences; economically parts of China modernised (industrialised, urbanised, and grew) due to integration into the world economy, while others remained traditional (agrarian, rural and stagnant); politically, new concepts such as liberalism and socialism arrived, while older ones such as Confucianism remained. But in other ways imperialism unified China. At an ideological level, Chinese nationalism became a reality and could be used by political elites.

What was interesting and what shaped the attitude of the CCP to foreign relations in the 1950s was its analysis of imperialism's influence on China. Basically, the CCP leadership believed imperialism had split Chinese society, underdeveloped the economy and undermined the autonomy of the Chinese state. The CCP believed that if China threw out the imperialists and redefined her relationship with the outside world then a strong, independent state could unite and develop China. The geographic and social origins of the CCP also influenced what was an inferiority/superiority complex *vis-à-vis* the West. By the mid-1930s, once located in Yenan after the Long March, the movement turned intellectually towards China-centred, parochial, and ultimately peasant-based solutions to Chinese political and economic problems; the new location in the hinterland was culturally traditional, away from the more cosmopolitan and socially more diverse littoral provinces.[13]

Nationalism had an impact on policy in two ways. Firstly the Chinese believed that political and economic relations with the outside world, while useful for improving China's global status, were not vital; indeed by opening up fully to world economic forces the power of the Chinese state might be undermined and Chinese economic development hamstrung by dependency on the West. Secondly, as Levine argues, the Chinese communist leadership's perception of the West produced a hypersensitivity to symbolic foreign policy issues, such as those outlined by the CPG to explain its failure to reciprocate on Britain's offer of relations.[14] The Chinese leadership, imbued with a hostile attitude towards the West, wanted to dictate the political terms of trade. Mao, with little experience of western culture and a strong sense of the historical legacy of imperialism, adopted a negative attitude to integration. He acknowledged that while 'Britain has shown herself more enlightened and more realistic compared with America, an imperialist nation is basically an imperialist nation'.[15] In March 1949 Mao informed the Seventh Central Committee of the Communist Party of China that:

> We are willing to establish diplomatic relations with all countries on the principle of equality, but the imperialists, who have always been hostile to the Chinese People, will definitely not be in a hurry to treat us as equals. As long as the imperialist countries do not change their hostile attitude, we shall not grant them legal status in China.[16]

Ta Kung Pao embodied the common view of British recognition when it stated: '[Britain] is not prepared to forsake an opportunity to make a few pence'.[17] The confidence pervading the CCP in the aftermath of its victory in the civil war intensified Chinese anti-imperialism. The CCP, aware that nationalism was an effective unifying force, broadcast blatantly jingoistic propaganda. For C.P. Fitzgerald, China's decision to sacrifice the convenience of diplomatic contact with Britain was 'well worth the moral prestige at home'.[18] The mistreatment of foreign nationals in China was institutionalised anti-imperialism and the CCP was not unduly concerned by the possible repercussions of this policy on its relations with the West. The PRC wanted to end imperialist influence within China. It was only by removing the last vestiges of imperialism from Chinese soil that the Chinese nation could redefine its relations with the West. In 1952 Chou En-lai, in an address to China's foreign envoys, outlined the essence of China's attitude to the West.

> The imperialists still want to retain some privileges in China in the hope of sneaking back in. A few countries intend to negotiate with us about establishing relations, but we prefer to wait for a time. The remaining imperialist influence in China must be eradicated first, or the imperialists will have room to continue their activities. Although their military forces have been driven out, the economic power they have built up over the past century is still strong, and their cultural influence in particular is deep-rooted. All this will undermine our independence. We should therefore clean up the house before entertaining guests, that is, before establishing relations with them.[19]

Nevertheless there was a degree of flexibility in the Chinese attitude: ultimately, the Chinese were willing to establish diplomatic relations with Britain.[20] This haughty but ultimately accommodating line can only be explained in terms of China's national interest. The ideological line emanating from the CCP was confused and more often than not contradictory. At times, particularly in propaganda aimed at internal audiences, Mao portrayed the West as a monolithic imperialist bloc, in which Britain was subservient to the US. A decision to refuse relations with Britain was compatible with this line. Yet, on occasions, he expressed notions of exploiting contradictions between imperialist countries. In his report to the Seventh Chinese Communist Political Consultative Conference, he noted that: 'Quarrels among the different groups of the US bourgeois and of the British bourgeois have also increased.'[21] This line suggests China wanted relations with Britain as a means of intensifying differences between Britain and the US. However, a more coherent and consistent influence on China's foreign policy alignment was Mao's belief that there was an important division between the ruling elite and the masses in Britain. Mao adhered to the traditional Marxist-Leninist line that perceived imperialist nations as internally weak and thus destined to fall. According to this theory, relations with a reactionary western ruling clique would betray and confuse the revolutionary masses and undermine the chance of a socialist revolution in that country. Indeed, instead of establishing relations with the British government, the Chinese established contact with left-wing, socialist and communist groups in Britain. In October 1949 the PRC sent a telegram to a 'Five-man Independent Group' of British Labour Party MPs, representing the extreme left of the party. The PRC also established contact with the British-China Friendship Association and, predictably, with the Communist Party of Great Britain (CPGB).[22] In a September 1950 telegram from the PRC, acknowledging the thirtieth anniversary of the CPGB, Mao declared that 'the Communist Party of Britain is the only hope of the British working class for attaining freedom and peace'. He signed off by offering his best wishes 'for attaining final victory'.[23]

A stronger influence on the CCP leadership was its desire not to rely solely on political and economic contact with the Soviet Union. The CCP was not a homogeneous, monolithic body and hence there was a range of opinions on Sino-Soviet relations. Figures such as Liu Shao-chi wanted close relations with the Soviet Union; others such as Chou En-lai desired contact with the West. However, the different strands within the CCP coalesced around Mao. The Chinese leader desired independence from Moscow, a position reinforced by tough Soviet bargaining at the negotiating table early in 1950. It was evident to

Mao that Soviet economic aid was not going to be adequate to fund post-war economic reconstruction. And, moreover, the price enacted by the Soviet Union would be politically and financially costly. The major political and economic concessions given away by the CPG to the Soviet Union included Port Arthur (Lushun) and Port Dalian for use as naval bases, Soviet control of the Changchun railway, and, in Inner Mongolia, Sinkiang and Manchuria, exclusive foreign rights over mineral exploitation and a degree of informal political control that undermined Chinese sovereignty in these territories.[24] In addition, the ideological gap between the two main leaders of the communist world was more evident after the conference. Mao perceived himself as an independent thinker and believed that the Chinese revolutionary model was more applicable than the Soviet one for promoting Marxism-Leninism in Asia; Stalin hated having his intellectual credentials undermined by a questionable communist. It is clear that Mao believed that China's relationship with the Soviet Union was threatening the nation's independence: China was replacing one imperialist (the West), with another (the Soviet Union). As Chinese nationalism was a more potent force than socialist internationalism, this dictated at least some contact, especially at an economic level, with the West. (These issues will be explored further in Chapter 7.)

LIBERALISM CONFIRMED: BRITISH POLICY TOWARDS CHINA

Labour government policy did not change before June 1950. The British government continued to operate within the liberal framework established by recognition. Ernest Bevin, the British Foreign Secretary, publicly reaffirmed that recognition had been the right decision taken at the right time: 'I searched my conscience as to what alternative there was. I came to the conclusion that the advice I gave to the Cabinet was right and, in a few years time, I think it will turn out to have been right.'[25] In the cabinet, Bevin labelled the British approach 'entirely realistic' and, in March, in conversation with Robert Schuman, the French Foreign Minister, he argued recognition had strengthened Mao's negotiating position with Stalin.[26] In private, however, Bevin expressed doubts about recognition. He informed his cabinet colleagues that Britain's 'position must be regarded as profoundly unsatisfactory'.[27] In March 1950, at a meeting with the China Association, he stated: 'It was a case of holding the balance between the East and the West; in the middle of these two grinding stones we are in danger of being ground.'[28] The Foreign Secretary perceived China's refusal to establish diplomatic relations as embarrassing – a blow to Britain's status as a world power – and regretted diverging from the Americans on this issue. Moreover, a number of other developments began to undermine the whole basis of Britain's China policy. Firstly, British businessmen were facing severe difficulties in China and it was becoming clear that the PRC might end Britain's economic stake on the Chinese mainland. Secondly, the Chinese had signed the Treaty of Mutual Alliance with the Soviet Union, seemingly cementing economic and political ties with the Soviet Union. Thirdly, Sino-American relations had deteriorated in the early months of 1950, bringing into some doubt American recognition of Communist China.

However, the rationale behind British policy remained intact. There was no advantage to be gained from writing 'China off as irretrievably lost to Western democracy'. Bevin reaffirmed that contact with the West provided the 'only hope of influencing China not to commit herself finally and irrevocably to the Kremlin'.[29] He argued the policy was a 'hard one from which we must expect to derive no early or material benefits',[30] but behind this magnanimous liberal façade were real national 'material' interests. Britain had to provide the PRC with a vested interest in the economic and political *status quo ante* in Asia because British economic interests in China, Hong Kong and Malaya were thought to depend on Chinese integration into the world economy and into world institutions such as the UN. The alternative to seeking a *modus vivendi* was to isolate China politically and restrict economic contact with the PRC. These policies would have tightened the bond between the Soviet Union and China and caused difficulties with left-wing groups at home and with the Asian Commonwealth abroad.[31] More importantly, they would have worked against British business interests. The government could have withdrawn its officials from China and frozen Chinese financial assets but it did not want to jeopardise trade with China nor the position of Hong Kong. In his meeting with the China Association in March 1950 Bevin admitted that, without British recognition, the position of British businesses in China would have been far worse.[32] In addition, the government believed a more confrontational containment policy *vis-à-vis* China might encourage Chinese intervention in South East Asia.

In the aftermath of recognition the British government changed the emphasis but not the direction of policy towards China. The government refused to concede to the grievances outlined by the Chinese, and instead attempted to work for China's admission to the UN and tried to influence the direction of American policy towards China. It is to these three aspects of policy that we now turn.

PRIDE AND PREJUDICE: THE BRITISH RESPONSE

The British government responded to the three specific grievances highlighted by the PRC with legalistic and, at times, pedantic arguments.[33] The upshot was that Britain did not meet Chinese demands. The British response was influenced by some deep-rooted and complex considerations, but it was also reactive and thus shaped by a determination to maintain 'face' with the Chinese. The British government's commitment to containing communism in Asia made further concessions too problematic. The Foreign Office had hoped that the Chinese would overlook the anti-communist tone of British policy in South East Asia, especially in Malaya, but China had highlighted policies such as Britain's recognition of the Bao Dai regime in Indochina and British abuses of human rights in Malaya. After January 1950 there was no question of the British changing or toning down these policies. The Foreign Office informed Hutchison that: 'We cannot conform our policy outside China to the wishes of the People's Government.'[34] Such concessions may have undermined the struggle to maintain western power and economic dominance in Asia. The government had to consider the impact of any change in policy on Anglo-American relations. Initially, Britain planned to complement recognition with a positive vote in the UN and the withdrawal of Britain's diplomatic representative from Taiwan. But Oliver Franks, the British ambassador in Washington, advised Bevin not to jeopardise Anglo-American relations by voting for a Soviet resolution in the Security Council. In the early months of 1950 the American administration pressed the British government not to allow the aircraft in Hong Kong to fall into communist hands and not to take any initiative to break the deadlock in the UN.

Political alignments in Britain also made concessions problematic. The Labour government did not want policy towards China becoming an internal party issue, nor a party-political issue. Since 1946, the left-wing of the Labour Party had promoted a non-aligned foreign policy. As a result of international developments such as the Berlin Blockade and Prague Coup and also because of the economic importance of Marshall Aid, they had lost ground both within the party and in the country. But it was the left-wing of the Labour Party that now pressed for further concessions to the PRC and which criticised the government's contradictory stand on recognition. Left-wing MPs such as Tom Driberg (Labour, Essex, Maldon) and Richard Crossman (Labour, Coventry, East) argued that Britain had delayed recognition for too long and now needed to secure a seat for Communist China in the UN.[35] With a general election in February, the Labour Party did not want to be accused of appeasing China in the Far East; as matters stood in February 1950, the Labour Party could claim it had attempted to establish relations and that the ball was now in the Chinese court. Even after the election, the Foreign Office was aware that the issue could potentially embarrass the government. In May the Foreign Office decided that the press must not be informed of Britain's response to a further non-committal Chinese communication: 'A skeleton must be kept in the cupboard, however much it may rattle and disturb them of [a] night.'[36] A number of Conservative Party MPs, including Fitzroy Maclean (Conservative, Lancaster), David Gammans (Conservative, Hornsey) and Julian Amery (Conservative, Preston, North), criticised a policy that was 'bound to serve encouragement to all communist and pro-communist elements in Asia, and bound to discourage anyone who was disposed to resist communism'.[37] Some others, such as Walter Fletcher (Conservative, Bury and Radcliffe), desired the roll back of Chinese communism. He stated:

We have got to think in terms of taking the new offensive. We are accepting far too easily that China has been conquered by Communism. It has not. A thin veneer of red paint has been put over China, but below it there are great movements which, if they are properly fostered will lead, as we have seen in south east Europe, to other powers arising which are anti-Communist.[38]

The Conservative Party front bench did not advocate roll back, but neither did they want further concessions to communism. Winston Churchill, the leader of the opposition in the House of Commons, and Anthony Eden, the shadow Foreign Secretary, accepted the legal rationale behind recognition but were concerned by the potential consequences for the Malayan Insurgency and for relations with the US and the 'white' Commonwealth. On 24 May 1950, Eden declared that he 'did not think then, and I do not think now, that [the] decision was fortunate either in its timing or in its method'.[39]

The Foreign Office also believed that China's intransigent position reflected traditional Chinese negotiating tactics; the Chinese were deliberately delaying relations to test British sincerity and hopefully to force further concessions. Bevin, using the discourse of employers, declared: 'They must return to work pending negotiations. What it amounts to is that they are on strike. They are holding up the work and that will not do.'[40] In March he informed a delegation of the China Association that, if Britain tried to negotiate formally with the PRC, it would merely provoke China to up her price.[41] Underpinning Britain's failure to concede was an unwillingness to undermine British prestige. A further initiative would be portrayed as weakness and would bring into question Britain's determination to resist communism in Asia. In a disinterested tone, Sir William Strang, Permanent Under-Secretary at the Foreign Office, declared: 'this thing may sort itself out given time and patience', but above all else, 'Britain must be vindicated if relations did breakdown'.[42] Relations must be established 'without loss of dignity or the sacrifice of any principles'.[43]

Dissatisfied with its response, Hutchison advised the Foreign Office to concede to Chinese demands. He did not believe that the Chinese were being deliberately obstructionist and that they would establish relations when Britain cleared up the ambiguities regarding Britain's attitude towards the PRC. He argued that personal contact with Chinese officials could break down their misconceptions about British policy; he noted that his contacts with Chinese officials had not proved to be acrimonious and suggested an approach be made to Chang Han-fu, the Chinese Vice-Foreign Minister for Foreign Affairs.[44] Hutchison, inclined to accept Chinese statements at face value, failed to appreciate the ideological and political hurdles precluding harmonious ties. But he did appreciate that the Chinese wanted relations.

SIT DOWN AND BE COUNTED

The authors of the San Francisco Treaty had assumed that if there was a dispute over the membership of one of the permanent seats in the UN Security Council, the UN as a body would cease to exist. There was thus no constitutional precedent for the situation confronting the UN in 1950, whereby the Chinese Nationalists were the incumbent power in the Security Council but the Chinese communists were claiming their seat.[45] However, despite these legal obstacles there is no doubt that the PRC, which governed 450 million people, had a legitimate right to be seated in the UN, a world organisation. The problem was that neither the US nor the Soviet Union (for most of this period) wanted the admission of Communist China. The US sought to isolate the PRC; and the Soviet Union wanted to tie the Chinese communists to the Soviet bloc. On 13 January 1950, a resolution to the UN Security Council seeking to admit China was rejected. It had been introduced with China's agreement by the Soviet Union but was probably a deliberate Soviet attempt to discredit the UN and forestall Chinese membership.[46] The US and France, along with temporary Security Council members Cuba, Ecuador and Egypt, voted against, whilst Britain abstained. Thereafter the Soviet Union boycotted the Security Council in protest, a response agreed to by Mao.[47]

Subsequently, the British government, in conjunction with Trygve Lie, Secretary-General of the UN, sought to break a deadlock which undermined Britain's overall strategy of integrating China into the world community. Initially Britain worked behind the scenes to persuade members of the Security Council to alter their vote; but then, after June 1950, the government decided to reverse its original decision to abstain when a future resolution on Chinese admission came to a vote. In addition, Lie, deeply frustrated by US intransigence, tried to arrange a special meeting of the Security Council, with the Soviet Union present, to discuss the question.[48] All these approaches failed because the American administration held the key to China's admission. At this stage it did not lock the door on membership but did keep it firmly shut.[49] In May, Acheson informed Bevin that 'it was difficult to give way on the question of Chinese representation without appearing to be giving in to Russian intransigence and blackmail'.[50] Consequently, the US administration rejected initiatives by Lie. Meanwhile Cuba, Ecuador and Egypt clearly understood that a vote for Communist China meant opposing US interests and hence did not alter their voting policy.[51]

It is worth focusing for a moment on the British government's decision to change its voting policy in the UN. This may seem a trivial and ultimately ineffectual development but it is important for two reasons: firstly, it threatened a serious disagreement with the US; and secondly, it indicated that the British government desired a universalistic UN as a counterweight to American power.

The decision to reverse British voting policy was taken in June 1950. Attlee and Bevin, prompted by Kenneth Younger, temporarily in charge of the Foreign Office because of Bevin's ill health, agreed that at the next meeting of a subsidiary body of the UN, Britain would vote for China's admission.[52] The decision was legitimised within the liberal policy framework: China's admission to the UN would integrate the PRC more closely into the world community, reduce its reliance on the Soviet Union and moderate its behaviour. It was also argued that this initiative might break the diplomatic deadlock between Britain and China. Younger informed Attlee and Bevin that 'it seems to me far too early to assume that Peking will not eventually want relations with us and will not be prepared to do trade with us'.[53] William Strang believed 'we should have done better to vote for the admission of the representative of the People's Government once we had conveyed *de jure* recognition'. Elser Dening, Assistant Under-Secretary of State in the Foreign Office, noted that 'our attitude in the UN has been one of the main reasons for our failure in establishing relations'. Hutchison reaffirmed that a positive vote in the UN could be enough to secure diplomatic relations.[54] However, this thinking was a departure from a previous consensus that Britain should not 'run after the Chinese'; even Younger had previously minuted that, until China established full diplomatic relations, 'I think we might well sit on the fence'.[55] Clearly other factors explain the reversal.

Of some significance were forthcoming votes to admit Communist China to UNICEF, ECOSOC and ECAFE. These were going to be extremely close and thus a British abstention, if it prevented the PRC's admission to one of these bodies, would publicly discredit Britain's liberal stance. More importantly, Asian nations, in particular India, were pressing strongly for China's admission to the UN. Before the Soviet resolution was tabled in January 1950, Sir Benegal N. Rau, the head of the Indian delegation at the UN, suggested that the Security Council should refer the question to a tribunal. After the Soviet walk-out, he suggested that the rules of the Security Council be amended to allow a simple majority of UN members to decide the admission of new delegates.[56] These feasible solutions were rejected by the US and Britain. The Foreign Office, and undoubtedly Attlee, wanted to defuse the resultant Indian charges of western intransigence. There was also pressure from within Britain. The British press supported British moves to persuade others to vote for China's admission and were concerned that a stalemate could seriously damage the UN. By June 1950, even *The Times* branded Britain's voting policy 'grotesque and undignified'.[57] Meanwhile, Labour Party MPs on the left of the party criticised the government's anomalous position. By June, even Bevin admitted that British policy had 'made us look rather ridiculous in the light of our actions in recognising the Peking Government'.[58]

However, the main reason for the shift in policy was the government's desire to bring the Soviet Union back into the Security Council. The British initiative was a response to developments in Moscow rather than in Peking. The Labour government was extremely worried that if the Soviet boycott proved permanent, the UN would come to represent western nations, thus forcing the Soviet bloc to establish an alternative organisation to represent the communist world, a development which would intensify the cold war, isolate the Chinese communists from the West and could cause non-aligned nations, including India, to withdraw from the UN. The Labour government held an idealistic view of the UN: it maintained the international order and provided a forum for discourse between hostile powers. Consequently the UN had to be a collective body, even if this meant a Soviet veto over the collective security element of the UN constitution.[59] Evidence to suggest that the US had rejected this universalistic concept heightened British concerns. Elements within the Democratic administration, which had traditionally placed emphasis on the UN as a body for collective security, had become frustrated by an organisation perceived to be a vehicle for communist propaganda.[60] Moreover, by 1950, the rightwing of the Republican Party and a large proportion of the US press wanted the Soviet Union permanently excluded and viewed the Soviet boycott as an opportunity to circumvent the Soviet veto.[61] These opinions were underpinned by a belief that the Soviet boycott would be permanent anyway, given that for the communists UN membership was incompatible with world revolution.[62] In fact the converse was actually true. By May, with a North Korean offensive imminent, the Soviet Union wanted to return. At the end of May, Younger reported that Stalin seemed to be anxious to return to the UN if the problem of a seat for China could be resolved.[63] This was a view confirmed by G.N. Zarubin, the Soviet ambassador in London.[64] The UN department of the Foreign Office, impressed by the UN's success in settling the Kashmir dispute while the Soviets were absent, did not want the British government to respond.[65] But Bevin agreed to trade a seat for Communist China for the return of the Soviet Union. Plans were laid to approach the Soviets in Moscow. However, the outbreak of war in Korea scuppered these diplomatic moves.

CONTAINING THE COMMIES: US POLICY TOWARDS CHINA

Before turning to British attempts to shape the direction of US policy towards China, it is essential to explain in what ways and why American thinking on China was changing in 1949 and 1950. The actual nature of American policy towards the Chinese communist regime in 1949 and 1950 remains a controversial issue amongst American historians.

John Lewis Gaddis, one of the most prominent American historians on the cold war, argues that the US had the same long-term aim as Britain: to divide China and the Soviet Union.[66] He notes that during the Korean War, the US attempted to isolate China. This would increase China's reliance on the Soviet Union which would in turn aggravate tensions between the communist powers. Most historians accept this was the basic geo-strategic rationale behind policy during the war, but disagree whether the US adopted this approach as early as 1949. Gordon Chang argues that, in 1949, the US had ruled out recognition and, by the autumn of that year, policy was being formulated as an attempt to isolate the PRC politically and economically.[67] Nancy Bernkopf Tucker and Warren Cohen argue that, while the US State Department adopted a cautious approach to Communist China, it was working towards the recognition of the Chinese communist regime.[68]

Whatever the exact position of the US administration in 1949, what is evidently clear is that American policy towards China shifted dramatically in the first six months of 1950.[69] By May 1950, the US administration had moved away from an internationalist approach towards a strategy based on containment. China would be contained by political, military, economic and 'psychological' weapons. The administration sought to delay China's admission to the UN, to curtail Sino-Western trade and to increase military pressure on the PRC. By June 1950, both the US and Britain were legitimising their policy towards China in terms of restricting Chinese communist expansion and promoting and exploiting tensions between China and the Soviet Union. The State Department believed that its policy would, by forcing the Chinese to rely economically and politically on the Soviet Union, cause tensions between Chinese nationalism and Soviet internationalism, and deepen divisions within the CCP between those for and those against a close alignment with Moscow. Equally, the State Department argued that economic difficulties in China, exacerbated by a curtailment of trade with the West, would increase popular discontentment with the CPG.

The change in American policy can be attributed to a number of factors. Firstly, this new US policy was founded on American intelligence and diplomatic reports from China. McConaughy, the American consul-general in Shanghai, reported a 'swelling tide of popular discontent [and] hostility toward [the] new regime, which has spread here and apparently throughout the country with startling rapidity during [the] past two months and seems destined [to] grow *pari passu* with economic crisis'. He argued that while there was no real resistance to communist rule at the time, if a rebellion broke out it would quickly gain wide support.[70] In January 1950 a CIA report argued that if a 'difficult' situation developed, then 'many Chinese will hold the USSR and the Peiping regime jointly responsible for the famine and inflation that is bound to arouse widespread discontent in the coming year'.[71] Secondly, the deterioration in Sino-American relations in the early months of 1950 had an influence on American thinking. During January and February 1950, due to Chinese attacks on US nationals and the CPG's vehemently anti-American propaganda line, the administration concluded that China was intrinsically hostile. China's refusal to establish relations with Britain and the signing of the Sino-Soviet Treaty in February 1950 confirmed American thinking. Thirdly, it was influenced by public and congressional opinion in the US. Not formulated within the bipartisan foreign policy structure of the late 1940s, Democratic policy towards China was an important target for Republican critics of Truman's foreign policy.[72] Uniting isolationists and 'Asia firsters', the so-called 'China Lobby' represented the Chinese Nationalists in the US and included important figures such as Senators Robert Taft (Republican, Ohio), William F. Knowland (Republican, California), H. Alexander Smith (Republican, New Jersey), a member of the Senate Foreign Relations Committee, Styles Bridges (Republican, New Hampshire) and Richard Nixon (Republican, California). It was a powerful force in US politics. It was closely associated with the Roy Howard and Scripps-Howard newspaper chains, with Henry Luce (*Time* and *Life*), and prominent columnists, such as Joseph and Stuart Alsop. The China Lobby was intrinsically tied to advocates of roll back in the administration and to MacArthur, through his intelligence chief, General Charles Willoughby.[73] This lobby played on the American public's sentimental attachment to China and to Chiang Kai-shek, a Christian and wartime ally, and heightened growing paranoia about the threat communism posed to the American way of life. In January 1950 Richard Nixon had Alger Hiss, a former State Department official, condemned for perjury after allegations that he was a communist. In February Senator Joseph McCarthy (Republican, Wisconsin) made a speech at Wheeling in West Virginia, claiming that there were over 200 communist sympathisers in the State Department, whilst subsequent diatribes from McCarthy attacked State Department officials, especially Acheson, whom he associated with the so-called 'loss of China'. Hardliners within the American administration and in Congress were clearly trying to change public perceptions of the communist threat in order to influence the direction of the administration's policy.[74] With congressional elections in November

1950, more liberal elements within the administration felt the need to depoliticise the controversy surrounding policy towards China by rejecting accommodation with Communist China. The *Manchester Guardian* admitted: 'it would take only the triumph of the Chinese Communists at Lake Success to set the Republicans ringing the fire alarms in every state of the union'.[75] John Lewis Gaddis agrees that the political environment in the US, coupled with Chinese hostility towards the US, forced the administration to retreat from a moderate line which waited for tensions between China and the Soviet Union to develop, towards a policy which was driven by an ideological distaste for Chinese communism.[76]

In 1950 there were different shades of opinion in the US administration which shaped American policy. Within the State Department, Philip C. Jessup and Walton Butterworth wanted a more moderate line on China, believing this could engender Sino-Soviet divisions; but Rusk, who replaced Butterworth as Assistant Secretary of State for Far Eastern Affairs on 28 March 1950, wanted a harder line on Chinese communism.[77] The Department of Defense rejected recognition of Communist China. General Douglas MacArthur, the Supreme Allied Commander in the Far East, harbouring designs on a 1952 nomination as Republican presidential candidate, argued the PRC posed a far greater threat than the Soviet Union. Acheson's stance on Communist China remains a subject of historical debate. Some historians argue he wanted recognition, while others argue he had ruled it out. What is clear is that in the months before the Korean War, Acheson was under increasing pressure from the Pentagon and from right-wing Republicans to opt for a tougher line. President Harry Truman, a vehement anti-communist, was sympathetic to the Department of Defense and sensitive to congressional opinion, having spent ten years as a senator. At the end of 1949, Acheson persuaded Truman that the administration should disengage support from the Chinese Nationalists and moderate its line on the communists. Truman was highly sceptical about the possibility of Titoism in China, but was disillusioned with Chiang Kai-shek. However, in 1950, with growing Sino-American hostility and evidence of a close relationship with the Soviet Union, Truman's position on China hardened.

Differences within the American administration coalesced in the spring of 1950. American thinking on the cold war was standardised and radicalised by National Security Council Directive 68 (NSC68). This secret internal document advocated a massive programme of rearmament, funded by the American public, and legitimised by reference to the Soviet threat to Europe and to 'civilisation itself'.[78] The rationale behind the new policy can be interpreted as a justifiable response to a real Soviet military threat or as a Machiavellian attempt to redirect American and western resources into military production, away from domestic consumption. The latter aimed at restructuring and stimulating American and European economic development and was to be legitimised by the creation of a 'Red Threat' myth. What is certain is that it was partly a response to developments in Asia: to the emergence of Communist China and a Sino-Soviet alliance, to nationalist and left-wing threats to American spheres of influence and to the European empires in Asia. According to Bruce Cumings:

> NSC-68 was about the end of the atomic monopoly, it was about the absence of bipartisanship in the wake of the victory of the Chinese revolution, it was about how to jump start the advanced economies, it embodied the year long debate in Washington over containment and rollback, and finally it was about fear.[79]

NSC68 globalised the American commitment to containment – the US would now overtly aid anti-communist movements (however un-representative and repressive) in Africa, Asia and Latin America.[80] In terms of American policy towards China, it meant a new American commitment to defend Taiwan, together with huge sums of American aid for the island's economic development; a propaganda campaign against Communist China; no diplomatic relations between the US and China; and a curtailment of trading links. Policy was confirmed and further radicalised by the outbreak of the war in Korea in June 1950.

SCHEMING, SCHISM AND THE SPECIAL RELATIONSHIP

The shift in US policy on China threatened to jeopardise British at-tempts to integrate China economically and politically into the world and posed important questions about Britain's relationship with the US. When formulating policy towards China in 1949, the British government had assumed that US policy would realign with that of Britain. The Foreign Office argued that pressures within the US would delay but not prevent US recognition of the PRC, because ultimately Taiwan would fall to the communists and right-wing sympathisers of the Chinese Nationalists would be marginalised. The US decision to disengage from the Chinese Nationalists (to be discussed in Chapter 2) seemed to vindicate British thinking. Oliver Franks, the British ambassador in Washington, argued that American recognition would come in three months once the State Department had prepared 'public opinion', while the Foreign Office thought it would arrive after the congressional elections in November 1950.[81] However, as early as March 1950, Acheson confided to James Webb, Under-Secretary of State, that he had 'strong doubts about the value [of the] present British position, both from a general political stand point, a commercial stand point and [because of its] effect on South East Asia'.[82] Acheson informed Franks that he was disturbed about the distance between the Atlantic powers on China and believed the British government was 'leaning over backwards to placate the Chinese Communists'.[83] In May, Livingston Merchant informed Esler Dening that: 'There comes a point where recognition can become a symbol of humiliation rather than a beacon. From the beginning [the] US did not feel immediate recognition was [the] proper answer.'[84] He argued that even if Taiwan fell, US recognition of Communist China might not occur for 10 to 12 years.[85]

The distance between the powers over China presented the British government with a dilemma: should it continue to seek a *modus vivendi* with the PRC or align policy with the US? Bevin believed that the US had 'no positive policy – or indeed any policy – towards China at all',[86] arguing that it was possible for Britain and the US to have conflicting policies as long as Anglo-American relations were not prejudiced.[87] However, this was not going to be the case. British and American policies were about to diverge over the seating of Communist China in the UN. At the May conference, Acheson made it clear to Bevin that the US strongly opposed China's admission to the UN and would not support the British initiative to bring the Soviet Union back into the UN Security Council. It was only the outbreak of the Korean War which prevented China's admission to the UN and hence a public schism between Britain and the US over policy towards China.

Ultimately, in response to British pressure, the government still believed that US policy would align with Britain's. After NSC68 such thinking was redundant and, in any case, opportunities to influence the American policy-making process were limited because the US administration could not be seen to be yielding to British pressure. At the time, the British government misunderstood the domestic pressures on the American administration. The Foreign Office argued that Acheson was paying far too much attention to his domestic troubles and perceived right-wing opponents of the administration as isolated extremists; it felt temporary, election-induced considerations were clouding the wider needs of global strategy. A traditional perception of the American political system, which portrayed public opinion as changeable and foreign policy as following such popular vacillations far too closely, conditioned thinking. Franks, by contrast, appreciating the severe pressure on Acheson, argued that the atmosphere in Washington was so 'charged and embittered' that Acheson had become 'acutely conscious' that the Democratic administration was 'struggling for their Asian policy in Washington'. He went on to argue that 'in the China situation both what they did and what we did had a direct bearing on their struggle'. At a more fundamental level, however, neither Franks nor policy-makers in London understood the radical changes undergone by American strategic thinking on the cold war in Asia. They did not believe that intervention to prevent Taiwan's fall was feasible and thus believed a Sino-American accommodation inevitable. However, as the next chapter will explore, an integral part of this new American policy was a long-term commitment to Taiwan – a development which made diplomatic relations between America and Communist China extremely difficult and highly unlikely in the short term.

This new US policy threatened to seriously destabilise Anglo-American relations. The consequences of this development were potentially profound. A schism over policy towards China could have jeopardised American support for European economic recovery. The powerful anti-Chinese communist lobby in the US could, in the event of a failure of Britain to support hardline American policies towards Communist China, mobilise support in Congress and amongst the American public to block important sections of the programme of US military and economic aid to Britain. It is interesting that, as early as March 1950, Acheson indicated to Franks the stakes the British and American governments were playing for on policy towards China. Franks informed London that:

> members of Congress were being hotted up to attack aid to Britain under the European Recovery programme and the military Defence Assistance Programme but that the purpose in doing this was, by attacking us, to attack the policies of the State Department [on China] and himself and so carry the present campaign against him a stage further.[88]

This was no idle warning, but a real threat. Since 1947 Marshall Aid, now at the end of its first phase (1947–49), had been vital to British economic growth, facilitating infrastructure developments and raising industrial output. In the early 1950s the debates about the extent to which the US government should fund further European economic re-covery during the second phase of Marshall Aid (1949–51) were in-tensive and many sided. The State Department, under the Anglophile Acheson, wanted the American financial commitment to western Europe to be continued and for the US to accept western European trade discrimination indefinitely. By comparison, the US Treasury wanted less aid and more stringent adherence by the European powers to the post-war international economic system, as symbolised by GATT and the IMF, which aimed at moving towards world free trade and the short-term settlement of trading deficits. Equally, in Congress, there was a large body of opinion that was extremely sceptical about the worth of US aid to Europe; congressmen saw American taxpayers' money being spent by 'socialist' countries, such as Britain, on welfare measures. These debates were not resolved until the summer of 1950, when the Korean War made it imperative for the US government to ensure that western European countries had the dollars to rearm.[89] Consequently, after the Korean War had broken out in June 1950, the trade-off between maintaining a liberal policy towards China and en-suring good and hence prosperous relations with the US became more politically explosive and economically vital. It was a trade-off that policy-makers in Britain now had to face full on.

CONCLUSIONS

The PRC's reaction to Britain's offer of political relations was charac-terised by a 'teach the imperialists a lesson' mentality and by an under-lying desire for limited and controlled contact with the West. It resulted from a complex intertwining of influences: by a realisation that total isolation from the world was neither possible nor desirable, by a desire to play politics with the Great Powers, and by a historically and ideologically derived desire for economic and political independence. Between January and June 1950, the British government played a patient game, but from a Chinese perspective this was a hypocritical and in-transigent one. The government underestimated the historical legacy of imperialism on Chinese attitudes: history mattered to the Chinese communists. Throughout the period, the government continued to ad-here to its existing liberal policy. Britain maintained a basic level of business and diplomatic representation in China, worked behind the scenes to secure China's admission to the UN and attempted to steer the US government towards a liberal policy on China. The British position would have been clearer if accompanied by a positive vote in the UN and by the withdrawal of diplomatic representatives from Taiwan, but at the time these policies could not be justified because of their impact on Anglo-American relations. By June 1950 British government policy depended on a more liberal American policy towards China, thought inevitable once Taiwan fell. In actual fact, the US had by then renewed its commitment to the island.

2 The Origins of 'Two Chinas', 1950–54

The early 1950s were the formative years for Taiwan's post-war development. The island remained capitalist, integrated into the world economy and under Chinese Nationalist control. The emergence of 'Two Chinas' had a profound influence on the course of Anglo-Chinese-American relations. This chapter will consider how the respective positions of the US, China and Britain ensured that Taiwan remained in the hands of the Chinese Nationalists; it will analyse how the US increased informal economic and political control over the island of Taiwan; and it will determine how Britain tried to reconcile its far eastern strategy with a deepening American commitment to a non-communist Taiwan.

CHINA'S REUNIFICATION: PLANNED BUT NOT EXECUTED

Between 1950 and 1954, the seizure of Taiwan was one of the most important foreign policy objectives for the Chinese People's Government.[1] In 1950, while discredited and moribund, the KMT remained an alternative source of loyalty for anti-communists within China and amongst Chinese communities in South East Asia. The Nationalists also posed a military threat to the CPG. Nationalist guerrillas were operating in south China; Nationalist forces were stranded in the Yunnan-Burmese border region and in North Vietnam; and the Nationalist blockade of the Chinese east coast was hindering coastal transport and contributing to difficult economic conditions in trading centres such as Shanghai and Amoy. The Chinese communists, well aware of the close contacts between the US military and intelligence organisations in the Far East and the Chinese Nationalists (and Taiwanese independence leaders in Japan), also wanted to preclude an American political or military commitment to a key strategic base – a potential invasion launching pad.[2] A successful invasion of Taiwan would have ended the Chinese Civil War, reaffirmed the new regime's nationalist credentials and released resources for Chinese economic development.

Whether an invasion would actually have 'reunited China' in 1950 remains debatable, but until the outbreak of the Korean War an invasion was certainly expected and being planned for. Evidence from Soviet and Chinese archives indicates that Mao wanted Taiwan taken by the summer of 1950, and that the People's Liberation Army (PLA) was planning an assault from 1949 onwards.[3] Both the British and American governments, relying on evidence from intelligence sources, believed that Taiwan would fall in 1950.[4] Although the Chinese Nationalists were a powerful military force, with an estimated 300 000 troops on Taiwan and naval and air supremacy over the PLA,[5] numerical strength disguised a profound collapse in morale and a lack of effective leadership; some observers felt internal subversion alone would end Nationalist control.[6] Moreover, lacking economic ties with Japan and China, Taiwan's economy was in a desperate state, and thus the government could not, without running up an inflationary budget deficit, support the military forces on the island.[7] Two factors made an invasion of Taiwan in 1950 more risky in the short term: the CCP's failure to infiltrate the Nationalist political structure or to gain a wide base of popular support amongst the Taiwanese,[8] and the PLA's lack of equipment for, or extensive experience of, amphibious warfare.[9] But evidence from the Soviet and Chinese archives suggests an invasion was still possible in 1950 and inevitable by 1951. Sergei Goncharov, John Lewis and Xue Litai note that Stalin's attitude towards an invasion changed dramatically in 1950. In 1949, fearing US retaliation, Stalin refused to provide China with military aid, but by 1950, desiring a confrontation with the US to solidify Sino-Soviet relations and prevent China's possible alignment with the West, he actively encouraged the capture of Taiwan and agreed to supply the necessary military equipment.[10]

By publicly declaring the Taiwan straits neutral and by sending the Seventh Fleet to the area after the outbreak of war in Korea, the US prevented a military clash between Nationalist and communist forces, and guaranteed the long-term survival of 'Two Chinas'. The CCP nevertheless reaffirmed that it was 'fully determined to wrench Taiwan from the control of the American aggressors and to destroy completely this wasps nest of the Chinese reactionary bands'.[11] America's intervention made Chinese military planning redundant.[12] After June 1950, instead of firm indications that an invasion was imminent, there were now only vague references in the Chinese press to the eventual recovery of the territory. The Chinese transferred 30 000 troops back to the area in July, but this was a defensive measure against a possible Nationalist attack. Thereafter the Chinese refrained from linking US aggression against their territory (including Taiwan) with articles 1 and 4 of the

Sino-Soviet Treaty which sanctioned Soviet military assistance in the event of such an attack.[13]

Whether the Chinese would have accepted a political as opposed to a military solution to the Taiwan problem in the 1950s remains unclear. During the summer of 1950, the Chinese sought assurances that the US would, once the Korean War had come to an end, withdraw protection. Nevertheless, the Chinese failed to outline what they would accept as a valid proposal to defuse tensions. This stance tends to suggest that the Chinese would have rejected a formula which failed to uphold their sovereignty. The Cairo and Potsdam Declarations of 1943 and 1945 had reaffirmed that Taiwan would return to China after a peace treaty had been signed with Japan. An independent territory under the Nationalists, the Taiwanese, or temporarily under the authority of the UN, while more amenable than under American control, would have been unacceptable to the Chinese. The US position on Taiwan and the subsequent failure of the UN to formulate a solution certainly influenced China's perception of American intentions in the Far East, and hence ultimately affected its decision to enter into the Korean War. At the same time, even if China's sovereignty over Taiwan had been reaffirmed, it is unlikely that the Chinese would have been distracted from intervention in Korea. Once the Chinese had intervened, a solution that reconciled the conflicting positions of China and the US over Taiwan was impossible. The Taiwan problem was not settled on Chinese terms; instead, as British policy-makers discovered over the course of 1950, it was the US which determined the future status and shaped the political and economic structure of the island.

PEDANTIC LEGALISM: BRITAIN'S RELATIONS WITH TAIWAN

After a period of strained relations during the 1940s, Britain's relationship with the Chinese Nationalists reached a new low in January 1950, when Britain recognised the PRC and simultaneously de-recognised the Chinese Nationalist regime. Although Britain no longer recognised the Chinese Nationalists as even the *de facto* government of Taiwan, E.T. Biggs remained as Britain's diplomatic representative on the island. The British government anticipated trade with Taiwan and wanted Hong Kong to remain the entrepôt centre for the Taiwanese economy. However, it believed trade would be with a communist and not a Nationalist Taiwan.[14] In the meantime, the Bank of England froze the Chinese Nationalist sterling account, whilst tight visa restrictions in Hong Kong and Taiwan prevented movement between the two islands. It was consideration of Anglo-American relations that forced Britain to maintain some contact with the Nationalists. The British government originally decided to withdraw representation, but opposition from Oliver Franks, the British ambassador in Washington, forced a reversal. With the Pentagon and Republicans in Congress advocating an American commitment to the island, Franks believed a withdrawal of British representation might prejudice discussion of the Taiwan issue in the US.

At this stage the retention of contact with the Chinese Nationalists did not imply British support for a non-communist Taiwan. But the intensification of the cold war, coupled with a radical shift in US thinking on Taiwan, forced changes in the British government's attitude. At first, between June and October 1950, the government worked for a compromise solution to defuse tensions over Taiwan's political status; and then, from November 1950 onwards, it effectively, if not publicly, accepted a non-communist Taiwan. This was a policy that threatened to jeopardise the whole basis of the British government's policy towards China.

PREVENTING AND ENSURING 'TWO CHINAS': ANGLO-AMERICAN POLICIES TO OCTOBER 1950

In January 1950 the US administration began to disengage from the Chinese Nationalist regime.[15] A presidential statement on 5 January 1950 and a speech to the National Press Club by Secretary of State Dean Acheson reaffirmed that Taiwan was a part of China and that the US would 'not pursue a course which will lead to involvement in the civil conflict in China'; the Economic Co-operation Administration's programme would continue to supply economic assistance, but the US would not provide military aid or advice to the Chinese Nationalists, nor would it intervene to prevent the island falling to the communists.[16] American reasoning reflected strategic and political considerations. Truman and Acheson, disillusioned with Chiang Kai-shek's regime, accepted that without massive American intervention the island would fall; equally a public denial of support would hopefully deflate the domestic debate over the direction of US policy towards China, by undermining Republican critics and preventing the army, in particular MacArthur, from increasing assistance to the Nationalist regime.[17]

Officially, US policy reversed because war broke out in Korea. The US declared Taiwan neutral, a status to be maintained by an American naval presence. Neutralisation can be viewed as a pragmatic response to a new military situation. Taiwan tied down communist forces in south China, kept naval and aerial communication lines open and, by reaffirming the American commitment to contain communism, improved the morale of UN and South Korean troops.[18] But the decision to prevent Taiwan falling was actually taken in March 1950 and reflected a fundamental change in US thinking on the cold war in Asia. The globalisation of the American containment strategy, culminating in the adoption of NSC68, gave the island a symbolic importance. In May, Dean Rusk, the new Assistant Secretary of State for Far Eastern Affairs, argued that it was time to 'draw the line' on Taiwan, for it was 'important politically if not strategically'.[19] A plan was set. The US navy would prevent an invasion; a political coup would remove Chiang Kai-shek and install Sun Li-jen as leader. A UN trusteeship over the island would reduce western and Asian criticism. The Korean War altered the plan; the fleet still intervened but saved Chiang as well as Chinese Nationalist rule.[20]

Although between the early spring of 1950 and the outbreak of the Korean War the British government began to doubt the direction of US policy, it made no attempt to pressurise the US over this issue. The British government realised that the US military wanted to save Taiwan and was supplying covert military assistance to the island. After MacArthur had arrested Thomas Liao, a Taiwanese independence leader, in March 1950, Guy Burgess, an official in the Far Eastern Department and a spy for the Soviets, became convinced that the Supreme Commander for Allied Powers in Japan would intervene to save the Nationalists.[21] At the end of May 1950, Biggs noted that it was 'just possible that [the] Americans may reverse her policy and send forces from Japan at the last moment to prevent communist occupation'.[22] Ernest Bevin, the British Foreign Secretary, even considered raising Taiwan at the meeting of foreign ministers in May, but confirmation that the State Department was reassessing its whole strategy was not given until 5 June 1950. Even then, the Foreign Office reaction was critical but not alarmist. William Strang, Permanent Under-Secretary of State at the Foreign Office, remarked that 'there are the seeds of trouble here'; while Robert Scott, Assistant Under-Secretary of State at the Foreign Office, argued that 'unsuccessful American measures to defend Formosa would be much worse than outright abandonment'.[23] The British government had misjudged the US position on this issue and had overestimated China's ability to successfully invade Taiwan in 1950. Given the paucity of information on which they were based, these misconceptions were understandable; but even post-June 1950

the assumptions that had underpinned British policy continued to do so.
From the British government's perspective, neutralisation was 'a difficult, delicate and potentially very dangerous development':[24] it prolonged the Chinese Civil War, made the return to normal relations between China and the West extremely problematic, raised tensions in the Far East, and might, if the Chinese had launched an attack on Taiwan, have resulted in war between China and the US. During July, Chinese statements indicating an intent to invade and evidence of Chinese troop movements into the coastal provinces adjacent to Taiwan compounded British worries.[25] In the event of a clash, the British Chiefs of Staff wanted to delay military support to the US for as long as possible, but acknowledged that, if there was a prolonged conflict, then British forces would have 'to join in'.[26] US policy undermined the British strategy for dealing with communism. It also threatened world peace and provoked widespread criticism of US policy. The Indian government, and in particular Jawaharlal Nehru the Prime Minister of India, believed that the development was indicative of a US administration out of step with Asian attitudes. Nehru argued that the linking of Taiwan with the war in Korea had convinced the PRC that the US was planning aggression against the Chinese mainland. In July, Nehru informed Attlee that a solution was required to prevent a possible head-on collision between America and China over Taiwan.[27] The French government, concerned by developments, wanted Britain to try and influence the direction of American policy.[28] Bevin resisted pressure from within the cabinet and from the Chiefs of Staff for a strongly worded denouncement of US intervention, but recognised that tensions had to be reduced. In July, Bevin implored Acheson to play down the Taiwan question and reaffirm that its future status should be settled on the basis of the Cairo Declaration.[29] By the end of the month, he began to step up pressure for a UN resolution, which endorsed neutrality but tied it to a formula to settle Taiwan's status. Bevin wanted to forestall a Chinese invasion and prevent the issue from becoming 'a septic focus tending to poison relations between the Democracies'.[30]

Unfortunately, at this stage, all possible formulae dealing with the future of Taiwan were problematic. The return of the island to the Chinese mainland would be fiercely resisted by the Chinese Nationalists and was, in any case, incompatible with American policy. The retention of Taiwan by the Nationalists was unacceptable to the PRC and to the majority of Asian nations. The most viable solution in 1950 appeared to be independence. Taiwanese nationalism had emerged during the period of Japanese occupation, while the brutal suppression of the

Taiwanese rebellion in March 1947 had engendered hatred and distrust of Chinese Nationalist rule.[31] Unfortunately, by 1950, the Taiwanese independence movement was weak and divided, with its leaders,
such as Thomas Liao, exiled in Japan and in Hong Kong.[32] Moreover,
as a result of the repression of 1947, the Taiwanese had no political
base on the island, and with Nationalist control over the majority of
large-scale industrial and commercial concerns, Taiwanese business
activity was confined to the small-scale sector. Consequently, if Taiwan was declared independent, the Nationalist regime would need to
be replaced, either by an independent Taiwanese government or, more
realistically, by an international trusteeship. Even if possible, independence
was unacceptable to the Chinese communists and to the Chinese Nationalists. A demilitarised independent Taiwan was more amenable to the
PRC than a Nationalist Taiwan, but, even if the US and the majority
of UN members accepted this solution, it still left the vexed question
of what to do with one million Chinese Nationalists resident on the
island; they could not be left on Taiwan, if independence was to be
credible or feasible, and could not, on humanitarian and political grounds,
be returned to the mainland.

Ultimately, no compromise solution was possible because one was
not in US interests. On 19 July Truman made an address to Congress
to reaffirm that 'the neutrality of Formosa is without prejudice to the
political questions affecting that island',[33] and at the end of August the
US agreed to place the question on the UN agenda. A number of reasons
prompted the US to pay lip-service to a settlement. Firstly, there was
concern in Washington over the strain the issue was placing on Anglo-
American relations.[34] Secondly, General MacArthur, by visiting Taiwan
and sending a controversial address to the 'Veterans of Foreign Wars'
advocating a US military commitment to the Nationalist regime, had
undermined an attempt by the US administration to play down the scale
of US involvement on the island.[35] MacArthur wanted to increase military
aid to the island, to incorporate Taiwan into his military command and to
use Nationalist troops in Korea and against China. The State Department
acted now because it did not want the US military to use Taiwan to justify
a policy of roll back against Communist China. Thirdly, the Chinese
communists intensified a propaganda campaign highlighting American
interference in the Chinese Civil War. On 24 August Chou En-lai
stated that the UN should condemn US policy towards the island and
introduce 'immediate measures to bring about the complete withdrawal
of all the US armed invaders from Taiwan'.[36] Fourthly, a solution to
settle Taiwan's status had to be formulated before the Korean War

ended, when the rationale for an American naval presence would cease.

To be acceptable to a large number of UN members and to have any chance of reducing tensions over the issue of Taiwan, a UN resolution had to combine UN control with a coherent solution to deal with the island's future status. The British advocated that the UN assembly should uphold the basic tenets of the Cairo and Potsdam Declarations, with a UN commission studying when and how, and not if, the island would be turned over to the communists.[37] The PRC and Asian nations would have supported this solution but it was unacceptable to the US. Although there were different shades of opinion within it, there was no question of a US administration sanctioning the return of Taiwan to Communist China. The State Department wanted a liberal, non-communist regime, whereas the Pentagon was willing to acquiesce in Chinese Nationalist control.[38] At the foreign ministers meeting in September 1950, Acheson rejected a UN resolution drafted by the British government; he argued that, instead of emphasising the Cairo Declaration, a clause should be inserted which took 'into account the interests of the people of Formosa ... on an equal level as the Chinese claim'.[39] Despite being aware that US military supplies were reaching the island,[40] the British government had underestimated the US commitment to Taiwan; the US was merely using the UN to legitimise neutrality. As the American position became clearer, the Indians and Canadians, as well as the British, distanced themselves from the UN resolution. Even before China had intervened in the Korean conflict, it had become extremely unlikely that there would be a UN-sponsored attempt to defuse tensions over Taiwan.

China's intervention in the Korean War in November 1950 made the immediate return of Taiwan to China impossible, but, at the same time, made it more self-evident that if there was to be a general political settlement reducing tensions in the Far East then the question had to be on the political agenda. Nehru was adamant: Taiwan had to be handed back to China if a world war was to be avoided. He wanted a formula that reaffirmed the Cairo and Potsdam Declarations on Taiwan – but did not necessarily cede Taiwan to China – coupled with China's admission into the UN, to be offered to the Soviet bloc as the price for a peaceful conclusion to the Korean War.[41] Bevin and Attlee agreed. During his December conference with Truman, Attlee argued that, if the Korean War was prolonged, the UN should establish a commission to consider the future status of Taiwan.[42]

By December 1950, however, no solution could reconcile US and Chinese attitudes. The chance of Taiwan being returned to China as part of a general settlement for the Far East was remote and the Chinese would not accept a solution that did not return the territory to China. General Wu Hsui-ch'uan, the PRC emissary at the UN in New York, made this emphatically clear:

> Whatever decision the United Nations General Assembly may take on the so-called question of the status of Taiwan, whether it be to hand over the island to the United States so that it might administer it openly under the disguise of 'trusteeship', or 'neutralisation', or whether it be to procrastinate by way of 'investigation', thereby maintaining the present state of actual United States occupation, it will, in substance, be stealing China's legitimate territory and supporting United States aggression against Taiwan in opposition to the Chinese people. Any such decision would in no way shake the resolve of the Chinese people to liberate Taiwan, nor would it prevent action by the Chinese people to liberate Taiwan . . .[43]

The Americans, by contrast, could not agree to any political solution promising to return the territory to China. *The Times* acknowledged that this was the issue 'which sticks most in the American gullet'.[44] At the Washington conference in December 1950, between Attlee and Truman, the US President agreed to a special commission to gather information on the problem (nothing came of this); but underlying American opposition to a general settlement involving a concession over Taiwan was made emphatically clear to the British delegation. Acheson informed them that:

> It is hard to believe that this [the Korean War] is merely a burst of Chinese military fervour; and if we gave them Formosa and make concessions, they would then be calm and peaceful. On the contrary if we give concessions they will become increasingly aggressive. We may not be able to do anything about this on the mainland, but we can on the islands.[45]

By the early months of 1951, the British government accepted that impasse had been reached. Herbert Morrison accepted that 'Formosa looks like bedevilling the foreign policy of His Majesty's Government and the US government for as far ahead as can be foreseen'.[46] When, in May 1951, MacArthur accused Britain of wanting to hand over Taiwan to a 'potential red enemy', the British government was forced to retreat further.[47] On 11 May, Morrison stated that while the UN would consider the question 'at the appropriate time . . . it would be premature to discuss the future of Formosa so long as the operations continue in Korea'.[48]

In theory, the British government still wanted Taiwan returned to China; in reality, British thinking had begun to shift towards independence for the island, an idea now even more problematic in 1951 than it had been in 1950. The Nationalists, now firmly entrenched, had repressed the independence movement; and, perhaps because of the social revolution unleashed on the mainland from 1951 onwards, the Taiwanese had begun to view Nationalist rule as the better of two evils. While in 1950 the British consul reported that the idea of independence had gained prominence amongst the Taiwanese, by 1951 he argued that Nationalist rule had been accepted.[49] In any case, the scale and breadth of American financial support to the Chinese Nationalists made talk of independence redundant.

CONSTRUCTING AN INFORMAL US EMPIRE ON TAIWAN

Over the course of the early 1950s American policy towards Taiwan had two components: firstly, in order to guarantee the security of the Nationalists and to extend American influence, the US significantly increased economic and military aid to the Chinese Nationalist regime; secondly, in order to transform Taiwan into a viable and attractive anti-communist state, the US promoted economic, political and military reform. These two elements were closely linked, reform being essential to ensure Taiwan would not become dependent on American financial support, while aid was a prerequisite for the transformation of the Taiwanese state. Within a month of the outbreak of the Korean conflict, US policy-makers privately declared their aim was to establish an economically viable 'show window for democracy'. Over the summer of 1950 Acheson, Dean Rusk and George Kennan began considering the necessary political, economic and military reforms needed to achieve this goal.[50] There was, however, an inherent contradiction in the American position. In order to maintain Taiwan as a strategic stronghold against communist encroachment and then, as the Korean War intensified, as a potential launching pad for action against China, massive military expenditure and tight political control were necessary. These policies threatened the island's economic viability and made political change more problematic.

The impact of US aid and reform proposals on the Taiwanese economy in the early 1950s was profound and guaranteed the long-term viability of the Chinese Nationalist regime. The Taiwanese economy, with a solid agricultural and industrial base, sound infrastructure, a highly

Table 2.1   US Aid to Taiwan, 1951–54 (US $ million)

Fiscal Year	Stabilisation	Development	Total
1951/2	130.0	24.2	154.2
1953	58.6	13.3	71.9
1954	59.4	17.6	77.0
Total	248.0	55.1	303.1

Source: NSC Planning Board Staff study, 30 March 1953; DDRS 1988, 406.

educated labour force and managerial and administrative personnel from the mainland, had the necessary prerequisites for economic development, but it was American aid which allowed the economy to overcome grave short-term problems.[51] As Table 2.1 indicates, American aid had two objectives: stabilisation and development. In total, stabilisation accounted for 82 per cent and development 18 per cent of aid in this period. The division of aid by the National Security Council (NSC) into these two components seems arbitrary, but does indicate the depth of the US commitment to a non-communist regime.

With Nationalist foreign exchange reserves virtually exhausted in the spring of 1950, and with the collapse of Taiwanese export markets in China and Japan, American aid, coupled with an import substitution strategy (introduced in 1951), allowed the Taiwanese economy to bridge its foreign exchange gap. In the 1950s, with the US financing between 30 and 47 per cent of Taiwanese imports, US aid ensured the economy received valuable sources of raw materials and manufactured goods for economic reconstruction.[52] American military and economic aid also underwrote a Taiwanese budget deficit, the product of a small tax base and excessive military expenditure. Aid allowed the Nationalists to continue military preparations without undermining the island's economy; most economic historians agree that without foreign aid, the economy would have entered a new inflationary cycle in 1951.[53] American aid helped overcome a Taiwanese investment and savings gap; it provided the economy with capital and, by reducing demand-pull inflation and by restoring confidence in the regime, promoted savings and stopped excessive capital flight from Taiwan.

The US did not want to underwrite the Taiwanese economy indefinitely and argued that economic and military reforms were needed to ensure sustainable economic growth on the island. Military reform proved difficult. The Nationalists were extremely reluctant to change military structures and, more importantly, to reduce the size of their forces in line with government revenues. The US had more success in influencing Nationalist economic policy but Chiang's regime was more receptive to reform in this area after the experiences on the mainland in the 1940s. The Nationalists were determined to reduce and prevent further inflation and were amenable to land reform, especially with the US-inspired Joint Commission for Rural Reconstruction aiding and promoting change in rural areas. The Nationalists, still under the influence of Sun Yat-sen's interventionist doctrines, and the Americans, with their faith in economic liberalism, were not in total agreement on economic policy, but there was a basic understanding that a strong economy was an essential prerequisite for political stability.[54]

If US policy towards Taiwan succeeded in stabilising an economy which was already fundamentally sound, it guaranteed the survival of a political system which was politically redundant and ideologically bankrupt: Taiwan did not become a 'show window for democracy'. The Nationalists retained a monopoly of political power, with Chiang Kai-shek dominant and his son Chiang Ching-kuo, in control of the intelligence network, groomed to succeed. Chiang introduced some minor changes to the political structure such as reducing the influence of the CC Clique and modifying the Central Committee, but these consolidated his own power base and maintained KMT dominance; they did not move Taiwan towards a liberal political system.[55] Although the Chinese Nationalists encouraged independence leaders to enter Taiwan in the first six months of 1950, this was only a ploy to gain credence in the US; once the territory had been declared neutral, the regime once again suppressed independence sympathisers, arresting 12 independence campaigners during 1951 – including Peter Huang and Joshua Liao – thus driving the independence movement underground.[56] Campaigners remained active in Japan; Thomas Liao made appeals to the UN and to Attlee during the course of 1951. But they had no base on Taiwan. The Nationalists introduced a pilot self-government scheme for provincial and local government in 1951, but significant power was not vested in these bodies; the provincial governor, who did wield some power at that level, was a KMT appointee.[57] Political change on Taiwan required US pressure. Once China had intervened in the Korean conflict, political reform became a secondary concern; the US came to accept that the removal of Chiang had become an 'exceedingly difficult, perhaps impossible task', and one which threatened Taiwan's political stability and military strength.[58] Chiang was a reactionary figurehead with no real support on the island, but he was the only Nationalist capable of holding together a party that, historically, had been weak and factionalised. The Americans were helping to create a economically viable but politically repressive, strategic bulwark against communism.

CEMENTING THE ANTI-COMMUNIST BULWARK

Japanese recognition of the Chinese Nationalists in 1952 as the government of Taiwan was a profound development. There was now no chance of a trade-driven reconciliation between Japan and China; the PRC would view the Japanese as lost to the American camp and the US determined to encircle China. In 1951 the British and the US had disagreed over who could participate in the Japanese Peace Treaty – Britain wanting an invitation to the PRC; the US to the Chinese Nationalists – but they had eventually agreed that neither 'Chinas' would sign. In theory this allowed the Japanese government to enter into relations with either Chinese state.[59] In 1951 the British Conservative government had sought to prevent US pressure on the Japanese to recognise the Chinese Nationalists and had received a guarantee from Acheson that the US would refrain from doing so.[60] Early in 1952, however, Yoshida Shigeru published a letter indicating the exact opposite. Eden had been personally rebuffed; British views ignored; and Chinese Nationalist control of Taiwan further legitimised. The importance of China as a market for Japanese products and as a source of raw materials made relations with Communist China economically useful for Japan but politically (and hence economically) the Japanese could not afford to jeopardise relations with the US. They had to align with the Chinese National-ists. Given Britain's acceptance of the Japanese Peace Treaty, this development reaffirmed China's perception of Britain as subservient to the US and made a future political settlement in the Far East, which incorporated Taiwan, even more problematic. In January 1952 Chang Han-fu, the Chinese Vice-Minister of Foreign Affairs, made a direct link between the Japanese Peace Treaty and Anglo-American collaboration:

> Since the conclusion of the Second World War, Britain's Government policy towards the US government has always been one of betraying the interests of the British people and of abject servility towards the US government. Since the British government participated in the San Francisco Peace Conference and hastened to be among the first to ratify the unilateral Peace Treaty with Japan, it cannot but submit to the US government's policy of forcing the Japanese government

to pledge to conclude a Peace Treaty with the Chinese KMT reactionary clique, of acting with hostility to the Chinese People and of intensifying the preparation for a new aggressive war in the Far East.[61]

British policy towards Taiwan rather drifted in the wake of this development. Thereafter the government became more committed to a non-communist Taiwan, but did not attempt to reconcile its desire for political settlement in the Far East with the American commitment to Chinese Nationalist control of the island. On Foreign Office advice, Eden agreed that Taiwan be 'held in suspension until the general Far Eastern situation has clarified and until a satisfactory Korean settlement has been achieved'.[62] Churchill was willing to acquiesce in American policy. He suggested that the British government accept Japan's recognition of the Chinese Nationalist regime, as long as it did not cover their claim to mainland China.[63] And in May 1953 he wrote to Gladwyn Jebb and argued that 'it would be very shabby of the Americans to desert Chiang whom Roosevelt rammed down my throat in the war, and of whom they despised too soon because of the corruption which General Marshall felt in his regime'.[64]

The Conservative government's commitment to a non-communist Taiwan sprang from a number of factors. Firstly, the Chinese Nationalists, under American guidance and with American economic and military aid, were turning Taiwan into an economically and politically viable state. Secondly, a British stand advocating the 'reunification of China' was not going to guarantee a *modus vivendi* between China and Britain at this stage. Thirdly, the British Chiefs of Staff believed the territory was a useful means of maintaining the maximum military pressure on the PRC.[65] Fourthly, Commonwealth criticism of US policy was muted and not as significant an influence on the new Conservative government: India wanted Taiwan returned to China but no longer demanded this as a means of securing peace; Australia and New Zealand, more closely tied to the US as a result as the ANZUS treaty, were willing to accept an anti-communist Taiwan. Finally, and most significantly, there would be no reversal in the American commitment to Taiwan in the short to medium term and Britain would not jeopardise Anglo-American relations for the prospect of a wider political settlement in the Far East incorporating Taiwan. Indeed, in December 1951 Robert Scott suggested that British support for a non-communist Taiwan could dramatically improve Anglo-American relations:

The Americans take a keen interest in this, partly for strategic and partly for domestic political reasons. To us it is less important than policy towards China or the defence of South East Asia; and if yielding a little on the Formosan issue helped us to secure American agreement on these bigger issues, I consider that it would be worth our while to do so. It is true that any Japanese arrangements with Chiang will irritate Peking, but the major irritant to Peking is the denial of the island – on which the Americans are agreed.[66]

CREATING AN INVASION LAUNCHING PAD

By 1952, American policy was shifting away from a defensive concept of Taiwan as a safe haven for the Chinese Nationalists and towards building up the island as a political and economic alternative to communism in Asia. Chiang wanted to return to the mainland and had, since 1950, lobbied the US administration to remove the restrictions placed upon his forces (whether he believed a successful invasion was possible is questionable). Karl Rankin in Taiwan was a strong advocate of Nationalist raids on mainland China, which he argued would relieve pressure on Indochina, divert Chinese forces from Korea, and raise the morale of anti-communist forces throughout the Far East.[67] The use of Chinese Nationalist forces in Korea and against the mainland had been under consideration in Washington since China had intervened in the Korean War. Throughout most of 1951 and 1952, the US Joint Chiefs of Staff advocated establishing 'ready units in the Chinese Nationalist forces capable of overt military action outside Formosa',[68] and considered providing air and naval support to allow the Nationalists to hold beachheads in south China – so stimulating resistance to the communist regime. With the Korean War ceasefire talks not promising any progress during 1952, the US actually began to train Nationalist forces for offensive as well as defensive operations.[69]

A decision to de-neutralise Taiwan was taken by President Eisenhower, supported and prompted by Secretary of State, John Foster Dulles, at the end of 1952. The President, having made an election promise to end the Korean conflict, believed that unleashing Chiang would increase pressure on the Chinese to reach a settlement; he reasoned that the PRC would not want to have a long-term commitment in Korea if it perceived a threat to its position on the mainland. De-neutrality could force the Chinese to divert troops and material to Fukien and Kwangtung; it could also stimulate resistance in China and could improve morale amongst Chinese Nationalist forces. Eisenhower wanted to retreat from the containment strategy inaugurated by the Democratic administration; he did not believe the US had the military or economic resources or the political will to use American ground troops to resist communist expansion in Asia. Instead Asian troops would meet the communist threat on the ground. The de-neutralisation of Taiwan sprang from this new policy direction. It was also influenced by Dulles's thinking on how to deal with Communist China. He wanted Communist China isolated politically and economically, and pressurised militarily. Three elements of US policy towards Taiwan secured these three aims. By upholding the Chinese Nationalist seat in the UN, it isolated the PRC politically. By tying Japan to Taiwan, it reduced pressure from within political and business circles in Japan for stronger Japanese economic ties with the Chinese mainland, and thus ensured China's exclusion from any future Asian trading bloc. Finally, by de-neutralising Taiwan, the Chinese Nationalists became a more significant military threat to China. Some historians, notably John Gaddis, have argued that this policy was a coherent strategy aimed at forcing China into greater reliance on the Soviet Union to induce Sino-Soviet tensions and hopefully a schism in the communist bloc.[70] Others, notably Nancy Bernkopf Tucker, have argued Dulles was influenced by domestic political factors. She argues Dulles deliberately adopted a hostile line towards China to pacify the right-wing of the Republican Party, to allow the administration more room to manoeuvre and to prevent these elements attacking Dulles personally.[71] Eisenhower was amenable to any policy which diverted the attention of the right-wing of his party, which had wanted Senator Robert Taft (Republican, Ohio) as the party's presidential candidate.

What is perhaps surprising is not that Eisenhower de-neutralised Taiwan in January 1953, but that the Democratic administration had not done so in 1952. The reluctance of the State Department, under Acheson, to take such an initiative is partly explained by allied opposition. Acheson, for example, dismissed a proposal by Admiral William Fechteler for a naval show of strength in 1952, arguing that 'if anything does happen now we will really be in trouble with our allies'.[72] Of greater significance, however, were the different nature of Pentagon–State Department relations under the two administrations. The Democratic administration was concerned about the degree of Pentagon control over the Chinese Nationalists and over American military advisers on Taiwan. Acheson, in particular, was extremely reluctant to cede any scope for independent action to the US military establishment in Washington or the Far East.[73] Acheson feared that if the US encouraged Chiang to adopt a more aggressive stand towards Communist China, it might become involved in a general war in the Far East. Eisenhower, by comparison, trusted the US military to keep a grip on Chiang and prevent him from invading the mainland.

The British government opposed de-neutralisation because it argued it would not contribute to the military defeat of the Chinese in Korea, would prolong the Korean War and would make a general settlement in the Far East more difficult. It was also argued that, by interfering with coastal shipping routes, it might be detrimental to the position of Hong Kong and to British shipping interests in the area. Finally, the government also felt that de-neutralisation would cause pronounced disagreements between Asian nations and the West.[74] Most significantly, the government thought it brought the risk of a general war between China and the West far closer. The US, and even the Soviets, might be brought into a Far East conflict if Chiang fulfilled his promise to invade the mainland. At the same time, a number of factors moderated the government's position. Firstly, while the Foreign Office and the Chiefs of Staff remained concerned about Nationalist military plans, especially after the large-scale assault on the island of Tungshen in July 1953, they did not believe that the Chinese Nationalists were likely to invade China unless the US provided extensive military aid, logistical support and naval and air cover. Tamsui believed that, while the US would increase small-scale Nationalist raids on communist-held islands, it would not encourage a major assault on the mainland.[75] Once Dulles had confirmed to Eden that the US did not contemplate increasing its military assistance to the Nationalists and did not want Chiang to return to the mainland, British concerns subsided.[76] Secondly, after a prolonged and intensive debate on far eastern affairs during the presidential election campaign, the government fully expected a toughening of US policy. Thirdly, while Nehru publicly denounced the American initiative as imprudent, in private he acknowledged that this had been a decision based on political rather than military reasoning and hence was unlikely to lead to war in the Far East.[77] Fourthly, Britain could not afford to allow differences over Taiwan to jeopardise relations with the US, the cornerstone of British foreign policy. It was the American failure to consult fully with Britain on the decision to de-neutralise Taiwan, and not the policy itself, which caused the British government most concern. Eden claimed he had not been informed of the decision, prompting the Labour Party to demand a parliamentary debate on the issue. As the blame lay as much with the British as with the Americans, the Foreign Secretary then rightly backed down. As the British and Amercian archives show, the British government had failed to probe the US deeply on the matter in 1952, and then in January, at the meeting between Churchill and Dulles, the Prime Minister had actually agreed that Chiang should be unleashed.[78]

The American administration had no intention of underwriting Chiang's return to the mainland. Eisenhower and Dulles did not want such a military commitment. The State Department was reluctant to supply military equipment to Taiwan: before agreeing to the shipment of bombers in 1953, it sought assurances from the US military in the Far East and from Chiang that these aircraft would not be used against the mainland without sanction from Washington.[79] Despite pressure from the Nationalists and from the US military, the State Department did not extend US naval protection to the numerous off-shore islands between Taiwan and China and did not use Nationalist troops in Korea. Nevertheless, these policies reflected a number of perceived military drawbacks and not any lack of political commitment to the Nationalists.[80] Indeed, the US fully supported a policy which developed 'the capabilities of the Chinese Nationalist armed forces for the defence of Formosa and for such offensive operations as may be in the US interest'.[81] The US encouraged liaison between the Nationalist and guerrilla forces operating in China and encouraged small-scale naval and aerial attacks on communist-held offshore islands and on communist positions on the mainland. In July 1953 the US acquiesced in a large-scale Nationalist attack on Tungshen, an island off the Chinese mainland held by communist forces using an estimated 10 000 Nationalist troops.[82]

As we will discover in Chapters 4, 8 and 9, a key aim of British policy in the early 1950s was a general political settlement in the Far East, which would ease Sino-Western tensions. Despite Taiwan being the most intractable obstacle to such a settlement, the Conservative government did not formulate a coherent strategy for its future status. The Labour Party was more forward-thinking; it advocated independence for Taiwan. The party leadership, the parliamentary Labour Party and constituency parties saw Taiwan's status as symbolic, representing a misconceived and dangerous US approach to the Far East, which failed to take into account Asian susceptibilities. It was seen as an issue which could preclude a Far East settlement and drag the West into a war with China. At the Margate conference in October 1953, a resolution declared that:

> the problem of Formosa should be referred to the people of Formosa. Formosa should be neutralised for a period and Britain should be prepared to contribute to an international naval force for this

purpose. Therefore, the people of Formosa should be enabled freely to determine their own destiny.[83]

In January 1955, Attlee proposed that Chiang should be exiled and the island de-neutralised with a plebiscite to decide whether the island should join China.[84] The Foreign Office, promoted by Robert Scott, also sought independence for Taiwan, under a temporary UN trusteeship but with the UN eventually admitting two separate states: Taiwan and Communist China. Scott argued that India would propose the return of Taiwan to China in the aftermath of a Korean armistice and hence Britain had to formulate a positive alternative which prevented a division between the Asian Commonwealth and the US. He believed a solution possible. The Chinese communists might 'waive their claim to Formosa' and recognise Taiwan as an independent territory if Taiwan's status was linked to Chinese co-operation in a Korean settlement and if Taiwan was demilitarised.[85] Eden, however, rejected a change in the British position. He did not believe that the Chinese communists would accept the linking of Taiwan with a general settlement in the Far East, and argued that the attitude of the US administration and the hostility of American public and congressional opinion towards rapprochement with the PRC made it unlikely that the US would accept this solution. He believed that any compromise solution to settle Taiwan's political status was dependent on a realistic US attitude. The US administration would have to recognise the Chinese Nationalists as the government of Taiwan, thus renouncing their claim to the mainland. This was highly unlikely in the 1950s. Basically Eden did not want to jeopardise Anglo-American relations. Instead, Britain would try and moderate American policy towards Communist China, but would not take an initiative to foster a Sino-Western rapprochement. Eden's attitude was realistic and pragmatic but at the same time cautious and unadventurous. A diplomatic initiative over Taiwan may have allowed China's admission into the UN and may have changed China's perception of the West. As matters stood in 1953, however, a solution to the problem of Taiwan awaited an easing of Sino-Western relations.

CHINA, TAIWAN AND THE WORLD DIVIDED

The continued existence of a hostile Chinese Nationalist island under American protection intensified the cold war in Asia and presented a seemingly non-negotiable obstacle in the way of a general political settlement. Throughout this period, the Chinese gave no indication that they would accept a compromise solution which did not reaffirm their sovereignty over the island: there was no talk of independence, trusteeships or regional autonomy for Taiwan by the CCP.[86] Meanwhile, the depth of the American commitment reinforced Chinese communist perceptions of the US as an insincere and intrinsically hostile power, which wanted to challenge the PRC's political and military hegemony. Chinese communist propaganda increasingly argued that the US had assumed the imperialist mantle from Japan. The CCP brandished the San Francisco Conference, which resulted in Japan's recognition of Taiwan, as an 'obvious attempt at pairing off the two servile offshoots of its own spawning': Taiwan and Japan.[87] The CPG exploited the Taiwan question, using it to appeal to Chinese nationalist sentiment, to appeal for Asian unity against the West and to promote the CPG as the only advocate for peace in the Far East.[88] The attitude of the CPG, however, did vacillate, and to some extent moderate, over the course of the early 1950s. Whereas in 1952 the Chinese communists were still, in theory, actively advocating liberation, by 1953 they confined their propaganda to opposing the Chinese Nationalists, no longer promising an invasion of Taiwan. The Chinese were now more anxious to reduce tensions and prevent a clash between China and the West. The Americans had succeeded in forcing the Chinese onto the defensive over Taiwan and indeed the PLA began redeploying troops to defensive positions adjacent to Taiwan. The Chinese press dismissed de-neutralisation, but not as violently as might have been expected; there was no official statement by the Chinese government denouncing the new American initiative.[89] The Chinese began to link American policy towards Taiwan with a wider attempt to drive a wedge between the US and its allies. Commenting on Eisenhower's speech announcing the de-neutralisation of Taiwan, the *New China News Agency (NCNA)* argued that the American decision would cause 'widespread fear and uneasiness in Western Europe and Asia', and would, moreover, 'widen still further the gulf between the US and the other capitalist countries'.[90] Chou En-lai stated that if there was a war in the Far East, the Chinese would drag Taiwan into the conflict in order to stimulate contradiction in the western bloc.[91]

CONCLUSIONS

Until November 1950, Britain wanted and worked for Taiwan's return to China. This solution, however, was incompatible with a deepening

American commitment to the island. Once China had intervened in the Korean War and the Americans had rejected a compromise solution, British thinking radically changed. In 1951 the Labour government advocated independence for Taiwan, and in 1952 and 1953 the Conservative government accepted Chinese Nationalist control. The continued existence of a hostile regime, supported by the US, made a wider political settlement between China and the West extremely problematic. A solution to defuse tensions over this question has proved elusive into the 1990s. The Chinese reaction to British and American policies was hostile and non-accommodating; they would not accept informal American control over a part of China. This was an attitude which, as we shall see in Chapter 5, contrasts with the PRC's acceptance of British rule in Hong Kong.

3 Roll Back not Relations, June–October 1950

Let China sleep for when she awakes the whole world will tremble.

Napoleon

The Korean War, between the Democratic People's Republic of Korea (DPRK) in the north and the Republic of Korea (ROK) in the south, escalated into an international conflict when the UN intervened to prevent the fall of Syngman Rhee's pro-western regime. The war tightened cold war geo-strategic alliances and entrenched cold war political and ideological divisions. The presence of western military forces in Korea and in the Taiwan straits and the tightening of the western economic embargo on the PRC cemented the Sino-Soviet alliance, intensified Chinese anti-imperialism and accelerated the transformation of Chinese society. In the West, more nuanced approaches to Communist China were the casualties of war. The first part of this chapter will examine how war affected the British liberal policy framework; how the British government dealt with pressure to establish an economic embargo on China; and how it sought to gain China's admission to the UN. The second part will analyse the impact of war on British attempts to moderate American policy towards China. The third section will explain why Britain agreed with an American decision to extend the Korean War into North Korea, a decision that ultimately resulted in war between China and the West.

LIBERALISM CONTINUED: BRITISH POLICY TOWARDS CHINA

Sino-British relations did not deteriorate in the early months of the Korean War but the political impasse between Britain and China became entrenched. The status of British representatives in China did not alter.[1] But there was now no real chance of an end to the diplomatic impasse; any economic or political concessions to the communists in a time of war would be misinterpreted as appeasement. Even Hutchison now admitted there was nothing that could be done.[2] Nevertheless, the

53

British Foreign Office still held out hopes of full diplomatic relations with China. James Tang alludes to a plan to send Elser Dening to Peking to meet the Chinese government, a scheme in the back of Bevin's mind since the spring of 1950.[3] The mission was postponed because of China's intervention in the Korean War.

War in Korea did not change British government thinking: economic and political contact with China remained essential. British businessmen wanted trade and representation, and a diplomatic presence was now also required to negotiate a withdrawal of some commercial assets.[4] Domestic political opinion (left-wing groups, the left of the Labour Party and pacifist organisations) wanted a liberal approach. The British government did not want to 'drive China into Soviet hands'. The attitude of the Indian government continued to shape the British approach. The Indians did not want the Korean War to affect the West's attitude towards China.[5] Britain did not want Indo-British relations to deteriorate.[6] India was important to the British economy and India, with close diplomatic ties with Peking, could perhaps moderate China's response to Korean developments.

What the Korean War did was to intensify simmering Anglo-American differences over China. Britain wanted to maintain economic contact and work towards China's admission in the UN; the US wanted an economic embargo and China's continued exclusion.

TRADE NOT MILITARY AID

China required industrial goods for economic reconstruction; but goods such as metal products, machinery, machine tools and chemicals had a strategic value, augmenting China's military capacity. (A nation's industrial base is closely related to its military capabilities; if imported strategic goods and semi-strategic exports were not used directly to produce military equipment, then they could satisfy domestic demand, allowing resources to be transferred into military production.) The West faced a dilemma: whether to integrate China into the world economy or whether to hinder the development of its economy by restricting trade. The British government instinctively believed that, despite the hostilities in Korea, longer-term political and economic considerations had to be taken into account: an internationalist strategy had to prevail. The new hardline American stance on trade with the Chinese communists threatened the whole basis of such thinking.

An embargo on China presented huge logistical and political problems. How were the allies to control exports, especially re-exports from countries hostile or ambivalent to such measures? How would Hong Kong, as the international entrepôt centre for the Chinese economy, be included? And what about the Soviet North East Asian ports such as Vladivostok? More importantly, an embargo was unwanted: Britain still desired economic ties with China. Trade with the communists had a geo-strategic rationale: it provided an avenue of contact between the Chinese and the West; might undermine the isolationist and expansionist impulses of the Chinese communists; and might reduce their reliance on the Soviet Union. But underpinning British reluctance to extend economic controls against China were economic considerations.

The state of the British economy remained weak. It was imperative to increase exports and, because of the chronic shortage of dollars, find areas of supply, such as China, which were outside the dollar bloc. The President of the Board of Trade, Harold Wilson, and the Chancellor of the Exchequer, Sir Stafford Cripps, argued that a trade embargo against China would be a 'grave prejudice to the national economy'.[7] At the back of cabinet minds was the vision of a world divided into communist and capitalist trading blocs. Would the US press for restrictions on trade with the Soviet Union in semi-strategic goods, including rubber and machine tools? Soviet grain and timber were vital to the British economy. An alternative source would be the US which would be a further drain on British supplies of dollars. The government also had to take into account the position of British traders and industrial concerns. After having encouraged British firms to stay in China, would commercial interests view a trade embargo on the Chinese as a betrayal of their interests? Equally, if Britain imposed a unilateral trade embargo, would the French, Germans and Japanese gain a foothold in the Chinese market at the expense of Britain? (If trade had to be restricted then it would have to be done multilaterally through the Paris Co-ordinating Committee and not unilaterally as a result of pressure from the US.[8]) Trade sanctions against the Chinese communists threatened the prosperity and perhaps the future status of Hong Kong. Simply stated: Hong Kong was an entrepôt centre which relied on the international trade with China, a curtailment of which could cripple the colony's economy and perhaps undermine its political stability. Moreover, in 1950, Hong Kong was undergoing a minor economic boom because the Chinese economy had begun to recover from 13 years of war and a high proportion of China's trade was being processed by the colony. Hong Kong was making money again. Hence the British government did not want to lose the colony and so resisted trading sanctions.[9] The Foreign Office, the Colonial Office and British officials in Hong Kong agreed that if the colony restricted its exports to China, the PRC would start to question Hong Kong's value to them as a crown territory. Worse case scenarios entered the Whitehall discourse. With Chinese troops released from a possible invasion of Taiwan, and Chinese prestige slighted by Truman's intervention in the Chinese Civil War, a Chinese invasion could not be ruled out. Economic retaliation was more probable, but even so, if the Chinese simply withheld vital food and water supplies, British rule would become untenable. It was the intensity of American pressure, coupled partly with a realisation that China was not preparing for an invasion of the colony, that forced Britain eventually to tighten restrictions on the trade between Hong Kong and China.[10]

Initially, the Labour government ignored American demands. The cabinet meeting of 4 July 1950 imposed an embargo on exports to North Korea but deferred a decision on wider trade restrictions on China.[11] Attlee set the parameters: 'We should keep the question of our economic policy towards China separate from that of any embargo on North Korea.'[12] In July, the authorities in Hong Kong were informed that 'there is no present intention of making any major change in our policy *vis-à-vis* the Chinese: China was not a prohibited destination'.[13] As Britain, under the auspices of COCOM, was already restricting strategic exports to China, the government believed further sanctions unnecessary. The Foreign Office argued that the Americans would not stop at denying strategic exports to the Chinese but would add non-strategic items of trade to the list. 'We must, in fact, be prepared to face American pressure to take action which would involve the abandoning of our interests in China and the imposition of drastic controls over all trade, including normal civil requirements.'[14]

Although the British government had been co-operating with the Americans since July 1949 – when the US initiated attempts to curb strategic goods to China – the two powers had always approached this problem from different angles. The Americans saw the controls set up in 1949 as the bare minimum, but for the British these were the maximum. There had never been a cabinet consensus on the issue and hence in July the Prime Minister was extremely reluctant to broach the issue to the cabinet.[15] By July, the Ministry of Defence argued that Britain's controls on strategic exports to China were totally inadequate; it did not advocate an end to commercial contact with China, but did want a new balance drawn between the requirements of trade and defence.[16] Chinese inquiries about items such as steel rails, copper wire, wireless sets and heavy-duty tyres had increased dramatically: there was no point denying these goods to the North Koreans if they were easily available in China. The Ministry of Defence did not believe that the system of informal controls in Britain was working; it wanted export licences to be applied and international lists extended.[17] Bevin regarded the government's position as incomprehensible, doing little to alleviate the position of British business and liable to cause serious tensions in Anglo-American relations. Bevin conceded to Attlee that the number of strategic goods reaching China may have been 'of negligible proportion'. But argued that 'the psychological effect of our refusing to impose the controls proposed by the US [would] create resentment out of all proportion to the question of their practical effect, and would seem to have no advantage in the context of our policy to China'.[18]

The confusion and controversy surrounding the export of oil to China deepened divisions within the government. In May 1950 the American government stopped trade by US oil companies – the largest suppliers of petroleum to the Chinese mainland – and demanded a total western oil embargo.[19] Shell, in collaboration with the Foreign Office, agreed not to enter into any long-term contracts to supply oil products to the Chinese but honoured its existing commitments. Shell was to export only 26 000 tons to China, accounting for 5 per cent of total Chinese demand in 1950.[20] On the outbreak of war the government refused to reverse its policy. The British government informed the US administration that Shell supplies were for the Chinese domestic market only and thus not of any strategic importance. The Foreign Office believed the US administration was not only aiming to stop strategically important products, such as aviation and petroleum fuels, but also goods such as kerosene, which had only domestic uses. But since fuel shortages were one of the main constraints on the North Korean advance, and there was evidence that Shell supplies were reaching the North Koreans from China, this position became politically untenable.[21] The Americans exerted extreme pressure on the British government. American officials informed Lord Tedder, the British representative at the Joint Staff Mission in Washington, that if the South Korean regime fell, a scapegoat would have to be found; with British petrol fuelling the Korean People's Army advance it would be British export policy.[22] Under pressure from Bevin and the Chiefs of Staff, and with the *S.S. Fusus* at sea due to unload 750 tons of motor spirit at Tientsin, the cabinet authorised the requisitioning (for 'military purposes') of Shell's oil stocks in the Far East and intercepted the tanker. An embargo had been placed on the export of oil to the Chinese market.[23]

In due course, during the summer of 1950, the British government was forced to introduce further restrictions on trade with the Chinese. It removed the differential between strategic controls on exports to the Soviet Union and to China and tightened controls in Britain and her territories in the Far East to ensure that these and existing restrictions were enforced.[24] But instead of establishing institutional procedures, in the UK and/or through COCOM, to codify controls, British measures were introduced in a piecemeal fashion; additional goods were added to an informal list of prohibited items and Hong Kong's controls were gradually adjusted. The British government was slow in implementing an effective scheme for controlling exports to the Far East, and, once established, the system was cumbersome, inefficient and inconsistent; it confused British industrialists, did nothing to improve relations with the Chinese and placed severe strains on the Anglo-American relationship. The government thought the system would be temporary and would be removed when the Korean War ended. China's intervention in Korea and the consequential vehemence of opposition by America to trade with China ensured the embargo would become draconian and remain in place until 1957.

MEMBERSHIP DENIED

After 25 June 1950 China's admission to the UN became linked to a settlement of the Korean War. The Indians formulated a peace initiative which linked a ceasefire for the Korean War with China's admission to the UN and its recovery of Taiwan. The US government rejected this plan. The British government was divided on the Indian approach and as a result its policy vacillated. On the one hand, Britain wanted Communist China in the UN and desired a ceasefire in Korea; on the other, if China were admitted it would increase communist morale and indicate to the PRC that it was in its best interests to follow the diplomatic line of the Soviet Union.[25] Moreover, the UN resolution sanctioning UN collective security in Korea had been made possible by the absence of the Soviet delegate. If the Chinese and the Soviets were allowed to return to the Security Council before the end of the fighting, they could veto any further resolutions on Korea. Even the Foreign Office now acknowledged that previous efforts to circumvent the Chinese Nationalists had been 'sadly misplaced energy' because the Chinese Nationalists were now useful members supporting western resolutions on the Korean War.[26] The attitude of the US had also to be borne in mind. Pierson Dixon, Deputy Under-Secretary of State at the Foreign Office, noted that: 'The Americans have made it plain that they do not want the Chinese, followed by the Russians, in the UN at the moment and if we took part in bringing this about the strain on our relations with the Americans would be considerable.'[27] Attlee reduced the matter to a basic equation: it was 'unrealistic to risk alienating US opinion for the sake of making further gestures towards the Chinese communists'.[28] Attlee told the cabinet, 'we must reject any suggestion of a bargain, by which a representative of the Chinese government would be admitted to the Security Council, in return for a settlement of the Korean situation'.[29] The vote by a British delegate accepting Chinese communist credentials to the ECOSOC was thus cancelled.

Nevertheless, Britain's position on China's admission did change in August 1950. The return of Y.A. Malik to assume the Presidency of the Security Council altered the situation. When the Security Council reconvened in September 1950, the Soviets would raise Chinese communist credentials. Moreover, the Soviets and the Indians had now indicated that the problem would be 'raised on its own merits' – detaching the seating of China from a Korean resolution.[30] The issue might have eased a Korean ceasefire. Behind the obscure procedural reasoning was the same liberal line used to justify recognition: China's admission might influence the international behaviour of the PRC and reduce its reliance upon the Soviet Union. Bevin informed Acheson that:

> if the issue comes up in the Security Council in the way I have suggested [by the Soviets, but not linked to Korea] ... it will to my mind be the straightforward one of whether we drive China further into the Soviet camp with consequences which may be very serious for world peace or whether we admit her to the UN and put her good behaviour to the test, with the possible result of gradually drawing her away from Russia.[31]

A seat in the UN may well have moderated China's perception of the West and tied it more closely to the international community. In 1950, after the UN had intervened in the Korean War, the Chinese attacked the UN but never denounced the organisation. Indeed the Chinese attacked US imperialism by drawing on international law; they argued the administration was violating the UN charter by its decision to neutralise the Taiwanese Straits, and argued that the absence of a Chinese communist delegate invalidated all UN resolutions. On 25 September a spokesperson for the Ministry of Foreign Affairs stated that: 'The

Chinese people are continuing to observe closely the attitude in the UN of these self-contradictory countries whose deeds do not accord with their words.'[32] The failure of the UN to admit China at this juncture was a set-back: it reinforced the Chinese view of the West as intrinsically hostile. It is uncertain whether China's admission to the UN at this moment would have resulted in full diplomatic relations between Britain and China, but the Chinese had always justified their refusal to establish relations by reference to British policy in the UN. In September 1950 Chou En-lai reiterated: 'the reason the negotiations have been fruitless is that, while the British government recognises the People's Republic of China, it favours permitting the so-called Chinese representatives belonging to the reactionary Kuomintang clique to continue their illegal occupation of China's seat in the United Nations'.[33] Full diplomatic relations may then have followed China's admission to the UN.

The British government's thinking continued to be influenced by Asian and British political opinion. Most Asian governments believed that a newly emergent anti-imperialist, nationalist government had to be seated in the UN. Nehru declared that 'so long as a nation of 450 million people remains outside a world organisation, that organisation cannot be regarded as fully representative'.[34] Asian sentiment was important because Britain did not want to strain its relationship with the Indian government. Attlee admitted that this problem was one that might cause a cleavage between the West and Asia.[35] Bevin agreed that 'The good effect of such a vote would be that the position would not arise in which the Asiatic countries by and large were voting on one side and all the Western powers either voting on the other or abstaining'. But Bevin did not believe that communists would behave once in an organisation; between 1921 and 1940, as General Secretary of the National Transport and General Workers' Union, he had fought to rid the union of communist influence. Instead he said that Chinese communist membership of the UN would expose the PRC for what it was to the rest of Asia, which might be 'of the greatest value in solidifying South and South East Asia against China'.[36] At the back of British minds was the thought that the problem, if not treated with care, could split the world into two camps. The domestic political reaction to the government's vacillating policy varied across the political spectrum. The Conservative opposition welcomed the decision to exclude China from the UN. Anthony Eden stated, rather inelegantly, that 'it adds to the difficulty and danger of re-opening that question before the UNO, until the Korean conflict is resolved'.[37] By contrast the left of the Labour Party still favoured admission. Sidney Silverman, invoking a 1906 speech by Lloyd George on Germany, argued that it was not possible to have a policy of encirclement and collective security at the same time.[38] Judging by the number of letters reaching the Foreign Office, constituency Labour parties were sympathetic to the Silverman line and critical of the Labour government one. Indeed Bevin addressed his critics at the October party conference. He informed delegates, 'I have no doubt if the statesmen of China do not indulge in aggression and upset the show again, if a little patience is shown and events are handled carefully, that . . . the new China will find herself associated with the rest of us in trying to build a new world'.[39] The British press supported the government's position on this question. *The Times*, hesitant about doing 'something to benefit the Russians', viewed the issue pragmatically: China's admission was inevitable and if not admitted, the UN, as a body, would be discredited. The *Daily Worker*, adopting the Soviet propaganda line, argued the issue was 'the burning need of the hour to save peace'.[40] The attitude of the British public was difficult to judge on this question. The Foreign Office rather condescendingly argued that the British public would not be able to understand how communism could be attacked for aggression in Korea in the Security Council and then admitted to the ECOSOC.[41] Yet the British public were never as vehemently opposed to the Chinese communists as the American public; they would probably have accepted the admission of China, especially if not tied to a settlement of the Korean War.

However, there was a major problem preventing China's admission: the US did not want Communist China to have a seat in the UN. In August and September 1950 the State Department did not close the door on China's admission, and indeed inferred to British policy-makers that it might compromise its position before the Korean conflict came to an end. But, in reality, the US could not contemplate the presence of the Chinese in the UN before the congressional elections in November, and probably for a long period thereafter. Acheson and Dean Rusk informed the British embassy in Washington that Chinese support for North Korean aggression had to be taken into account and that equally US public opinion would not accept Communist China's membership at this time.[42] However, when the Indians threatened to raise the question on its own merits, the US initially appeared to compromise its position. Rusk informed Oliver Franks, the British ambassador in Washington, that 'if we could not have a marriage by consent, there was at least a chance of a shotgun marriage'.[43] Rusk suggested that, instead of the issue going to the Security Council, it should be referred to a credentials committee, which would lay down the procedure for the admission of China to the UN. This was not an ideal solution: it would delay admission and would not facilitate a settlement of the Korean War. But the Foreign Office accepted it as a face-saving device to prevent a public airing of differences between Britain and the US. Within a week, however, the US had rejected the solution and returned to a straightforward vote in the UN.[44] As Latin and South American nations, who made up a sizeable proportion of the UN at this time, would not vote against the US, the administration had effectively blocked China's admission. A subsequent Indian resolution on the admission of China to the UN was defeated.

The British government believed that the political climate in the US had precluded a realistic US attitude. With public opinion highly agitated and the Republicans willing to exploit this question, the seating of Communist China was an extremely sensitive one for the Democratic administration. Senator Millard E. Tydings (Democrat, Maryland) reminded the American administration that the issue was a potentially explosive one. He submitted a resolution to Congress requesting the President to use his veto in the Security Council in order to block the admission of China to the UN.[45] Bevin argued that after the November congressional election, Britain could, with the support of other nations such as France and India, moderate the American position to 'secure a change-over in Chinese representation in the UN'.[46] British thinking was misconceived, however. What the government did not understand was that the whole basis of US thinking on the admission of China to the UN was at odds with that of the British. The US administration was determined to prevent the communists taking up a seat. American reasoning was infused by morality: the Chinese were hostile to the US, they had violated the resolutions of the UN in their support of the North Koreans and were under the dominance of the Soviet Union.[47] Equally, there was a rationale to the US position. The administration wanted to isolate the Chinese from diplomatic contacts with the West because it did not want to provide revolutionary communism with another actor for the UN stage. The Chinese would instead be forced to rely on the Soviet Union to be their voice in the UN, a role which would cause tensions between the two powers. Nor did the US want the status of Taiwan to be complicated. If a Chinese communist delegate was admitted to the UN, he or she would undoubtedly raise the status and future position of the island. This was the most important factor, indicating how central the decision to keep Taiwan non-communist had become. Taiwan was now integral to the

American containment strategy for the Far East; it pacified domestic critics of US foreign policy and was the polemical issue at the heart of internal power struggles within the US administration. Finally, the US did not attach much importance to the universality of the UN; if collective measures could be introduced without the presence of the Soviets and the Chinese, then so be it. Even if the Chinese had not intervened in Korea, it was highly unlikely that the US would have allowed China a seat in the UN.

BAILING OUT THE GOOD SHIP ANGLO-AMERICAN

> We are like the crew of a sailing ship in the path of a typhoon, indulging in a petty and sometimes ill-natured squabble about the theory of revolution.[48]

Tensions over the admission of China to the UN and the introduction of a strategic embargo had proved that while differences over China would not sink the Anglo-American ship, they could divert it seriously off course. The British government realised that it would have to align its policy closer to that of the Americans. The Foreign Office admitted that: 'We and the Americans cannot afford the luxury of mutually conflicting policies in China and the Far East.' However, the Korean War had actually widened the gap between the Atlantic powers.[49] As a result, Britain and America no longer fought over the control of the ship, which the Americans would guide through the storm. But disagreements over a future course continued below deck. Britain wanted the western response to the Korean War separated from western policy towards China. Once the war came to an end, China would be admitted to the UN, Taiwan would be returned to China and Sino-Western trade could be developed. During the war interim solutions would prevent a divergence between the Americans and the Indians and pacify the Chinese communists. By October 1950, however, this policy had clearly failed; the future of Taiwan remained uncertain, no formula to admit the Chinese communists to the UN had been agreed, and trade with the communists had been subject to discrimination.

The approach of the British government was based on the premise that Britain could successfully moderate US thinking. Britain, the old experienced head, would guide the naive, hot-headed and inexperienced Americans in the ways of world affairs. Esler Dening epitomised British attitudes:

We hope that by communicating our views to the State Department, we may to some degree influence them to approach the problem from an angle different from which they have hitherto approached it. They appear to have judged Chinese intentions without much regard for what the Chinese are likely to be thinking themselves.[50]

The British government misunderstood American administration thinking on China and totally overestimated British influence in Washington. As early as 11 July 1950, Acheson informed Bevin that he did not see 'any likelihood of harmonising our policies towards China by any significant changes in the basic attitude on which US policy is founded'.[51] The American administration would not compromise on the admission of China to the UN nor consider a solution which defused tensions over Taiwan. Acheson did not believe concessions would deter the Chinese from an aggressive move in Asia. He informed Bevin:

There can be little doubt that Communism, with China as a spearhead, has now embarked upon an assault against Asia, with immediate objectives in Korea, Indochina, Burma, the Philippines and Malaya and with medium range objectives in Hong Kong, Indonesia, Siam, India and Japan. We doubt that they will be deflected from their purpose by temporary accommodation, particularly if this accommodation is obtained by them at a time when their conduct is aggressive and in violation of the Charter.[52]

The Korean War had actually focused and hardened US thinking on the cold war in the Far East: the US was now determined to isolate the Chinese politically and economically. Previously such thinking, epitomised by the American commitment to Taiwan, had been difficult to articulate and implement because of allied and Asian opposition. The Korean War gave the US greater leverage over the attitude of its allies. The geo-strategic rationale underpinning American policy seemed more relevant, that is the administration believed war in Korea would heighten tensions between China and the Soviet Union. The State Department's Office of Intelligence Research epitomised American strategic thinking when it noted:

They [the Chinese communists] would be impressed not only by the relative weakness or ineptitude of the USSR in its Korean adventure, but also by the threat of the new military posture of the US in the Far East, a threat that had all but been created by Soviet blundering. As a consequence the strength of the Chinese communist ties to the USSR would be significantly weakened.[53]

John Lewis Gaddis argues that thoughts of dividing China and the Soviet Union became less significant during the Korean War, but clearly the strategy still had a pervading influence upon American thinking.[54]

US government policy was reinforced by the changing bureaucratic power balances within Washington and the reactionary political climate in America. There was an ongoing battle within the administration between those advocating a more aggressive anti-communist strategy for the Far East – 'roll back' – and those who wanted to contain communism.[55] The war, by enhancing the Pentagon's position within the bureaucracy, gave hardliners the ascendancy.[56] Moreover, with congressional elections pending, any compromise by the US administration on the admission of China to the UN, the future of Taiwan or on trade with the communists would have been exploited to the full by the Republican Party. The war deepened popular anti-communism, making accommodation between the US and the PRC politically difficult. Even if Acheson still believed that China should be integrated into the world community, his difficult relationship with Congress and the strength of popular and bureaucratic opposition to the Chinese communists severely constrained his scope for flexibility. Viable solutions, which could have stabilised the situation in the Far East, were out of the question.[57]

During the summer of 1950, fear of global war re-entered both the British public and governmental consciousness. The fear was that the US might escalate the Korean conflict into a war between America/ Britain and the Soviet Union/China. Fear of escalation permeated discussion in the British cabinet. Bevin branded the US a 'law unto themselves as regards their Far East strategy'. He argued US policy towards Taiwan had 'caused alarm and despondency because there was now the possibility of a conflict between the US and China'.[58] Bellicose statements by the American military establishment, and in particular by General Douglas MacArthur in Tokyo, heightened British concerns: the language was that of roll back. Alvary Gascoigne, Britain's representative in Tokyo, reported that by September 1950, after his Inchon landing success, the General was in the 'mood to defy all-comers': if the Chinese communists did not come to him he was liable to come to them.[59] Given MacArthur's links with the Chinese Nationalists, would he use Nationalist troops in Korea or in China as the tools of roll back? The Foreign Office questioned the degree of control Washington exercised over the General.[60] Given Chinese concerns about a possible imperialist attack on the mainland, the American strategy could only increase the chance of war between China and the West.

The British government argued that conflict between China and the West was to be avoided because of its impact on Britain's policy towards China and because of its potentially damaging consequences for the British economy. War would place a severe burden on British military resources. The various military dimensions were complex, but put simply, war required extra men for Korea and also for British territories in South East Asia. The reinforcements would have to come from somewhere, either from already overstretched theatres in Europe, the Middle East, or from the Commonwealth, which might cause severe political difficulties with Asian members given this was a conflict between the West and Asia. The British Chiefs of Staff argued that, in the event of a war between the US and China, the Americans would have to be persuaded to delay a request for British military assistance. But, in the case of a prolonged war in the Far East, they admitted that Britain would, whatever the consequences, supply the necessary support.[61] War would also require a programme of rearmament in Britain. Clearly this can be viewed from a number of perspectives. Firstly as a Keynesian type demand-side boost to the economy, stimulating an increase in output and employment. But equally defence spending can be perceived as detrimental: unbalancing the structure of the British economy by crowding out private investment in consumer durables, causing an overheating of the economy and balance of payments problems. This latter consequence of war was at the forefront of British ministerial thinking given the shortage of dollars (needed to pay for raw materials and capital goods) and because of Britain's reliance for raw materials on Sterling Area countries which already held large sterling balances in London.

Given these preoccupations, the government's support for the extension of the Korean War from a war to contain alleged North Korean aggression into a military conquest of North Korea needs to be explained.[62] The decision, initiated by the US, supported by Britain and sanctioned by the UN, represented an intellectual and ideological shift away from a strategy of containment to a policy which strove to roll back communism in Asia. It was a decision that resulted in war between China and the West because the PRC intervened to prevent the collapse of the DPRK. We will consider briefly why the Chinese intervened in the next chapter, but for the rest of this chapter the focus will be on British and American decision-making.

American policy-makers looked upon roll back as a means of uniting Korea: a neat solution to the Korean problem and a way of pacifying Republican critics of Truman's foreign policy. Once the Korean

War was settled, the administration could divert military resources and shift the US politically towards Europe. The administration did not believe the PRC or the Soviet Union would intervene to uphold the DPRK. The Chinese communists, preoccupied by domestic difficulties, were not thought to be the dominant influence in the Korean peninsula. The US believed the Soviet Union had shied away from a military commitment to save the North Korean state and hence would not now intervene: a decision which would increase tensions between China and the Soviet Union.[63] The administration's strategy was formulated as NSC81/1 and agreed by Truman on 11 September. The decision to advance north was taken before MacArthur's plan to break the Korean stalemate by launching an amphibious attack behind North Korean lines at Inchon; but once this had succeeded MacArthur pressed strongly for the removal of constraints on military operations and on 27 September the administration approved a move north of the 38th parallel, the political boundary between North and South Korea.

The British government endorsed the American decision because it thought a victory was possible. But equally Bevin was extremely worried that if Britain did not publicly support the US then there would be a severe backlash by the American public and also by the American administration.[64] Bevin was also confident that Acheson wanted to limit the conflict to Korea and thus accepted American assurances that UN forces would avoid military action close to the border with Manchuria. Cabinet and Foreign Office minds were on post-war nationwide elections to unify Korea – a neat political fix to stabilise the peninsula. As William Stueck notes, the British government focused on the consequences of not supporting the move north and missed an opportunity to restrain the US, its stated objective.[65]

The British decision was taken despite clear evidence that China was willing to intervene. In the months before intervention, Chinese propaganda prepared the Chinese people for a conflict with the West and troops and equipment were moved north to the Chinese-Korean border. The British Foreign Office received reports of troop concentrations and movements from consuls in Canton, Kunming and Mukden, from Hutchison in Peking, from Chinese Nationalist sources (usually Taipei) and from British intelligence. As early as 18 August 1950, there were reports that Mukden and Antung had been reinforced and, by September, Hutchison reported large Chinese troop movements into Manchuria.[66] Famously and publicly, in September, Chou warned of an imminent Chinese intervention in the Chinese press and via Panikkar to the Indian government.[67] The British Chiefs of Staff understood the dangers of roll back. Sir John Slessor, Marshal of the RAF, criticised American plans to cross the 38th parallel. His concerns were shared by Admiral Lord Fraser and Field Marshall Sir William Slim, the other Chiefs of Staff. As warning signs of Chinese intervention increased, Chiefs of Staff reservations mounted; they wanted any action north of the 38th parallel restricted to undermining a future North Korean offensive.[68] Despite this, Bevin dismissed Chinese warnings as bluff, an attitude which only moderated slightly when Chou reiterated to Panikkar that if UN forces crossed the 38th parallel then China would intervene. Bevin's reasoning was myopic: he did not want Britain blamed for a military reversal. Bevin failed to view developments from the Chinese perspective. He believed that the Chinese could be pacified by assurances, given by India, that UN forces would not impinge upon Chinese sovereignty and that the PRC would be invited to discuss the question of Taiwan in the aftermath of the conflict. Bevin failed to appreciate the depth of China's distrust of the West, the product of a century of imperial exploitation, exacerbated by a failure to seat China in the UN and by the neutralisation of Taiwan. Attlee had growing doubts about extending the conflict into the north, but acceded to Bevin's opinion.[69]

In the months leading up to Korea, Britain's assessment of the Chinese communists and their relationship with the Soviet Union had been shifting and the conflict in the Far East seemed to confirm the direction of British thought. The 'wait and see' attitude evident in 1949 had been replaced by a more calculated assessment of Communist China's intentions in Asia: China was bent, for revolutionary and nationalistic reasons, on an expansionist strategy. This change had come about because China had rejected Britain's offer of diplomatic relations and because of growing evidence of Chinese military and political support for anti-colonial movements in South East Asia. A.E.E. Franklin argued that 'For Mao, the Chinese Revolution, apart from its importance in its own right, means China exists as a solid base for the extension of Communism in Asia'.[70] The Korean War sent shock waves through the military and political establishments in Britain and Asia. It heightened tensions and altered the strategic balance in East Asia. With the US preoccupied on the Korean peninsula, perhaps by preconceived communist design, British thoughts focused on communist infiltration in Indochina, Burma, Malaya and Hong Kong. The US decision to neutralise Taiwan merely exacerbated fears. If the Chinese had cancelled the planned invasion of Taiwan, they might want to regain the initiative elsewhere. The Chinese had extensive troop reserves in Fukien province opposite Taiwan, in Kunming on the border of Indochina and an estimated 200 000–300 000 in Canton, all of which were theoretically available for intervention in South East Asia.[71] The Foreign Office believed that the Soviets and the Chinese, rather than competing for the revolutionary leadership in Asia, were now revolutionary accomplices. It argued that with the Soviets instigating events in North Korea, the Chinese might intervene in South East Asia. China had rejected relations with the West and had adopted a Soviet-style propaganda line on Asian affairs.[72] By October 1950, the Foreign Office was preoccupied by the prospect of Chinese intervention against Taiwan or in South East Asia and not in Korea. It believed the Soviet Union was the dominant influence in the North Korean state.

Hutchison disagreed with the Foreign Office analysis. He argued that, in the aftermath of their victory on the mainland, the Chinese were preoccupied not with overseas expansion but rather with domestic considerations: 'I still feel sure that the Chinese government have every intention of keeping clear of international hostilities at least until they have firmly established internal political, social and economic conditions on a sound basis.'[73] The Foreign Office rejected such thinking. Franklin stated emphatically: 'Their [the Chinese communist's] whole foreign policy alignment is such as to make one question the validity of the point made by Mr. Hutchison in this respect.'[74] His assessment was nearer the mark than the alarmist predictions of the Foreign Office. The CCP needed to consolidate its political base in China. Bandits, some of whom were sympathetic to the Chinese Nationalists, needed suppressing, while Party control needed to be imposed throughout China. The second priority was the economy. The Land Reform programme, the guarantor of peasant support, awaited extension to the south of the country; industrial rehabilitation was incomplete; currency and prices needed to be stabilised and plans needed to be made for socialist planning. The clear direction of policy was domestic. Mao wanted to consolidate the base of communist support in China. On 6 June 1950 Mao announced a pragmatic approach to the Central Committee of the CCP.

We must not hit out in all directions. It is undesirable to hit out in all directions and cause nation-wide tension. We must definitely not make too many enemies, we must make concessions and relax the tension a little in some quarters and concentrate our attack in one direction . . . In this way, the remnant Kuomintang forces, the secret agents and the bandits will be isolated, as will the landlord class and the reactionaries in Taiwan and Tibet, and the imperialists will find themselves isolated before the people of our country.[75]

Mao would hardly have made such a moderate, conciliatory statement if within one month he planned an extensive campaign of intervention in South East Asia.

The British government's misconceived assessment of Chinese communism and the Sino-Soviet relationship explains why Britain acquiesced in the march to the Yalu by UN forces. Evidence of Sino-Soviet collaboration was irrefutable. Soviet military and economic aid was arriving in China and Soviet technicians were present in Chinese factories and in the armed forces; Soviet air planes and pilots were based at Chinese air fields, whereas Soviet submarines, reportedly available for an attack on Taiwan, were stationed at Port Arthur and Tsingtao.[76] Growing international tensions between the West and the East had drawn Moscow and Peking much closer together. British diplomacy would not succeed in 'driving a wedge' between Moscow and Peking. Western restrictions on trade with China had made the Chinese much more dependent economically on the Soviets, and heightened tensions within the Far East reaffirmed the strategic importance of the Sino-Soviet treaty to the Chinese communists. The decision by the US administration to intervene in the Chinese Civil War (the Chinese communist propaganda line) ensured that, on psychological, strategic and political levels, the Chinese would turn to the Soviet Union. China feared that the US was trying to establish a hegemonic position in the Far East so that China would have to rely on the Soviets. Hutchison acknowledged as much: 'It seems most probable that the general effect of President Truman's statement will be to force China over into [an] ever closer alliance with and greater dependence upon Russia.'[77] The Foreign Office interpreted the Korean War as a Soviet 'offensive to expel Western influence from the Far East'.[78] The Chinese had been consulted on the decision to invade the south and, by agreeing, had delineated Korea as a sphere of Soviet influence. As matters stood in September 1950, the British government did want Korea to remain in Soviet hands, and equally argued that without a quick military solution the Soviet Union might force Chinese intervention in the area. Robert Scott, Assistant Under-Secretary, epitomised the Foreign Office thought: 'Chinese intervention could not be ruled out and the key to the situation thus seems to be to finish the job in Korea as quickly as possible in a way which will convince the Chinese that they need not fear American aggressive intentions towards them, or permanent occupation of North Korea by hostile forces.'[79] The British were viewing developments from a Soviet and not a Chinese perspective.

Assigning responsibility for the instigation of the conflict in Korea is difficult but Kim Il Sung probably took the initiative in June 1950, with tacit approval by the Soviet Union and the PRC. According to Goncharov, Xue and Lewis, and Kathryn Weathersby, material from the Chinese and Soviet archives indicates that a decision by Stalin to remove a Soviet veto over a North Korean offensive was crucial. He did this because North Korea was not capable of launching an attack without Soviet support, because Kim had convinced him that the US would not intervene and because he saw it as a convenient way to tie China to the Soviet Union and possibly embroil them in a conflict with the West.[80] Bruce Cumings disagrees with this analysis. He argues that North Korea had the capacity to invade the south and that the Chinese had become the dominant source of political and military support to the north.[81] Whatever interpretation is believed, one fact remains: this was essentially a civil war, one aided but not instigated by the global forces of communism.

At the time, the Foreign Office misconstrued the strategic balance between the Chinese, the Soviets and the North Koreans. The fact that the Soviets were pressing for a settlement in Korea and would most probably accept an American advance north of the parallel did not necessarily mean that the Chinese would. Bevin and Attlee both believed that a UN advance into North Korea would strain China's relationship with the Soviet Union because the Soviets would acquiesce in a western military settlement for Korea. It was the British chargé d'affaires in Peking, Hutchison, rather than the British Foreign Office who grasped the complex nature of Sino-Korean-Soviet relations. Although he had originally thought that the Russians initiated developments in Korea, his opinion changed over the summer of 1950. On 28 September he pronounced that:

> China was the prime mover in setting off the Korean war ... In Korea, China's national interests are directly concerned. The independence of Korea from domination by any other foreign power has always been (and must, I think, remain) of paramount importance in the foreign policy of any Chinese Government ... The possibility even of Soviet domination of Korea could hardly, in my opinion, be regarded with any equanimity by the Chinese Government.[82]

CONCLUSIONS

In the months leading to China's intervention in the Korean War, Britain had hoped to align its Far East strategy closer to that of the US while retaining the basic elements of its thinking towards China: that diplomatic and economic links should be maintained with the Chinese regime. Britain had tried to work towards compromise solutions on the admission of China to the UN, regarding the future of Taiwan and the economic embargo on China. The British government had tried to influence the direction of Chinese and US policy. It wanted to prevent the escalation of the conflict in the Far East and hopefully, in the longer term, provide the Chinese with an opportunity to establish a new framework for their relations with the West. The strategy failed and, by November, China and the West were involved in a far eastern war. Britain had misunderstood both US policy towards China and the attitude of the Chinese towards events in the Far East. Contradictions were inherent in the strategy: on the one hand the British government wanted to appease the Chinese, and yet on the other hand it acquiesced in a military advance to China's border.

4 Fear and Loathing, November 1950–October 1951

> Just ally this discipline, the acquirement of new arms and modern tactics, with the primitive barbarism of the Chinese masses, with their total lack of any idea of human protest, of all instinct of liberty, with their habit of servile obedience ... and you will understand how great is the peril which menaces us from the side of the East.
>
> Bakunin[1]

War between China and the West, fought on the Korean peninsular between November 1950 and July 1953, was a profound development: the first war between China and the West since the early nineteenth century. It forced the British government to face the contradiction at the heart of its response to Communist China: whether to continue to adhere to its liberal policy of maintaining political contact and encouraging economic relations or align with the Americans for broader macroeconomic and geo-strategic ends. This chapter will explore how the British government dealt with this dilemma. It will deal with four issues: the attempt to brand the Chinese communists as aggressors in the UN; the attempt to prevent China's admission to the UN; the organisation of a military response to Chinese aggression in Korea; and the introduction of tighter international economic sanctions against the Chinese. The initial sections of this chapter will place this crucial debate within its wider context by assessing the impact of war on Britain's position within China, on the contrasting British and American interpretations of Chinese intervention and on British attempts to broker a ceasefire for the Korean War.

LOOKING AFTER THE IMPERIALISTS

The heightened international tensions of late 1950 and 1951 intensified state and popular anti-imperialism and xenophobia in China. A fierce and prolonged anti-American campaign reflected genuine concern over US intentions but also formed part of a wider campaign to suppress counter-revolutionaries and to ruthlessly exploit nationalist sentiment to justify tighter communist control over China. Anti-imperialist slogans and speeches and the mistreatment of foreign missionaries, businessmen and officials all increased dramatically in 1951. Lionel Lamb, the new British chargé d'affaires, believed that the PRC 'would like to cut off contacts and build up a self-sufficient economy, getting rid of foreign traders, foreign teachers and foreign missionaries'.[2] The Chinese had found the 'magic prescription for converting xenophobia and nationalism into civic conscience and patriotism'. War tightened bureaucratic controls on foreign, diplomatic and trading interests. The Chinese began to avoid 'like the plague' contact with British citizens;[3] Britain's consular representatives in sensitive areas such as Mukden and Tiwa were expelled;[4] foreign nationals found themselves imprisoned, mistreated or held against their will; British traders and industrialists were desperate to leave China; and relations between the Chinese and the other foreign representatives in China became strained. K.M. Panikkar, the Indian ambassador, requested a transfer, and there were evident tensions between the Soviet embassy and the Chinese.[5] Fear, frustration and isolation pervaded the foreign community in China.

Why then did the PRC not throw out British diplomatic representatives and businessmen in 1951 – a move that would have proved its revolutionary and nationalist credentials? Lamb believed the Chinese wanted to humiliate Britain. But this rather cynical view does not fit the facts: Chinese propaganda was not overtly anti-British and expulsion would have emphasised communist power much more dramatically. More plausibly, relations gave the Chinese a degree of flexibility, and also an important tactical asset. The Chinese communists wanted a seat in the UN; to drive a wedge between the Atlantic powers; and to illustrate their independence from the Soviet Union to internal and external audiences. Although the CCP stressed the importance of following the Soviet line, the leadership continued to emphasise the Chinese character of the revolution and Mao's unique contribution to communist thought. An article in the *Peking Daily* by Ch'en Po-ta on Mao's thought epitomised the ideological and propagandist line adopted by the CPG during 1951; entitled 'The Thought of Mao is the Union of Marxism-Leninism and the Chinese Revolution', it argued that Mao had applied the doctrine of Marx and Lenin to 'the concrete facts of the Chinese revolution' and thus had drawn together the confused threads of the Chinese revolutionary experience.[6] Finally, the CCP leadership realised that trade with the West was vital for economic development and useful for moderating western attitudes.

The British government's attitude towards relations with the CPG was tempered by developments in China. The government's hopes for a revival of business fortunes and for full political ties faded, and while Hutchison thought relations possible, Lamb, his successor, did not believe the CPG wanted relations and he even went so far as to question whether it was worth remaining in China, his half-hearted conclusion being that 'it is worth the price even though there is precious little to show by way of tangible dividend'.[7] Equally, in London, China's intervention in the Korean War was perceived by some as the 'inconclusive end of a somewhat melancholic chapter'.[8] Nevertheless, diplomatic and business contacts remained a barometer on Chinese developments and a means of keeping the door open to peace and therefore the government refused to withdraw officials or encourage businessmen to leave the country. On 10 November Bevin informed the cabinet that: 'I still regard it as an important contribution to mutual understanding that relations between two countries should be re-established on a formal basis of recognition and the exchange of Ambassadors and that the Chinese government should be represented in the UN.'[9] Bevin informed Acheson that withdrawal from China would be 'an empty gesture which would do us harm and not harm China'.[10] Instead Britain used its contacts to reassure the Chinese of UN intentions regarding Korea; in November 1950 Bevin told Hutchison to inform Chou En-lai that UN forces would not violate Chinese territory.[11] Moreover, British business interests still desired governmental representation in China, with the China Association, concerned about the closure of British consuls in China, demanding that offices be reopened at the first opportunity.[12]

TO PACIFY OR STIGMATISE?

It was war between China and the West and not political and economic relations with China which preoccupied the British government in the period after November 1950. With the atmosphere in Peking reported as 'tense' and Chinese propaganda 'so worded as to try and destroy any confidence in the statements of the United Nations Organisation, USA, or democratic countries about confining the present conflict to Korea',[13] British government predictions became alarmist. It feared that the Korean War could escalate into a general war in the

Far East, and believed that the 'shrewd' and 'calculating' Chinese were ready for such a war. It argued that the attack on UN forces had been well planned and supported by an internal and external propaganda campaign. It also noted that industrial and military equipment had been moved to coastal sites as a precautionary measure against coastal bombing by UN forces, and that provisional plans had been made to transfer the Chinese capital from Peking to the relative safety of a city in the centre of China. British business interests in China reported that the Chinese authorities were moving 'stuff' out of Shanghai.[14] A sense of their own geography and history gave the Chinese confidence; the vastness of China would draw western forces into an arena where the People's Liberation Army had defeated Chinese Nationalist armies, trained and equipped by the West.

Nevertheless, although the Chinese communists were prepared militarily and psychologically to meet the threat of western encirclement, the Foreign Office did not believe they desired war with the West. Chinese intervention in Korea was not the same as Japanese or German aggression in the 1930s: the overriding political and economic drive to conquer was missing. The Chinese would seek to influence rather than conquer. Bevin drew a comparison with the Soviet Union:

> Just as Russia has sought to erect a barrier ring of satellites for her own defence, so the Chinese leaders aspire to create a Union of Chinese Socialist republics from Tibet through South East Asia to Formosa and Korea. In the case of China, the instinct towards isolation from the outside world goes back many centuries. Consciously or unconsciously the Chinese may be seeking to reproduce the old system of a Chinese Empire and ring of vassal states.[15]

Historians agree that China's intervention was defensive. Although China did not intervene in order to impress the Soviet Union with China's military and political commitment to world communist revolution,[16] it has become clear from evidence surfacing from the Chinese archives that the CPG was planning to intervene in the Korean War well in advance of October 1950. It is also now evident that the CCP discussed intervention with the Soviet leadership and sought military support from the Soviet Union, only for Stalin to warn the Chinese against a large-scale offensive and to initially deny the Chinese military aid – a stand which caused Mao to temporarily cancel military plans.[17] Bruce Cumings and Qiang Zhai, by contrast, have argued that China's intervention in Korea was determined primarily by the close political and ideological bonds between the CCP and the North Korean Workers' Party.[18] They argue that the Chinese could not let their fellow Asian communists down. What is evident is that the decision to intervene was based on a belief that the US imperialists might not stop at the North Korean border but would attack China.[19] The Chinese believed that the UN advance into North Korea represented a real threat to their territorial integrity.

> We have no intention of encroaching on any country; it is aggression against our country by the imperialists that we oppose. As everyone knows, the Chinese people would not be fighting the US forces if they had not occupied Taiwan, invaded the Democratic People's Republic of Korea and pushed on to our northeastern borders. But since the US aggressors have launched their attack against us, we cannot but raise the banner of resistance to aggression.[20]

A US-sponsored imperialist assault against China was a constant theme of Chinese propaganda. Chou drew close parallels between Japanese aggression against China and American imperialism in the Far East:

> The US imperialists are pursuing the policy of MacArthur in the East, using Japan as their base, inheriting the mantle of Japanese militarism and taking their cue from history since the Sino-Japanese War of 1894. They are following the old maxim that anyone wanting to annex China must first occupy its Northeast and that to occupy the Northeast he must first seize Korea . . .[21]

Such statements highlight an ingrained, subconscious Chinese fear of Japanese-style aggression against China. The CCP leadership's main objective was to prevent Korea being used as a strategic springboard for an attack on China.[22] The Chinese interpretation was reinforced by an ideological belief that a conflict between capitalism (the US) and communism (China) was inevitable. However, China had entered a transitional period which required peace and not war. Chou, in an address to the meeting of the Chinese People's Consultative Conference, announced China's intervention in Korea but ended on a sobering note: he reminded delegates that in the 'meantime, economic construction must not be suspended'. He told them that China had to 'rehabilitate key branches of heavy industry, proceed unswervingly with water conservancy, railway and textile projects and try to raise people's living standards'.[23]

The British government accepted that China's intervention had been defensive, a response to a perceived threat from the US. The cabinet, the Chiefs of Staff and the Foreign Office were in agreement:

We have . . . to face realities. The Chinese have worked themselves up to a conviction that the US has aggressive designs against them. Their continued expulsion from the UN under what they regard as US leadership and continued US recognition of Chiang has helped to foster this impression of American intentions, however unjustified it might be.[24]

The government believed that as Chinese moves did not represent naked aggression, a Korean ceasefire and ultimately a general settlement for the Far East were possible. It argued that both required concessions to the Chinese. Attlee believed that if it was the choice between a ceasefire and a general war in the Far East and that if the former required major concessions to the Chinese then these had to be offered.[25] The price was already set: a seat for Communist China and the return of Taiwan.

The initial British attempt to achieve peace centred on the idea of a buffer zone, an area to guarantee the sanctity and security of Chinese territory. It was proposed by the Chiefs of Staff, who recognised that, once the Chinese had intervened, it would be impossible for General MacArthur to hold any military line in North Korea without air attacks on Chinese and North Korean bases. Unfortunately, the scheme was not formally offered to the Chinese until 24 November, by which time a successful Chinese offensive had eased their territorial insecurities.[26] Chou En-lai rejected it on 22 December, and dismissed a further resolution calling for a ceasefire on 11 January. Instead, the Chinese demanded a complete withdrawal of foreign troops from Korea.[27] If an offer had come earlier, the Chinese may have accepted a partial UN withdrawal, but at this stage the British government did not have the political will to try a radical approach. Bevin thought the buffer zone plan dubious and was only persuaded by the strength of opinion among the Chiefs of Staff.[28] He stuck to his view that the Chinese were not committed to an all-out offensive to oust the UN from mainland Asia – based on the belief that if they had wanted to defeat the UN forces, they would have done so much earlier. This was a miscalculation. Once committed to North Korea, the Chinese required significant safeguards for their borders and for the North Korean regime. Bevin also rejected a further possible chance of a peace when Britain failed to support Chinese demands for negotiations before a ceasefire. He did not believe that the US would accept such a settlement and that, if it was adopted as a formal UN initiative for peace, the administration might bypass the UN and act unilaterally in the Far East. Bevin admitted that the basic problem was that the US would not accept the principle of talks with, never mind concessions to, the PRC.[29] Once the British government had realised as much, it kept the door open to negotiations, more in hope of postponing punitive American sanctions against China than in anticipation of peace.

The Labour government's primary objective was to prevent a general war between China and the West.[30] It wanted to avoid such a war for a whole range of reasons: war would shatter hopes of a *modus vivendi* with China, drain British military resources, make British control of Hong Kong and possibly Malaya untenable, divide Asia and the West (perhaps threatening Asian membership of the Commonwealth) and overcommit the US in Asia, thus limiting the resources to build up the West. In any case, British strategic thinkers did not believe a war against China could be won. Attacks against the Chinese mainland would be pointless given that there were few suitable targets in China for bombing raids and that the use of economic and political sanctions would irritate but not endanger the regime.[31] And ultimately such a war might, by invoking the strategic clause of the Sino-Soviet Treaty of February 1950, precipitate a global conflict.[32]

The British government was concerned that while neither the Chinese nor the Americans desired a general war, both appeared willing to accept one. Ernest Bevin, not as alarmist as many of his colleagues, acknowledged that the situation was precarious and that the US response was uncertain, but he did not believe the US would precipitate a general war. He informed Attlee that: 'it is not, I think, in the character of the American people to provoke a war, or to commit an act of aggression, nor does their constitution lend itself to action of this nature'.[33] But he did think that there was a risk that the US government, by some ill-considered or impulsive action, or series of actions, might find itself in an exposed position from which it might drift into hostilities.[34] Consequently, a role for British diplomacy emerged: it would mitigate American naivety. The British government would influence the American decision-making process by using the representatives of the Chiefs of Staff and Oliver Franks, the British ambassador in Washington, who was in close contact with the American State Department, and by sending over the British Prime Minister to discuss the matter with the President.

Although the US did not extend the war into China, this option was under constant consideration by the Truman administration. In the first month of China's intervention, the threat of a nuclear or conventional air strike against the Chinese mainland was acute, with even Acheson initially advocating limited war against China. By January, talk of escalation had subsided; the US had ruled out strikes against the Chinese mainland unless China widened the area of the conflict, or began an extensive air offensive against UN forces in Korea.[35] The US administration came to accept that a war with China would be prolonged and probably inconclusive and might bring the Soviets into the conflict. British pressure gave further weight to these considerations but did not act as a block on US military measures. In this respect Attlee's December conference meeting with Truman had an influence at a most crucial time, drawing the US away from a self-conscious desire to punish China towards a slightly wider consideration of the position of its allies: Britain and France.[36] At the same time, it must also be appreciated that the military sanctions were not abandoned but rather postponed. By the spring and summer of 1951, attacks on the mainland were again under consideration, this time to encourage China to agree to a ceasefire and as retaliation against a Chinese air assault on UN forces in Korea.[37] On this occasion, while the British government initially opposed US plans, Herbert Morrison, the new British Foreign Secretary, eventually sanctioned attacks subject to British concurrence.[38]

These differences over ceasefire arrangements and attacks against China highlight the huge gap which had emerged between Britain and the US over policy towards China. The British government's position was clear: China's intervention in the Korean War must not be the precursor to China's isolation – politically and economically – from the western world.

> We must act in the belief that it is possible for the present day Great Britain and present day China to live together in amity and to mutual advantage; and our policy must constantly seek avenues which lead to this desirable end and to avoid all courses which tend to increase tensions and hostilities, or which tend to cut off any of the channels through which mutual advantage may flow.[39]

Attlee, in his December meeting with Truman, informed the President that 'it was a mistake to let China think that Russia was her only friend', as 'China might become an important counterpoise to Russia in Asia and the Far East'.[40] The Prime Minister wanted the UN to reject the roll back of Chinese communism and to respond to the newly emergent Chinese threat within the confines of a containment strategy. He thought any other strategy would be counterproductive, merely exacerbating China's sense of insecurity and deepening her hostility towards the West, driving her further into the Soviet orbit and encouraging expansionist impulses. In stark contrast, American policy towards China now aimed at undermining communist power on the mainland. This had always been implicit in American far eastern strategy, but, with Chinese military successes in Korea, such thinking was formulated and adopted as policy. National Security Council document NSC48/ 5 recommended that the US should undermine the political, economic, social and military base of communism in China by 'inflicting heavy losses on Chinese forces on Korea' and by 'expanding and intensifying, by all available means, efforts to develop a non-communist leadership and influence the leaders and people in China to oppose the present Peiping regime and to seek its reorientation or replacement'; stress was given to encouraging and sponsoring anti-communist elements in and outside China, particularly in south China.[41] The administration did not believe opposition groups could overthrow the Chinese regime but thought they would 'occupy considerable [Chinese] military strength'.[42] Whether the administration actually embarked on large-scale, covert attempts to undermine the communist regime is uncertain, but the direction of US thought is starkly evident.

The American stance was an emotional, political and tactical response to the domestic and international environment. US intelligence sources believed there was a non-communist core in the Chinese state, that political parties operated as underground cells, and that KMT generals such as Chang Chih-chung, Chen Ch'en and Lang Yun, and bankers and industrialists such as Hou Teh-peng and K.P. Chen, remained in powerful positions in China. These assessments confirmed what the administration wanted to hear: that the Chinese regime was not firmly in the saddle and that pockets of resistance in China could be exploited.[43] Some reports reaching Washington even suggested prominent members of the government such as Chou En-lai could be detached from the communist regime.[44] The administration came to believe that by delaying economic expansion and thus causing unemployment and inflation, the Korean War could stimulate internal opposition to and deepen tensions within the Chinese communist regime. It argued that such a policy could force the Chinese to rely even more heavily on Soviet military and economic resources, thus making Communist China a liability for the Soviets, leading eventually to 'a schism in the Peiping regime itself'.[45] By 1951, a consensus had been reached in Washington that friction and tensions in the Sino-Soviet relationship should be encouraged by isolating China. This strategy was no subtle attempt to detach China from the Soviet Union. On 18 May 1951, Dean Rusk, in a speech to the Chinese Institute in America, argued that Manchuria had become a 'Slavic Manchukou'.[46] Such blatant propaganda did not increase Sino-Soviet tensions and merely intensified the American public's intolerant attitude towards the PRC. The US was too reliant on Chinese Nationalist intelligence for developments in China and was too inclined to believe evidence of internal difficulties, especially in the south of the country. In actual fact, opposition in south China had no political overtures, was not co-ordinated, was for the most part pure banditry and faded away as the Chinese communists reinforced their grip on power. Throughout the first six months of 1951, lawlessness was publicised in the Chinese press and linked to American and KMT activities, but this merely indicated that Peking had the problem well under control.[47] The British Foreign Office's assessment of the domestic situation in China was far more accurate than the American one. While the US believed the Korean conflict would provide the climate for revolt and rebellion, the British judged correctly that it would merely result in more vigorous control measures in China.

The hardline American approach was a result of movements of political unrest in the US rather than in China. In 1951 there had been an emotive backlash against communist intervention in Korea and the American public demanded retribution. Republican critics demanded the roll back of the Chinese communist regime. The Truman administration had to respond to such pressure because, even after sanctioning the roll back of the North Korean state, the administration was still open to criticism for 'being too soft on communism'. Truman's decision to relieve General MacArthur of his command, because of his conduct of the war, intensified the domestic controversy surrounding the most appropriate policy to be followed in the Far East.[48] The administration feared that Republican critics in Congress would coalesce around MacArthur, who was advocating air attacks on the Chinese mainland. The fear was that too moderate a line on China could endanger the administration's relationship with Congress and thus reduce the power held by the executive to shape domestic and foreign policy.

The British government remained convinced that a hardline moralistic approach was counterproductive. As the American response turned towards military, political and economic measures against Communist China, Britain had either to alter its position, or face the consequences of a policy breach with the Americans. Divergence came over four issues: branding China the aggressor in the UN, seating the PRC in the UN, tightening and widening the economic embargo and introducing military sanctions against the Chinese.

SANCTIONING AGGRESSION

> The Americans feel they have failed to punish the Chinese for their aggressive behaviour in Korea. This leads to frustrations and a moral struggle resulting in the attempt to find another way of punishing the aggression now that military means have failed.[49]

The American demand, first voiced in November 1950 and made on 19 January, for a UN resolution branding the PRC the aggressors in Korea threatened the whole base of British policy towards China, endangered Anglo-American relations and divided the British government. The British government argued that declaring China an aggressor would symbolise Britain's alignment with the US, making rapprochement between Britain and China difficult. Britain's representative in Peking believed it 'would probably reverse any inclination which the Chinese may have to declare themselves now as willing to establish regular diplomatic relations'.[50] Once named by the UN as the agent of aggression, China could not be admitted to the organisation and Taiwan could not to be returned: such measures would now be rewards for aggression. China's reply of 17 January had not ruled out a settlement of the war; Hutchison had been instructed to delve further. But if the resolution was passed, the Chinese would be convinced that the US wanted to punish them, and there would be no further progress towards peace.

The Foreign Office was right: political and economic sanctions against the Chinese would inevitably follow a resolution. On 18 January Acheson informed Bevin: 'it is foolish just to say the Chinese are aggressors and not do anything further about it'. The US wanted the UN Collective Measures Committee (CMC) to be instructed to explore the option of sanctions against China.[51] The government believed that any measures would convince the Chinese that the US was to embark on an aggressive campaign against the Chinese state, and hence draw them closer to the Soviet Union, reduce trade with the West and increase the possibility of a general war in the Far East.[52] And in addition the government was concerned that the issue threatened to divide the Commonwealth. At the Commonwealth conference of January 1951, Nehru had informed Bevin that he questioned whether it was possible to align with the Americans, as their policy would preclude negotiations with the Chinese.[53] Pierson Dixon noted that 'a war between the US and China would divide Asia. If, however, war with China can be avoided, there is a good chance of carrying the Asian peoples with us, in our resistance to world wide communist aggression.'[54]

Despite this reasoning, a decision by the British government not to vote on an American-inspired resolution to brand China an aggressor in Korea had profound consequences. With China at war with the West, the American administration and the American public were in no mood to countenance an independent British position. Indeed Acheson, in close contact with Franks on this question, argued that, by delaying sanctions, the administration had brought themselves 'to the verge of destruction domestically'. He argued that if the UN failed to denounce the Chinese there would be a wave of isolationism in the US.[55] In the aftermath of the congressional election of November 1950, and with the US facing the possibility of a humiliating military defeat in Korea, prominent American politicians such as Senator Robert Taft (Republican, Ohio) and ex-President Herbert Hoover were demanding a retreat from a global role. At the beginning of the Eighty-Second Congress, in January 1951, Senator K.S. Wherry (Republican, Nebraska) and Representative F.R. Coudert, Jr. (Republican, New York) introduced resolutions opposing the despatch of US troops abroad without congressional approval.[56] Could the British economy and military establishment, so dependent on the US, afford the consequences of a negative vote? The American commitment to Europe was politically insecure: Marshall Aid was coming to an end and the NATO treaty bill was due to be ratified.

In early 1951 these debates intensified and polarised differences within Britain over the direction of British foreign policy. The British left, both within and outside the Labour Party, demanded a British foreign policy that was more independent from American influence. Left-wing MPs such as Michael Foot (Labour, Plymouth, Devonport), Richard Crossman (Labour, Coventry, East), Barbara Castle (Labour, Blackburn, East), Ian Mikardo (Labour, Reading, South) and Tom Driberg (Labour, Essex, Maldon) criticised an American response to Korean developments which they believed had brought the world to the verge of war.[57] Constituency Labour parties lobbied their MPs and pressed the Foreign Office; they had long advocated China's admission to the UN and the return of Taiwan to China, and now argued these concessions were essential to secure peace in the Far East. Labour Party activists and Labour MPs did not want the government to jeopardise Britain's relationship with Asian nations, especially socialist India, for the sake of relations with capitalist America. In December 1950 the Horsham constituency circulated to all constituency Labour parties a resolution which condemned US policy in the Far East, supported China's admission to the UN and argued that Britain should not go to war with

China. The National Executive Committee of the Labour Party received 68 replies, with only four opposing the Horsham resolution.[58]

The left-wing press, including the pro-communist *Daily Worker* but also socialist periodicals such as *Tribune* and *New Statesman*, which had backed the original UN moves in Korea, dismissed US policy as war-mongering. A survey taken at this time indicated that 25 per cent of Labour Party voters now believed that the US was more likely to start a war than the Soviet Union.[59] Bodies such as the National Peace Council, an organisation set up in 1950 to publicise the dangers of war in the Far East, did not want China condemned for aggression. On 8 January it set up the Peace with China Council, under the Chairmanship of Lord Chorley, a Labour Party peer. It was not aligned to any political party, refusing communist requests to participate, but was radical and expressed popular concerns about the direction of American policy in the Far East.[60] The Council demanded the return of Taiwan to China and Communist China's admission to the UN and it vehemently opposed the extension of the Korean conflict. By comparison, the Conservative Party rejected concessions and wanted Britain to align with the US in the Far East.[61] It was left-wing interest and pressure groups, however, that probably reflected a real concern within the country over developments in the Far East. Public fear that a general war might break out in the Far East was at its greatest in the aftermath of Truman's statement and during the early months of 1950; it then subsided during 1951 as the Korean conflict reached a stalemate, once MacArthur had been dismissed by Truman, and once peace talks had commenced in Kaesong. Basically, the common people did not want war, especially not in far-off China; and they were willing to accept concessions to the Chinese, be they communists or not.

Initially, the British cabinet decided to vote against an American resolution in the UN. With Bevin bedridden, opposition to the resolution coalesced around Kenneth Younger, the Minister of State. He argued that if the cabinet voted against their convictions just to support the US, they would 'forfeit their independence and their self respect'.[62] The majority of the cabinet agreed, with only Attlee, Morrison, Hugh Gaitskell, Chancellor of the Exchequer, and Lord Jowett, Lord Chancellor, dissenting. The cabinet vote was a conscious attempt to forge an independent policy line, reflecting opposition on the left of the Labour Party and within the country as a whole to American foreign policy. Unfortunately or fortunately, depending on how one views the importance of Anglo-American relations for Britain at this time, the decision was reversed. Under pressure from the Foreign Office, the Americans agreed to a last-minute concession on the wording of the resolution, and thus the issue went back to the cabinet on 26 January. By then, there had been a concerted campaign by Attlee and by Gaitskell to ensure a change of policy. On 1 February Britain branded China an aggressor in the UN.

The debate on whether to vote for the resolution symbolised a foreign policy dilemma that had troubled the Labour government since 1949: whether to align with the Americans on policy towards China even though the government disagreed with US thinking on how to deal with the threat posed by communism in Asia. The positive vote on 1 February did not signify an end to this dilemma; and nor was it a reversal of thinking, for, ever since recognition of the PRC, the government had disagreed but not publicly diverged with the US. Nevertheless, with the direction of British policy debated extensively within the government and in the public realm in December 1950 and January 1951, the resolution on aggression had symbolic importance. There was an immediate backlash from left-wing MPs and pacifist groups. G.D.H. Cole wrote in the *New Statesman* that 'if great Britain gets dragged into a war with China by the Americans, I shall be on the side of China'.[63] The National Executive Committee of the Labour Party received a large number of resolutions from constituency Labour parties criticising the government's far eastern policy. Between 16 January and 12 February 1951, out of a total of 86 resolutions received, 24 opposed the resolution branding China and demanded China's admission to the UN; and even by 9 April 1951, 20 of the 70 resolutions received opposed the government's position.[64] This was the most prominent issue of the day. By polarising differences between the right and the left of the Labour Party, the cabinet decision may have contributed to Aneurin Bevan's resignation from the cabinet in February 1950.[65] Indeed, outside of government, Bevan became more fiercely critical of US policy towards communism in Asia and supported more fully a revisionist socialist foreign policy. The reversal of the cabinet position indicated that the Anglo-American relationship would continue to be the bedrock on which British foreign policy was built. It also ensured that Britain could continue to try and moderate US policy in the Far East. Bevin, the architect of Britain's post-war foreign policy, informed Attlee that the cabinet should imagine 'what it would be like to live in a world with a hostile Communist bloc, an unco-operative America, a Commonwealth pulled in two directions and a disillusioned East deprived of American support'.[66]

The majority of the British press – *The Times*, the *Manchester Guardian*, the *Observer* and the *Daily Telegraph* – aware of administration and public attitudes in the US, agreed that Britain could not risk a rift with the US. The liberal and right-wing press was forthright; the *Daily Telegraph* pressed for further sanctions against the Chinese and the *Economist* argued 'the policy of conciliating Peking which was highly dubious at the start never paid a single dividend and is now patently bankrupt'.[67] There remained, however, a residual feeling that the US was adopting the wrong approach. Even after China had rejected the UN ceasefire proposals, the British press continued to support a strategy which sought a negotiated solution to the Korean War, and which eventually allowed a general settlement, with Communist China admitted to the UN and Taiwan returned to the PRC.[68] The *Observer* summed up the attitude of the British press: 'the best that could be claimed for it was that we chose the least of alternative evils'.[69] The *Manchester Guardian* argued that in the aftermath of the resolution the government had to press the US to agree to moderate its line with the Chinese. Britain wanted to see China admitted to the UN, Taiwan returned to China and a military stalemate prevented.[70]

Following the UN resolution, the British government continued to oppose sanctions against the Chinese, which would be counterproductive and 'only make it harder to get the Chinese to negotiate', thus increasing their hostility towards the West and leading 'to more violent counter measures on the part of the Soviets'.[71] Sanctions were seen as 'dangerous, double-edged or merely useless' and the government wanted the peace process to be given a chance before sanctions were introduced.[72] In UN speak: the work of the Good Offices Committee had to take precedence over recommendations from the Additional Measures Committee (AMC).[73] But these further British efforts were undermined by an American determination to press even more forcefully for sanctions which were thought essential to 'convince the enemy that a cessation of hostilities is in his interest'. The US administration did not believe the Chinese desired a ceasefire and needed action before the American public lost patience. Indeed, if the wheels started to move in the AMC, it might distract and undermine a potentially bitter and politically loaded testimony to the Congressional Select Committee by MacArthur on his conduct of the Korean War.[74] The US administration and the American public demanded military, political and economic retribution. They got them despite British protests.

A SEAT FOR PEACE?

War between China and the West initially failed to alter the British position on China's admission to the UN. On 14 December the UN General Assembly postponed a decision on China's admission to the UN pending a commission's report; but the question still threatened to arise in a number of subsidiary bodies such as the Universal Postal Union, the Trusteeship Council and the Economic Commission for Africa and the Far East. Over this prospect the British position was legalistic but clear: if these bodies could deal with such a substantive question, then the British representatives thereon would vote for the seating of a Chinese communist delegate. British reasoning was sound. China's admission was vital if there was to be a far eastern political settlement. It was strongly advocated by the Indian government and by public opinion and left-wing groups in Britain.[75] Moreover, a failure to seat the PRC would have serious repercussions for the future working of the UN: it was absurd that a nation the size of China was not represented on the Universal Postal Union and the Economic Commission for Africa and Asia.

American pressure forced a reversal of Britain's voting policy in the UN. The US administration wanted political sanctions to accompany the resolution branding China the aggressor in Korea. The British government did not think the moment was right for political sanctions. Bevin informed Acheson that voting should still 'be based on recognition of facts alone and should not be connected with moral approval or condemnation'.[76] Moreover, legally, the aggression resolution had steered the UN into uncharted waters. G.G. Fitzmaurice, a legal adviser at the Foreign Office, sardonically noted: 'if you do not recognise the existence of the Government which is misbehaving, and if you deny that it represents the state, then how can you hold the state responsible for what its government is doing'.[77] Moreover, outright rejection of a seat for Communist China would damage the very fabric of the UN; if a Soviet veto on political sanctions against China was circumvented by the General Assembly – by using the 'Uniting for Peace Resolution' – this could drive the Soviets out of the UN. The Soviets were promoting the World Peace Congress, a body the British Foreign Office believed to be the basis of an alternative Soviet bloc organisation. The scenario was complex and hypothetical but the outcome clear: the world divided into two camps. Britain viewed the UN as a meeting place of different and, quite often, hostile states, where problems could be discussed and hopefully resolved. If a split was inevitable, it would have to be accepted; but to maintain the political and moral high ground and to prevent a large group of nations declaring themselves neutral, the West must 'avoid action which might precipitate it'.[78] Fortunately, partly because of allied apprehension, the US retracted demands for political sanctions against the Chinese, turning their attention to the introduction of an economic embargo on China.

Nevertheless, the vehemency of American opposition to Communist China's admission forced a reconsideration of British voting policy in the UN. Legally the situation was messy. Robert Scott argued that British voting policy would throw up some 'queer' results, with the CPG represented on a subsidiary body of a committee upon which a Chinese Nationalist delegate was seated: British policy had become 'logical to the point of illogicality'.[79] Politically the balance had tilted. A positive vote on a subsidiary body would have negligible influence in Peking but prove politically embarrassing to Britain in the US. At the December conference, the US administration had agreed to differ with Britain over China's admission; but, during the first months of 1951, with votes pending that could have secured China's admission onto a number of bodies, Washington stepped up pressure on London.[80] The imminence of the Soviet tenure as President of the Security Council (June 1951) brought the problem to a head. Consequently, Acheson suggested a compromise solution, whereby an agreed Anglo-American moratorium would postpone a vote in the UN.[81] As such a moratorium was a procedural motion that had priority over substantive resolutions – such as ones raising the admission of new members – it could prevent a vote on China's admission. This was a reasonable face-saving compromise for the British government and thus the 'moratorium agreement' was introduced on 5 June 1951. It immediately prevented a vote in the Trusteeship Council which may have admitted a Chinese delegate. It remained the basis of Anglo-American policy until there was peace in Korea.

A TRADE WAR WITH CHINA

The British government did not want war against China in Korea accompanied by economic warfare against the Chinese mainland. The reasoning against an extensive trading embargo on China remained pervasive. Extending and tightening restrictions on British exports and on British financial services and shipping interests would be detrimental to the British economy: a source of materials, a market for British goods and invisible earnings would be lost.[82] The economy, with the additional burden of massive re-armaments expenditure, remained in dire need of foreign currency, export earnings and 'soft currency' areas of supply. Any further trading controls would merely exacerbate the already desperate position of British business in China and, perhaps most significantly, affect the economic viability of Hong Kong. British business interests vehemently opposed restrictions on trade with China, which would seriously jeopardise international trade: Sir Arthur Morse, the Chairman of the Hong Kong and Shanghai Banking Corporation, argued that 'to plunge the sword into the delicate texture of international trade and finance may cause irreparable injury and shatter faith in the sanctity of contract'.[83] The majority of British merchants in China believed that the Chinese economy was just beginning to expand and that the Chinese still preferred British goods; they were extremely apprehensive about the impact China's intervention would have on Britain's licensing system for goods to China.[84] Business interests operating in China and Hong Kong feared an economic embargo would make their position untenable. The Board of Trade was concerned that moves towards a more extensive embargo would also be the precursor for an embargo against the whole Soviet bloc. The Foreign Office argued that economic sanctions were politically unwise; they would merely irritate the Chinese, intensify their concern over capitalist encirclement and increase their economic and hence political reliance on the Soviet Union.[85] The Chiefs of Staff agreed. The West would commit a 'psychological error' by imposing further sanctions; they would merely provoke Chinese aggression elsewhere.[86]

For domestic political, economic and strategic reasons, the US wanted tighter economic sanctions on China. Immediately upon China's intervention in the Korean conflict, the Americans placed a total embargo on all trade with the Chinese and froze Chinese assets in the US. Once the Chinese had been declared the aggressor in the UN, the Additional Measures Committee was established through a US initiative. The aim: to introduce a UN economic embargo against China.[87] The administration argued that economic sanctions would increase international pressure on the Chinese and undermine the stability of the Chinese state. The American public was extremely critical of trade with communist states and Republican politicians were pressing for an embargo on all trade with China. The domestic environment in the US gave the issue a political edge. Right-wing Republicans, in particular Senator Joseph McCarthy and General MacArthur, criticised Britain for trading with 'the enemy'. In June 1951 Senator James P. Kem (Republican, Missouri) introduced an amendment to a US act which stopped foreign aid to any nation trading outside the US embargo.[88] In August the Mutual Defense Assistance Control Act (the Battle Act) allowed US aid to be discontinued to those nations who shipped strategic goods (category A) to communist countries. The administration pressurised the British government over two economic issues: Hong Kong's restrictions on China and UN economic sanctions against China.

Hong Kong's economy had been severely affected by the war in Korea because British and especially American sanctions had severely curtailed the colony's trade. Immediately after China's intervention in Korea, the US government restricted US exports to the colony, arguing, with justification, that US goods were being re-exported to China.[89] An economy which relied on US cotton for the nascent textiles industry and on the earnings generated by servicing American trade with China and the Far East was placed under severe strain. In London, the Colonial Office vehemently criticised the US administration, and the Board of Trade argued that the only solution that would satisfy the Americans was for the Hong Kong economy to be in American hands.[90] In Hong Kong, relations between the colonial authorities and the US administration became acrimonious.[91] In response to such a development, the Foreign Office tried to divert, moderate and postpone American demands for a harder stand. During February, Foreign Office officials proposed that either Franks should try to use his influence over Acheson or Attlee should approach President Truman over Hong Kong. Robert Scott disagreed, arguing that given the strength of feeling in the US any approach would be counterproductive. The implication was clear: Hong Kong would have to resign itself to the loss of American raw materials.[92] However, as Chapter 5 will explore, the government did begin to modify American thinking on Hong Kong. The US came to accept British arguments that if restrictions became too severe it would 'present China with an almost irresistible temptation to fish in those troubled waters'.[93] In the early 1950s, neither the British nor the Americans wanted the Chinese to catch the Hong Kong fish.

During 1951, the American administration also began to complain about the scale and type of British exports to China, the number of British ships trading with China and the amount of smuggling taking place through colonial ports. American complaints were more often than not justified. In the aftermath of intervention in Korea, Chinese communist purchases of raw materials and manufactured goods rose steeply, Hong Kong's and Malaya's trade with China increased dramatically, and Chinese orders stimulated demand throughout South East

Asia. There is evidence, in British as well as in American sources, that the communists were smuggling strategic and semi-strategic goods through Hong Kong, India and Macao.[94] At the time, the Americans were especially concerned over the level of rubber exports from Ceylon and Malaya to China, which directly augmented China's war-making capabilities.[95] Consequently, in March the government agreed to introduce a system to control re-exports from Hong Kong to China, restricted the export of pharmaceuticals and rubber, and improved smuggling surveillance. (Exports of rubber were limited to those needed in peacetime; but as China had already received their civilian requirements of rubber for 1951 (20,000 tons) by May 1951, the new British position meant an effective embargo on rubber exports to China.) Robert Scott argued that the point had been reached when 'the risk of further alienating China was less than the risk of allowing her to have material calculated to enable her to build up her military position'.[96] In addition, the government also accepted a UN selective embargo, passed on 17 May, which required all UN members to:

> Apply an embargo on the shipment to areas under the control of the Chinese People's Government of the People's Republic of China and the North Korean authorities of arms, ammunition and implements of war, atomic energy material, petroleum, and items useful in the production of arms, ammunition and the implements of war.[97]

Britain disagreed with such a universal embargo but by May 1951, with the chances of a ceasefire remote and American pressure intensifying, the government compromised and agreed to support the embargo. The government could not afford a politically damaging disagreement with the Americans on this issue. The Chinese reaction was predictably damning: the resolution was labelled an 'instrument of aggression'; Chou branded Britain an enemy of China; the *Peking Daily* argued that the 'Labour Government is the most submissive slave of the US and her most shameful accomplice'.[98]

The government feared that the embargo would be the first in a series of moves that would lead, ultimately, to a naval blockade of China. The Foreign Office, in submitting to a UN selective embargo, sought some assurance from the Americans that this would not be the first step towards a total economic embargo. At the time, the selective embargo on China was difficult to administer, inefficient and would not – if that was the US aim – seriously damage the Chinese economy. The only measure which would satisfy US public opinion and Republican critics and which might cripple the Chinese economy was a total embargo on trade with China. The only way to ensure a total embargo was effective would be a naval blockade of the mainland. This policy, under active consideration by the Joint Chiefs of Staff since January 1951 and constantly advocated by the US Navy – in particular Admiral Forrest Sherman and Admiral William Fechteler – was rejected by the State Department.[99] The State Department recognised that such an action could escalate the conflict and bring into question the viability of Hong Kong. British opposition had a role to play here but the American government's reluctance to press for a total embargo had deeper roots. Basically, the State Department did not believe a total economic embargo would be effective. It would damage a number of sectors of the economy and hamper China's economic growth in the long term, but in the short term would not seriously affect China's economic or military capacity. Although the economy required imports, it was not dependent on them. The modern industrial sector, in particular textile production, relied on foreign imports, but it was not a significant proportion of the economy; and while the Chinese relied on oil from noncommunist areas, the economy was not dependent on this energy source.[100] The US administration admitted that sanctions were actually needed as much for their moral and political as for their economic impact.[101] At this stage, to have universal support and hence to have maximum political impact, it was necessary for the US to go through the mechanism of the UN to introduce sanctions; and in order that they would be voted through, measures had to be moderate and flexible. If the US had pressed for a total UN embargo, it would have been rejected by the membership.

TALKING PEACE WITH CHINA AND AMERICA

On 10 July 1951 the initiation of peace talks for a Korean armistice revitalised British hopes for a removal of sanctions against China and an eventual political settlement. Assessing why at this moment the Chinese decided to push for peace is difficult but it is probably safe to assume that while the Soviets may have stepped up pressure, the Chinese took the initiative. Lamb argued that the cost of the war, the loss of a significant number of troops and the demoralised and economically devastated state of North Korea prompted the Chinese to enter discussions.[102] Essentially, however, the Chinese wanted a ceasefire because their war aims were limited. All the same, the resultant ceasefire talks in Kaesong proved acrimonious and unproductive. This was because America's hostile attitude towards China, the imposition of economic sanctions, obstacles to China's admission to the UN and extensive military and economic aid to Taiwan reinforced China's hostility to the West and thus made peace difficult to achieve.

The British government was actually willing to admit China to the UN and to ease the economic embargo on China in order to achieve peace. As Robert Scott pointed out, if China's admission to the UN brought about a Korean settlement under UN auspices it would 'be cheap at the price'.[103] Britain's liberal approach thus remained in place. Sino-British trade continued to be the prime underlying influence on British policy: trade influenced Chinese attitudes, was advantageous to the British economy and essential for Hong Kong and British traders in the Far East. The Board of Trade, in close contact with the China Association, argued that the shift from informal to formal controls was causing British traders great difficulties and it therefore wanted the embargo eased. The British Chamber of Commerce in Shanghai argued that the main problem was not the goods restricted by the UN, but the uncertainty surrounding the wider and more extensive controls enforced by the British government; discrepancies and ambiguities were causing the traders in China and Hong Kong embarrassment and undermining trade.[104]

The failure of the ceasefire talks postponed British thoughts of removing political and economic sanctions, but, even if a ceasefire had been obtained, the US would have vetoed the compromises necessary to achieve a more liberal approach to China. The US administration foresaw a prolonged period of economic and diplomatic isolation for China. The political and geo-strategic influences on its policy also remained intact. There was a presidential election in 1952 and the administration could not afford to allow the Republican Party to criticise a moderate line on China. More fundamentally, concessions to the Chinese were incompatible with the wider aims of NSC48/5 which were to isolate the Chinese and undermine social support for the regime. The US warned the British government that any change in policy towards China would undermine the credibility of the UN and encourage the Chinese to commit aggression elsewhere, perhaps in Indochina. Acheson reaffirmed that the US wanted the 'moratorium agreement' to operate for 'as long as aggression continued'. The new US ambassador in London, Arthur Ringwalt, blamed the force of McCarthy's diatribe against China.[105] Equally, the State Department continued to press for tighter controls on Sino-British trade. The impasse at the ceasefire talks had actually hardened the US position on China. The scale of the

American military presence in Korea increased, restrictions on military operations outside Korea were removed, a vigorous campaign of covert operations in China was sanctioned and pressure within the US administration for a naval blockade of the Chinese mainland intensified.[106]

Consequently, at the September meeting with US officials, Morrison reluctantly agreed to strengthen military forces in Korea, to tighten the economic sanctions against China and to continue the 'moratorium agreement'.[107] The government did not believe these measures would facilitate a solution to the Korean dispute, but they would hopefully prevent unilateral American initiatives. Since February 1951, the British government had attempted to moderate US policy while agreeing in the last resort to align policy with the US. The new US proposals threatened not only Britain's long-term aim of a political settlement with China, but also, crucially, revitalised British fears about a general war in the Far East.

CONCLUSIONS

By October 1951, the British government came to the reluctant conclusion that a political settlement for the Far East was going to be elusive; the Chinese were in no hurry for a military ceasefire in Korea, while the US would not compromise to achieve one. A solution to the 'China problem' required a 'global rapprochement between the West and the Soviet bloc' – such a development was extremely unlikely in the early 1950s.[108] Throughout this period the Labour government had been working within the parameters of its existing policy towards China: that China had to be integrated, diplomatically and economically, into the world community. The government had, as a result of Korean developments and because of the US position, changed its policy; but on the eve of the inauguration of Churchill's government, US thinking was again threatening to undermine the basis of Britain's position. The Conservative government's response to this pressure will be assessed in Chapters 8 and 9, but first we need to turn to the imperial and economic forces behind British policy towards China.

5 Empire Retained: Hong Kong, 1950–54

Hong Kong is always connected with fatal pestilence, some doubtful war or some internal squabble.

The Times, 1859[1]

In the nineteenth century, the British acquisition of Hong Kong symbolised western imperial encroachment in China and highlighted the weakness of the Chinese empire.[2] In the twentieth century, Hong Kong became a target for Chinese nationalists; in 1925 and 1926 there was a Chinese boycott of trade with Hong Kong and a general strike of Chinese workers within the colony. By the early years of the Second World War, Britain's hold on Hong Kong seemed untenable: the colony was occupied by the Japanese, whilst the US administration pressurised the British government to return the colony to China after the war.[3] Nevertheless, in the immediate post-war period, Britain retained the colony. Three changes explain this turnaround. Firstly, the new Labour government wanted an imperial possession in China; secondly, the US administration no longer pressurised Britain to return Hong Kong to a war-torn and potentially communist China; thirdly, China, weak and preoccupied by civil war, did not demand its return.[4]

In 1949, however, the balance changed: China was politically united and the communists were vehemently anti-imperialist. This chapter will examine why Hong Kong did not return to China in the 1950s. It will begin by assessing why the British wanted to retain the colony. It will then turn to explain how the British colonial authorities dealt with civil war in the colony, communism on their doorstep and an economic embargo on trade with China. Next it will examine how these developments affected Anglo-American relations. Finally, it will analyse communist attitudes to Hong Kong and determine why China did not demand or take back the imperial enclave in the 1950s.

EMPIRE CONFIRMED

Portrayed as a shop window for capitalism, prosperity and political freedom, Hong Kong underpinned Britain's strategic position in the

Far East. The British Labour government argued that withdrawal would undermine British prestige and bring into question British resistance to communism. Ernest Bevin labelled Hong Kong the 'Berlin of Asia'. Clement Attlee believed anti-communism in Asia would crumble if Hong Kong was lost.[5] The Chiefs of Staff were emphatic: a 'failure to hold Hong Kong in the face of an attack by Communist China would have grave repercussions for the Allied position in South East Asia and [the] Far East, and would be very damaging to British prestige generally'. Britain could not hand Hong Kong to the communists, nor sacrifice 'the lives of all who have sought our protection there'.[6] Talk of handing back Hong Kong was the talk of appeasement. With the exception of some enlightened anti-imperialists on the left, few within Britain advocated handing back Hong Kong.

Both Labour and Conservative governments were also acutely aware of Britain's economic reliance on the empire. Bevin held pragmatic and nationalistic views on the imperial question: he declared that he was 'not prepared to sacrifice the British Empire because if the British Empire fell . . . it would mean the standard of life of our constituencies would fall rapidly'.[7] This view of the colonial question struck a chord with most of his cabinet colleagues and mirrored the stand of key Whitehall departments: the Foreign Office, the Colonial Office and the Treasury.[8] Such thinking influenced British policy towards Hong Kong between 1950 and 1954: Hong Kong was an essential component of a British empire which would guarantee Britain's diplomatic status as a global power and underpin Britain's economy in the post-war world.

The British government perceived Hong Kong to be economically important to the British economy in the 1950s. The British government was reluctant to surrender an estimated £150 million invested in Hong Kong; whilst the colony, despite suffering from recession, bought on average over 1.2 per cent of British exports in the period 1949–54. Throughout the 1950s Hong Kong ran a trading deficit with the UK (see Chapter 7 for a breakdown of Hong Kong's trade with Britain).[9] Significantly, Hong Kong, reliant on imported raw materials and foodstuffs from the Chinese mainland, also ran a trading deficit with China and thus the colony provided the Chinese with sterling with which to buy British exports; Hong Kong estimated Chinese holdings of sterling at £100 million in the early 1950s.[10] In addition, the Treasury did not want to sacrifice Hong Kong's ability to support the pound. Hong Kong was a part of the Sterling Area, which, because colonial currency balances held in London augmented central reserves, was of vital importance in maintaining the international status of the pound.[11] Hong Kong's sterling balances increased from £67 million in 1950 to £132 million in 1954. This was a small proportion of overall sterling balances which totalled £4205 million in 1950 and £4422 million in 1954, but as a proportion of the sterling balances held by the colonies during this period Hong Kong represented approximately 10 per cent.[12] As Catherine Schenk has indicated, the situation in Hong Kong was slightly more complex than in other colonies because a free market for US dollars operated. By allowing UK and non-UK residents to exchange sterling for dollars, this financial arrangement made the colony a potential drain on Britain's reserves; and also, by allowing the US to settle sterling debts outside the central reserves, it reduced transaction income for British bankers in London. Schenk argues the free market was allowed partly because it would be administratively expensive to close the gap but mainly because the free market supplied 90 per cent of the colony's dollar requirements, reducing Hong Kong's burden on the central reserves. The Colonial Office viewed the free market as essential for Hong Kong's economic and political stability, because, by allowing raw materials (especially raw cotton) to be imported, the free market was vital for Hong Kong's industrial sector. In addition, the Treasury and Board of Trade argued that the free market also benefited British foreign exchange controls as it allowed large insurance companies and investment trusts to buy dollar securities and thus acted as a safety valve for sterling, reducing pressure for a relaxation of exchange controls in Britain.[13] Schenk asserts that the free market indirectly 'allowed the UK to reduce liability to the dollar area and to increase holdings of dollar assets which added to hard currency invisible earnings'.[14] The financial impact of Hong Kong on the British economy is difficult to unravel; but what is clear is that British officials in the Treasury, the Board of Trade and the Colonial Office perceived Hong Kong to be a net earner of dollars, and its sterling reserves a support for the pound. Finally, Hong Kong was cheap to run. The colonial authorities raised revenue from duties on the import–export trade and from indirect taxation and thus after 1947–48, when Hong Kong received a grant of £12 million, Hong Kong was not a drain on London. Until 1948 Hong Kong was under direct Treasury control but thereafter, because the colony was 'rolling in money', checks were not needed.[15] Consequently, the colony made fewer financial demands than any other territory.

However, the claim made by the Colonial Office that the loss of Hong Kong would have been a 'serious blow' to the British economy in the late 1940s and early 1950s is clearly an overstatement.[16] Hong Kong was more important to certain British business interests than to the British economy. And it was this rather than broader macro-economic factors that influenced the government's attitude. From the 1920s onwards, British firms had reacted to the rise of Chinese nationalism and the resultant encroachment on extra-territoriality by relocating headquarters and reorienting investment to Hong Kong.[17] British mercantile concerns were conscious that Hong Kong had become the bedrock of their position in the Far East. In a letter to the Foreign Office in 1945, G.W. Swire, of Swire and Sons Ltd, argued that if Hong Kong was returned, British firms would get out of China altogether.[18] In the early 1950s, Hong Kong was the most attractive base for economic contact with China. The colony was the most significant conduit for China's trade with the West and, with the Nationalists continuing their blockade of the Chinese east coast, Hong Kong was the most important access route for trade between China and South and North East Asia. The decision by the PRC to restructure China's import and export trade, by reducing the role of foreign merchants and placing control of foreign trade in the hands of government agencies, meant that throughout the 1950s the PRC began to conduct much of China's trade through its organisations in the colony. In this period British businessmen established good working relations with the various Chinese communist agencies operating in the colony, such as the buying agency Universal Development Corporation, a development which made businessmen increasingly aware that trade with China could be best conducted through Hong Kong. Frank King notes that the Hong Kong and Shanghai Banking Corporation was heavily involved in financing China's trade through the Bank of China's Hong Kong office, and indeed facilitated the export of key commodities throughout the Korean War period.[19]

EMPIRE RULED

British policy-makers acknowledged that if the Chinese wanted the return of Hong Kong then British rule was untenable. The CCP could destabilise the colony in a number of ways: by using its influence in trade unions and in schools to start popular disturbances, by sending in the troops, or by introducing an embargo on trade with Hong Kong.[20] At the beginning of the period, the Foreign Office and the Colonial Office thought it inevitable that the CCP would pressurise for the return of the colony; and the British government remained acutely conscious of Hong Kong's vulnerability throughout the 1950s. However, during the period, evidence accumulated to suggest that the PRC would not immediately demand the return of Hong Kong. Communist agents in the colony implied to British officials that Hong Kong was safe; the CCP prevented its cells in the colony from orchestrating a general strike or student protests; Chinese troop levels in Kwangtung were relatively small and Chinese propaganda against Hong Kong was muted.[21] As the last section of this chapter will explain, the PRC was placing national economic interests before its ideological adherence to anti-imperialist and Marxist-Leninist thought. Basically, Hong Kong provided the Chinese economy with valuable goods and services and, most crucially, with foreign exchange with which to import capital goods for industrialisation. The PRC was reverting to the Canton system of trade of the late eighteenth and early nineteenth centuries as a means of controlling contact with the West. This tacit communist acceptance of a British colony on the Chinese mainland guaranteed that British business would have a base in the Far East even after a withdrawal from China. But there was no calculated trade-off being made within Whitehall with the loss of foreign direct investment in China being balanced against the retention of Hong Kong. British governments never had that level of confidence in the retention of a far eastern empire: the short-term political future of Hong Kong was always thought precarious.

How would Britain deal with the threat communism posed to Hong Kong? Firstly, the government would not raise the question of Hong Kong's status with China; and, if the Chinese did, Britain would consider declaring Hong Kong an international port. Attlee believed that 'If we made it a point of prestige that we should retain Hong Kong as a British possession, it might become a matter of prestige for the communists to force us to withdraw from it'.[22] Britain would not raise Hong Kong's constitutional position with the Chinese at this juncture, a position that did not change even when war in Korea had heightened international cold war tensions. In November 1950 Esler Dening, on a visit to the Far East, rejected any international settlement for Hong Kong; Britain's position under international law was weak and any reference to the case would publicise and hence complicate matters: 'It is of course a sleeping dog at the moment and the longer it sleeps the better.'[23] Secondly, Britain would administer Hong Kong in a liberal manner: communist activity in Hong Kong would be controlled but not suppressed. The colonial authorities would allow organisations with links to the PRC (or the Chinese Nationalists) to continue to operate but preclude overtly political activity and suppress illegal actions. A minimum garrison, insufficient to repulse an external assault, would ensure internal security. The Foreign Office, the Colonial Office and Hong Kong agreed that a basic aim of the CCP's strategy *vis-à-vis* Hong Kong would be to take control of labour, educational and cultural organisations. If successful the CCP would be in a position to challenge British possession.

In theory, British colonial policy reflected the traditional liberal approach to maintaining the political, social and economic order in Hong Kong. Historically the colony had allowed the free movement of capital and labour into and within the territory: colonial authorities had refrained from intervening in economic matters and Hong Kong had been a haven for political dissidents from mainland China, admitted on the understanding that they would not continue their political activities in the colony. British strategy concentrated on highlighting the higher standard of living and the existence of greater political and economic freedoms in the colony. Ironically, the most emphatic statement of this basic ideology came from Soviet spy Guy Burgess: in March 1950 he declared:

> We cannot fight communism with force, but with facts. The facts are that living conditions in Hong Kong are still better than those inside China and the fundamental rights such as those of freedom of speech and the press and liberty of movement are still basically preserved . . . All inhabitants of this colony, whatever their race or persuasion, will be given equal privileges under the law, but none will have special privileges.[24]

In practice it was not ideological considerations which shaped how the British government ran Hong Kong, but rather the weakness of the British colonial state's position in the early 1950s *vis-à-vis* the CCP, the financial cost of any more authoritarian measures and the fact that some restrictive measures would have hampered economic activity in the colony.

In practice the colonial authority did not have the power to contain communism in Hong Kong because its position was too tenuous and because the British government did not want trade and diplomatic ties with the PRC jeopardised by vigorous anti-communist policies in the colony. Bevin informed Charles Johnston of the far eastern department that 'we must do everything we can in Hong Kong to prevent [and] avoid incidents which give additional ammunition to the Chinese communists'.[25] The Foreign Office line engendered tensions between London and Hong Kong. Alexander Grantham, the governor, whilst accepting that political contact with China was useful, argued an excessively moderate attitude would undermine local opposition to communism and encourage more overt communist activities.[26] But ultimately Britain was too weak to prevent communist influence in Hong Kong. The Colonial Office and the authorities in Hong Kong recognised, and were extremely concerned by, the colony's vulnerability to communist insurrection. Arthur Creech Jones, the Secretary of State for Colonial Affairs, admitted that 'Hong Kong must often be at the mercy of events over which she has little control . . . [it] would be a rash man who tried to minimise current difficulties or to forecast what the long term prospects might be'.[27] He acknowledged that:

> There is abundant evidence that a part of the present communist tactics is to attempt to undermine the authority of government wherever possible in British colonial territories, and with the rising tide of political consciousness among colonial peoples, there are other influences at work, which, if they develop in the wrong way, may give rise to subversive movements.[28]

Consequently, Hong Kong had to accept Chinese communist infiltration in trade unions, societies and in the press. A vigorous campaign to reduce communist influence would alienate non-aligned sections of society and drive political organisations underground, encouraging a shift to terrorist methods, a development that would make it difficult to monitor signs of forthcoming political insurrection – a precursor for any radical change in the PRC's policy towards Hong Kong.[29] The CCP could have easily and quickly ended colonial rule in Hong Kong, given that the colony could not be successfully defended against a military attack from the mainland. Britain would have very little warning of an attack and, in any case, the resources were not available to reinforce the British military presence.[30] The security forces in Hong Kong could not deal with a public insurgency accompanied by an overt external offensive by Chinese communist forces. During the summer of 1950 it was Hong Kong and not Malaya that provided a brigade for the war in Korea.[31] There was no evidence of communist agitation at the time, but a clear assumption was made: even if the Korean War was part of a wider communist offensive then the loss of Hong Kong would have to be accepted.[32]

By contrast, Hong Kong adopted stringent and restrictive measures against KMT activities. The authorities could not be seen to be acquiescing in Chinese Nationalist activity on the island; if the CCP believed that Hong Kong was becoming a base for the Chinese Nationalists it might step up its activities within the colony. A Hong Kong Special Branch report declared that 'the dangers of allowing Hong Kong to be used as a National intelligence and guerrilla base are obvious. Apart from the political implications, the presence of roaming guerrilla bands in the New Territories are a constant source of danger to law and order.'[33] The government wanted to avoid the escalation of civil war in the territory and realised that the KMT, a disintegrating political and military movement, was likely to resort increasingly to violent and overt means of resisting communist control in Hong Kong.

Hong Kong's industrial relations policy highlighted Britain's strategy for meeting the communist threat. In 1949 Chinese Nationalist influence declined and the CCP's grip on the labour movement tightened; but at the beginning of 1950 the trade union movement remained spilt fairly evenly between the Hong Kong Federation of Trade Unions (FTU), linked to the CCP, and the Hong Kong and Kowloon Trade Union Congress, sympathetic to the Chinese Nationalists. The KMT still retained the dominant position in most trade unions, but the communists had taken control of the powerful public utility unions. This communist control of the trade union movement was a direct challenge to colonial rule.[34] The British cabinet acknowledged it 'gave occasion for communist interference and for [the] weakening of our internal grip on the colony from a strategy point of view'.[35]

In January 1950 a bitter and protracted tramway workers' strike heightened cabinet concern: it thought that such a symbolic dispute between capital and labour might allow communism to extend its influence. The traditional industrial strategy of the colonial authorities in Hong Kong was based, in theory, on non-interventionism: the government only intervening in the process of arbitration between labour and capital if a dispute contravened the law. Hong Kong argued that Chinese workers preferred an unofficial, personal and direct approach that isolated the exact nature of the problem and which would initiate a process of bargaining 'so ingrained in the Oriental mind' that it would achieve a solution.[36] The Labour government, however, believed that Hong Kong's industrial relations policy needed to be changed to meet the new economic and political situation in Hong Kong. Bevin argued that, as workers would not turn to communism if the government was acting on their behalf, Hong Kong must arbitrate and conciliate.[37] He believed that as matters stood the lack of corporate institutions bringing together employers, workers and the state made the settlement of disputes more problematic. But because the Hong Kong authorities rejected state intervention and because unrest in the tramway workers' strike subsided, the Labour government did not force change. Industrial relations did not re-emerge as a political issue in Hong Kong. As Steve Tsang has indicated, however, the colonial authorities actually sided with and intervened on behalf of the employers. When the tramways strike escalated in January 1950, the authorities issued a warning to the union to cease political speeches and, on 30 January, broke up a political rally, arresting and deporting leading union officials and preventing tram premises from being occupied.[38] This government intervention proved crucial in determining the outcome of the strike. A subsequent compromise between the union and the employers ended the dispute on 11 February, whereby allowances would in future be negotiated and dismissed workers would be allowed to return to work. The Hong Kong authorities, closely aligned at a social and political level to the tramway employers, had in fact used the strike to break the power of the FTU.[39]

The strike proved to be a turning point in Hong Kong's labour relations. Trade union membership fell, the movement was divided by internal disputes and communist influence collapsed. The strike was followed by a period of relative industrial peace and then, from June 1950, communist influence in the trade union movement declined. Most dramatically, the political standing and financial health of the FTU diminished, attendance at meetings declined, funds dried up and the appeal of its political propaganda waned. In June 1950 cracks began to appear in its affiliated membership, with some members of the three most left-wing unions (the Tram Workers' Union, the Motor Drivers' Union and the Postal Workers' Union) proposing a rival organisation.[40] Economic and political factors explain this development. Firstly, rising unemployment during the Korean War and concessions by employers undermined the radicalism of Hong Kong's workforce. Secondly, the FTU lost credibility during the tramways strike because some of its key officials were deported by the authorities, and, more significantly, because it had not thrown its full weight behind the strike. It could be argued that these developments vindicate the interventionist approach of the Hong Kong authorities. But this is not the case. What really explains the FTU hesitancy, weakness and eventual decline is the attitude of the PRC. The Chinese government did not want a general strike nor even token disputes.[41] The PRC played a minor role in the tramway workers' strike, providing moral support and a number of advisers from Canton but not extensive political or financial support. Over-zealous local officials in Hong Kong and Canton had, by trying to organise a general strike, attempted to instigate political insurrection in the colony; but the PRC, not wanting to destabilise Hong Kong, withdrew support from local trade unions. The decline in trade union activity in the colony in the aftermath of the strike was not the result of suppression by the Hong Kong authorities, but the product of CCP compliance with the British empire, an issue we will return to in the final section of this chapter.

WAR AND EMPIRE

The outbreak of the Korean War and China's subsequent intervention changed the British approach to governing Hong Kong. A harder, more stringent anti-communist line was taken. A number of factors brought the change about. Firstly, the colonial authorities demanded greater powers because they feared that the economic recession caused by the economic embargo on China would stimulate social unrest. Secondly, given that the Korean War reduced trade with China and lessened the possibility of better diplomatic relations between Britain and China, the Foreign Office removed its veto on new measures and on more extensive powers for the Hong Kong government. N.C.C. Trench, an official in the Foreign Office, commenting on a proposal by Hong Kong for tighter immigration controls, noted that: 'I do not think that we can really put much faith in the belief that if we are nice to the Chinese, they will be nice to us too.'[42] The colonial authorities in Hong Kong also argued that as support for the CCP had tailed off they could introduce more repressive measures without courting unpopularity in the colony. In January 1950 the CCP, riding on the back of the prestige gained by reuniting China, had widespread sympathy within the Chinese community. By June 1950, however, communism had lost ground in the territory. There was scepticism about CCP domestic policy; the Sino-Soviet Treaty had been greeted with 'very mixed feelings'; and China had failed to establish full diplomatic relations with Britain, 'a centre from which the prestige and influence of the Peking government would have radiated'.[43] Then after June 1950, public morale in Hong Kong was seriously affected by the war in Korea. Hong Kong authorities reported 'a gloomy foreboding regarding communist intentions towards Hong Kong'; while, in the aftermath of China's intervention in Korea, there was widespread anxiety about a general war.[44] Consequently, the colonial authorities believed they could suppress Chinese communist activity without losing public sympathy.

Moreover, the authorities thought that the communist position in Hong Kong was vulnerable and could be attacked. They believed that the communists were losing ground in the trade union movement because 'most workers wished to be left in peace' and 'did not wish to be "taken for a ride" to serve communist political ends'.[45] They admitted that communism had made significant gains in the arena of education – exploiting the 'impressionability of youth, and the natural patriotism of the young' – but also thought that the CCP had not gained the loyalty of all students nor gained control over most schools. Steve Tsang argues that the lack of government funding for education forced working-class parents to send their students to trade union funded schools; but even then, because of strict government controls on outside financing and indoctrinated teaching, the local communists failed to exploit the situation.[46] The two most prominent CCP-controlled schools in 1950 were Heung To in Kowloon and Pai Kiu in Hong Kong, but, even by then, the colonial authorities had closed down three schools. And then, during 1950, they deported Lo Tung, the communist official responsible for education.[47] Above all else, new measures were possible because neither the British government nor the Hong Kong authorities believed China would retaliate against anti-communist British policies. In 1952 the CCP orchestrated a propaganda campaign against the colony, suggesting a Chinese move to take back Hong Kong, but, while alarmed by developments, neither Hong Kong nor London believed the CCP planned a military assault or a campaign of subversion within the territory.

Three administrative changes in the colony highlight the more discriminatory and radical measures introduced during the war: an extension of expulsion powers, tighter controls over the press, and a reversal of thinking on constitutional reform. We will discuss how and why the British government changed its position on each of these issues in turn.

Immigration controls epitomised the vexed problems involved in administering Hong Kong in this period. An 'open door' policy, allowing the free movement of capital, labour, raw materials and finished goods to and from the colony was essential for Hong Kong's prosperity. However, political and economic pressures forced the introduction of controls. In 1949, to prevent mass immigration while at the same time allowing legitimate entry and exit of traders and other temporary visitors, immigrants were forced to produce travel documents. In 1950 tighter immigration controls to expel squatters, the destitute and communist activists from Hong Kong were introduced, because unemployment was high, food supplies inadequate and the colonial authorities feared communist infiltration. (According to Hong Kong, its controls were still allowing communists and the destitute to enter the colony with the 'tacit assistance of the Chinese authorities behind them'.[48]) Initially, the Foreign Office was reluctant to accept new controls – potentially 'a large spanner thrown into the works of the discussion now proceeding in Peking' – but with continued impasse in Peking a quota system was introduced at the border; any immigrants with northern dialects were excluded.[49] The heavy flow of migrants into Hong Kong ended and there was no serious Chinese communist reaction. Thereafter, China's intervention in Korea, representing a 'sudden deterioration in the security situation', provoked the colonial authorities to invoke the 1949 Expulsion of Undesirables Ordinance, a development which Hutchison objected to but which the Foreign Office, under pressure from the Colonial Office, sanctioned.[50] In 1952 the authorities expelled communist activists; in January 13 well-known CCP members, active in the local film industry, and three prominent trade union officials were deported.[51] Unlike the deportations of 1950, these provoked a more severe reaction from China, but no popular protest in Hong Kong itself.

War in Korea allowed tighter press censorship in Hong Kong. In 1950 and 1951 freedom of the press in Hong Kong meant an uncensored and unregulated communist press circulated in the colony. Increasingly, however, critical and propagandist reporting by Chinese communist newspapers led the British authorities in Hong Kong to introduce controls. In 1952 Hong Kong prevented the distribution of *Nan Fong Yat Pao* and banned the publication of *Ta Kung Pao*. The British chargé d'affaires in Peking astutely observed that the step was 'a flagrant denial of the rights and freedoms which we pretend to uphold'.[52] In 1950 the *New China News Agency*, an organ of the CCP, should have registered with the Hong Kong authorities, but neither Hong Kong nor London forced the issue, fearing retaliatory action against British interests in China. In 1952 the Foreign Office line changed and the Chinese registered the agency.[53]

Constitutional reform for Hong Kong, publicly announced in 1946 and under consideration in London and Hong Kong between 1946 and 1952, was abandoned by the British cabinet in September 1952. The political system in Hong Kong had remained, for the most part, unchanged since 1843. The colonial authority comprised four components:

a governor; an Executive Council, made up of the governor, nine official members and three unofficial members; a Legislative Council, composed of the governor, nine official members and eight appointed unofficial members; and an Urban Council with five official and eight unofficial members.[54] The system was not democratic. Real power in the colony, vested with the governor and supreme authority, lay in London; the government had the right to make laws, to veto Legislative Council decisions and to appoint and instruct the governor. As part of a wider movement to introduce colonial reform, the Labour government proposed constitutional reform for Hong Kong, a process which culminated in the 1947 Young Plan to introduce municipal self-government and reform the Legislative Council.[55] These and other subsequent proposals, revised and debated at length in London and Hong Kong, were abandoned indefinitely in 1952.

As Tsang has outlined in his comprehensive study of this question, a number of complex intertwined factors explain the failure to democratise the Hong Kong political system in the 1950s. Firstly, the British government feared that more democracy in Hong Kong might provoke opposition from the PRC and might allow communist elements to gain power in the colony. Secondly, in the 1950s political reform movements were weak and there was a lack of popular interest in democracy in Hong Kong. This was a product of the economic difficulties of the 1950s which turned people's minds to survival and not to political rights. It also resulted from the incorporation of various Chinese business elites into the political system, which allowed them informally to influence government policy behind the scenes, as clearly seen in their response to the tramway workers' strike in 1950. As demands for democratisation were muted and internalised, there was not much pressure on the colonial authorities to introduce reform. Nevertheless, Tsang lays the blame with a Labour government that failed to push through change and, ultimately, with a Conservative government that was uninterested in reform. Moreover, he argues that throughout the period the Colonial Office vigorously opposed reform, while Grantham, who believed the most appropriate form of government for Hong Kong to be a 'benevolent autocracy', constantly demanded more dictatorial powers from London. Tsang notes that the governor had spent a major portion of his career in Hong Kong and this experience, in particular of Chinese agitation in Hong Kong in 1925, had shaped his perceptions of the Hong Kong Chinese, who, he argued, would align with the Chinese government in Peking in a dispute over the future of Hong Kong.[56]

Hong Kong's unusual status compounded some of the dilemmas faced by the British government and firmed up opposition (or apathy) towards reforms in Hong Kong. The basic problem was that if the franchise was extended and the Legislative Council democratised, the CCP could undermine British control through the electoral process, but that if, alternatively, reforms were so framed so as to prevent an elected majority from gaining control of the Legislative Council, local political aspirations would not be satisfied and this might provide the catalyst for a stronger pro-democracy movement. Neither local Chinese elites nor the British state wanted either of these outcomes. In 1946 the Colonial Office had mistakenly assumed that Hong Kong could be treated like any other colony. But in actual fact developments in Hong Kong depended on, and severely affected, Sino-British relations. In 1950 and 1951 Creech-Jones and James Griffiths, Colonial Secretaries in the Labour governments, postponed a decision on democratisation until the situation in the Far East stabilised, but refused to drop constitutional reform from the agenda. The crucial change came in 1952 when Churchill and his Colonial Secretary, Oliver Lyttelton, abandoned reform.[57] The real block on change was in the colony. Hong Kong's governor, the Colonial Office and, to some extent, the Chinese merchant community in the colony believed democracy would jeopardise the political stability and economic prosperity of the colony.

The most significant short-term impact of the Korean War was on Hong Kong's economy. In 1950 the colony benefited from the recovery of the Chinese economy and from the Nationalist embargo of Shanghai which diverted much of China's trade, notably with Japan, through Hong Kong. Exports from Hong Kong to mainland China rose from HK$585 million in 1949 to HK$1260 million in 1951, a rise of some 115.38 per cent. Sir Arthur Morse, the Chairman of the Hong Kong Shanghai Bank, acknowledged that Hong Kong had benefited by the diversion of Sino-Japanese trade from Shanghai to Hong Kong.[58] The Korean War dramatically curtailed the growth of Hong Kong's trade with China. Exports increased by 27.3 per cent in 1951, but in 1952 fell by 67.58 per cent and only rose by 3.85 per cent in 1953. In the longer term, the collapse accelerated a restructuring of the Hong Kong economy away from a reliance on the re-export trade with China towards manufacturing. In 1948 there were an estimated 1600 factories in Hong Kong employing 60 000 people, and contributing 10 per cent of Hong Kong's total exports, whereas by 1955 the colony had 2594 factories, employing 200 000 people, and contributing 30 per cent of Hong Kong's exports. Hong Kong also began to diversify and extend its trading ties with the Asian and global economies; in 1938 75 per cent of Hong Kong's trade was with China, in 1949 the corresponding figure was 50 per cent and in 1955 it was 15 per cent.[59] Manufacturing benefited from cheap, educated and skilled labour and a well-connected, experienced and capital-rich entrepreneurial class, many of whom were recent emigrants from the mainland. In the short term, however, a number of developments dislocated the economy: the strengthening of British controls, the total American embargo on trade with China (permanent) and on trade with Hong Kong (partial and temporary), the tightening of Japanese controls, and the 1951 UN embargo on trade with Communist China. (See Chapters 3, 4 and 8 for the implementation of the embargo.) The PRC, unable to obtain certain imports from Hong Kong and fearing its assets held in Hong Kong would be seized, was reluctant to maintain trading balances in the colony. But it was the American embargo on trade with China which had the most dramatic impact on Hong Kong's economic position. In 1950 trade between Hong Kong and the US had accounted for over a third of Hong Kong's total trade; the colony was an entrepôt centre for American trade with China and the Far East and the US supplied vital raw materials for Hong Kong's industry. Once China intervened in the Korean War, US exports to Hong Kong and imports from the colony fell dramatically, and although US restrictions on trade eased somewhat in 1952 and 1953, US trade with or through Hong Kong did not reach its levels of 1950.

By undermining the economy, causing widespread unemployment and reducing living standards in the colony, economic sanctions threatened to destabilise Hong Kong's political order. Hong Kong's economy had already been dislocated by civil war on the Chinese mainland, with social conditions in the colony deteriorating in the aftermath of huge immigration from the mainland. Social and economic conditions improved in the early months of 1950; the flow of migrants was stemmed and Hong Kong's economy benefited from post-war economic reconstruction in China. But the dire social problems had not been fully alleviated by this short-term upturn in entrepôt earnings and were exacerbated by the economic recession caused by the Korean War. Hong Kong had a substantial squatter population because its housing stock was inadequate and unable to cope with the massive increase in migration in the late 1940s. Unemployment in the colony also remained high – amongst Hong Kong's squatter population it was estimated at 30 per cent in June 1950. It could thus be argued that the conditions were ripe for revolution. Indeed there had already been an acrimonious and politically influential strike by the tramway workers, whilst trade unions continued to demand a general strike. The authorities in Hong Kong and the Colonial Office in London feared that the economic embargo, by reducing the value of the imperialist enclave to the PRC, might encourage a CCP inspired and funded revolution. In December 1950 the colony strongly opposed the introduction by the US of special licensing restrictions on trade with Hong Kong which prohibited US shipments of cotton, black plate, tin plate, petroleum products and other raw materials essential for Hong Kong's industry and for the entrepôt trade with China.[60] The Foreign Office recognised that any measures that reduced the economic value of the colonial territory to the communists would be to Hong Kong's detriment; but wider political and strategic considerations forced the government to introduce tighter controls over the export of strategic and semi-strategic goods from the UK to Hong Kong and from Hong Kong to China. In July 1950 strategic controls were secretly placed on Hong Kong's exports to China, and in June 1951 Britain, in compliance with the UN embargo on trade with China, publicly announced that exports of certain goods to China from Hong Kong were prohibited. The government successfully lobbied the US for a relaxation of its controls on its exports to Hong Kong, but this concession did not radically change the amount of goods and raw materials arriving from US sources. The British government did not want to jeopardise control of Hong Kong; but two considerations prevailed. Firstly, Britain could not resist the embargo, as economic and political relations with the US were more important than the economic well-being of the colony. And secondly, it seemed unlikely that the PRC would use the Korean War as a pretext to regain Hong Kong. It is to these two issues that we now turn.

THE AMERICANS AND THE BRITISH EMPIRE

> The situation in Hong Kong is, in fact, not comparable to that elsewhere. Apart from the special preoccupation of the Hong Kong Government with the maintenance of internal security, it is at present inevitable that the divergence of British and American policies towards China should manifest itself strongly in Hong Kong.[61]

Hong Kong was at the heart of the contradiction inherent in Britain's policy towards China. Britain's retention of Hong Kong necessitated economic and diplomatic contact with China, but wider political, economic and strategic interests demanded an alignment of policy with the

US. The British government was willing to damage the Hong Kong economy and possibly bring into doubt the political viability of Hong Kong by acquiescing in American measures against China, as evidenced by the introduction of the economic embargo and by capitulating to American pressure over the Hong Kong aircraft case. At the same time, the British government sought to deal with the contradiction in policy by using Hong Kong to moderate American policy towards China and by seeking an American commitment to the defence of Hong Kong.

In January 1950 the disputed ownership of 70 Chinese aircraft in Hong Kong epitomised British government dilemmas. Ownership of the planes formerly belonging to the Chinese Nationalist Aviation Corporation (CNAC) and the Central Air Transportation Corporation (CATC) was claimed by the PRC and an American company which had close links with the Chinese Nationalists. The case was in the hands of the Hong Kong courts.[62] The communist claim was sound: the aircraft were in CCP hands. On 12 November 1949 Chou En-lai had issued a directive to the managing directors declaring the two corporations to be Chinese communist property; on 3 December 1949 he had issued a public statement on the question; on 13 January 1950 the Head of the Civil Aviation Bureau of the CPG had instructed the managers to take over the assets of the CNAC and CATC. The president of the CATC and the majority of its employees had defected to Communist China. The American case was more tenuous. Civil Air Transport (CAT) had been set up and registered in the US for the specific purpose of preventing the aircraft falling into communist hands.

The political implications of the case were so profound that the British cabinet and not the Hong Kong courts dictated the outcome of this case. The British government faced a dilemma. A decision to uphold the US claim might preclude full diplomatic relations with China.[63] On the other hand, the US administration made it clear that it did not want the aircraft in communist hands, an outcome which would boost communist morale and augment Chinese air capabilities.[64] Moreover, American domestic politics complicated the issue. CAT was owned by Claire Chennault, a forceful advocate of the roll back of Communist China, who had close links with the Chinese Nationalists and with right-wing politicians in Washington. Bruce Cumings notes that from the summer of 1949 CAT was partly funded by the CIA and the airline symbolised, and was an integral part of, plans to roll back communism in Asia.[65] Allowing the aircraft to return would antagonise the US administration and right-wing opinion-makers, and, by stimulating a public debate on British policy, make it more difficult for the administration to align US policy on China towards British policy. Oliver

Franks, the British ambassador in Washington, warned that US public opinion, manipulated by the right-wing press and by Congress, could turn against Britain. The popular interpretation of developments would be dogmatic and critical: US interests were being unfairly treated by a British court in Hong Kong. The cabinet, persuaded by the arguments of Ernest Bevin and the Chiefs of Staff, prevented the aircraft returning to China.[66] In a classic British legal fudge, the aircraft were prevented from returning to China by an order in court making the issue *sub justice*. In May 1951 the Chief Justice of Hong Kong judged in favour of the PRC; but in July 1952, after an appeal by the US company, the sale of the aircraft to Civil Air Transport was sanctioned.[67]

During the Korean War, Hong Kong became a tool to moderate American thinking on economic and military sanctions against China. The government line was straightforward: Hong Kong was important in the fight against communism; could be lost to the West by economic and military sanctions against China; and hence policy towards China must be moderate. The Foreign Office played on the importance of the colony. A memorandum by the British embassy in Washington declared that Hong Kong was 'a window in the Modern Great Wall of China . . . an example of justice and enlightened Government which provides hope for a better future for many who live outside China', while functioning as an important listening post on developments in Communist China.[68] The colony was a strategically important harbour, which in Chinese hands would disrupt travel in the South China Sea. An *aide-mémoire* to the State Department, on 1 February 1951, declared that 'Hong Kong is important to *both* [my italics] [the] US and the UK, since it is a symbol of strength and stability of the British Empire throughout Asia'.[69] In January 1951 Bevin informed Franks that if China was named as the aggressor in the UN and sanctions were imposed upon the PRC, it 'would give China strong provocation to take action against us in Hong Kong and elsewhere in the Far East'.[70] The new Conservative administration continued to use Hong Kong as a way of gaining leverage over American policy in the Far East. In 1952 Eden informed Acheson that Hong Kong would be lost during a general war and would face a grave crisis if an economic embargo was introduced.[71] (The vulnerability of Hong Kong did not concern Churchill; he admitted that, in the event of further American measures, Hong Kong would 'suffer gravely', but believed Britain had to support fully US policy in the Far East.[72])

The US administration accepted to some extent British arguments that British control over the colony made it difficult for Britain to support American strategy towards China. In November 1950 Dulles informed Senator Lodge that: 'The British appeared to feel that their position in Hong Kong was immune so long as they could persuade the Chinese communists that they were trying to get Formosa back for them.'[73] Similarly, a brief for Churchill's visit to Washington in January 1952 noted that:

> A basic factor in the British attitude is their feeling of military and economic insecurity. The exposed position of Hong Kong necessarily affects their attitude towards China and increases their fear that the US might permit itself to be drawn into a major war with China, with resulting disastrous effects to Hong Kong and to the Eastern defence effort.[74]

Indeed it appears that the vulnerability of Hong Kong did add weight to the arguments against more stringent economic and military measures against China. In March 1951 Dean Rusk informed Acheson that Hong Kong was of 'psychological importance', and if it fell as a result of US inspired sanctions, it would cause tensions in the Anglo-American relationship and reduce American prestige in Asia.[75] By the end of the Korean War, the US administration had adopted Bevin's analogy to describe Hong Kong: a document written for the White House in December 1953 declared that 'we do not have the advantage of a "West Berlin" in relation to Communist China. The closest thing to it is the crown colony of Hong Kong.'[76] Hong Kong was an outpost of capitalism, a listening post on the Chinese mainland and a base for anti-communist activities against the PRC in South China by the CIA and Chinese Nationalists: it was a potential bridge-head for an invasion. Significantly, Hong Kong became strategically and symbolically important to 'rollbackers'. Consequently, the State Department used Hong Kong's vulnerability to resist pressure from elements within the administration for more extensive measures against China. The ploy worked because it played on differences within the Department of Defense over Hong Kong. The defence establishment was divided on Hong Kong; some, such as General Collins, the US Army Chief of Staff, argued the loss of Hong Kong had to be reconciled; but others, notably Admiral William Fechteler, Chief of Naval Operations, and Admiral Arthur Radford, Commander in Chief (Pacific), did not want the territory sacrificed. In 1953 Radford informed John Allison, the Assistant Secretary of State for Far Eastern Affairs, that 'the benefit to be derived from a blockade would not outweigh the dangers to Hong Kong and the possible loss of that island to the communists'.[77]

The shift in US thinking on Hong Kong allowed the British government to obtain an American military commitment to the defence of Hong Kong. The British Chiefs of Staff argued that Britain needed US support to be able to resist a Chinese assault. In June 1950 Franks and Hubert Graves, counsellor at the Washington embassy, immediately raised the issue with the State Department; Franks asked George W. Perkins, Assistant Secretary of State for European Affairs, why there was no reference in Truman's statement on Korea to Hong Kong. In October 1949 the National Security Council had ruled out US support for the defence of Hong Kong. The Department of Defense was initially reluctant to reverse the decision. Louis Johnson and George Marshall were adamant: they would not 'associate the military position of the Western World in Asia with the retention of Hong Kong' because Hong Kong could not be defended against a communist assault. By 1952 and 1953, however, while the Department of Defense reaffirmed that the US would not accept an 'implicit assumption by the US of responsibility for the UK positions in the Far East, such as Hong Kong and Malaya', there had been a shift in policy.[78] The US realised that 'the successful defence of Hong Kong, in addition to having psychological advantages, would have a considerable effect on deterring communist aggression elsewhere in South East Asia'.[79] If sufficient notice of a Chinese attack was available the US would reinforce Hong Kong. In April 1954 Eisenhower informed Congress that an American commitment to the defence of Hong Kong was dependent on a British commitment to collective security.[80]

In the 1950s an American commitment to the defence of Hong Kong was problematic: it might have entangled Britain in a major Sino-American conflict. R. Scott informed the Chiefs of Staff that 'it might be dangerous to obtain an American guarantee for participation in the defence of Hong Kong if such a course was likely to draw us into war with China'.[81] An American commitment to defend Hong Kong might result in the establishment of a beachhead in south China from which anti-communist forces could undermine communist control: it might mean the roll back of Chinese communism. General MacArthur had raised this strategy in 1951, and Radford and Fechteler renewed it in 1952 and 1953. Once China had intervened in Korea, Washington stepped up intelligence gathering in Hong Kong, began to assess the strength of bandit activity in south China and promoted an anti-communist 'Third Force' within Hong Kong. Hong Kong was a clear-cut military commitment, 'whereas putting troops in jungle areas elsewhere in Asia, which could absorb almost unlimited numbers, would be more likely to fall in with Soviet strategy'.[82] The Operations Co-ordinating Board in the White House, recognising the value of Hong Kong as a source for covert activities in China, declared that 'the British would probably be very reluctant to use, or permit [the] use of their proximity to China, but it might be worth exploring with them'.[83]

The Colonial Office and the authorities disliked US overt and covert activities in Hong Kong and China. Grantham informed London that Hong Kong could not be used 'as a front-line base for operations against world communism'.[84] The Foreign Office was sympathetic to such views; Lloyd argued that the US was 'overdoing it to the point of farce', while Robert Scott admitted that 'American irresponsibility in Hong Kong may provoke Chinese retaliation and it is we who will suffer – not the Americans'.[85] But an American role had to be accepted:

> The Americans are apt to be insensitive and rather clumsy in coping with a situation [so] that the patience of the Hong Kong authorities must be sorely tried. Nevertheless, in the interests of Hong Kong itself, as in the general British and American interests, it is essential to make the effort.[86]

ACCEPTING EMPIRE ON THE DOORSTEP

Given the PRC's anti-imperialist ideological bent and the anti-communist policies adopted in Hong Kong, why did China not regain Hong Kong? The British Foreign Office thought they would. Charles Johnson, the head of the China and Korea department, stated:

> They clearly do not want the pot to boil over immediately, but the fact that they are heating it more frequently than before, makes it look as if, while they probably have no hard and fast timetable, their thought is becoming crystallised and that in their mind der Tag, while still in the remote future, is far less remote than it was.[87]

However, as previously noted, communist elements in trade unions and within the education establishment did not attempt to subvert the political process in the colony. There was no evidence that CCP-controlled schools encouraged students to participate in civil disobedience. In 1950 the Special Branch of the Hong Kong police force obtained a secret directive to CCP members in Hong Kong; this instructed the CCP to reduce its public activities, to tighten party cells if relations with the UK deteriorated and to prevent the destruction of their archives in the event of a war.[88] The CCP did not plan a campaign to subvert British rule in Hong Kong.

The Chinese position on Hong Kong hardened from late 1951 onwards. Chinese newspapers adopted a more aggressive line, criticising the policies adopted by the Hong Kong authorities towards schools, trade unions and private residents.[89] The expulsion of seven cinema workers in January 1952 and then the suspension of *Ta Kung Pao* in May 1952 were catalysts for a Chinese propaganda campaign in Hong Kong. Protest meetings were held and there were articles in Chinese newspapers, including the *Peking People's Daily* and *Sin Wen Jih Pao* in Shanghai, strongly criticising British policies. On 10 May the Ministry of Foreign Affairs declared that 'the Chinese people cannot possibly tolerate such seriously hostile acts of the British government'; and on 20 May Huan Hsiang complained about the persecution of Chinese residents in Hong Kong.[90] The PRC declared Hong Kong an American sphere of influence, a base for aggression towards China. In January a protest meeting in Canton declared the expulsion of the cinema workers to be 'part and parcel of British imperialism's subservience to the US government's aggressive plans. They show that the British imperialists are working hand in glove with Chiang Kai-Shek's bandits in Taiwan.'[91] In February 1952 Chou publicly declared that 'at the behest of [the] Americans, the British government in Hong Kong has been allowing remnant KMT gangsters to infiltrate into Kwangtung from Hong Kong.'[92]

Chinese propaganda began to imply retaliation. In January 1952 the *NCNA*, quoting the Shanghai *Sin Wen Jih Pao* on the expulsion of the cinema workers, argued that: 'The British government of Hong Kong must bear full responsibility for the consequences of this vicious outrage.' In February Liu Chiang-yu, the Chairman of the Kwangtung TUC, declared: 'The British imperialists, who seized Hong Kong by armed force over a century ago, have been persecuting the Chinese for a long time, for which a final reckoning has not yet been made.' Peking Radio announced: 'we will never tolerate the unscrupulous and tyrannical opposition of our compatriots by the British imperialists on the Chinese soil they seized by force'. In May the *NCNA* informed Britain: 'If you perversely continue in the wake of American imperialist despotism, the Chinese people will undoubtedly fight you resolutely to the end to safeguard the legitimate right of Chinese residents in Hong Kong.'[93] In subsequent months, there were further incidents: the Chinese authorities banned the use of Hong Kong currency in south China; the number of border incidents between China and Hong Kong increased; and the Chinese declared that they were considering measures to protect Hong Kong citizens from imperial suppression. The propaganda campaign was not a precursor for intervention; it was a warning to Britain not to transgress the mark in Hong Kong. As Tsang notes, it was a reminder to the new Conservative government that a close alignment with the US might jeopardise Britain's hold on Hong Kong.[94]

China's failure to incite political subversion in Hong Kong may have reflected the CCP's lack of an effective party organisation in the territory. There is some evidence to suggest that support for the CCP within Hong Kong was not as strong as expected; the communists had not obtained total control over labour, educational and cultural establishments and the KMT remained, albeit much diminished, a political force in the colony. More importantly, many of the colony's inhabitants did not have close allegiance to either the KMT or the Chinese communists. The CCP had certainly found it more difficult to gain the support in Hong Kong than it might have expected. There was definitely an element of dissatisfaction with communism in Hong Kong. Having migrated from China to escape the economic and political realities of life there, Chinese residents in Hong Kong often established ties with the PRC simply to preclude attacks on relatives in China. But any failure of the CCP organisation in the colony must be attributed to the fact that the CCP did not attempt a concerted campaign to gain the support of the Hong Kong Chinese. If it had wanted to, there is little doubt that the PRC could have used its political might to establish a dominant influence in the economic and cultural life of the colony; by threatening retaliatory action against Chinese relatives on the mainland, or by threatening to overthrow British rule, it could have given Hong Kong residents a vested interest in accepting communist influence.

The PRC neither reaffirmed the legality of the treaties underpinning British control, nor raised Hong Kong's future status with Britain. The consensus amongst historians is that in 1949 the Chinese became reconciled to British possession of Hong Kong. James Tang alludes to a secret directive from the CCP, instructing local communist agents in Hong Kong not to undermine the British colonial government.[95] Steve Tsang notes that top communist officials in Hong Kong returned to the mainland in 1949 and refers to a meeting in September between Lo Lung-chi, the leader of the Chinese Democratic League, and Mao Tse-tung, at which Mao inferred that he had accepted British control of Hong Kong.[96] Sergei Goncharov, John Lewis and Xue Litai note that Mao rejected a suggestion made by Stalin in 1950 that the CCP invade Hong Kong.[97] In 1952 it was more extreme left-wing groups within China who raised the issue of sovereignty, with the PRC leadership, by contrast, merely reminding Britain that Hong Kong 'depended entirely on the materials and manpower of the Chinese people'.[98] The PRC did react when Hong Kong impinged upon its authority. In 1951, when Hong Kong requisitioned the Chinese tanker *Yung Hao* carrying a cargo of oil for China, the PRC sent a protest letter to Lionel Lamb and requisitioned the holdings of the Shell Company of China Ltd. In August 1952, when a Hong Kong court ruled in favour of the US company in the Hong Kong aircraft case, the authorities in Shanghai requisitioned two British-owned dockyards. In November 1952, after an unfavourable judgement on the remaining 31 aircraft, the Shanghai authorities expropriated British-managed water, gas and electricity undertakings and a British shipping company.[99] However, more often than not, Chinese propaganda targeted US imperialism and British rule in Malaya, not Hong Kong.

Unquestionably, the new Chinese regime wanted to extend Chinese sovereignty over Hong Kong but it did not want to do so in the early 1950s. The New Territories were to revert to China in 1997; after the 99-year British lease, signed in 1898, expired, there was no possibility of China renewing the agreement. As Hong Kong was not really viable without the New Territories, a vital source of agricultural produce for the island, it could be argued that China was awaiting a time when Britain would be forced to negotiate with China. Wenguang Shao argues that the CCP Central Committee held a long-term view on the Hong Kong problem.[100] If the Chinese did have such a long-term perspective, it was because China had a vested interest in maintaining British rule. The reluctance of the PRC to tread on British susceptibilities over Hong Kong is clear evidence that it did not want to jeopardise these advantages.

A number of reasons for China's acquiescence can be hypothesised. Firstly, but less plausibly, there were strategic considerations. In early 1950 an invasion of Taiwan was the priority for the PRC and once the Korean War had broken out, and more especially once China had intervened in that conflict, Chinese military resources were too stretched to contemplate an assault on Hong Kong. After November 1950, the PRC may have feared that an attempt to seize Hong Kong might precipitate American intervention in south China, resulting in a general war between China and the US in the Far East. Strategic apprehension may explain why China was reluctant to launch a military campaign but it does not fully explain why China did not raise the question of Hong Kong's sovereignty, either directly with Britain or through an international body such as the UN. The Chinese may have feared a forthright policy on Hong Kong would align Britain closer to the US, a development which could remove Britain's moderating influence on American policy in the Far East. Asian nations would have disapproved of a military assault on Hong Kong, but would obviously have accepted a political end to British imperial rule. Hong Kong may also have proved difficult to administer. Tang notes that in 1951 Peng Chen, a member of the Politburo, declared that 'to take Hong Kong now would not only bring unnecessary technical difficulties in the enforcement of our international policy, but [would] also increase our burden'.[101] Harold Hinton argues that the PRC did not want the 'onerous and chaotic responsibility of administering Hong Kong', while C.P. Fitzgerald believed that because Hong Kong would be less prosperous under Chinese rule, a take-over would have reflected badly on the PRC.[102] Firmly in control in China, the CCP may have been less inclined to try and win popular support by raising the question of sovereignty and, moreover, did not want to be pushed into military action. Hong Kong was a valuable means of contact with the West; the colony provided the PRC with a communications' network for contacting agents and overseas Chinese residents in South East Asia and was an important source of intelligence on western and Chinese Nationalist activity in the Far East.[103]

Above all else, the economic benefit China derived from Hong Kong is the key to understanding the Chinese position.[104] As the next two chapters will show, the PRC wanted to end the presence of western economic interests on the mainland but still wanted to trade with Britain. As a result Hong Kong was an important source of imports for China and was a route for Chinese exports. In 1950 the PRC took over the existing official Chinese government trading, banking and insurance corporations within the colony and signalled China's acceptance of Hong Kong's vital position by establishing a number of new organisations to deal with trade. The Korean War and the resultant stringent economic embargo placed on China undoubtedly undermined the worth of Hong Kong to the Chinese communists. Hong Kong trade with China fell significantly from its peak in June 1950; and while a great amount of smuggling undoubtedly occurred, the colony was not as significant a source for strategic goods thereafter. At the same time, it is important not to exaggerate the impact of the embargo. In some respects, the war enhanced the economic importance of Hong Kong. It was difficult for Britain and the US to introduce an economic embargo on the mainland unless they accepted the loss of Hong Kong and, with the Nationalists firmly entrenched on Taiwan and continuing their block-

ade of China's east coast, Hong Kong was a key coastal entry point
for China. Crucially, Hong Kong was throughout this period a vital
source of foreign exchange for China.[105] The Chinese communists,
embarking on a strategy of industrialisation, required foreign exchange
to import the capital goods necessary to overcome the structural problems of the Chinese economy. The Chinese received export credits
and a loan from the Soviet Union but these were insufficient to meet
all China's import requirements, and from 1954 onwards Soviet loans
had to be paid back, resulting in a drain on China's foreign exchange.[106]
Trade with Hong Kong allowed China to gain foreign exchange without entering into binding long-term trade deals that would have reduced the PRC's room for manoeuvre and which would have increased
China's reliance on trade with the West. The PRC was using Hong
Kong to maintain trading contacts with the global economy without
suffering the socially divisive and politically weakening consequences
that it associated with a fully open door policy. China was reverting to
the early nineteenth-century Canton system of trading with the West:
the barbarians would remain in Hong Kong.

The PRC acceptance of Hong Kong partly explains the dynamics of
its relationship with Britain in the period. Firstly, because the Chinese
communists maintained economic and diplomatic contact with Britain
through Hong Kong, there may have been less pressure on the Chinese to establish formal diplomatic relations with a British government. Secondly, with the PRC not taking the initiative over the imperialist
enclave, an over-sympathetic Chinese communist response to British
recognition may have been misconstrued within China. It could have
caused tensions between radicals and moderates within the CCP hierarchy and may have encouraged liberal pro-western elements within
the Chinese population. At the same time, China's recognition of Hong
Kong's importance meant that it could not adopt an overly hostile policy
towards Britain; both powers had vested interests and influence to
protect.[107]

CONCLUSIONS

Hong Kong remained British because the colony provided the PRC
with valuable foreign exchange earnings and contact with western
merchants. Consequently, during the early 1950s, the Chinese acquiesced in tighter British control over life in the colony and also accepted growing American involvement in Hong Kong. The British

government wanted to retain Hong Kong for economic, political and geo-strategic reasons. British businessmen wanted Hong Kong because, as the next two chapters will indicate, British investment in China had collapsed and the structure of Sino-British trade had undergone profound changes. Consequently, Hong Kong had become the most important base for trading with China, an important centre for funding and shipping far eastern trade, and an industrialising economy which needed British capital and mercantile expertise.

6 Ending Informal Empire: British Business in China, 1950–54

As long as capitalism remains what it is, surplus capital will be utilized not for the purpose of raising the standard of living of the masses in a given country, for this would mean a decline in profits for the capitalists, but for the purpose of increasing profits by exporting capital abroad to the backward countries.

> V.I. Lenin, *Imperialism, the Highest Stage of Capitalism*

In October 1949 China entered a new epoch; it had been united under an anti-imperialist Marxist-Leninist regime which wanted to reorder Chinese economic and social life and redefine its external economic relations. The People's Republic of China posed a threat to Sino-British trade and to British foreign direct investments in China and Hong Kong. The plight of British far eastern economic interests in this period has been examined by a number of historians.[1] This chapter will address a number of issues: how did British business respond to the emergence of a Communist China? How did the Chinese authorities expropriate foreign economic interests? What factors determined the Chinese attitude? How did the British government respond and what does this indicate about the relationship between British business and the British government?

By 1950, the character and composition of British investments in China itself were complex and diverse, with a number of different components, including commercial and industrial enterprises operating in China and British firms selling to the Chinese market from the UK. Agency houses, including Jardine, Matheson and Co. and Butterfield and Swire, specialised in buying, insuring, shipping and selling Chinese raw materials such as tung-oil, eggs and raw cotton, and were the most important aspect of British business in China; others included banks, notably the Hong Kong and Shanghai Banking Corporation, insurance companies, public utilities, department stores, hotels and coastal and ocean-going shipping firms. As British multinationals had been slow to invest in China during the inter-war years, manufacturing concerns in China were of less importance than commercial ones;

Table 6.1 British Investments in China, 1930 and 1936
(US $ million and % of total in brackets)

Type of Investment	1930	1936
Banking and Finance	115.6	302.0
	(12.0)	(28.5)
Import–Export	240.8	243.9
	(25.1)	(23.0)
Real Estate	203.3	202.3
	(21.0)	(19.1)
Manufacturing	173.4	179.8
	(18.0)	(17.0)
Transportation	134.9	61.4
	(13.9)	(5.8)
Communication and Public Utilities	48.2	48.6
	(5.0)	(4.6)
Mining	19.3	15.8
	(2.0)	(1.5)
Miscellaneous	28.9	5.1
	(3.0)	(0.5)
Total	964.4	1058.9

Source: Hou Chi-ming, *Foreign Investment and Economic Development in China, 1840–1937*, Cambridge, Mass. 1965, p. 226.

nevertheless, Lever Brothers, Shell and British American Tobacco had all established large units in China, employing Chinese workers, using Chinese raw materials and supplying markets in the Far East.[2] Britain's commercial and industrial position in China centred around Hong Kong and Shanghai. China was a market for a large number of British manufacturers who had sent commercial agents to exploit market opportunities in China. Although the size of Britain's economic stake has been estimated at between £110 and £300 million at 1941 prices, the actual extent of Britain's economic contact with China is very difficult to estimate.[3] Indeed, the subsequent problems suffered by British firms between 1950 and 1954 must be placed firmly within the context of a longer-term restructuring and relative decline of Britain's stake in China. Britain's share of the Chinese market – which had always been more significant for the British empire (India) than Britain proper – had been squeezed by foreign competition and indigenous Chinese production from the end of the nineteenth century onwards. But Britain did dominate throughout the period in 'service industries': notably shipping, banking and insurance. British companies funded, transported and guaranteed China's trade. Whereas ICI estimated their assets to be worth

£296 000 at 1941 prices in 1947, the corresponding figure for the Hong Kong and Shanghai Bank was £3 272 000.[4] Even so, after 1914, Britain's economic position in China experienced a decline relative to other countries, and any growth resulted from firms in China reinvesting their profits and not from inward investment.[5] In addition British companies were beginning to collaborate more closely with local Chinese business and political elites as a means of maintaining their position in the face of growing Chinese nationalism and the British government retreat from a confrontational imperialistic policy towards China. Osterhammel argues this manifested itself in a number of Anglo-Chinese joint-stock companies, market sharing between Chinese and British firms and an increasing reliance by British concerns on the Chinese Nationalist regime to suppress popular labourism and control anti-imperialist sentiment.[6] By 1937 British businesses in China were closely intertwined into China's economy and society, increasingly independent of the British government and, having stopped remitting sums to home, had fewer ties to the British economy.

The British government did not believe the PRC could reconcile communism and Chinese nationalism with the presence of foreign business interests in China. Bevin argued diplomatic recognition of the PRC would not provide 'any immediate panacea' for Britain's trading interests in China.[7] Experts on Chinese communism in the Foreign Office viewed Chinese attitudes towards foreign business interests as consistent with their ideological and political leanings. Nevertheless, fortified by moderate statements made by Chinese communists in 1949 and by optimistic reports from British businessmen on the ground in China, the British government argued that, while the position of commercial and industrial enterprises in China was very doubtful in the long term, in the short term the PRC would not destabilise the Chinese economy by expropriating foreign investments. Moreover China, united under a regime committed to national economic development, needed to replenish a capital stock destroyed or depreciated during 13 years of warfare. As a fair proportion of China's industrial and infrastructural capital stock originated from Britain, the Chinese might favour Britain as a source for imports over Japan, Germany, France and the US. The British government believed the Chinese would have to rely on British mercantile interests located in China and Hong Kong to fund, insure and ship this trade. The position of British (and multinational) industrial enterprises may have been untenable; they would be nationalised. But British mercantile concerns in the Far East located in China and Hong Kong could be viable in the longer term. The moderate political

line on the PRC was designed to aid the activities of British mercantile companies, enterprises that could act as a conduit for British exports to China and underpin the British presence in Hong Kong.

China adhered to a 'United Front' policy during its initial stages of
economic reconstruction. The Chinese bourgeoisie, driven by intense
anti-imperialism, were allied with the working class and the peasantry
to overthrow the forces of feudalism and imperialism in China.[8] As
Mao Tse-tung declared in *The Chinese Revolution and the Chinese
Communist Party*, 'the spearhead of the revolution will be directed at
imperialism and feudalism rather than at capitalism and capital private
property in general'.[9] The state nationalised basic industries such as
coal, steel and power generation, took control of the railway network,
and expropriated the assets of certain businessmen tied to the previous
Chinese Nationalist regime.[10] The Chinese bourgeoisie were allowed
to continue but a number of restrictions were placed on their activities. Chou En-lai, the Chinese Prime and Foreign Minister, argued that:

> We endorse the existence of private capitalist enterprises. However,
> our aim is to guide them away from the old capitalist road and onto
> the road of New Democracy. We intend to move towards socialism
> gradually, carefully and methodically over a long period of time.[11]

China's communist leadership did not want an extremist left-wing assault on capitalism in urban areas; initially economic considerations
had to take precedence over political and ideological requirements. The
PRC's moderate policy towards the Chinese bourgeoisie contrasted with
its more hostile position towards foreign capitalists operating in mainland China.

For economic, political and ideological reasons, the PRC wanted to
throw out the resident foreign communities in China. Economically,
the new Chinese state did not want to rely on private foreign investment and would not, for financial as well as for ideological reasons,
allow foreign economic interests to remit profits from China. Politically, the Chinese leadership believed that the foreign community represented a threat to Chinese communist control; it was an alternative
source of loyalty for the Chinese middle classes. The attitude of the
CCP was justified by an ideological stance which blended Marxist-
Leninist thought with economic nationalism and responded to a historically derived perception of the impact of western imperialism on
China.[12] Basically, imperialism had made China dependent on the West
(and Japan) and divided the loyalties of the Chinese people; as a result, it had under-developed the Chinese economy and weakened the

Chinese state. The aim of CCP economic policy was to make China strong and independent; and the means was greater control over economic forces. Mao believed that western capitalism, allied with the old feudal landlord class, had turned China into an economically dependent, semi-feudal colonial society. He believed that the Chinese hinterland embodied the real soul of China because it had been untainted by western cosmopolitanism and individualism; if China could rid itself of western influence then the Chinese people could unite and rebuild the nation. Even Chou En-lai, one of the most moderate and pro-western thinkers in the CCP hierarchy, who, unlike Mao, had spent time abroad and in the Treaty Ports, wanted to redefine China's relationship with the West. In a speech delivered in December 1949 he declared:

> Old China was dependent on imperialism not only in the economic sphere but also in the spheres of culture and education; it was exploited economically and polluted ideologically. That was very dangerous. It is now time to expose and eradicate the evil influence of imperialism.[13]

Despite these overriding factors, there was initially some flexibility in the Chinese attitude towards western economic interests. Western firms did not suffer direct expropriation but were allowed to operate in the short term. Beverly Hooper alludes to a speech by Mao in which he stated that while the imperialist era was over, a more flexible attitude would be adopted towards foreign economic and cultural interests.[14] Wenguang Shao points to evidence, leaked during the Korean War by the Chinese communists, that the PRC had established a Foreign Enterprises Administration Bureau to ascertain the precise position of foreign-owned firms in the Chinese economy; its work included drafting a set of procedures and rules governing the proportion of foreign capital allowed in joint foreign-Chinese industrial concerns.[15] This evidence does not conclusively prove that the PRC was prepared to acquiesce in western capital investment in China; the Foreign Enterprises Administration Bureau would probably have codified, rather than prevented, discrimination against foreign firms. Even if the Korean War had not broken out, western enterprises in China would eventually have been forced to withdraw.

The PRC did not immediately want to expropriate western economic contact within China for a number of reasons. Firstly, by not immediately nationalising these concerns, the Chinese kept diplomatic and economic options open. The Chinese communists reasoned that the existence of a British economic community moderated Britain's diplomatic stand on China; the PRC might have hoped that the British government would be more willing to resist American demands for a harder line because businessmen remained in China. Although diplomatic nuances may have influenced the way in which policy towards foreign capital enterprises evolved, the prime considerations were financial and economic. By allowing foreign interests to operate, the PRC managed to expropriate funds from the remaining firms without damaging the Chinese economy or making a large number of Chinese workers redundant. The CCP, lacking experience in urban industrialised areas, did not have the technical and administrative knowledge to manage large industrial and commercial units.[16] Indeed, early attempts to harness revolutionary forces within Chinese cities had proved to be less than successful. (Suzanne Pepper argues that the CCP had difficulty adapting its revolutionary and essentially rural-based ideology to the urban environment during the civil war. From 1947, the CCP hierarchy had introduced an 'anti-leftist' campaign; in urban areas, this manifested itself as a campaign to protect the national bourgeoisie.[17]) The Chinese economy was in such a precarious state in the aftermath of the civil war that ownership was less important than broader macroeconomic considerations: the control of inflation, stimulating investment and maintaining employment. The Chinese required economic contact with western merchants and hence did not want to prejudice the attitude of foreign firms by expropriating their China-based investments. Finally, the continued existence of foreign businesses did not weaken the CCP's political position: by humiliating the last vestiges of the western informal empire in China, the PRC still harnessed Chinese nationalist and anti-imperialist sentiment to coalesce a wide base of support for its regime.

Chinese policy presented foreign firms operating in China with a peculiar set of constraints that made their position increasingly untenable.[18] On the supply side, the Chinese authorities, operating through centralised buying agencies, made it difficult for foreign companies to obtain raw materials. Foreign firms were also prevented from dismissing workers and setting their own wage rates. Local trade unions determined wage rates; and while foreign firms could lobby the CPG's Labour Bureau, it tended to reinforce the position of the local trade unions.[19] On the demand side, western firms found it increasingly difficult to sell to a depressed and discriminatory Chinese market. Moreover, in sectors of the Chinese economy in which foreign firms had previously dominated, such as insurance, banking and the wholesale trade,

of the deflationary strategy, were reduced, taxation levels fell and re-strictions on access to foreign exchange were partly lifted. The CCP publicly admitted that the balance between private and public sectors of the economy needed to be readjusted. Mao declared that the CCP 'should introduce suitable readjustments in industry and commerce and in taxation to improve our relations with the national bourgeoisie rather than aggravate these relations'.[29] In the summer of 1950 the Korean War stimulated demand within China and, coupled with a slight eas-ing of the Chinese Nationalist blockade, the position of Chinese and, to a lesser extent, foreign business interests stabilised. Encouraged by developments, the China Association argued that the PRC now genu-inely wanted to revive trade and industry. Firms within China did not believe profits would flow, but thought that their financial position would stabilise, allowing them to remain in China in the short term.[30]

China's intervention in the Korean War in November 1950, by height-ening international tensions between the communist bloc and the West and by radicalising Chinese domestic policies, ended misplaced busi-ness optimism. When the Korean War broke out in June 1950, British businessmen in the Far East and the China Association in London had accepted, albeit reluctantly, the extension and tightening of an em-bargo on strategic goods for China, but at the same time had pressu-rised the British government to resist American demands for more comprehensive controls on semi-strategic goods, on the entrepôt trade through Hong Kong and on shipping and financial services in the Far East. The British government, wanting and needing far eastern trade, vehemently opposed economic warfare against the Chinese mainland. With China's intervention in the war in Korea, however, it could no longer resist pressure from the US administration for measures to un-dermine the Chinese economy. The US believed an embargo on trade with China would hinder the Chinese advance in Korea, curtail Chi-nese industrialisation and increase China's reliance on the Soviet Union, thus engendering tensions in the Sino-Soviet relationship. (The Demo-cratic administration had been sympathetic to measures of economic warfare since 1949, but it was the Korean War and vocal pressure from right-wing Republicans in Congress which coalesced this as policy.) The subsequent tightening of existing measures and the introduction, in May 1951, of a UN embargo on trade in strategic goods with the PRC severely curtailed Sino-British trade and further undermined the position of British business in China and Hong Kong. The business community in Shanghai believed the economic embargo was doing 'im-measurable harm' to British interests within China.[31] But the increasingly critical line of the British community in Shanghai and the China Association had a limited influence on the British position on the economic embargo. By contrast, the government pressurised the US to ease the severity of the embargo against Hong Kong.

During 1951 and 1952, the PRC was starkly exposed as a regime which wanted to eradicate the economic as well as the political influence of the bourgeoisie in Chinese society. The *san fan* and *wu fan* (three and five anti) campaigns, launched in 1952, symbolised for foreign firms the irreconcilability of Chinese communism and capitalism. The *san fan* campaign aimed to eradicate corruption, waste and bureaucracy; the *wu fan* campaign waged a struggle against capitalists 'violating the law by bribery, tax evasion, theft of state property, cheating and stealing economic information'.[32] F.C. Teiwes views the *san fan* campaign as a general attack on urban non-communist economic and political values, replacing the traditional arbiters of social relations, the family, the school and the workplace, with the authority of the state and the party.[33] The campaigns undermined bourgeois influence in the party and in society by using the *chengfeng* (self-rectification) methods developed during the Yennan period. (Whether these revolutionary methods of political control were suitable once the CCP was in power is questionable.[34]) By unleashing and further institutionalising the revolutionary consciousness of Chinese workers and by significantly increasing state control over the private sector of the economy, the campaigns exacerbated the difficulties faced by foreign businesses and brought many to the conclusion that private business had no future in China. This trend was reinforced by a long delayed acceptance that while the Chinese wanted trade with the West, they did not necessarily want resident foreign merchants acting as middle men. The British business community came to believe that rather than improving their prospect of trade, the maintenance of extensive commercial and industrial interests in China may have been hampering the development of future trading contacts. The withholding of exit permits for foreign businessmen was also proving a severe strain on individuals. In February 1952 the British consul-general in Shanghai reported that 'British merchants and the residents in general have now just about abandoned all hope for the future and are thinking hard about how they can get out'.[35] In Peking, Lionel Lamb, the British chargé d'affaires, acknowledged that: 'There can now be little doubt from recent events that the avowed policy of the CPG is to eliminate private interests from trade and industry.'[36]

By the end of 1951 and certainly by early 1952, the majority of British concerns had made the decision to withdraw. The continued heavy remittances to China from headquarters in Hong Kong and the UK, the increasingly harsh treatment of businessmen and the decline in trading opportunities resulting from the tightening economic embargo on the Chinese mainland finalised attitudes. In January 1952 Sir Arthur Morse, the Hong Kong Bank's Chairman, acknowledged to W.R.M Cockburn, Chief General Manager of the Chartered Bank, that 'the general policy was to get out of China as quickly as possible'.[37] What is surprising is not this decision but its timing. The majority of firms did not take the final decision to leave China until the end of 1951 and the beginning of 1952; before then, a number of firms, including British American Tobacco, had entered into negotiations with the Chinese authorities but most had not made a definite decision to leave. Reluctance to confront the issue of withdrawal resulted from a number of factors. Firstly, British business interests thought a forthright approach might jeopardise future trading contacts with China and, possibly, the prosperity and security of Hong Kong. Secondly, the British government failed to take the lead; it was initially reluctant for firms to leave China, and then, once reconciled to their departure, did not make the necessary diplomatic or financial resources available. Thirdly, divisions within the British far eastern business community, between those who concentrated on trade and those who owned industrial units, made the formation of a common front *vis-à-vis* the Chinese authorities problematic: manufacturing concerns were willing to relinquish all their assets to secure an exit from China, whereas trading concerns with fewer liabilities wanted to maintain a trading link with the PRC. As 'service' concerns dominated the Chambers of Commerce in China and the China Association in London, the impetus for withdrawal only came when they accepted that trade could be continued through Hong Kong: a gradual realisation. Fourthly and most significantly, the Chinese authorities made it extremely difficult for British firms to leave.

The decision to leave China brought to a head a problem that had troubled businesses since 1950: how would firms secure their exit from China? The official Chinese government position was that if foreign firms were not breaking the law they were free to close down. In practice it was extremely difficult and potentially very costly for firms to do so. If a firm wanted to close, it had to negotiate redundancy payments with its Chinese employees and meet all outstanding orders and financial commitments such as taxation and fines. As employees' trade unions, often by using the Chinese courts, negotiated with foreign firms at a local level, the Chinese dictated the terms of closure. British firms faced an impossible situation. Imperial Chemical Industries (ICI) estimated that while it were losing £225 000 a year, if it chose to liquidate it would face 160 000 redundancies and a possible minimum expenditure of £400 000.[38] Although the cost of withdrawal was high, it was not prohibitive; with no future in China and their employees unable to secure exit permits, most firms began to negotiate a way out of China. The majority accepted that they would need to sacrifice their fixed and working capital assets against liabilities such as redundancy payments, taxation claims and fines. The essential problem was that closure was not in the interests of the Chinese authorities or the employees of foreign firms; the firms were remitting large sums to China and, even when factories were not producing, workers' wages were guaranteed. Moreover, foreign-owned property would, in time, be handed over anyway. Lamb acknowledged that 'the Chinese, being also communists, are all the more determined to squeeze the maximum out of capitalists and in particular out of foreign capitalists from whom they can, in addition, secure badly needed foreign exchange. Being bullies as well, they will press harder at any sign of weakness.'[39] It was only after the Geneva Conference in 1954, at which China, the Soviet Union, Britain, France and the US negotiated a temporary settlement to the Indochina crisis, that a mass exit of British firms was possible. By 1955 the majority of firms had left. The decision to wait until after the Geneva Conference to settle the question of British business in China suggests the PRC deliberately used foreign economic interests to prevent diplomatic and economic isolation by the West during the Korean War, when American pressure for a total economic embargo on China was at its most intense. Equally by 1954 the new regime was confident that it could dictate the subsequent nature of economic relations between itself and Britain. China had emerged as a world power: it had fought the forces of the UN to a stalemate in Korea and had achieved a diplomatic coup by forging a settlement in Indochina, and no longer needed to humiliate western businessmen.

British businesses and the China Association requested government intervention to aid their position. In 1950 the China Association, British insurance companies such as Lambert Bros. and Lloyds, and British shipping companies such as Williamson and George Grimble and Sons, requested government action to break the Chinese Nationalist blockade and to stop air raids against British property on the mainland.[40] (The blockade was not the root cause of business difficulties in China; the British commercial community exaggerated its importance.) Government intervention to break the blockade was unrealistic and implausible: it would have infringed upon Chinese sovereignty, have damaged Sino-British relations and have been rejected by the US, which was tacitly supporting the blockade.[41] In March, Bevin informed a delegation from the China Association that 'the day had gone when you could give the Admiral the tip and turn a blind eye'.[42] There were, however, other measures that could have been introduced. The China Association requested financial support to guarantee the losses of British firms and to support vital services within China, such as social clubs and public utilities, which firms could no longer afford to subsidise. It also demanded the dispatch of a high-standing British diplomat to co-ordinate a strategy for closing British enterprises.[43]

Between 1951 and the end of 1952, the British business community discussed two possible approaches to facilitate withdrawal from China: a collective approach by all British businesses and government-sponsored negotiations with the PRC. John Keswick, Chairman of the Chamber of Commerce in Shanghai, suggested co-ordinated action between firms, supported by the British government.[44] He argued that such an approach would provide a stronger bargaining position and would prevent individual firms from prejudicing the position of others during negotiations. At the time, British American Tobacco (BAT) was negotiating a deal which relinquished its assets in return for exit permits for its staff. The consul-general in Shanghai reported 'widespread regret that they should have pursued a solitary and secret agreement to its logical conclusion without endeavouring to save more firms from the wreck'.[45] In addition, business interests wanted to use the inducement of a trade mission and future trading contracts to secure the release of firms. Meanwhile, the China Association wanted a multilateral approach, informing the PRC that remittances were being stopped because Britain faced balance of payments difficulties.[46]

In 1950 and indeed throughout the period under consideration, the British government was reluctant to intervene on behalf of British commercial interests in China. The government rejected all suggestions forwarded by business interests and instead issued a number of mild notes protesting about the treatment of British businesses: in May 1950 it suggested a meeting between John Hutchison, the British chargé d'affaires, and the Chinese government; in September 1951 Lamb discussed the issue with foreign diplomats in China; and in July 1952 a note was sent to the CPG informing it that British firms wished to close down.[47] The British government neither developed a strong policy advocating exit nor a concerted strategy to alleviate the position of businesses. Its attitude was hypocritical; by informing British businesses that economic links with China were central to government strategy, the government had implied a moral backing for British business activities in China. British businessmen, and even Hutchison in Peking, felt Britain's 'moral obligation' to its citizens in China had been relinquished. Some within the British merchant community in China, such as C.C. Roberts of Butterfield and Swire, blamed the government for persuading them to remain in China. Others, such as Sir A. Morse of the Hong Kong and Shanghai Banking Corporation, accepted that commercial reasoning had dictated the decision to remain in China.[48]

The official policy of the British government was to maintain 'a foot in the door' and initially, despite the grave difficulties faced by businesses in China, the government encouraged them to try and ride the storm. At a meeting in March 1950 with Tony Keswick of the Jardine Matheson company, Esler Dening, Assistant Under-Secretary of State at the Foreign Office, rejected demands for a government-sponsored approach to ascertain China's price for the closure of British firms: 'If even one firm did this, the Communists would come to the conclusion that they need only continue their present tactics for the whole of our investment in Shanghai to fall into their lap.' Dening did not believe the Chinese would adopt a policy of hostage capitalism. He argued that 'it had not been part of communist tactics to inflict bodily harm on western nationals, and I doubt whether they would adopt these tactics in China'.[49] And yet Bevin, who had always been sceptical about the opportunity for business in China, had, as early as April 1950, taken up a more pragmatic position: he now accepted that the position of British businesses in China was untenable. He did not believe the Chinese government was deliberately discriminating against these business concerns, but argued that 'the communists are indifferent to the fate of British interests and it may even be that by a simple policy of inaction they are conniving at their liquidation'. He admitted to the cabinet that: 'The total loss of a great proportion of British investment at Shanghai must therefore be faced in the very near future.'[50]

While increasingly resigned to an imperial retreat from the Chinese mainland, neither Labour nor Conservative governments believed they could alleviate the position of businesses in China. When Bevin met Tony Keswick in March 1950, he admitted that he did not think the British government could do much to aid businesses.[51] In Peking, John Hutchison argued that any attempt to raise the plight of British businesses with the Chinese would produce a rebuff and could make the negotiations over diplomatic relations more problematic.[52] The Foreign Office and the Board of Trade argued that a government-to-government approach would be counterproductive: it would formalise the whole issue and encourage the Chinese to take a more intransigent line. A draft cabinet paper declared that 'any increased pressure against the Chinese would, as a result of a general deterioration in the political situation, probably make the release of the firm's staff more difficult'.[53] (The Foreign Office may have suspected the China Association was pressing the British government into a corner on this issue: if British actions did not ease the position of foreign firms, then the government would be in a potentially embarrassing position.) The cabinet ruled out extensive financial and diplomatic support to the 'Old China Hands'.[54] There was cross-party support for the government's non-interventionist policy towards Britain's economic stake in China. In 1950 Eden argued that the government should assist British business but should not 'embark on a policy of appeasement over the matter of economic interests in China'.[55] By 1952, Eden, now Foreign Secretary in Winston Churchill's Conservative government, whilst promising to give all the help he could to British firms in China, had, in reality, washed his hands of this 'terrible chapter in our history'.[56]

Most significantly, there was a financial rationale underpinning nonintervention. The Treasury, the Board of Trade and the Foreign Office acknowledged that assistance was neither feasible nor astute given the long-term prospects of firms operating in China: it would be money thrown away. In 1950 the Board of Trade and the Treasury rejected a deal that relinquished assets in return for enabling closure, which would reduce British invisible earnings, 'would be a sign of weakness' and 'would prejudice the position of British concerns all over the world'.[57] And then subsequently the Treasury rejected controls on remittances which it argued could not be watertight and might not be effective. The Treasury position was ambiguous: 'we should do our best to help the firms, the individual and our own balance of payments'.[58] Significantly, financial intervention might have jeopardised the position of Hong Kong. If the government introduced remittance controls these would have to be applied to Hong Kong as well as to China in order to be effective. The Hong Kong authorities strongly opposed measures that 'could not fail to intensify the increasingly hostile attitude of the CPG towards Hong Kong and would probably be regarded as the forerunner of other and more extensive measures likely to remove the remaining economic usefulness of the colony'.[59] J.B. Sidebotham, at the

Colonial Office, agreed that 'unless stringent controls over all remittances to China are introduced, which is not practical politically, we do not think the attempt to introduce partial controls, merely to cover remittances from these particular firms, will serve any useful purpose'.[60] And moreover it might provoke Chinese retaliation against Hong Kong.

CONCLUSIONS

In returning to the questions originally posed, a number of conclusions are clear. Firstly, the British government responded to the emergence of a Communist China by adopting a liberal international policy which attempted to facilitate economic and political links with the new regime, a policy dictated by economic and geo-strategic considerations. Britain sought to defuse cold war tensions in the area, reduce China's reliance on the Soviet Union, and, crucially, maintain a formal and informal empire in China. Secondly, this policy was, for the most part, a failure. British firms were not nationalised but faced discriminatory supply and demand side problems which made their position untenable and induced them to remit sums to China. British governments refused to intervene to aid the withdrawal of these firms. By comparison, the Chinese allowed the continuation of a formal empire in Hong Kong.

The attitude of the British government towards British far eastern businesses allows some tentative conclusions about the nature of the British state and its relationship with overseas financial concerns. Firstly, it is clear that British far eastern businesses did not dictate to and control state external policy: there were conflicts of interest and disagreements. British Labour and Conservative governments placed wider macro-economic and geo-strategic considerations before the interests of far eastern business: they accepted an economic embargo on the Chinese mainland despite intensive business pressure and they did not give their full support to businesses trying to negotiate an exit from China. But there was a wider symbiosis of interest: both wanted to maintain an imperial presence in the Far East. It was these companies who benefited from the retention of Hong Kong, a base which allowed them to continue to trade with China. There was no wider macro-economic questioning of the consequences of this on the British economy by the British state: it was assumed to be in the nation's interest.

7 A Most Unfavoured Trading Nation: China, 1950–54

> A trade not so much subject to the commercial principles of supply and demand but subordinate to political considerations and restrictions necessitated by national economic causes.
>
> Mr E.H. Stewart, *Manchester Chamber of Commerce*[1]

This chapter will examine a range of factors explaining changes in Sino-British trade in 1950–54. The first section will assess and explain the PRC's attitude towards trade with Britain. It will examine CCP thinking on economic development and explore the dynamics of Sino-Soviet bloc economic relations. The second section will assess how British businessmen and the state organised trade with China. As previous chapters have dealt with the imposition of the economic embargo on China, this one will concentrate on the responses of businessmen and the state to Chinese attempts to break the embargo in 1952 and 1953, an interesting development because new merchants and industrialists emerged who were willing to challenge the dominance of the 'China Association' group of traders. The chapter will begin with a look at statistical trends in Sino-British trade.

SINO-BRITISH TRADE

On examining China's trade with the outside world it is clear that the period 1950–54 was one of profound change. The majority of China's trade was with the Soviet bloc and in particular with the Soviet Union, which provided 62 per cent of China's imports and bought 48.7 per cent of China's exports in the period. By comparison, China's trade with the non-communist world (the US, Britain, France, Japan, Germany and Hong Kong) declined; imports from these countries fell from 39.8 per cent of total Chinese imports in 1950 to 12 per cent in 1954, while China's exports to these countries fell from 56.8 per cent of total exports to 15.5 per cent in 1954 (see Tables 7.1 and 7.2).[2] Equally, the commodity composition of China's trade shifted. China stopped importing

Table 7.1   China's Imports from Selected Countries, 1950–54 (US $ 10 000)
(with % of total trade in brackets)

	1950	1951	1952	1953	1954
Britain	4 091	1 955	1 366	6 719	4 609
	(7)	(1.6)	(1.2)	(4.9)	(3.5)
Hong Kong	852	19 979	13 510	12 161	8 848
and Macao	(1.4)	(16.6)	(12)	(9)	(6.8)
US	14 263	791	5	nil	nil
	(24.5)	(6.6)			
Japan	2 614	1 195	108	312	1 460
	(4.5)	(0.9)	(0.09)	(0.2)	(1)
West	1 067	1 552	476	2 885	1 322
Germany	(1.8)	(1.2)	(0.4)	(2.1)	(1)
France	383	436	77	1 774	956
	(0.6)	(0.03)	(0.06)	(1.3)	(0.7)
USSR	18 519	49 731	65 217	77 762	70 461
	(31.9)	(41.4)	(58)	(57.6)	(54.6)
Eastern	403	5 267	16 182	16 011	25 117
Europe*	(0.6)	(4.3)	(14.4)	(11.8)	(19.4)
TOTAL	58 000	120 000	112 000	135 000	129 000
IMPORTS					

* Eastern Europe comprises Romania, Hungary, Czechoslovakia, Poland and the German Democratic Republic.

Source: *Statistical Yearbook of China 1981*, compiled by State Statistical Bureau, PRC (English Edition), Hong Kong 1981.

consumer durables and concentrated on importing producer goods.

There are a few points to note about the level and pattern of Sino-British trade in the period 1950–54. Firstly, the level of Sino-British trade vacillated greatly: rising, falling and then rising again. Secondly, while the commodity composition of British imports from China remained unchanged – the majority of imports comprising foodstuffs and raw materials – the commodity composition of British exports to China did change; the level of manufactured goods fell, while the level of raw materials and basic materials rose (see Tables A2–4 in the appendix). Thirdly, Britain's share of China's total trade fell in the period from 7 per cent in 1950 to 3.5 per cent in 1954, but it should be noted that relative to other non-communist countries Britain's performance compares favourably (see Tables 7.1 and 7.2). Fourthly, Britain was

Table 7.2   China's Exports to Selected Countries, 1950–54 (US $ 10 000) (with % of total trade in brackets)

	1950	*1951*	*1952*	*1953*	*1954*
Britain	3 260 (5.9)	1 552 (2)	1 215 (1.4)	2 985 (2.9)	2 459 (2.1)
Hong Kong and Macao	15 514 (28)	19 445 (25)	16 874 (20.5)	16 808 (16.4)	12 960 (11.2)
US	9 549 (17.3)	8 (0.001)	0.3	0.2	nil
Japan	2 105 (3.8)	1 195 (1.5)	108 (0.1)	312 (0.3)	1 460 (1.2)
West Germany	875 (1.5)	200 (0.2)	231 (0.2)	322 (0.3)	751 (0.6)
France	208 (0.3)	36 (0.04)	165 (0.2)	618 (0.6)	561 (0.4)
USSR	15 325 (27.8)	49 731 (65.4)	65 217 (79.5)	77 762 (76.2)	70 461 (61.2)
Europe Europe*	1 925 (3.5)	13 493 (17.7)	14 479 (17.6)	18 467 (18.1)	19 300 (16.7)
TOTAL EXPORTS	55 000	76 000	82 000	102 000	115 000

* Eastern Europe comprises Romania, Hungary, Czechoslovakia, Poland and the German Democratic Republic.

Source: *Statistical Yearbook of China 1981*, compiled by State Statistical Bureau, PRC (English Edition), Hong Kong 1981.

running a trading deficit with China. Finally, Britain's trade with China (and Hong Kong) was at a historically low level and fell as a proportion of Britain's total trade. Between 1950 and 1954, British exports to China averaged only 0.17 per cent of total British exports. It is worth emphasising that the corresponding figures for 1913, 1922, 1936 and 1947 were 2.36 per cent, 2.8 per cent, 1.27 per cent and 1.07 per cent. British trade with Hong Kong has to be taken into consideration as much of it came from or ended up in China. But although the level of British–Hong Kong trade began to rise significantly in the late 1940s, it stabilised in the early 1950s, with Hong Kong's trade with China actually falling in 1952 (see Tables 7.3 and 7.4).[3] It could be argued that China's declining share in Britain's trade in the 1950s was part of a long-term trend.[4] But it must be remembered that for much of the

Table 7.3   Total Trade between Britain and China, 1946–54 (£)
(with % of total British trade in brackets)

	Imports	Exports
1946	2 696 832	7 856 304
	(0.21)	(0.81)
1947	7 171 090	12 824 258
	(0.41)	(1.07)
1948	8 201 085	8 717 340
	(0.4)	(0.52)
1949	3 622 320	2 406 002
	(0.16)	(0.13)
1950	10 324 328	3 591 022
	(0.4)	(0.16)
1951	7 669 804	2 676 319
	(0.2)	(0.09)
1952	3 011 897	4 541 249
	(0.09)	(0.16)
1953	10 222 182	6 161 377
	(0.31)	(0.22)
1954	8 958 694	6 825 913
	(0.27)	(0.24)

Source: *Annual Statement of the Trade of the UK with Commonwealth Countries and Foreign Countries*, vol. 1, London 1946–54.

period after the First World War either China or Britain were at war or suffering economic dislocation and hence it is unsurprising that trade experienced a downturn in the preceding decades. In actual fact, as the second part of this chapter will show, short-term political and ideological considerations and not long-term economic factors explain the historically low level of Sino-British trade in the 1950s.

THE PRC AND FOREIGN TRADE

In the 1950s the CCP leadership wanted to shield the Chinese economy from world economic forces. The CPG pursued a policy of import substitution. Consequently, Chinese bureaucrats controlled China's trade with the outside world in order to stimulate industrialisation. The domestic currency was overvalued to allow cheaper imports and to discriminate against exporters, whilst access to foreign exchange and export licences were controlled by state trading agencies to ensure that China imported capital and not consumer goods.[5] In short, China sought to

Table 7.4   Total Trade between Britain and Hong Kong, 1946–54 (£)
(with % of total trade in brackets)

	Imports	Exports
1946	392 337	6 052 984
	(0.03)	(0.62)
1947	2 088 387	12 828 745
	(0.12)	(1)
1948	5 510 467	20 705 250
	(0.2)	(1.25)
1949	10 265 175	28 033 758
	(0.46)	(1.5)
1950	12 049 441	28 049 037
	(0.47)	(1.29)
1951	14 472 046	36 056 665
	(0.38)	(1.33)
1952	6 390 066	29 045 278
	(0.19)	(1.06)
1953	8 312 423	27 297 481
	(0.25)	(1.01)
1954	11 129 480	24 074 510
	(0.32)	(0.86)

Source: Annual Statement of the Trade of the UK with Commonwealth Countries and Foreign Countries, vol. 1, London 1946–54.

build up heavy industry and did not exploit its comparative advantage, which would probably have been in textile and farm products.[6] This policy was ideologically derived. In Chinese communist thought there was an underlying emphasis on nationalism rather than internationalism. This intellectual current was evident in a speech by Chou En-lai at a 1949 national conference on agriculture, iron and steel production and civil aviation. He informed delegates that:

> In building our country, which should we chiefly depend on: domestic capabilities or foreign aid? Our answer is domestic capabilities – in other words, we must chiefly rely on ourselves. Small countries have to do that, and it is even more necessary for China, a big country with 450 million people. There is no question that we need to be self-reliant economically and independent politically.[7]

The CCP's attitude towards trade was heavily influenced by its perception of the impact of imperialism on China. The CCP believed that trade with the outside world had underdeveloped the Chinese economy because China had become economically dependent on the West. It argued that because China had become a market for western consumer goods and a source of raw materials for the West, Chinese industry had been underdeveloped. Moreover, the practical experiences gained in the struggle against the Japanese and the Chinese Nationalists had reinforced the ideological basis of economic self-sufficiency. During the war with Japan (1937–45) and during the Chinese Civil War (1945–49) Chinese communist areas had been self-sufficient. Suzanne Pepper notes that the Chinese communists would only trade with KMT-held areas for vital goods unobtainable in communist areas.[8] CCP trading policy was also a product of an economic and social base of support for the communist movement which was agrarian, peasant-based and located in the rural hinterland: such economic systems, such people and such areas did not trade a great deal.

However, the deep roots the Chinese communist movement had in agrarian areas also meant that the Chinese communists were reluctant to follow the Soviet strategy for heavy industrialisation, which meant the forced collectivisation of agriculture to mobilise capital and labour for industry. The CPG could have adopted a slower evolutionary path to industrialisation, with the gradual switch of resources from the agricultural to the industrial sector, achieved by either socialist planning or by a state-led pricing system. But the CPG wanted to industrialise quickly because it believed this would guarantee economic development and political independence. In addition, after 1950, the CPG controlled a more diverse national economy, in which there were industrial and commercial enterprises in the coastal provinces that historically had been reliant on western markets, western technology, and western credit, insurance, shipping and port facilities. The CCP had to adjust its previous autarkic policy to its new social base. The Chinese economy had also been devastated by the war with Japan and then the civil war with the Nationalists. According to Chinese figures, between 1937 and 1949 Chinese industrial production had fallen by 50 per cent, heavy industrial production by some 70 per cent, grain production by 22.1 per cent and cotton production by 48 per cent.[9]

Consequently, China's development strategy needed foreign capital goods and technical knowledge. This required foreign exchange. The Chinese had two ways of securing it: by trade and by aid. We will examine aid from the Soviet Union, which presented political and economic problems for the CPG, in due course. But despite this aid, and partly because of the drawbacks it entailed, trade was an important means of gaining foreign exchange. However, in order to gain foreign exchange from trade China needed to sell primary products, including farm goods such as grain, cotton, eggs, vegetables and minerals such as coal. The Chinese did not view this kind of trade from a liberal perspective but instead saw trade through mercantilist spectacles: exports were useful to gain foreign exchange but were a drain on the national resource base and could foster dependency. There was no question of the Chinese communists building up certain industrial and agrarian goods such as cotton, silk, rice or tea as export sectors. The Chinese also viewed trade statically and not dialectically. Trade would be used initially to overcome capital and technological shortages and to fill gaps in the socialist plan. The Chinese report on the First Five Year Plan reaffirmed that 'on condition that it benefits our construction, we should continue to develop trade with other capitalist countries to increase imports of certain necessary materials'.[10]

Given the close political ties between the PRC and the USSR and Soviet economic aid and trading credits to China, the CPG obviously relied heavily on the Soviet Union as a source of imports in this period. Nevertheless, the Chinese communists also wanted a diverse trading base, which would ensure that China gained technologies and industrial supplies from a range of countries. Even in 1949, Mao argued that while the Soviet Union would be China's main trading partner it was 'necessary to do business with Poland, Czechoslovakia, Germany, Great Britain, Japan and other states'.[11] By 1952 and 1953, with China embarking on its First Five Year Plan to industrialise and with the western economic embargo impacting on, if not severely damaging, the Chinese economy, the leadership initiated moves to encourage trade with the West. In September 1952 Yeh Chi-chuang wrote that: 'if these countries [the West] exert their efforts to remove such artificial obstacles, they will be able to trade with us on a basis of equality and mutual benefit'.[12] Consequently, in 1952 and 1953, with the UN embargo severely restricting imports into China, the PRC took a number of initiatives to try and circumvent controls on trade and to break the growing political and ideological consensus behind economic warfare in the West. In 1952 western firms were invited to attend a Moscow international economic conference that 'aimed at restoring normal commercial relations between the two camps in the world, to develop foreign trade of the various countries with a view to promote production, increase the number of employed and raise the standard of living of the people'.[13] Nan Han-chen, a Chinese communist delegate at the conference, indicated that the PRC was 'very desirous of establishing the maximum amount of trade with the British people'.[14] In the aftermath of the conference, the CPG established a branch of the Chinese

National Import and Export Corporation in East Berlin to act as an institutional link for businesses wanting to trade with China.[15] In 1953 the Chinese held an economic conference in Peking, inviting businesses from the West to attend and discuss future trade deals.[16]

The CPG still maintained an extremely cautious approach to external economic relations. This had always been inherent in Chinese communist thinking. In a telegram sent from Moscow in January 1950, Mao stated:

> Concerning the question of export-import trade, please pay special attention to making a comprehensive calculation of the total varieties and volume of exports and imports with such states as the Soviet Union, Poland, Czechoslovakia, Germany, and Hungary, as well as Great Britain, France, the Netherlands, Belgium, India, Burma, Vietnam, Thailand, Australia, Japan, Canada, and the United States for the whole year of 1950, or otherwise we will find ourselves in a *passive* position.[17]

The emphasis placed on the word *passive* refers directly to the CCP leadership's desire to avoid economic dependency: the Chinese wanted to be active and in control. Chou En-lai argued that:

> It is all right [*sic*] for us to do business with imperialist countries now if the terms are favourable. We shall neither refuse it nor ask for it. The habit of relying on imperialism, a habit formed over the last hundred years and deep-rooted among some people, has to be broken.[18]

Consequently, the CPG wanted to change the organisation of China's trade, replacing a system in which individual capitalists conducted China's trade with a system in which the state was the sole agent. The involvement of the state hindered the development of China's trade but the most problematic feature of China's trading system was the CPG's non-involvement in multilateral systems of payments. Unsurprisingly, the PRC was not a member of GATT but nor, rather more surprisingly, was it a member of the Council for Mutual Economic Assistance, established by the Soviet Union in January 1949. This meant that China could not run up trade imbalances with the outside world and trade was bilateral. Interestingly, the PRC came to accept that it was often more convenient and cheaper to trade through old established merchants located in Hong Kong.

This system resulted partly from the CCP leadership's determination not to rely too heavily on trade with the Soviet bloc, a desire which also explains why the PRC sought trade with the West in the mid-1950s. Before turning to examine how the West responded to these Chinese overtures on trade, we will briefly determine why trade with the Soviet bloc posed problems for the PRC.

Between 1950 and 1954, PRC–Soviet bloc economic relations changed; intra-bloc trade increased significantly and the Soviet Union provided financial aid and technical support for Chinese economic reconstruction. The Chinese communist leadership was by no means united over how and to what extent China should integrate into the communist economic system. Some leaders such as Liu Shao-chi, the Secretary-General and Vice-Chairman of the PRC, and Chen Yuan, the Minister for Economic Planning, sought a tight adherence to socialist internationalism. Others, and most importantly Mao, were determined to retain as much autonomy in economic decision-making as possible and thus did not want to become too reliant on the Socialist camp for supplies of capital goods and foreign exchange. These differences probably narrowed in the 1950s, when it became obvious that trade with and aid from the Soviet bloc was inadequate to accomplish Chinese development plans and that Moscow had set a high political and financial price for such support.

Although China gained capital goods from the communist bloc, this trade proved costly and extremely difficult to organise. In April 1950 the PRC signed a trade agreement with the Soviet Union and between late 1950 and 1954 signed similar agreements with other communist countries. The Chinese supplied primary products to the Soviet Union and Eastern Europe and they in turn supplied industrial machinery, chemicals, rubber and textiles.[19] (For a commodity breakdown of China's trade with the Soviet Union between 1950 and 1954, see Table A7 in the appendix.) However, from an economic perspective, it is questionable whether it was in the interests of the Soviet Union or Eastern Europe to exchange capital goods for Chinese raw materials. In 1952 and 1953 a number of Eastern European countries re-exported Chinese products at prices which were often lower than those prevailing in China or Hong Kong; this tends to suggest that Eastern Europe was either obtaining raw materials extremely cheaply, by exploiting China's demand for industrial and military supplies, or was forced to buy Chinese goods by the Soviet Union. In 1953 the East German Minister of Foreign Trade admitted that there had been problems in developing trade with China. Indeed, in April of that year, targets for trade between East Germany and China were lowered from those brokered in 1950.[20] These difficulties were partly the result of China's reluctance to integrate fully into the communist economic system, which was a direct result of the CCP leadership's concern about retaining economic independence.[21]

Aid from the Soviet Union presented the Chinese with a possible way of preventing the long-term economic dependency of 'unequal exchange'. Aid could be used to close capital and technological gaps without the need to sell vast quantities of primary products. The Sino-Soviet Treaty of Friendship and Mutual Alliance, signed in February 1950, provided the Chinese with a $300 million loan, allowed the PRC some short-term trading credits and promised technical aid and the transfer of technology. In 1952 the Soviet Union supplied a further undisclosed amount of financial assistance.[22] Alexander Eckstein estimates that the Soviet Union provided China with a total of 5294 million yuan in credits between 1950 and 1957, of which 2174 million were supplied between 1950 and 1954. He notes that this figure exceeds the officially acknowledged level of Soviet aid to China and argues that the Korean War forced the agreements of February and April 1950 to be redrawn.[23] As Carl Riskin acknowledges, there is little doubt that the Soviet Union provided China with extremely valuable credits to enable it to overcome capital shortages.[24] Soviet aid, however, had limitations and hidden costs. The loan of February 1950 was repaid from 1954 onwards over a ten-year period at a 1 per cent rate of interest. This rate of interest was lower than market rates, but as the debt repayment was over a short period of time it may have absorbed between 10 per cent and 40 per cent of China's export earnings after 1954.[25] Moreover, the value of Soviet loans was further reduced by a 60 per cent devaluation in the value of the ruble. By 1953 it must have been obvious to the leadership of the CCP that Soviet aid was not sufficient to fund China's First Five Year Plan. In addition, in the early 1950s, the PRC also had to bear the political costs attached to Soviet aid. The 1950 treaty had provided the Soviet Union with exclusive and extensive influence in Sinkiang, Outer Mongolia and Manchuria. And, in order to exploit Chinese mineral resources in many of these areas, the treaty had also established five joint Sino-Soviet companies, which were dominated by Soviet managerial cadres. The treaty forced China to sell a certain amount of minerals to the Soviet Union and gave Moscow a veto over their sale to other countries.[26] To the Chinese leadership these concessions were similar to old-style extra-territoriality rights given to imperial western nations in the nineteenth and early twentieth centuries. Moreover, as these concessions were in the non-*han* periphery of China, the CPG may have been concerned

Table 7.5   Chinese Repayment of Loans and Interest and Foreign Exchange
Payment to the USSR, 1950–57
(million of currency indicated)

	Loans (Yuan)	Repayment of all Debts and Interest (US $)	Net Foreign Exchange Payment to the USSR (US $)
1950	94	0.4	0.4
1951	94	0.4	0.4
1952	94	0.8	0.8
1953	141	1.7	1.7
1954	141	62.4	62.4
1955	305	208.9	208.9
1956	117	200.4	169.3
1957	23	209.8	16.7

Source: Feng-hwa Mah, *The Foreign Trade of Mainland China,* Edinburgh
1972, p. 162.

that elites in these areas might be more willing to establish close ties
with a foreign government.[27]

A few conclusions can be drawn from this examination of China's
policy towards foreign trade. Firstly, that ideological influences on the
PRC partly explain the low level of Sino-British trade. China did not
want to become dependent on trade with the West and established
cumbersome institutions to ensure it could control the extent and direction of trade. Secondly, the low level of Sino-Western trade in the
period cannot simply be blamed on the Chinese because the PRC wanted
more extensive trade with the West. We must then turn to examine
British business and state attitudes towards trade with China.

A STATE-SET BUT NOT A STATE-LED TRADING POLICY

Chapters 3 and 4 of this book discussed the British government's introduction of an economic embargo against China. This embargo partly
accounts for the changing direction of China's foreign trade and certainly
caused the severe slump in Sino-British trade in 1951 and 1952. The
embargo may also have encouraged the Chinese to set up stringent and
cumbersome trading institutions, whereby western goods had to arrive
in China before Chinese goods were released. The latter part of this
chapter will assess lobby group and British government attitudes towards
Chinese attempts to increase Sino-British trade in 1952 and 1953.

LOBBYING FOR TRADE: PRESS, POLITICAL AND BUSINESS OPINION

In 1952 and 1953 opinions on trade with China held by the press, within political circles and by businessmen differed. The press was generally against trade with China, whereas party-political opinion and business lobby groups were in favour. However, there were also important divisions within all these groupings. On the political side, there were differences between left and right. On the economic side, there were differences between merchants and industrialists and, interestingly, because a new set of Sino-British trading organisations emerged, between mercantile lobby groups.

The press greeted cautiously the new opportunities to trade with China. The majority of British newspapers tended to view the possibility of trade from a political rather than an economic angle. The *Observer* noted that 'such olive branches contrast strangely with Peking's ceaseless hymn of hate against Britain as well as America'.[28] The press concentrated not on the prospects for trade but rather on Chinese recalcitrance in Korea, the extremism of Chinese domestic campaigns and the transformation of China into an orthodox communist state. Most newspapers argued that China wanted trade because the Soviet bloc had failed to supply all of China's needs, hence threatening Chinese plans for industrialisation.[29] During 1952 and 1953, *The Economist* dismissed the Chinese initiatives to increase trade as unimportant and warned that western unity on the embargo should not be sacrificed because of international trading rivalries. Moreover, it did not believe that trade with China had much potential in the long term given that the Chinese economy was moving towards self-sufficiency. It argued that in the short term there were better markets elsewhere for products demanded by the Chinese, whilst Chinese raw materials were not vital to the British economy.[30]

The question of trade with China, and East–West trade more generally, had become an important party-political issue. In the House of Commons, Labour Party MPs voiced their desire to see trade develop with China and were perturbed by rumours that West German, French and Japanese companies were fulfilling orders for exports to China. Trade with China also became an important issue within the Labour Party. Desmond Donnelly (Labour, Pembroke) declared that 'we shall be arriving too late with too little and with no chance of success'; in November 1953 Stephen Swingler (Labour, Newcastle-under-Lyme) pointed out to Peter Thorneycroft, President of the Board of Trade, that Japan had recently signed a £30 million trade agreement to supply steel plate and copper to China; Sidney Silverman (Labour, Nelson and Colne) still hoped Lancashire textiles could exploit the massive China market, lost to the Japanese in the inter-war years.[31] A diverse range of Labour Party MPs including Hugh Gaitskell, the shadow Chancellor, Harold Wilson, Emrys Hughes and Ian Mikardo all agreed that trade should be encouraged. Attlee epitomised the party-line when he declared: 'I want to see flowing East and West trade in Europe. I want to see trade with China.'[32] The Labour Party perceived such trade as essential for defusing East–West tensions. There was also grass-roots pressure on the Labour leadership over this issue. In a survey of resolutions from constituency and ward parties sent to the National Executive Committee, out of a total of 91 replies, 24 demanded that the party press for greater East–West trade. This was clearly a promi-nent issue within the party and one to which the leadership had to respond.[33] Out of power, and conscious of the polarisation between the right and the left on foreign policy, the Labour front bench may have been using government inflexibility on the economic embargo as a means of unifying the party.

Press and political debate was intense because British businesses attended the Moscow and Peking conferences and signed trade deals with the PRC. At the Moscow conference, British firms agreed to sup-ply £3.15 million of textile goods, £3 million of chemicals and £3.5 million of metal products, and, in return, China agreed to supply soya beans and seed oil to the value of £5.5 million, eggs and egg products to the value of £2 million and bunker coal worth £2.5 million.[34] In Britain, in the aftermath of the Moscow conference, these business-men formed the core of the '48 Group of British Traders with China' and a number of unofficial bodies, including the London Export Cor-poration, set up by Jack Perry, and the British Council for the Promo-tion of International Trade, under the Chairmanship of Lord Boyd-Orr, were established to promote trade with the East, including China.[35] In Berlin, the Chinese established the China Committee for the Promo-tion of International Trade. In 1953 the firms represented by these or-ganisations attended the Peking economic conference. These organisations were severely critical of the lacklustre response of British business-men and the British government towards trade with China. The British Chamber for the Promotion of International Trade argued that the longer Britain restricted trade with China 'the more harmful will be its effects on British trade'.[36] In 1952 and 1953 these organisations did not have the finance to handle large-scale transactions with China and could not in any case circumvent the economic embargo on China.[37] But their contact with the Chinese begs two questions: why did the China Association not attend the Moscow and Peking conferences and why did it not set up similar trade deals through Berlin.

Between 1950 and 1954, the attitude of the China Association towards Sino-British trade changed. The cautious optimism about trading prospects evident in 1950 had ebbed away. Three factors explain this change: the Chinese government's attitude towards businessmen operating in China, the reorientation of the Chinese economy towards the Soviet bloc and the tightening of the western economic embargo on China. Nevertheless, even in 1952 and 1953 the Association still believed there was scope for trade between Britain and China. Indeed trade with China increased in the aftermath of the Moscow conference and did so until the end of 1953. As a result, the China Association believed that if the economic embargo on China was lifted, substantial new contracts could be signed with the PRC. Moreover, by 1952, whilst most of its representatives had come to the conclusion that the Chinese did not want merchants resident in China, they also recognised that China wanted to trade with them through Hong Kong.

Competition from other traders made the China Association set of traders even more determined to exploit any opportunities for trade with China. When China had intervened in the Korean War, the China Association had opposed the imposition of tough controls on trade but had accepted some restrictions as inevitable; it reasoned that if universally applied, these would not disadvantage British firms *vis-à-vis* Western European, American or Japanese rivals. But as German, French, Japanese and Australian trade with China began to increase in 1953 it intensified pressure for a change of government policy.[38] There was a feeling amongst British businessmen that Japanese, German and French merchants especially were stealing a march on them by circumventing the economic embargo on China. The British government, aware of the sensitivity of this question in the US, may have been more vigilant than its European neighbours in ensuring the embargo was not breached, but, at the same time, as *The Economist* acknowledged, there was also a 'whispering campaign' throughout Europe, with merchants believing others were 'getting fat slices of the alleged Chinese pie'.[39] The establishment of new Sino-British business organisations was a more threatening development. The China Association feared that the contracts struck in Moscow and Peking by these groups would jeopardise their grip on Sino-British trade, because while new firms could not circumvent the UN embargo they could, once the Korean War had ended, use their contacts to gain a foothold in the Chinese market. By 1953, there was a growing consensus within the China Association that if an armistice was signed and the embargo lifted then the China Association firms might lose out in the race for Chinese contracts for China's First Five Year Plan.

Given their desire for trade with China, the decision by the China Association firms not to attend the Moscow and Peking conferences, and their reluctance to use Berlin to establish contacts with Chinese communist trading organisations, needs to be explained. In 1952 the China Association strongly opposed the Moscow conference and afterwards the majority of its members were reluctant to trade through East Berlin.[40] In 1953, despite being more positive about the Peking conference, China Association firms did not attend. There were two reasons for this stand. Firstly, as we shall see, the British government put pressure on these firms neither to attend the conferences nor to trade through Berlin, and, secondly, most China Association firms objected vehemently to the possibility of trade with China conducted through Berlin or Moscow. These new ways of trading with China circumvented the traditional Sino-British trading structures in Hong Kong and China. British agency houses, such as Jardine Matheson and Butterfield and Swire, who had worked to establish contacts with Chinese communist elites on the mainland and also, importantly, in Hong Kong, were directly threatened by these new institutions for organising Sino-British trade. John Keswick, of Jardine Matheson, admitted: 'It is part irksome that these ridiculously uninformed businessmen should go hobnobbing with the Chinese at a time when we are being squeezed to death by them.'[41] Equally, British shipping companies such as Wheelock Marden and Co. Ltd and Mollers Ltd, British insurance companies such as Lloyds, and British banks such as the Hong Kong and Shanghai Banking Corporation and the Chartered Bank of India, Australia and China, with close business and social links with traditional British firms trading with China, might lose out if the communists in Berlin and Moscow insisted on using their own transport links with China.

In 1952 and 1953 divisions began to surface within the China Association between mercantile and industrial firms. In contrast to their mercantile counterparts, manufacturing firms showed far more interest in the Berlin and Moscow avenues of trade. Frustrated by the economic embargo on China, fearful of foreign competition and aware that the Chinese were moderating their attitude to enable foreign firms to deal with the PRC more easily, these firms wanted to establish direct contacts with Chinese state trading organisations.[42] With the CPG needing large quantities of industrial chemicals, ICI, in particular, showed a great deal of interest in the Moscow conference. Afterwards, once China had placed orders for chemicals worth £3 million with another British firm, H.J. Collar, the company's representative in the China Association, met Liu Shu-chang and Shih Li of the Chinese National Import and Export Company in Berlin.[43] In 1952 and 1953 there was also growing interest from other British firms, which had close contacts with British mercantile firms in China and Hong Kong, in the new trading contacts. The Manchester Chamber of Commerce showed considerable interest in the Moscow and Peking conferences and argued that if the China market was reopened then the British and the Japanese economies would benefit. The Chamber of Commerce also argued that this development would reduce competition from Japan, especially in cotton piece goods, in the Sterling Area.[44] In 1953 Platt Brothers, the Lancashire textile manufacturers, attended the Peking conference. A couple of developments closed the gap that was beginning to emerge within the China Association and, more generally, between mercantile and industrial firms. Firstly, Chinese officials informed British merchants that the PRC was not completely satisfied with East Berlin as a conduit for China's trade with the West, and that they still wanted to use old established merchants in Hong Kong who had a knowledge of the Chinese market and who could be dealt with informally and in a flexible way.[45] Secondly, the British state put pressure on British firms to reject the Chinese initiatives and continue to trade through Hong Kong and through British mercantile firms.

During 1952 and 1953, the British government refused to bow to political or business pressure to follow up China's overtures for trade. The government discouraged British firms from attending the Moscow and Beijing conferences and from establishing contacts with the Chinese National Import and Export Corporation in East Berlin.[46] In 1953, when the Foreign Office and the Board of Trade received enquiries from the China Association, the Federation of British Industry and from individual firms interested in attending the Peking conference, the government informed all these parties that while it would not prevent them from attending, it would prefer firms not to go. Anthony Eden, the Foreign Secretary, speaking in Parliament, laid the blame for the low level of Sino-British trade squarely with the communists:

> It is pretty heavy work for our people when we have done all we can, for instance, to take up the offers of the so-called Moscow Economic Conference and we do not even receive an answer. Trade is a

two way traffic and if people do not answer one's communications, one cannot get very far.[47]

The Conservative government was extremely critical of attempts by businesses to establish new trading contacts with China and against using East Berlin as a conduit. A symbiotic relationship continued to exist between the China Association and the government. A government policy that worked against the interests of this organisation by promoting other businesses was out of the question. The government's reasoning was dressed up in cold war rhetoric. For example, when Winston Churchill personally advised MP B. Drayson (Conservative, West Riding, Skipton) not to go to the Moscow conference,[48] he was acting on information supplied by Eden suggesting that Drayson and his wife 'played the communist game'.[49] Equally, and more publicly, Eden declared in the House of Commons that the British Council for the Promotion of International Trade was a communist front organisation. The two most prominent members of the London Export Corporation and the British Council for the Promotion of International Trade, Bernard Buckman and Jack Perry, were seen by the Foreign Office as fellow-travellers.[50] The government informed the Federation of British Industry that these businessmen were playing for political not commercial gain.[51] By comparison, the China Association was reliable and anti-communist. Closely tied to the British government, the China Association was regularly consulted and proved to be an important alternative source of information on developments in the Far East. More fundamentally, neither the China Association nor the government wanted new ways of trading with China to circumvent British companies operating in the Far East. British mercantile firms would find it difficult to survive or would have to diversify without substantial trade with China. From the government's perspective these firms were perceived to be important for the British and the Hong Kong economies. As these mercantile firms had close social and business ties with commercial business interests in London, they would continue to use British shipping, insurance and merchant banks located in Britain. As a result these firms were an important source of invisible earnings for the British economy.[52]

However, a mistrust of new patterns of trade cannot fully explain government policy on trade with China in the 1950s. It cannot explain why the government was reluctant for China Association businessmen to attend the Peking conference and nor can it explain why the government refused to co-operate with the China Association to develop a trade mission in Peking. The government knew that these two initiatives would certainly not have circumvented Hong Kong and British financial capital in the City of London, especially after both the China Association and the British government had received evidence that the CPG wanted to trade through businessmen with knowledge of the Chinese market. Equally it does not explain why the government vetoed an initiative by the China Association to set up a trade mission in London in 1953, a move that would have benefited all British businessmen wanting to trade with China. It is worth focusing on these developments in a little more depth before turning to a few explanations.

First raised in 1950, but debated in greater depth in 1952, British business interests in the Far East believed a trade mission in Peking would provide them with an institutional link with the Chinese market. British firms did not want to conduct their trade solely through Hong Kong, but rather wanted their own men on the ground in China to price and assess the quality of Chinese products and ascertain Chinese needs. With knowledge of the Chinese market, British merchants would have an advantage over foreign and other British merchants trading more directly. Hong Kong's Chamber of Commerce and the Chamber of Commerce in Shanghai supported the idea, the latter arguing that an offer of a trade mission should be the key and opening gambit in any negotiations regarding the exit of British firms from Peking.[53] The China Association was reluctant to link a trade mission closely to the withdrawal of firms from China, arguing that 'by giving priority in any discussion we may have with China to the subject of establishing the representative Trade Group, we are running a grave risk of embarking on a kind of Korean armistice talk, during which the men we want to get out of Shanghai will linger on'.[54] But by December 1952 the China Association had divorced the two issues; it informed the Foreign Office that it was 'just what is wanted at the present time'.[55] This switch came about because of competition from the new British businessmen and from European and Japanese merchants for post Korean War Chinese contracts. The change in attitude also came about because Chinese communists had suggested such a body to W. Lorimor, a British delegate to the Moscow conference.[56] Despite business support, the government rejected the idea of a trade mission. As a result business interests postponed further initiatives.

THE CHINESE MARKET ON HOLD

The government had to ascertain whether trade was possible given the state of diplomatic relations between Britain and China, whether trade with the West might help to engender tensions between China and the Soviet Union, whether trade with China was of value to the British economy and whether a British attempt to trade with China might endanger Anglo-American relations. We must explain why the Conservative government refused to allow a trade mission or allow British representation at the Peking and Moscow conferences?

Whether it was rational in a economic sense for Britain to be trading with China was even less certain in 1952 and 1953 than in 1950. The changing balance of the Chinese economy made China a far less lucrative market for the West. Structural changes in the Chinese economy simplified the country's export and import trade: China wanted capital goods but not consumer goods. This change worked against the dependent trading relationship desired by the West. In 1953 *The Economist* acknowledged that, 'Apart from a few . . . "sweeteners", there is no prospect of any substantial market for western consumer goods'.[57] Equally, there was no shortage of world demand for capital goods in the 1950s. *The Economist* acknowledged that 'To meet China's demands in this direction, British industry would have to disappoint better customers elsewhere'.[58] The Korean War, an armaments-driven Keynesian boost to the world economy, had vastly increased world-wide demand. In addition, the institutional framework for Sino-British trade made it risky and increased transaction costs. Since 1951, the Chinese had demanded cargo for cargo deals, had stipulated that letters of credit should be exchanged and that goods should arrive in China before releasing others for export. The British Board of Trade strongly objected to trade on this basis.[59] Given the consolidation of a socialist planning system in China in 1951 and 1952 and the nature of China's development planning, China would not be the most attractive market in the world in the 1950s.

However, if trade was of questionable importance for the British economy as a whole, the British government understood that it remained vital for certain business interests. The Board of Trade wanted to support British businessmen, and especially the China Association of traders, and was particularly concerned by the evidence surfacing that West German, French and even Japanese firms were gaining a foothold in the Chinese market.[60] Indeed there was a marked change in the Board of Trade's attitude once an armistice was signed in Korea.

Before July 1953 it did not want to jeopardise Anglo-American relations for the sake of Sino-British trade.[61] Peter Thorneycroft went so far as to argue that 'if the Americans felt strongly that a complete embargo should be introduced and all countries were willing to apply such an embargo, provided we came into line, I should not, on purely trade grounds, regard it as vital to preserve this trade'.[62] Once the armistice was signed, however, Thorneycroft advocated an easing of East–West trade controls. The Board of Trade was evasive in the House of Commons, arguing that 'trade depends essentially upon the trade policy of the Chinese People's Government and there are, in present circumstances, no steps which His Majesty's Government can usefully take'.[63] Within Whitehall, however, Thorneycroft did express concern about growing business and parliamentary pressure: he warned Eden that 'it is going to be very difficult to maintain for any length of time such extensive restrictions on trade with China, now that active hostilities in Korea have ceased'. He argued that the end of the economic embargo must not be linked with a political settlement in Korea, warning that 'we might well find that we should not in fact be able to hold the position at home so as to honour such a pledge'.[64] The Board of Trade, then, despite the limited importance of trade with China to the British economy, did not block the development of such trade. In 1952 the Board of Trade, in a letter to the China Association, declared that:

> China is likely to be near the end of the queue for scarce goods, but we would not, if we could avoid it, discourage manufacturers who have a long term interest in the market from continuing to cultivate it if they consider the prospect for future business justified them in doing so.[65]

In 1952 and 1953 the geo-strategic rationale for trading with China was reaffirmed by two developments. Firstly, as Chapter 8 will highlight, the British government had evidence of Sino-Soviet economic tensions. Secondly, the Soviet Union increasingly wanted to open up the Soviet bloc to more trade with the West. The Moscow economic conference had been part of a co-ordinated strategy by the whole Soviet bloc. The Soviets had arranged the conference and were probably instrumental in developing trading contacts through East Berlin. The Soviet Union had political and economic aims for initiating such developments. In 1952 and 1953 the Soviets were moving away from an autarkic development strategy and wanted to increase trade with the West; bottlenecks in their economy were holding up Soviet economic development and hindering trade with the Eastern European satellites and with China.[66] In addition the Soviet Union may have reasoned

that the prospect of trade with the eastern bloc might divide the West
– the US from its Western European allies – and also by diverting
China's trade through East Berlin, prevent China developing direct
economic ties with the West. According to the liberal policy framework established by British policy towards China, the British government should have exploited these developments by actively encouraging
and not restricting trade with China.

By 1952 there was a gut hostility in the Foreign Office to trading
with China because of Chinese intransigence in Korea and because of
China's failure to establish diplomatic relations in 1950: there was a feeling that the political ice had to be broken before British traders could
fish the Chinese waters. Eden accepted the advice of Robert Scott who
argued that Britain 'should not help the Chinese, who disrupt the traditional trade processes and channels, and [who] have been turning to
a barter basis'.[67] However, as Chapter 8 will show, the Conservative
government remained intrinsically opposed to the economic isolation
of Communist China. The Foreign Office remained convinced that a
lifting of the economic embargo on China was in the best interests of
Britain and in the 'general interest of the Western World'.[68] In September 1952 Charles Johnston, the head of the China and Korea department in the Foreign Office, acknowledged that:

> Our trade connection seems to offer a link through which we really
> can make the Chinese conscious of our existence and, if the link
> can be strengthened adequately without trade in strategic goods be-
> ing involved, we might in time make it strong enough to extend a
> certain amount of influence through it, particularly if Sino-Soviet
> relations get no easier in the meantime.[69]

It is not therefore a change in thinking on the economic and geo-
strategic importance of trade which explains the government's trading
policy, but rather the dynamics of Anglo-American relations.

As we shall explore in Chapters 8 and 9, in 1952 and 1953 the
Truman and Eisenhower administrations were still, for the most part,
tied ideologically to a policy which aimed at isolating the Chinese
economically and politically. Consequently, any unilateral initiatives
by the British government over trade with China would have angered
the Americans and hardened the attitude of the US public and the US
Congress towards Britain. In 1952 Johnston acknowledged that, while
a Chinese trade mission in London was advantageous, the American
public and the American administration would misrepresent and mis-
understand a British initiative to establish one.[70] In October 1952 F.S.
Tomlinson, the first secretary at the embassy in Washington, warned

that if Britain promoted trade with China 'whilst the Chinese communists are still actively intervening in the Korean War, we may have a
row with the American government and are practically certain to have
a good deal of public criticism'.[71] In November 1953, in a statement
of policy sent to the China Association, the government admitted that
unless public attitudes changed in America 'a major increase in our
trade with China would be likely to produce highly adverse reactions
both on relations with this country, and even towards the individual
companies concerned'.[72]

The British government had two priorities regarding trade with China:
to persuade the US not to introduce more stringent economic controls
on trade and, once an armistice had been signed, to persuade the US
to relax the embargo on China. The British government would not
jeopardise these aims by encouraging premature trading links with China.
It hoped that demands from American and Japanese businessmen for
an easing of the economic embargo, coupled with a toning down of
popular and congressional hostility towards trade with China, would
allow a US administration to adopt a more liberal stance on trade.
And it believed that British diplomacy could speed the process along.
As the next two chapters will show, this aim proved unachievable.

CONCLUSIONS

Sino-British trade rose in 1950, fell in 1952 and recovered in 1953.
Given that the Chinese economy was entering a period of economic
reconstruction, Sino-British trade in the early 1950s was at an artifi-
cially low level. The Chinese and British governments shaped the pattern of trade. The CPG did not want to rely on trade with the West
and reorientated the Chinese economy towards the Soviet Union. The
British government prevented trade in strategic and semi-strategic goods
with China and hindered British shipping interests involved in trade
with China. British Labour and Conservative governments resisted
domestic pressure from business lobby groups and from left-wing opinion
for an easing of the embargo on China. The government questioned
the economic worth of trade with China to the British economy: China
wanted capital goods and not British consumer goods. More importantly, the government could not afford the political trade-off involved
in adopting a more liberal approach: it believed that removing sanctions on the Chinese economy might have meant American political
and economic sanctions against Britain.

8 Stalemate and Restraint: November 1951–July 1953

I do not regard Communist China as a formidable adversary. Anyhow you may take it that for the next four or five years 400 million Chinese will be living just where they are now. They cannot swim, they are not much good at flying and the trans-Siberian railway is already overloaded ... I doubt whether Communist China is going to be the monster some people imagine.

Winston Churchill[1]

We have nothing to fear from Communist China: they are far too busy looking after 600 million people.

Clement Attlee[2]

British policy towards China did not change significantly under a Conservative government: Britain would leave the door open for an improvement in political and economic relations between China and the West and try to moderate American thinking on China. This strategy depended above all else on an armistice being signed for the Korean War, which would, Britain hoped, allow economic and military measures against the PRC to be scaled down, and then perhaps, in the longer term, with an easing of Sino-American antagonism, open the way towards closer diplomatic and economic contact between China and the West. Unfortunately, the process towards peace in Korea was arduous and drawn out. As a result, Churchill's Conservative government faced the same dilemma as Attlee's Labour government: to acquiesce in an aggressive US approach towards China or to follow a moderate liberal line.

CONSERVING CHINA POLICY

The Conservative government did not sever ties with the PRC. Anthony Eden, the Foreign Secretary, told Prime Minister Winston Churchill that this 'would not harm or frighten the Communists, but would lose us the listening post represented by our embassy in Peking'.[3] In January 1952, at the Washington conference between Churchill and Truman, the Prime Minister informed the President that British recognition, an

161

established fact, was difficult to alter.[4] In July 1952 he reaffirmed in the House of Commons that 'it is just at the time when things are disagreeable between countries that you need diplomatic relations'.[5] Nevertheless, Conservative leaders had never been enthusiastic about recognition of the Chinese communists; in 1949 Eden had reservations over its timing and Lord Salisbury had totally opposed the decision. James Tang notes that Churchill told Truman that if he had been in power in November 1950 he would have broken off relations with the Chinese.[6] By 1952 such views were not far removed from those of the Foreign Office. Robert Scott, the head of the Far Eastern Department, now acknowledged that British recognition had been hasty and legalistic. He wanted the British government to adopt a more confrontational position towards China: 'the Chinese do not play the game by established western rules and customs' and neither would Britain.[7] Lionel Lamb, the British chargé d'affaires, provided the justification for such an attitude. He informed the Foreign Office that he did not 'envisage any contingency in which they [the Chinese communists] might be inspired to take the plunge and offer to discuss seriously an exchange of ambassadors'.[8]

Nevertheless, the ultimate objective of policy remained a *modus vivendi* between Britain and China. Robert Scott, anxious to clear up ambiguities in the government's position, argued Britain must contain and embrace Communist China, with Britain 'resisting Chinese aggression, but at the same time seeking to live and let live'.[9] Conservative ministers remained sceptical over the notion of a *modus vivendi*. Churchill thought Britain could neither influence the course of events in China nor alter her relationship with the West. He perceived China as an American sphere of influence – a mind-set dating back to the Second World War. Eden, meanwhile, did not envisage a grand strategy aimed at a far eastern settlement and eventual accommodation with the Chinese. The Conservative government, however, still worked within parameters set by the Labour government because the economic, strategic and political rationale behind Labour thinking had not altered.

War in Korea and social revolution in China forced the Foreign Office to reassess Chinese domestic and foreign policies. The severity and brutality of communist methods of political control – especially the intensity and violence of the *wu fan* and *san fan* campaigns – surprised and shocked the Foreign Office.[10] Lamb reported that 'everyone trembles as the old loyalties of family, office and school are broken down to be replaced by loyalties to the people, a loyalty which, unless the party displays unusual moderation, must inevitably degenerate into subservience and dictatorship'.[11] He believed that whilst the mass mobilisation campaigns of the CCP were an intrinsically weak means of achieving political control, predictions of internal dissolution were hypothetical because the regime was 'very firmly in the saddle'.[12] Lamb reported that:

> All in all there is little cause for expecting – at present – that [the] traditional Chinese character will again threaten to undermine or even weaken the Chinese People's Government's grip on the nation's bodies and souls, not, at least, for some time to come. The government and the party now have everything under control – even sufficient to make some ostensible gestures of relaxation here and there. The vigilance of the security, however, remains hawk like, tireless and unfaulting and ever present.[13]

The Foreign Office foresaw little chance of the communist state disintegrating. Robert Scott argued that even if the PRC succeeded in alienating a number of groups within Chinese society, the political control the Chinese government enjoyed meant that any sort of opposition had 'little chance of developing in China'.[14] The Foreign Office was uncertain whether the Chinese communists would adopt an expansionist foreign policy. The Foreign Office admitted that while communist ideology promoted revolutionary communism, there were no pressing strategic or economic interests making the PRC expansionist. Nevertheless, in the 1950s a consensus was gaining ground in the Foreign Office and within the Chiefs of Staff that the Chinese might well intervene in South East Asia, an area of far greater importance to Britain than the Korean peninsula.[15] The British Foreign Office began to talk in terms of imperial dominoes falling in Asia. If Indochina, the most probable target of Chinese adventurism, fell to communism it would undermine Britain's already tenuous position in Malaya, a territory of prime economic, strategic and political significance. Moreover, this sort of reasoning raised questions about the Sino-Soviet alliance. Had, for example, the Soviet Union diverted China into South East Asia in order to weaken the West and prevent a Soviet-American confrontation in North East Asia?

In 1952 and 1953 the Foreign Office received evidence which reaffirmed the closeness of economic, political and military ties between China and the Soviet Union. The Chinese had accepted Soviet influence for ideological, economic and strategic reasons; they required an alliance with the Soviet Union to offset the threat of an American-Japanese economic and military bloc and to secure economic aid for reconstruction.[16] Nevertheless, the Foreign Office still believed that a 'wedge' could be driven between China and the Soviet Union. It argued that Sino-Soviet tensions might arise if the Soviet Union failed to provide the PRC with sufficient aid or attempted to extend its influence in China. Alternatively, the Foreign Office believed that dissatisfaction could emerge among the Chinese masses themselves in response to Chinese communist subservience to the flawed and imperialistic Soviets. Lamb argued that the repetitive and intensive campaigns, orchestrated by the Chinese communists to justify the importance of Soviet assistance, were 'not palatable to the inherently conceited Chinese character and can therefore scarcely be conducive to increased respect and affection'.[17] In 1952 there was no suggestion of a schism but there was evidence of differences between the Chinese Communist Party and the Soviet Communist Party. When Chou visited Moscow in August 1952, 'with the aim of further strengthening friendship [and] co-operation between the two countries', the Foreign Office noted that the talks had produced a public agreement over the Sino-Soviet Railway but no announcement on wider aspects of policy.[18] Alvary Gascoigne, ambassador in Moscow, suggested there may have been a secret agreement. The Foreign Office argued, however, that if the Soviet Union had committed itself to increase aid to China and to align more closely with the CPG on the Korean War, then this would have been made public. Eden accepted that the Korean conflict would have caused disputes over the level of military and political aid and over military and economic strategies for Korea.[19] The Foreign Office questioned whether the glorification of all things Soviet in the autumn of 1952 (culminating in the 'Sino-Soviet Union Friendship Month') might have been a propaganda cloak to disguise the lack of Soviet economic aid to China. It noted that Chinese economic affairs officials, including Chen Yun, had remained in Moscow after the majority of the delegation had returned to Peking. And in January 1953 Liu Shao-chi spent a further three months in Moscow, engaged in delicate and difficult discussions with the Soviet leadership. The Foreign Office admitted that without access to the decision-making process in the Soviet Union or in China its analysis was 'lacking in meat and rather superficial',[20] but it concluded that any tensions surfacing in 1952 and 1953 resulted not from a Chinese reaction to Soviet encroachment, but because of a Soviet reluctance to become further involved in China.

For British policy-makers the search for a *modus vivendi* and the division of the Sino-Soviet Union bloc thus remained complementary. The only means of causing tensions in the Sino-Soviet relationship was to reduce the military and political threat from the West and relax economic restrictions on the Chinese. The Foreign Office was not convinced that its strategy would produce a schism between China and the Soviet Union, but the alternative American approach could still not be contemplated – such a strategy would cause political difficulties at home, commit too many resources to the Far East and jeopardise co-operation between Asian nations and the West.

Even in 1952 and 1953, British government thinking was conditioned by a fear that the Korean War might escalate into a general war in the Far East. Churchill and Eden both acknowledged that Britain must prevent such a development.[21] Maintaining economic and political contact with the PRC was deemed essential for this end. Epitomising British thinking, Robert Scott stated: 'a policy of deliberately worsening relations with China would not only have an effect in the Far East, but would also set up an inevitable chain reaction resulting in a general deterioration of international relations and in an increased danger of global war'.[22] A general war was certainly less likely in 1952 and 1953 than previously, especially because, as noted by the Foreign Office, there was no public commitment by the Soviet Union to support China in the event of an attack by the US. Charles Johnston, head of the China and Korea Department, admitted: 'It is just possible China may be wishing to suggest to the world that Russia is more prepared to come to her assistance than is in fact the case; indeed China may be trying at the same time to get the Soviet Union more involved in Far East commitments.'[23] Interestingly, British and American thinking on this point had actually converged. As Rosemary Foot notes, the US administration was also questioning whether the Soviet Union would become involved in a far eastern conflict, causing the US to contemplate a more aggressive approach in the Far East.[24] (For details of changes in US policy see the later sections in this chapter and Chapter 9.) The closeness of British and American government assessments of Sino-Soviet relations suggests once again that an explanation for differences in US and British policies on China in the 1950s lies at home rather than abroad.

If British views on whether a war would break out in the Far East were opaque, then the reasons why Britain wanted to avoid such a war were crystal clear. From a British government perspective, a general war in the Far East had to be avoided because British military resources were seriously overstretched: they were already protecting Europe, the empire and being used to fight a war in Korea.[25] The government believed that a policy which sought to step up military and economic pressures on the Chinese would further drain British resources and increase the risk of Chinese retaliation against Hong Kong and Malaya. Although military expenditure and, in particular, rearming for the Korean War had provided a demand-side boost to the economy, they had also exacerbated structural problems at home. Basically, in 1950 and 1951 rearmament had been undertaken too rapidly and taken up too great a proportion of GNP. As a result, it caused inflation and destabilised the balance of payments, with a £300 million surplus in 1950 turning into a £400 million deficit in 1951.[26] On gaining office, the Conservative government had immediately raised interest rates to reduce consumption and investment, and had reduced the stockpiling of imported raw materials – thus completing the first post-war 'stop–go' cycle. As the Conservative government wanted to cut income and profit taxes in order to redistribute income, neither it nor the economy could afford a further round of rearmament.[27] The Conservative government had no real alternative but to adopt a non-confrontational approach to China.

Moreover, while Britain's economic foothold in China had been severely eroded and trade with China significantly reduced by the economic embargo and the reorientation of the Chinese economy towards the Soviet bloc, it was still in the government's interest to promote economic contact with China. As Chapter 5 proved, the government believed that Hong Kong, essential for Britain's position in the Far East, needed economic contact with China. And, as Chapters 6 and 7 indicated, British business interests needed and wanted more trade with China and continued to press the government to secure it.

In addition, the influence of the Asian Commonwealth remained important. The Foreign Office argued that if Asian nations became disillusioned with the West's policy, it could divide the world even more starkly into two blocs, with a group of non-aligned nations in between. This development could make Asian nations less amenable to anti-communist strategies and erode British 'influence' in the area. Scott, analysing the basis of the British strategy for opposing communism in Asia, noted:

> There is no single policy which will stop communism. Politically the aim should be to set up stable, friendly, and efficient governments based on popular support. The alternatives are to quit or to rule Asia on Colonial lines. The Western powers cannot afford to quit because of the political and the economic and strategic consequences, and they are no longer strong enough to do the second

(even if they wanted to) in the face of the political tides that have swept over Asia in modern times.[28]

Robert Scott was conscious that the communist world was courting Asian nations; he argued that China and the Soviet Union were trying to seduce India.[29] The Chinese government had indeed entered into a trading agreement to supply rice to India in 1953, while in 1952 an Asian Peace Conference, organised by the communist bloc, had as its central theme: western and Japanese imperialism in Asia. The conference had two aims: to distance Asian governments from the West and intensify popular hostility to western influence amongst Asian nations. Consequently, the British government was determined to counter these moves by ensuring policy towards China was broadly in line with its Asian allies. Commenting on American policy towards China, F.S. Tomlinson, in Washington, warned: 'dropping agents into South China may look like a defensive measure in Washington or New York, but would certainly look like a direct provocation in New Delhi, Rangoon or Djakarta'.[30]

Political considerations at home also ensured a moderate and conciliatory line on Communist China. Churchill's government, with a small majority in the House of Commons, could not allow its China policy to be exploited by the Labour opposition. Although deep divisions in the Labour Party over foreign and defence policy plagued the party in 1952 and 1953, both its right and left wings advocated a moderate policy towards Communist China and strongly opposed American military plans contemplating a general war between China and the West. In January 1954 Clement Attlee succinctly outlined his position in *Foreign Affairs*:

I think it unlikely that the Chinese people with their ancient civilisation are likely to swallow the whole Communist doctrine. Still less do I think that China is likely to become a docile satellite of Russia. But the more China is shut away from the Western world and forced to ally herself with Russia, the more strength will be given to her Communist masters.[31]

Attlee demanded changes in British government policy. He wanted China admitted to the UN, the trade embargo eased and an international settlement for the Taiwan issue. Equally, well aware of American cold war strategic thinking, he wanted the US administration restrained. In February 1952, for instance, the Labour Party, feeling that Churchill had acquiesced with dangerous US initiatives during his January conference with Truman, tabled a vote of censure in the House of Commons against the Prime Minister. The American bombing of the Yalu power stations in July 1952 produced another heated exchange between the two sides in the House. However, it was difficult for the Labour opposition to launch an attack on the Conservative government because, in actual fact, there were no fundamental differences between the parties over far eastern policy. Churchill, by outlining that the Attlee government had approved of UN attacks on Chinese air fields, successfully repelled a Labour attack in January 1952. Consequently, figures on the left of the Labour Party including Nye Bevan, Barbara Castle, Tom Driberg, Tony Benn and Michael Foot, as well as traditional dissenters such as Emrys Hughes and Sidney Silverman, took up the issue. During an April 1953 debate on further restrictions on trade with China, these Labour figures, notably Benn and Castle, criticised government acquiescence with the 'insidious encroachment' by the US over Britain's far eastern trade.[32] There was wide party support for the left's approach. Constituency Labour parties sent numerous resolutions to the National Executive Committee to express alarm at US policy, to demand a settlement in Korea and to insist on China's admission to the UN.[33] Despite the ideological distance between them, Bevan's views coincided with Attlee's over China: both believed China was neither an expansionist power nor a subservient ally of the Soviet Union and thus should be accommodated and not isolated.[34] The views of left-wing groups were a political brake on a Conservative government which was more willing to toe the American line.

Since the establishment of the PRC, public attitudes towards China had hardened. China's refusal to establish relations with Britain and the plight of British businessmen reduced public sympathy for the Chinese communists. More dramatically, China's intervention in Korea meant 'British boys' were fighting 'China men'. Media reporting of domestic developments in China increasingly emphasised the 'orthodox' nature of Chinese communism. Newspapers and periodicals on the left of the political spectrum approved of and supported the social revolution in China; the *News Chronicle* noted that the 'atmosphere was different, utilitarian in aspect yet fixed with a zest and zeal which no democratic country betrays'.[35] But, by contrast, the mainstream media became more vitriolic in its criticism. The major daily newspapers, such as the *Manchester Guardian* and *The Times*, argued that Chinese communist policies, especially during the *san fan* and *wu fan* campaigns, indicated the anti-capitalist and hence anti-western slant of the new regime. For *The Times*, the campaigns were an 'orgy of accusation and confusion', with an 'intensity which rarely seemed to count the cost'.[36] Nevertheless, neither press nor public wanted an anti-communist crusade against China. The British press was concerned by American policy in the Far East. The *Manchester Guardian* argued that the US was close to accepting MacArthur's plan for dealing with the Chinese and *The Times* rejected military or economic measures that would not necessarily damage China's military and economic strength.[37]

What all press, political, business and governmental groups agreed on was that a prerequisite for defusing cold war tensions in the Far East was an armistice for the Korean War. And all believed a moderate line with China was the best means of achieving one. Moreover, as Foot argues, despite the deadlock at the talks in Panmunjom, the Conservative government remained convinced that the Chinese desired peace; it did not perceive any real ideological, strategic or political obstacles preventing the Chinese from signing a ceasefire.[38] The Foreign Office still argued that if the West offered to discuss the status of Taiwan and a seat in the UN then the Chinese would agree to a ceasefire.[39] The Conservative government argued that a concession could save Chinese 'face' and break the deadlock in the armistice talks. Unfortunately, the Conservative government could not dictate how the West interacted with the PRC. Instead it had to concentrate on moderating American policy towards China.

BRITAIN, THE US AND CHINA

The US did not want a political settlement for the Far East: a *modus vivendi* between the Chinese communists and the West was out of the question. Instead the basic objective of US policy between 1951 and 1953 was to 'bring about changes in China which will eliminate the threat from that country to free world security'.[40] The establishment of an independent, self-sufficient and non-communist China was a long-term objective of US policy, but in the short term the US administration believed its strategy would deter the Chinese communists from committing further acts of aggression, force them to reach a settlement in Korea, make their control of China as difficult as possible and increase tensions between themselves and the Soviets. The US would minimise China's economic and diplomatic contact with the West, and would, if a ceasefire was not signed in Korea, threaten military action against the Chinese mainland.

The British Foreign Office argued US thinking on China was too inflexible in design and too ambitious in objective. Robert Scott thought the Kennan doctrine of containment plus *modus vivendi* had been corrupted into containment plus crusade against communism, leaving out 'any possibility of a return to a policy of moderation even if the Chinese were to show that they wished to reach a *modus vivendi*'.[41] By the summer of 1952, the British government argued that the American approach to the peace negotiations in Korea was making progress towards an armistice more difficult; previously, the Conservative government had worried that an armistice might have been concluded carelessly, thus threatening a resumption of hostilities. The Republican Party's victory in the November 1952 presidential elections exacerbated these concerns. John Foster Dulles, the new American Secretary of State, had a moralistic and ideologically driven hostility towards communism; and more generally, the new administration seemed unable to contemplate a policy which lay between friendliness and enacting maximum pressure on the communists.

British policy had to respond to American policy towards China and thus had three objectives: to prevent the US from intensifying military and economic pressure on the Chinese; to deepen the US commitment to resisting communism in South East Asia; and to persuade the US that China should be admitted to the UN. The aim was to 'get the Americans to deal with China as they deal with Russia, by recognition and by accepting them in the UN, whilst forming a collective security system to prevent aggression'.[42] The first step towards this goal would be a Korean armistice, as this would allow relations between China and the US to thaw and prevent the US from extending the war into China. The British government then hoped it could divert American resources into South East Asia and encourage a more moderate US attitude towards China. If it was impossible for the US 'to make any gesture towards Peking' then the British government would ensure that the US increased its commitment to supporting the containment of communism in South East Asia.[43] The Foreign Office believed that it might be easier to achieve these policy objectives under the new Republican rather than under the Truman administration. Robert Scott argued that, as Eisenhower and Dulles wanted to remove American troops from the Asian continent, 'a solution which promised to lead to a Pacific security system and to stop American casualties in Korea' might 'appeal to him [Eisenhower] even at the price of American recognition of China'.[44] The Chiefs of Staff, perturbed that America was 'loath to commit herself' to South East Asia, pressed for a more forthright US line on containment.[45] Despite the consensus view that the British government should try and shape US policy, there remained a marked difference of opinion between Churchill and Eden over the extent to which Britain should do so. Winston Churchill, uninterested in China and determined to improve Anglo-American relations, wanted responsibility for far eastern matters delegated to the US.[46] In January 1952 he informed Truman that 'the UK desire to help the US in every way possible and recognise that in the Far East there could be no UK priority or equality or leadership. The role of leader squarely belongs to the US and the UK will do its utmost to meet US views and requests in relation to that area.'[47] In July 1952 Churchill declared to the House of Commons that: 'I think we ought to admire them [the US] for the restraint which they have practised instead of trying to find fault with them on every occasion'; he would not follow the advice of the Labour Party which argued that Britain should try and force the Americans to recognise China while 'the fighting is actually going on'.[48] Eden, by contrast, wanted to influence American policy towards the Far East.

Ultimately, because Britain could not afford to jeopardise relations with the US, the scope for British influence over American decision-making was limited. The Anglo-American relationship was too fundamental to Britain. In addition, in the event of policy towards China diverging too markedly from that of the US, the government feared all influence over the direction of US thinking towards the Far East would be lost. As the priority was the avoidance of a general conflict in the Far East, the British government believed it had to retain its influence. And, consequently, as the next sections will emphasise, the government failed to moderate American thinking on China and was forced, in response to American pressure, to adopt an even less liberal line itself with the PRC.

ADMISSION DELAYED

The Conservative government's position on China's admission to the UN was consistent with the previous Labour government's. While in theory the government favoured a seat for China, war in Korea and American opposition to such a seat ensured that there was no change in the British position. The British embassy in Washington warned against diverging too far from American policy.[49] Churchill argued Britain must 'support America in not having Communist China in the UN'; and Eden agreed that the 'moratorium agreement' would be continued until an armistice had been achieved in Korea.[50]

Unfortunately, the Truman and the Eisenhower administrations wanted to ensure that even in the aftermath of an armistice in Korea, China would not be admitted to the UN. Consequently, tensions between the US and Britain arose again. Before both the 1951–52 and the 1952–53 UN sessions, the US proposed a tightening of the moratorium procedure by introducing a resolution to postpone all consideration of China's status during the whole UN session – regardless of whether an armistice was signed.[51] The British government refused to play ball. Eden wanted the issue 'to remain dormant so long as the Korean armistice negotiations were in train'.[52] John Pierson Dixon, Deputy Under-Secretary of State at the Foreign Office, argued that a new US motion might provoke a long and divisive debate in the UN and would send out a message that read: China should be politically excluded from the world community.[53] The Foreign Office was still determined to prevent the US from moving the UN from an universal body towards an anti-communist organisation, a shift in emphasis that might, by provoking the Soviet Union to withdraw from the UN, have divided the world into ideologically determined camps. Gladwyn Jebb, the permanent British representative at the UN, argued that the priority for Britain was actually not the admission of Communist China to the UN but 'to induce the Americans to agree not to take action which would gravely prejudice developments in the Far East and perhaps even endanger the existence of the UN itself'.[54] Robert Scott, perceiving the American initiative to be the 'thin edge of the wedge to open up a general review of our policy of recognition', wanted the government to take a firm stand.[55] In November 1951 the British government informed the US that while there would be no immediate change of British voting policy in the aftermath of an armistice for Korea, it preferred to avoid any language in the UN which tied its hands on this question indefinitely.[56]

The inauguration of the Republican administration, coupled with the prospect of an armistice in Korea, widened Anglo-American differences. In March 1953 Eden felt the need to publicly reaffirm that Britain found it 'quite impossible' for Communist China to be admitted to the UN while the regime was engaged in aggression in Korea.[57] The British government initially feared that Eisenhower would be too inclined to adopt the views of the UN held by the right-wing of the Republican Party, but, encouraged by Eisenhower's announcement that the UN should be a 'mirror of the world', soon began to hope that there might be a change in the American position.[58] Indeed, it may have only been opposition from the American public and from the right-wing of the Republican Party in Congress which prevented a change in the administration's position on the admission of Communist China to the UN. (The factors determining US policy will be discussed in Chapter 9.) In May 1953 Senator William Knowland (Republican, California) proposed a rider to a UN appropriations bill, which cut off US funds to the organisation if the Chinese communists were admitted.[59] Subsequently, Eisenhower succeeded in persuading leading senators to remove the amendment, but in the process agreed to seek assurances from the allies that they would not change voting policies in the UN. Anglo-American divisions over China's admission to the UN remained deep-rooted.

BARRICADES BUT NO BLOCKADE

Conservative government policy on economic sanctions against China was straightforward: Britain would resist the imposition of further sanctions against China while the Korean negotiations continued, and after an armistice would, depending on the attitude of the US, try and relax the embargo. The rationale behind this policy was the same as that underpinning Labour government policy in 1950 and 1951: the government believed that trade with China, and with the Far East more generally, was important for the British economy, a means of influencing the CPG, and essential for the economic (and hence the political) well-being of non-communist territories in South East Asia, including Hong Kong. The government's attitude was most clearly evident over the question of trade in rubber with China. In 1952 the American administration wanted to tighten controls on this trade, but the British government argued that this might destabilise colonial regimes in Asia. It justified these arguments by referring to unrest in the 'rubber circle'. The government argued that certain regimes, and in particular Ceylon, could not introduce tighter controls because they feared being branded too pro-western. In the Ceylonese case, the Ceylon government faced an election in 1952 and was conscious that the Indonesian government had just fallen partly because it was perceived by the Indonesians as too amenable to the West.[60] As Chapter 7 highlighted, of equal importance was increasing dissatisfaction within British business circles over the continuation of tight controls on trade in the Far East; this was from bodies such as the British Council for the Promotion of International Trade (an organisation associated with the Moscow and Peking economic conferences in 1952 and 1953 and sympathetic to international communism), but also from mainstream organisations such as the China Association. Consequently, the government was anxious not to impose unilateral controls that would allow other Western European countries to gain markets from British traders. Britain resisted American pressure for tighter controls. At the end of 1952, pharmaceutical companies – wanting to increase trade with China and worried by expanding Western European trade with China – successfully persuaded the government to ignore American demands for tighter controls and to relax restrictions on trade in drugs with the mainland.[61] However, financial interests continued to have primacy. The Ministry of Transport and the Board of Trade, for example, opposed any new restrictions because they would affect Britain's position as a 'commercial and maritime power'.[62] The most persuasive pressure came from the colonial authorities in Hong Kong, which were extremely anxious to relax restrictions and simplify the procedures for restricting goods unavailable to China.[63] On this issue alone, the Conservative government succeeded in persuading the US administration to ease its policy on China. The US administration agreed that if the colonial authorities ensured that US goods were not re-exported to China or used in the manufacture of goods arriving in China, then they would 'permit a reasonable flow of US material to Hong Kong'.[64] The British government accepted this concession, but was concerned by its arbitrary nature and wanted some machinery established which would guarantee that goods would arrive in Hong Kong. In actual fact the whole procedure was difficult to organise because it was virtually impossible, without setting up a cumbersome and politically damaging bureaucratic licensing system, to monitor end use and to check that US goods or raw materials were not being indirectly exported to China. The American administration probably realised as much but overlooked the practical problems 'because of the special situation and trade patterns of Hong Kong'. As Chapter 5 outlined, in the early 1950s the Americans perceived Hong Kong as strategically and politically important. When, in 1952, Truman demanded a British explanation for excessive trade between Hong Kong and China, Acheson reminded him that Hong Kong could not survive without trading with China.[65] Subsequently, this shift in the American attitude was exploited by the Conservative government which threw Hong Kong into the debating pot when it discussed a total embargo or a naval blockade with the Americans. (In addition, the government also began to exploit a recognition within some circles in Washington that the Japanese economy required access to the Chinese market; the Washington embassy suggested that Britain should ensure that Japan was 'tarred as black as Hong Kong' when the question of trade with China arose.[66])

Despite these modifications in the US position, British thinking remained at odds with prevailing thought in the US. Indeed the Democratic administration pressurised the incoming Churchill government to further curtail trade with Communist China: it wanted tighter controls and the introduction of new restrictions to prevent British flag ships from transporting strategic goods to China.[67] Ultimately, the British government acquiesced in these American demands because it feared that if it did not American public opinion would turn against Britain, thus damaging Anglo-American relations and reducing the government's influence over the process of policy formation in Washington. Tomlinson warned that: 'There are a large number of sincere and not otherwise unfriendly or irresponsible Americans who think it morally wrong to trade with China at all at a time when we are engaged in a war with China in Korea to which there is no end in sight.'[68] Initially, Eden, conscious of US public and governmental sensitivity over this issue, agreed to review British procedures, but at the same time, not wanting to give the impression that Britain would comply with a more extensive embargo on trade with China, resisted US demands for tighter controls.[69] It was the inauguration of an Eisenhower administration determined to tighten controls on trade with China that forced Britain to accept and introduce new measures. The Foreign Office argued strongly that if Britain refused to support further restrictions on trade with China, the US would unilaterally impose a total embargo or even a naval blockade. In addition, in 1953 evidence also reached the Foreign Office that British ships had recently carried strategic goods to China. Potentially, this was politically explosive news, which in the hands of the US press or the US government could affect British standing and hence influence in Washington.[70] In March 1953, therefore, the cabinet, by introducing a system of voyage licensing, prohibited British and colonial ships from carrying strategic goods to China. It also refused British bunkering facilities to ships carrying strategic goods and agreed to re-examine the list of goods embargoed to China.[71] Later in 1953, the British government introduced further measures, again in response to developments in the US. In May and June 1953 Senator McCarthy, during the Senate Investigation Subcommittee hearing on East–West trade, alleged that British ships were trading in strategic goods with Communist China and that two ships had actually aided the communists to move troops and equipment.[72] McCarthy's case was not based on conjecture; the two ships accused of transporting Chinese troops were under British jurisdiction, registered by Anglo-Chinese companies in Hong Kong.[73] Given the tense and emotional situation in the US, these allegations again threatened to undermine the credibility of the British government's policy towards China and reduce Britain's standing with the American administration and the American public. The government tried to let the storm pass and then attempted to undermine McCarthy's case.[74] Ultimately, however, there was very little the British government could have done to prevent instances such as these. Unless British businessmen had withdrawn completely from Hong Kong and all far eastern trade, McCarthy would always have had plenty of ammunition to fire at the British government. At the time, the British embassy in Washington concluded that Britain would simply have to await a more favourable American attitude towards trading with China, which it believed would arrive once a Korean armistice had been signed.[75]

DEBATING BOMBS AND BLOCKADES

Further differences between the US and Britain arose over the military and economic options the US thought necessary to secure and ensure peace in the Far East. The initial disagreement between the powers was over a warning statement which the US thought should accompany an armistice. The British government opposed an American proposal threatening a total economic blockade and attacks on the Chinese mainland, but accepted a compromise which removed direct reference to retaliatory measures against the Chinese mainland – instead referring more generally to an allied response to a breakdown in the negotiations.[76] As peace talks stalemated, the US administration began to consider further military and economic measures, which it believed might induce the Chinese to negotiate. The Truman administration had, since the summer of 1951, been formulating a series of such options. Foot argues that by 1952 the administration had come to the conclusion that if the Korean negotiations proved unsuccessful then military operations in North Korea would be stepped up, Yalu power stations bombed, Chinese air bases attacked, an embargo or a naval blockade imposed and covert operations within China launched.[77] In October 1952 the American ambassador in India, Chester Bowles, informed the Indian government – implying that it should pass such a message to the Chinese – that if there was no armistice then the US would extend the war in Korea.[78] In May 1953, the Republican administration endorsed Democratic administration thinking and, in addition, included the added option of nuclear strikes against the Chinese mainland. Foot argues that if there had been no armistice by May 1954, the US would have been ready to initiate these various courses of action.[79]

Any further measures against China were unacceptable to the British government. The Chiefs of Staff did not believe they would have seriously reduced China's military capabilities, nor forced the Chinese to accept an armistice in Korea, but argued that they would have 'considerably' raised the risk of global war and been 'misinterpreted throughout Asia as an imperialist war of aggression'. The Chiefs of Staff proposed an alternative strategy whereby the West would respond to further Chinese aggression only in the area where aggression had been committed:[80] they wanted the conflict contained and not expanded. They argued that a naval blockade would only affect some 5 per cent of Chinese national income and, if it was to have a significant impact on China's military capabilities, would have to include the Soviet-controlled ports. A program of bombing Chinese administrative centres, communication infrastructure, or strategic sights would only be effective if nuclear weapons were used – an option that could not be considered for moral, strategic and political reasons. The Foreign Office agreed with this assessment. Robert Scott indicated that 'the State Department planners seemed to overlook the fact that a policy of deliberately worsening relations with China would not only have an effect in the Far East, but would also set up an inevitable chain reaction resulting in a general deterioration of international relations and an increased danger of global war'.[81] Eden and Churchill were initially less forthright than the Foreign Office. In November and December 1951, during Anglo-American discussions over the warning statement, they opposed a naval blockade of the Chinese coast but viewed attacks against Chinese air bases as less problematic. By mid-1952, however, when Washington again proposed military measures Eden vigorously opposed them. By then Eden was more critical of the American administration's approach to the ceasefire talks and disturbed by its decision not to consult Britain when it decided to bomb the Suiho power station on the Yalu in July 1952. With a presidential election imminent in November, he suggested that the administration was playing politics. While Churchill disagreed and did not want the British government to simply reject any American proposal, Eden aligned himself with the Canadians and supported an Indian peace initiative to break the deadlock in the peace talks. In a modified form, the resultant Krishna Menon UN resolution was eventually supported by the US, but was subsequently rejected by the Soviet Union and then by the Chinese communists.[82]

THE POWER OF RESTRAINT

Judging from the above discussion, it could be argued that British pressure may have been important in preventing the US administration extending the war into China. It was aware that any aggressive moves against China would be opposed by the majority of its allies and certainly believed that, given the volatile nature of congressional opinion, any differences of opinion on China could bring into question American support for NATO and reinvigorate isolationist sentiment in the US. Barton Bernstein accepts that this was a significant factor preventing the US from extending the war into mainland China.[83] Foot agrees, noting that because the Truman administration doubted whether the Soviet Union would become involved in a far eastern conflict, an alternative constraining factor had been removed. Nevertheless, it is important not to overplay the role of allied restraint. Of greater significance was an acceptance within the Truman administration that if the US escalated the war, it might neither bring peace nor seriously damage the Chinese economy.[84] The administration realised that military victory could only be achieved by committing further troops to Korea. This was impossible for political reasons.

Furthermore, Britain's influence on the US attitude towards the Korean armistice talks was marginal. Dulles and Eisenhower fully supported a policy of raising the temperature in Korea by threatening to use nuclear weapons against the Chinese mainland.[85] Whether Eisenhower would have gone through with these implicit threats in the event of a breakdown of negotiations is debatable, but what is clear is that the administration had circumvented allied criticism.[86] In his memoirs, Eisenhower acknowledges that a decision to extend the war into China would have caused severe difficulties with Britain, but argues that in the event of such a policy being adopted, any rifts induced could have been healed.[87]

British influence was limited because the British government could not afford to jeopardise its influence over American policy towards China or relations with the US. The bombing of the Yalu power stations and the de-neutralisation of Taiwan had an important influence on British thinking: both emphasised that the Truman and Eisenhower administrations were willing to adopt a unilateral policy in the Far

East without consulting the British government. The British, as much as the Americans, did not want differences over the policy towards China to threaten US military and economic aid to Europe. Peter Boyle notes that senior figures in the Foreign Office, such as Pierson Dixon and Frank Roberts, were increasingly concerned about a possible return to isolationist doctrines in the US and hence advocated a moderate line to be taken with the US over policy differences.[88] The Truman administration increasingly linked public disillusionment in the US over allied policy in the Far East with possible congressional disapproval of the doctrine of collective security in Europe.[89] The Eisenhower administration realised that Britain relied on the US more than the US relied on Britain and hence was less willing to consult Britain and subordinate US policy to European demands.[90]

WARRING RELATIONS

Political relations between the PRC and the British Conservative government, strained for the majority of 1952 and 1953, were very much a diplomatic side-show to the main military attraction in Korea. There were, however, some interesting developments which highlight China's attitude towards contact with the West and which reaffirm that China wanted peace in Korea. Unsurprisingly, Chinese political speeches and Chinese press articles became increasingly critical of British policy in Korea and towards China. Chou En-lai confirmed that China 'should not only listen to their [the West's] words but must also observe their actions';[91] the status of Britain's chargé d'affaires did not alter, and by the end of the Korean War consular representation in China had been reduced to two posts. Articles in the Chinese press and speeches by prominent Chinese government officials highlighted Britain's subservience to the US and its hostility towards China. In October 1952 Chang Han-fu, the Chinese Vice-Minister of Foreign Affairs, declared that 'the Chinese people cannot but feel indignant at the outrageous acts of the British government in being repeatedly and openly hostile to the PRC'.[92] In January 1952 the *NCNA* reported that 'Britain is still bent on serving obsequiously' its masters in the US; and in July 1952 the *NCNA* expressed 'deepest anger at the British Conservative government, which is obediently following the American aggressive policy of military adventurism'.[93] The *NCNA* argued that the Hong Kong government was allowing the colony to become a base for KMT banditry on the mainland, a policy which was merely 'part and parcel of

[the] British imperialists subservience to the US government's aggressive plans'.[94] The Chinese highlighted what they saw as the serious divergence between the ruling elites and the people in capitalist countries, arguing that this was being exacerbated in Britain by the close allegiance between the Conservative government and the US – symbolised by aggressive British policies in the Far East, and stemming from a British economy reliant on American economic aid. The *Peking Daily* argued that the British people 'cannot but view with grave concern the role played by Churchill in Washington', and referred to 'surging waves in Britain'.[95] Chou En-lai informed a meeting of China's foreign envoys that 'we should unite with and win over the former colonial and semi-colonial states and also the people of capitalist and imperialist countries'.[96] Chang Han-fu declared:

> There is no doubt that the policy of servility towards America pursued by the British Government ... is one which is step by step dragging the British people and the peoples within the orbit of the British Empire into the abyss of war. Not only Britain but any country which is willing to adopt a submissive policy towards the US and to be the accomplice of the US Government, will inevitably confront its people with the threat of war.[97]

The Chinese propaganda line was ideologically driven but retained a degree of tactical flexibility, which, with hindsight, was a precursor of the slight thaw in Sino-British relations beginning after July 1953. This process culminated in the Geneva conference of 1954, which formalised the diplomatic status of British representatives in China. Chou En-lai, for example, declared that 'the function of diplomacy is to deal with relations between states ... Through diplomacy we ultimately gain access to the people, influencing them and winning them over. We should be clear about this dialectical relation.'[98] Chou's statement may have indicated that the PRC only wanted relations with socialist and communist organisations within capitalist countries – in order to encourage subversive action against the capitalist state – but this is a rather narrow ideological position. More plausibly, Chou was reaffirming that the PRC wanted political contact with western states in order to moderate the West's position on China, to deepen differences between the US and Britain, and because China needed western capital goods. This position resulted from a CCP belief that contradictions in the Anglo-American alliance would deepen and undermine a western attempt to destroy Chinese communist rule. The *NCNA*, commenting on Churchill's meeting with Truman in January 1952, stated that 'in addition to their other divergences, America and Britain can never iron out their differences regarding their imperialist policies towards China'.[99] Chou informed the Chinese People's Political Consultative Conference that China had to aim at 'increasing the internal contradictions within the camp of imperialism', and should try to place 'increasingly serious difficulties in the way of the frantic scheme of the American imperialists to attack the camp of peace and democracy'.[100] This propaganda line, aimed at internal and external audiences, overplayed the inherent contradictions between and within imperialist countries, but also reflected a concern that the US would extend the Korean conflict into a general war against the Chinese mainland. China wanted to induce Britain to adopt a conciliatory line and encourage a modification of American policy in the Far East.

The Chinese communist desire to prevent the Korean conflict being extended into a general conflict in the Far East also shaped their attitudes. In order to secure a ceasefire, the Chinese had dropped their original demands for a seat in the UN and the return of Taiwan and were willing to compromise on a *quid pro quo* basis with the Americans. They only adopted a hostile stance in response to American diplomatic or military intransigence and did not deliberately attempt to induce stalemate in the talks. In May and June 1952 the Chinese tried in conjunction with India to formulate a compromise solution regarding the POW issue – the key sticking point for the negotiations. This initiative for peace only foreclosed when the Americans bombed the power stations on the Yalu. In March 1953, it was a Chinese compromise over the POW question which again revitalised the armistice talks. The Chinese wanted to end a war which was imposing severe financial, economic and hence political strain upon communist rule in China. These Chinese attempts to break the deadlock in ceasefire negotiations, however, do not necessarily mean that the American policy of increasing the military, economic and political pressure on the PRC forced the Chinese to sign the armistice in July 1953. It is more likely that US policy towards China actually delayed rather than aided the achievement of an armistice in Korea.[101]

CONCLUSIONS

Chinese communist attitudes towards the West prove that it was the British approach towards dealing with the PRC which was most suited to achieving an armistice in Korea. It was British policy-makers who recognised that a policy of increasing military, political and economic pressure on China would make the Chinese communist leadership more intransigent and less likely to agree to an armistice. However, Britain was relatively impotent when it came to influencing the direction of American policy towards the Far East. This was clearly evident in discussions over a strategy to end the Korean War, but was even more starkly exposed when, in the period after the Korean ceasefire, the British government tried to persuade the Eisenhower administration to scale down military pressure upon the Chinese and to relax China's diplomatic and economic isolation.

9 Rapprochement Denied: July–December 1953

They have learnt nothing, and forgotten nothing.

Charles-Maurice de Talleyrand, 1796

The end of the Korean War should have allowed the West to end China's diplomatic and economic isolation. But instead China's trade with the West remained restricted, its seat in the UN denied and its territory threatened by military measures. To understand why there continued to be a block on China's integration into the world trading and diplomatic communities, we need to examine the dynamics of British and American policies towards China. This chapter will assess the British government's thinking on diplomatic and economic relations with China. It will then examine British attempts to formulate a political settlement aimed at defusing cold war tensions in the Far East. It will next turn to British attempts to persuade the US to tone down or remove military, economic and political sanctions against Communist China. Finally, it will, by analysing US policy towards China, assess why the British government failed.

RAPPROCHEMENT DENIED

There was a shift in Sino-British relations in 1953. Although British officials in Peking 'heard very little of what was going on in that teeming city behind the official facade'[1] and contact with the Chinese government was parsimonious and ineffectual, a number of developments indicated that there had been a thaw in Sino-British relations: British staff attended the May Day celebrations, Chou En-lai sent a message upon Elizabeth II's coronation, the CPG agreed to simplify the restrictions on the Queen's messenger service, to ease travel restrictions on foreign nationals and to reply more rapidly to British communications.[2] In August, when Chou En-lai praised Churchill's tough attitude towards Syngman Rhee, President of the Republic of Korea, he declared that at least the British were gentlemen and he could deal with them.[3]

Despite such developments, the British government decided that an improvement in Britain's relations with the Chinese would 'reflect rather than precede a general improvement in the far eastern situation as a whole'.[4] Consequently, the government viewed the shift in China's attitude as potentially embarrassing.[5] Lord Reading, the Minister of State at the Foreign Office, pedantically justified the British position. He argued that as the Chinese were adept at 'passing over the anomalies in silence', 'silence' was now the best policy for Britain to pursue.[6] Although the issue of political relations with the Chinese did not reach the cabinet, it is safe to assume that Eden and Churchill did not want to take any initiative on relations with China. Meanwhile, by the summer of 1953, with Anthony Eden and Winston Churchill stricken by ill-health, Lord Salisbury, an ardent critic of the British decision to recognise the PRC, was the acting Foreign Secretary. The government's attitude sprang from a number of considerations. The Foreign Office was unsure whether the Chinese actually wanted to formalise relations; C. Crowe noted that the CCP was 'politely evasive on issues of substance' while its general attitude towards Britain left 'much to be desired'.[7] The Foreign Office believed that the slight thaw in political relations was a Chinese tactical ploy. It argued that the Chinese did not genuinely want relations but rather wanted to exploit and exacerbate Anglo-American differences over China. Moreover, it argued that the perceived economic benefits to be derived from full diplomatic relations were limited, encouraging trade with but not facilitating the exit of British firms from China. At times, some Foreign Office officials discounted what they argued was the false optimism of the business world on trade with the Chinese, arguing that the PRC would maintain many policies which hindered trade between China and the West.[8] There may also have been a realisation that trade with China could continue through Hong Kong with or without full diplomatic relations between Britain and China. However, these considerations do not explain the attitude of the Foreign Office in 1953. A positive British response was impossible not because the Foreign Office took into consideration issues of prestige or the economic worth of trade but because the establishment of diplomatic relations so soon after an armistice would have affected Anglo-American relations. Indeed, as Chapter 7 indicated, the government, prompted by the Board of Trade, was still responsive to business pressure for contact with the new regime.

SETTLING THE BIGGER ISSUES?

Since intervention in Korea, the Chinese had made an explicit link between a settlement for Korea and a general political settlement for the Far East, including a solution dealing with the status of Taiwan and China's admission to the UN. In 1951 the Chinese downplayed these demands to facilitate ceasefire negotiations but, in the aftermath of the Korean armistice, Chou En-lai made it clear that a political settlement for Korea must be combined with a settlement of other political questions. By 1953, such a settlement seemed possible because the Chinese position on certain issues had altered. Significantly, the CPG did not directly broach the seemingly intractable problem of Taiwan's reunification with China and instead placed greater emphasis on China's right to UN membership.[9] This more moderate Chinese position was underpinned by a seemingly counter-ideological adherence to 'peaceful co-existence', whereby the PRC would improve its international position by diplomacy and not military expansionism. The PRC argued that an armistice in Korea had 'created favourable conditions for securing an easing of international tensions' and had proved that the settlement of all internal disputes could be achieved by means of peaceful negotiation.[10] Evidently, the PRC wanted to switch resources – severely stretched by war – to economic development. In September 1953, at the Chinese People's Political Consultative Conference, Chou admitted that the strain on state finances during the Korean War had delayed the economic transformation of China and implied that the Chinese wanted to avoid another conflict so that resources could be concentrated on the economy.[11] Other CPG policies such as the encouragement it gave to Ho Chi Minh to take the offensive in North Vietnam, and attacks it launched on Chinese Nationalist-held offshore islands in 1954 and 1955, appear to contradict 'peaceful coexistence'. But, as Shu Guang Zhang argues, these policies were underpinned by a belief that short-term belligerency would force the US to accept the political *status quo ante* in Taiwan and Indochina.[12] The Chinese communist leadership believed that a peace initiative combined with an assertive military position would prove the most effective means of causing difficulties between the US and its allies, improving China's relations with Asian nations and reducing diplomatic, economic and military pressure on the PRC, thus allowing the economic development of China.

The British government recognised that before there could be any prospect of a *modus vivendi*, the West had to retreat from its confrontational position *vis-à-vis* China: military and economic measures against

China had to be reduced and the PRC admitted to the UN. Nevertheless, the British response was extremely cautious. The British government wanted Sino-Western talks to discuss a Korean settlement, the conflict in Indochina, China's admission to the UN and the future of Taiwan; but, in the immediate aftermath of the Korean armistice, a conference between China and the West was deemed premature.[13]

The British government believed that a change in the West's position would have to await a political conference on the Korean problem. Churchill and Eden argued that any concessions to the Chinese before a conference would be premature: they would remove the incentive for China to agree to a political settlement and be perceived by the US as rewards for aggression.[14] Equally, the conflict in Indochina complicated the western approach to Communist China because the French and American administrations would not relax pressures on the PRC until the situation there had stabilised. More fundamentally, the status of Taiwan was such a vexed problem that it might in any case prevent a general settlement between China and the West. Despite some tentative attempts to formulate a solution involving independence and a UN trusteeship for the island, the Foreign Office ruled out an initiative on Taiwan. Eden did not believe the PRC would accept a solution which did not uphold its sovereignty, while the US could not, for strategic and political reasons, allow Taiwan to fall into communist hands. Rab Butler, the Chancellor of the Exchequer, informed the House of Commons that policy towards China would be 'reconsidered at the appropriate time after an armistice, but will not be automatically modified immediately on the conclusion of the armistice'.[15] The bottom line was that Anglo-American relations would not be jeopardised to achieve a general settlement in the Far East. Given the level of mistrust and antagonism between China and the US, the government did not believe that a conference would facilitate progress towards a general political settlement. The determining factor was the hostility of the US. If Britain advocated a conference, the US might not attend and its attitude towards China would harden, precluding any meaningful discussion. Eden informed the Prime Minister that: 'If we were to press prematurely for a five power meeting we should risk increasing our difficulties with the Americans over the Far East and thus play into the Russian hands.' Eden argued that a cautious approach was the most appropriate one; by taking developments stage by stage, starting with a conference on Korea, China's attitude could be assessed and the Americans would be given time to 'accustom themselves, by slow degrees, to the idea of working with the Chinese Communists'.[16]

In the meantime the government would try to moderate the direction of American policy towards China. In November 1953 Eden, outlining British policy, argued that:

> We should seek to convince the US government and encourage them to convince American opinion, of the rightness of our approach, based upon acceptance of the facts of the situation, the avoidance of provocation, gradual progress towards more natural trading and diplomatic relations and the need to keep a toe in the door in case a divergence between China and Russia develops and can be exploited.[17]

Britain could not pressurise the Americans too forcefully to relax military, economic and diplomatic measures against China: this would simply make the Americans more intransigent. At the Berlin conference of February 1954, the US agreed, albeit very reluctantly, to attend a five-power conference on the Far East.[18] The resulting conference, held in Geneva between 26 April and 21 July 1954, has been portrayed as a diplomatic triumph for Britain, the conference engendering an improvement in Sino-British relations and achieving a temporary settlement to the Indochina problem. These successes cannot be denied, but, at the same time, the conference failed to achieve a wider political settlement for the Far East. Even in the aftermath of the Geneva conference, China was not admitted to the UN and the majority of the economic measures against the PRC remained in place. The failure of the 1954 talks to re-integrate China into world diplomatic and trading communities indicates that in 1953 the British government failed to shift the basis of American policy towards China.

SANCTIONING A DETERRENT

The decision by the UN nations involved in the Korean War to issue a 'greater sanctions' statement in conjunction with the Korean armistice set the wrong tone for the post-war Far East. This statement threatened the Chinese with retaliatory military action – not necessarily confined to the area of immediate aggression – if they broke the terms of the armistice. The British government did not believe the statement would foster a political settlement nor, necessarily, prevent further Chinese aggression. And yet it agreed to support it. However, in the months preceding the armistice in Korea, Syngman Rhee adopted a belligerent and obstructive attitude towards the peace process. This heightened British concerns. If the Chinese and North Koreans retaliated against

South Korean aggression would this constitute grounds for UN action in North Korea or perhaps even in China? The agreement struck between the US and Britain was ambiguous on this point and could thus allow Rhee to instigate a conflict between the West and China.[19] Underlying British government misgivings was the justifiable belief that such a statement would be misconstrued by the British public and exploited by opposition parties.[20] In July, therefore, the government, in conjunction with the Canadians, suggested changing the 'greater sanctions' statement from a public declaration to a private communication with Peking. But the American administration, determined to prevent UN members from 'wriggling out' of the greater sanctions statement, stood firm. The allies acquiesced and a joint statement was issued on 7 August 1953.

Anglo-American differences over the warning statement were symptomatic of a wider divergence over the West's response to further Chinese aggression. The American administration's strategy involved using explicit threats of massive retaliation against the Chinese mainland to deter Chinese aggression.[21] In December, a Joint Chiefs of Staff contingency plan advocated nuclear strikes against military targets in China, a blockade of the Chinese coast and the use of Chinese Nationalist forces against the Chinese mainland. Although Dulles expressed reservations, the Pentagon and Eisenhower fully backed extending the war into China.[22] Anthony Short notes that the US planned to intervene in Indochina primarily to deter Chinese aggression in the area.[23] Subsequently, China received threats of massive military retaliation during the Indochina crisis of 1954 and during the Taiwanese Straits crises of 1954, 1955 and 1958.[24] Whether the US would have attacked the Chinese in the event of Chinese aggression is still open to question; there was certainly an element of bluff in American threats, with Dulles and Eisenhower recognising that a massive attack on China would alienate world opinion.[25]

By contrast, in the event of future conflict, the British Chiefs of Staff wanted military action confined to the immediate area of the hostilities and not taken against targets across the whole of mainland China. They believed the West should respond to renewed communist aggression in Korea by using conventional bombing (to destroy airfields and communications in Manchuria), by reinforcing ground forces in Korea and by introducing a localised blockade of the Chinese coast from Kwangtung to the Yalu.[26] If, by contrast, the PLA attacked Indochina, they argued that French troops should respond, with American air support confined to attacks on Chinese territory adjacent to the

Indochina border.[27] The British Chiefs of Staff wanted to avoid a general conflict in the area, which might have jeopardised Britain's retention of Hong Kong, alienated Asian opinion and precipitated a third world war. However, despite agreeing with the Chiefs of Staff, the British government failed to shape US strategic thinking. During the Bermuda conference between the US, Britain and France held in December 1953, Eden and Churchill strongly criticised American plans to use nuclear weapons.[28] But while Eisenhower reassured Britain that he would not be irresponsible in the use of nuclear weapons, he also reaffirmed that their use was central to American military planning.[29] Britain's scope for influencing the direction of American military thinking was limited because the government could not jeopardise its influence over an American response to future Asian conflicts, especially as the situation in Indochina was deteriorating quickly. Britain wanted to encourage the US to accept a negotiated settlement for Indochina and prevent direct American military intervention in the area.[30] This desire to maintain influence in Washington also made the government reluctant to press the US into a more moderate position on China's economic and diplomatic contact with the West.

PEACE SEAT DENIED

The British government wanted China admitted to the UN but decided that, despite the armistice in Korea, an actual shift in Britain's voting policy in the UN would have to await further political developments in the Far East. There would be no government concession before a political conference on Korea. Eden, writing to Churchill in January 1954, acknowledged that, 'I think we are all agreed that Communist China will have to be brought into the UN sometime if the organisation is to work properly; but she must first work [for] her passage'.[31] As James Tang notes, the Foreign Office was uncertain whether China wanted membership; it had evidence that the Chinese had established a permanent delegation to the UN in 1950 only to disband it in 1951.[32] More instrumental was the fear that by making a move on this issue the government would damage Anglo-American relations. Churchill informed the cabinet that: 'We should be well advised . . . to avoid [creating a] further cause of Anglo-American misunderstanding at the present time . . . we should make due allowance for the strength of this feeling, which was not likely to be influenced by considerations of logic or expediency.'[33] Eden, more committed to China's admission than his Prime Minister, was also unwilling to jeopardise relations with the US to obtain this goal.[34] Roger Makins in Washington and Gladwyn Jebb at the UN in New York were predicting a 'storm of protest' in the US if Britain changed its policy. They warned that, with congressional elections in 1954 and public feeling so emotional, it was highly unlikely that the American position would be reversed for a number of years.[35]

Left-wing groups and individuals on the left of the Labour Party campaigned to have China admitted but their influence was more on the attitude of the Labour Party than that of the government. Aneurin Bevan, the most prominent leader of the Labour left, argued that China's admission to the UN would be 'a giant stride towards the pacification of the world'.[36] The Labour Party front bench, whilst more willing to link the issue to a political conference on Korea, did not press the government too strongly. Morrison argued that 'it would be good business for the West if, when this Korea business is settled, China was admitted to the UN'.[37] The British press was deeply divided: the *Daily Herald* argued that China's admission was a vital step towards world peace, while the *Daily Telegraph* strongly opposed China's admission. The middle ground was held by the *Manchester Guardian* and *The Times,* who were sympathetic to China's admission but recognised the political difficulties that prevented a shift in voting policy before a political conference on Korea.[38] Parliamentary, press and public pressure made the Conservative administration stop and think but did not force its hand.[39]

It was not, however, domestic opinions but the attitude of the US which shaped the government's position in 1953. The problem was that the US administration still wanted to prevent China's admission to the UN. It reasoned that China's admission would reward the PRC for military aggression in Korea, represent a 'psychological victory' for communism, provide the CCP with a world stage and jeopardise the UN seat of the Chinese Nationalists.[40] Eisenhower and Dulles had reservations about China's permanent exclusion from the UN but reaffirmed that the US would oppose China's admission at least in the short to medium term. The British government succeeded in preventing the US from automatically continuing the 'moratorium agreement', now legally out of date after the Korean armistice.[41] In September the cabinet agreed that Britain would abstain if the US tried to introduce a motion that attempted to postpone the question for a further year.[42] But the government failed to get the US to link China's admission to a political conference on Korea. Moreover, the strength of US pressure forced the British government to harden its attitude towards China's admission. In November 1953, at the Bermuda conference, Dulles inferred that Britain could and should make a distinction between recognising the communist state and giving it moral support or political and economic aid. Consequently, in January 1954 Dulles urged Makins to take a stronger line politically against the Chinese communists, arguing that Britain had to prevent China from gaining a seat in the UN.[43] In January 1954 the government agreed to co-operate with the US to forestall, for the duration of the 8th session, any discussion of China's admission to the UN.

A TRADE WAR CONTINUED

Now that an armistice had been signed in Korea, the British government wanted economic sanctions on China eased. Trade was integral to British policy towards China – it integrated China into the world economy, made its economy less reliant on the Soviet Union and moderated the PRC's behaviour.[44] Churchill informed Eisenhower that he 'looked upon trade as a means of achieving the desired result of keeping China's nose above water'.[45] However, less altruistic reasons explain policy. As Chapter 7 highlighted, the government was coming under more intensive pressure from businessmen concerned by evidence that other nations, notably West Germany, were increasing trade with China. In addition, the government viewed Sino-British trade as essential for maintaining Britain's colonial and business presence in the Far East. The issue of rubber exports from Malaya is useful for highlighting the role that these forces played in shaping government policy. Eden raised the question of rubber exports with the US administration in December 1953. He informed the US that Ceylon and Indonesia were exporting rubber to China. The government wanted to ensure that Malayan rubber exports were not discriminated against, especially important because world-wide demand for rubber had fallen in the aftermath of the Korean War.[46] Earnings from Malayan rubber exports were important for the British economy because, as part of a Malayan trading surplus with the dollar area, they helped to off-set a British deficit with the dollar area. They were also vital to the Malayan economy and hence, to some extent, prevented further political instability in the colony.

However, it was political considerations which made an immediate relaxation of the embargo impossible. Before Britain could begin to encourage trading contact with the Chinese, there had to be an easing of international tensions in the Far East. The government agreed with the French and the Americans that controls would only be re-examined 'in the light of subsequent events'.[47] The government recognised that a relaxation might cause grave difficulties for Anglo-American relations and might harden American thinking towards a political conference between China and the West. Wenguang Shao believes the 'British government was entrenched in its dogma, unable to initiate any relaxation for fear of being out of step with the political tensions between China and the US'.[48] Shao's conclusion seems fair, but it must also be placed firmly within the context of American domestic politics. The attacks by Senator Joseph McCarthy (Republican, Wisconsin) on British trade with China continued into the post-Korean armistice period. In September 1953 McCarthy asked the British embassy in Washington to supply a list of ships that had been chartered on a bareboat basis to China. In November 1953 he publicly announced that between 1952 and 1953 trading by British ships with China had increased by 50 per cent. In December, on NBC, he declared that 'while Communist China has, in her blood stained dungeons, American young men, we should not give one dollar to any ally who is in turn shipping the sinews of economic and military strength to Red China'.[49] This was no time for the government to be taking a unilateral initiative or to be forcing the US to modify its position on the issue. Britain occasionally refuted McCarthy's allegations, but more often simply ignored them; the government feared further publicity would only stoke rather than extinguish McCarthy's fire. Lord Reading, Minister of State at the Foreign Office, rejected a Foreign Office proposal for a 'white paper' setting out British thinking on trade with the Chinese, arguing that any public reference to British policy would merely exacerbate the British and American governments' problems with McCarthy.[50]

There is some evidence to suggest that the American administration was more amenable to a shift in policy on trade than on military measures against the Chinese or over China's admission to the UN. The end of the Korean War had removed the strategic imperative behind economic controls. The administration recognised that pressure from allied nations for an easing of trading restrictions would mount in the aftermath of an armistice in Korea. And, more significantly, the administration realised that trade with China was useful for the Japanese economy.[51] Japanese politicians and businessmen were becoming increasingly restive about this issue. In July 1953 the Diet passed a resolution demanding that trade between China and Japan be eased to COCOM levels; when Japan had been admitted to COCOM, with the establishment of CHINCOM in September 1952, the Truman administration forced the Japanese to maintain controls tighter than COCOM levels.[52] Eisenhower, conscious of the burden that American aid to Japan placed upon state finances, wanted to increase Japan's trade with the world. He adopted a realistic and pragmatic approach to this problem; at a NSC meeting in November 1953 he announced that trade with the communist bloc should be judged by the criteria of 'net gain' and not based upon ideological considerations. He went so far as to state that he would send jet planes to the Chinese communists if he thought the US would gain from such a transaction.[53]

Despite evidence that American thinking was changing, there was no shift towards a more liberal trading policy. In June and July 1953 the administration sought a guarantee from Britain that the UN economic embargo on China would continue even after the signing of the Korean armistice.[54] The US rejected a suggestion that the London preparatory meeting of COCOM should discuss the issue of trade with China, arguing that any initiative had to await further progress towards a far eastern settlement. At the Bermuda conference in December 1953, Dulles reaffirmed that the US wanted to maintain economic pressure on the PRC and gave no indication when the UN economic embargo on China could be relaxed. He agreed that the West had to trade with China but still would not agree to remove the restrictions on this trade.[55] Even if there was a radical change in Chinese behaviour or a political settlement for Korea or Indochina, the Americans would not commit themselves to reducing economic pressure on the Chinese.

LEAVING IT TO THE AMERICANS

Anglo-American exchanges on these three issues illustrate that the American administration was opposed to any relaxation of the stringent measures introduced to meet Chinese aggression in Korea. Indeed, the US ensured economic sanctions, military containment and international exclusion formed the basis of the western approach to Communist China from the 1950s to the 1970s. The administration's policy was the product of two closely connected factors: domestic pressures within the US and its own strategic thinking.

The US domestic setting shackled the Eisenhower administration on three issues: trade with China, China's admission to the UN and over a political settlement for the Far East. Trade with Communist China was a highly sensitive political issue within the US and hence it was extremely difficult for the Eisenhower administration to relax trading restrictions without suffering severe criticism from the right of the Republican Party and especially from McCarthy. At the 169th meeting of the NSC, Eisenhower informed his colleagues that 'the great difficulty, of course, was in the public relations aspect of any policy which involved trading with Communist China. Demagogues would raise a hue and cry about building up the economies of nations who use their resources to kill our soldiers.'[56] Nancy Bernkopf Tucker argues that Eisenhower lamented this domestic political constraint.[57] Thomas C. Reeves notes that Eisenhower detested McCarthy but was extremely reluctant to publicly undermine the Senator from Wisconsin, especially as Robert Taft (Republican, Ohio), Senate Majority Leader, and William Knowland (Republican, California), Senate Majority Leader from January 1953, sympathised with McCarthy.[58] If the right of the Republican Party had any notion that the Eisenhower administration was yielding to British pressure on this question, America's scope for manoeuvre would have been curtailed. Equally, China's admission to the UN would also have caused grave political embarrassment, exacerbating tensions between the administration and Congress. The *Manchester Guardian* admitted that 'popular feeling [in the US] against Communist China would destroy the political career of any American in office who publicly advocated letting the Communists in the UN'.[59] The domestic environment precluded a political settlement with Communist China. In February 1954 when the US government agreed to attend a conference on far eastern matters, the reaction of the American right was extremely hostile. William Knowland, the Senate Republican leader, announced that 'the American people will not consent to a *Far Eastern Munich*'.[60] There was a domestic political market that ensured a non-liberal American approach.

Evidence from British and American government records suggesting that elements within the US administration considered a more flexible approach to China in 1953 reinforces the thesis that the domestic political climate acted as the main constraint preventing a change in American policy towards China. The Foreign Office noted that judicious private comments made by members of the US administration contrasted with their bombastic and moralistic public denouncements of Chinese communism.[61] Indeed the attitude of Dulles has been revised in the historical literature. Most commentators now acknowledge that his attitude towards communism was more complex than originally thought. Tucker believes that Dulles wanted a more liberal approach. She argues he advocated China's admission to the UN in 1951 and even by 1953 still believed that China would have to be admitted in the longer term.[62] Eisenhower's position on China was also more flexible than his public pronouncements and the traditional assessments of the President's policy have suggested. Eisenhower acknowledged that there was an inconsistency in the way the West was responding to communism: it had recognised the Soviet Union but not Communist China. He was also inclined to view trade between Japan and China as a means of stimulating tensions between China and the Soviet Union.[63] At the Bermuda conference, Dulles, in a private conversation with Eden, argued that his administration wanted to adopt more 'reasonable' policies towards China, but had to take into account the 'political dynamite' attached to a shift in America's China policy.[64] Tucker goes so far as to suggest that Dulles, 'under siege by the right-wing of his party', made a conscious decision to 'protect himself and policies he considered more central' by adopting a hardline over China.[65]

The British Foreign Office came to accept that societal hostility towards Chinese communism and political pressure would preclude an immediate modification of the American position. Nevertheless, it hoped that the anti-communist political culture in the US would change. The Foreign Office viewed American policy over the previous three years as a knee-jerk reaction to communist aggression in Korea reinforced by domestic hysteria against Chinese communism. Consequently, the Foreign Office decided to try and reshape the political debate within the US. To this end, Jebb and Makins privately attempted to influence the views of American politicians and journalists.[66] The Foreign Office believed that if the US public could be convinced that trade with the Chinese communists was in the best interest of the West, and would not merely benefit the communists, then it would be easier for the US to review its position on trade with China.[67] British reasoning was straightforward: if the US public was made aware of British thinking they would be more amenable to a shift in US policy towards China. The radical change in American attitudes towards Japan in the aftermath of the Pacific War may have had an important impact on Foreign Office thinking. By the early 1950s, the US public had seemingly come to accept Japan as a strategic ally and recipient of economic aid whereas previous public perceptions had been highly racist and confrontationist.[68] If this development was an influence, then the Foreign Office had both overestimated the shift in public attitudes towards Japan and overlooked the fact that, whereas the West had defeated the Japanese, American boys had died at the hands of the Chinese in Korea only to achieve a stalemate. More significantly, whereas in 1945 the shift in American attitudes towards Japan had been orchestrated from above, in 1953 the American political system did not want a conciliatory line on China.

The British government underestimated the degree to which US policy towards China was a coherent strategy for dealing with the threat posed by Communist China. In contrast to the British government which sought ultimately to forge a *modus vivendi* between Britain and China, US policy aimed at restricting diplomatic and economic contact with the communists and maintaining, without precipitating a further conflict in the Far East, a substantial military deterrent in the area.[69] In June 1953 the NSC declared that: 'It is important to our national security, as well as to the objective of obtaining an acceptable settlement in Korea, that political and economic pressure against Communist China be developed and maintained during the immediate post armistice period.'[70] In November 1953 the NSC formalised a policy of maintaining maximum economic, political and military pressure upon the PRC.[71] The American administration, recognising that its major allies disagreed with this approach, opposed British pressure to change the West's policy towards China.[72] The NSC did not feel that its allies would diverge significantly from their stance on China in the immediate aftermath of the Korean armistice, but argued that the allies would attempt to create 'an atmosphere in which resistance to communism and Soviet imperialism will be weakened'.[73]

In addition, the US administration wanted to make CCP control of China as difficult as possible.[74] The US administration did not believe that the political and economic isolation of China would engender political and societal movements that would seriously affect or even threaten Chinese communist rule – at least not in the short to medium term – but argued it would deny the regime international legitimacy and slow economic development, thus reducing the military resources available to China for aggression in the Far East. The US reasoned that economic and political concessions or any relaxation of military sanctions on China would merely allow the Chinese communists to consolidate their control more effectively and encourage further Chinese aggression.[75] Tucker argues that the American attempt to 'exile China beyond the pale' was based on a belief that if China broke out of America's ideological encirclement, then 'its internal political and economic health would be significantly enhanced, thus furthering the Mao regime's development, survivability and influence'.[76] Equally, isolation forced the Chinese to rely on Soviet aid and to acquiesce in the Soviet ideological line. It was believed that this might cause tensions between China and the Soviet Union by impinging on the Chinese communist's desire for political and economic independence. At this stage the question of providing an 'avenue of escape' for the PRC was deemed academic because the Chinese had not indicated that they wanted rapprochement with the West. The US administration actually argued that a hardline with China would stimulate 'a desire for an avenue of escape' and that only once this had become evident would the US re-examine its policy.[77] Gordon Chang notes that the US administration remained uncertain whether its main objective was the weakening of communist control in China or the weakening of the Sino-Soviet alliance, but argues that this contradiction was only 'apparent' and not 'substantive': in 1953 the aims were perceived to be linked.[78] John Lewis Gaddis argues that the Republican administration was continuing a 'wedge strategy' which was, in essence, the same as that advanced by the Truman administration, the key difference being that the Republican administration had successfully reconciled this strategy with the hostile political climate in the US.[79]

CONCLUSIONS

The Korean War had radically altered the way in which the West interacted diplomatically and economically with Communist China. In the aftermath of the Korean War, British attempts to move away from a confrontational position were tentative and generally ineffective. The slow progress towards a Korean settlement and the escalating conflict in Indochina made this transition more difficult, but it was the attitude of the US which precluded a change in the West's position. Whether the British government should have adopted a more independent line on China is ultimately a subjective question. Given the inconsistencies in American policy towards China such an independent approach may have forced the US to reconsider its policy. It may also have allowed a US administration to circumvent domestic pressures on it, by transferring the blame for a change in policy abroad to Britain. At the time, the British government could not contemplate such a strategy. It would have been far too risky. A more openly independent British foreign policy on China may have severely strained the Anglo-American relationship. In addition, given American thinking on China, it may have reinforced and not broken down the domestic constraint on the Eisenhower administration and also coalesced opinion within it around a hardline approach to China. The British government concluded that it was in its interest to maintain a united western policy in the Far East and to do nothing to jeopardise the basis of Anglo-American relations. There was no further Anglo-American divergence on far eastern strategy as there had been over recognition in 1949. By 1953, however, British government policy was out of step with political, press and business groups who wanted a more liberal policy towards Communist China. This situation contrasted with the unison between policy and public sentiment in the US.

Conclusions

THE STATE OF POLITICAL AND ECONOMIC RELATIONS

By the end of 1953, Sino-British political relations were at a low ebb, surpassed only by the deterioration in relations during the Cultural Revolution. From 1950 to 1954, political relations between an imperialist western state and a revolutionary Marxist-Leninist regime proved difficult. There had been diplomatic impasse for four years. China and Britain did not enter into formal, full, diplomatic relations and China was not admitted to the UN. The number of British diplomatic representatives in China fell and the status of those who remained was ambiguous and precarious. China did not have representation in Britain. Culturally, relations were also at a low point. In China, as war raged in Korea and the forces of social and economic change were unleashed at home, nationalism became xenophobic and jingoistic. In Britain, with bodies such as the Britain–China Friendship Association perceived as communist front organisations and the mainstream British press brandishing the PRC as a brutal revolutionary regime, popular perceptions turned: China was unstable and threatening. All wars breed contempt and hatred: the Korean War was no exception.

Economic relations between Britain and China underwent revolutionary changes between 1950 and 1954. Most dramatically, British foreign direct investments in China became financially and politically untenable. The CPG intensified and, more often than not, created demand and supply problems for British firms which meant they could not produce, buy or sell nor close down. Contemplated since 1950, and negotiated from 1952 onwards, the final exit of British firms was not achieved until 1955. British investment in China would not rise again until the opening of the Chinese economy in the 1980s and 1990s. Trade between Britain and China, at a historically low level in 1949, rose in 1950, collapsed from late 1950 to 1952 and then slowly recovered from 1952. Given that China wanted capital goods for post-war economic reconstruction and to aid a programme of heavy industrialisation, trade was low. The institutional framework for organising trade also changed, with Chinese state trading agencies replacing foreign and Chinese private companies. Increasingly these were located in Hong Kong, which the CPG accepted as a base for British and foreign busi-

199

nessmen and as an important source of foreign exchange. Hong Kong's economy, reliant on entrepôt trade, entered a severe recession; but its post-war economic restructuring away from commerce into manufacturing began, aided by the cheap and skilled labour, the entrepreurial talent and the capital which had entered Hong Kong from the mainland. Hong Kong is the only success story to tell. Other developments symbolised the resurgence of Chinese nationalism, highlighted Britain's imperial retreat and indicated Britain's political impotence with regard to Sino-British relations.

Several threads emerged from the complex weave of Sino-British-American relations. Changes in the pattern of international political and economic relations are explained by the impact of Chinese nationalist thought on the actions of the PRC, the impact of American political and economic hegemony, and the British determination to adhere to a liberal approach towards China.

CHINESE NATIONALIST THOUGHT

The Chinese state was the key actor shaping the international political economy of Sino-British relations. The PRC postponed formal political relations with Britain, adopted an obstructionist and intransigent attitude towards British nationals in China, made the position of British direct investments on Chinese soil impossible and sought to limit and control Sino-British trade. The Chinese position stemmed from a determination to prevent external influence over Chinese economic development. This attitude was ideologically derived, but the ideology was more nationalist than Marxist-Leninist and was profoundly influenced by the CCP's interpretation of the impact of imperialism on China. The CCP believed that contact with the West would be socially divisive and would undermine the power of the Chinese state, seen as the vital agent for achieving Chinese economic development. The Chinese did not simply believe there were political and social costs attached to an 'open door' policy, they believed integration into the world economy would underdevelop China. Capitalist forces needed to be controlled if China was to become economically prosperous and politically strong,[1] a Chinese view of the world that did not change until the 1980s.

There are some contradictions in the Chinese position that need to be explained: China accepted that Hong Kong was British and wanted some political and economic relations with Britain. Diplomatic factors partly explain the Chinese attitude. The Chinese leadership argued there were inherent contradictions within and between capitalist countries, which they sought to exploit – partly by improving political and economic relations with Britain. It believed these would lead to the inevitable decline of western societies. It could also be argued that the Chinese, fearful of the direction of American policy towards China, wanted to ensure that the British government was a brake on Amercian adventurism in Asia. As with similar British and American diplomatic nuances, however, there were more deep-rooted factors explaining their policy: geo-strategic reasoning legitimised but did not explain policy. A more important influence on Chinese foreign policy was China's determination to reduce its reliance on the Soviet Union. The Sino-Soviet relationship was a deterrent against the threat of a US attack, provided political and diplomatic support, and economic aid for reconstruction. The Soviet Union was also China's most important trading partner. Given the social base of the Chinese communist movement and the underdeveloped and uneven state of the Chinese economy in the early 1950s, the CPG could not generate growth and structural change by purely domestic means and hence it turned to the Soviet Union. The Soviet Union attached high political costs to aid, whilst Soviet capital and foreign exchange proved insufficient for Chinese development plans.[2] China wanted economic and political contact with the West because courting political relations with the western imperialists would give China some clout with the Soviet imperialists and would provide the CPG with some flexibility in its external economic relations. Hong Kong was especially important in this respect: it provided foreign exchange and contact with western merchants. Hong Kong was perceived to be a place where the social, political and economic costs of contact with the West could be reduced. Its role was similar to that of Canton in the early nineteenth century.

AMERICAN POLITICAL AND ECONOMIC HEGEMONY

After the PRC, the US had the greatest impact on the international political economy of Sino-British relations. In contrast to British policy, the Truman and Eisenhower administrations adopted an anti-liberal approach to Communist China. On the political side, US administrations did not to recognise the PRC, sought to prevent China's admission to the UN and tried to deny China a say in any future political settlement for Korea. On the military side, the US threatened to impose a naval blockade, to bomb Chinese cities (perhaps by using atomic bombs) and to unleash Chinese Nationalist forces. On the economic side, the US introduced an extremely stringent trade embargo on the PRC and curtailed Britain's and most of the western world's trade with China. There remained a certain degree of flexibility in the American attitude. Historians, even with different views on actual policy such as Gordan Chang, Rosemary Foot and Nancy Tucker, agree that there were a range of opinions on policy towards China within US administrations. These narrowed over the period but, as Rosemary Foot has argued, bureaucratic power balances, transformed by war in Korea, were an important influence on US policy. The Pentagon generally wanted a hardline, embracing containment and perhaps the roll back of Chinese communism, whereas the State Department wanted a containment policy which kept America's allies on board.[3] US administrations were reluctant to enforce a total western economic embargo on China, especially on Sino-Japanese trade, and also relaxed their own embargo on Hong Kong, a colony reliant on imported raw materials from the US and on the entrepôt revenue from US-far eastern trade. US administrations also expressed reservations about the worth of securing Communist China's long-term exclusion from the UN. But, even after the Korean War, the US refused to retreat from its hardline on China. The Eisenhower administration resisted pressure for an easing of the economic embargo, refused Communist China's admission to the UN, and remained committed to Taiwan as an anti-communist bulwark in the Far East. It was not until the Sino-American rapprochement in the early 1970s that the US recognised Communist China.

Historians are divided on what explains the US approach to China but a number of factors stand out. Firstly, Amercian policy was justified in internal memoranda as a rational strategy for stimulating tensions between China and the Soviet Union. The US approach forced the Chinese to rely diplomatically and financially on a Soviet Union which did not want to fund Chinese economic development, which could not effectively represent the CPG on a world stage and which would also try to extend its political and economic influence in China. The US argued that these tensions might eventually cause a Sino-Soviet schism and would certainly weaken and preoccupy the communist enemy. This strategy was influenced by the political climate in the US. Public opinion and the right-wing of the Republican Party, especially in the form of the China Lobby, were vehemently hostile to the Chinese communist regime and wanted the US to provide support for the Chinese Nationalists on Taiwan. The intensity of the political climate in America meant the administration had no choice but to apply maximum pressure on the Chinese. Doubts within US administrations about strategy towards China tend to reinforce the view that the American domestic environment precluded a more flexible approach. However, assessing the true impact of political sentiment on policy-making is difficult. The US position on China reflected but also exacerbated domestic hostility towards Communist China in the US. Administrations used public opinion to reinforce a hardline American position on China and popular anti-communism provided US administrations with the political authority to contain communism in Asia. This complex relationship between the US public and American foreign policy did not change until the Vietnam War shattered illusions of American power.

As was the case with Communist China's external relations, US foreign policy-making had an imperial slant. US policy towards Taiwan must be central to any analysis of Sino-American relations in the period. The US commitment to Taiwan ruled out any rapprochement with the PRC in the early 1950s. The decision to prevent Taiwan falling to communist forces and to finance Taiwanese economic development was taken before the outbreak of war in Korea, and then became set in imperial concrete once China and the West were at war in Korea. This decision was partly influenced by an American decision taken in 1947 to restore Japan as an industrial power in Asia; a decision which in itself resulted from a twin realisation that the US economy and US business needed Japanese recovery and that, without a stable non-communist China, Japan would be the only guarantor of US influence in Asia.[4] Consequently, and because Japan was being denied access to Chinese raw materials and Chinese demand for consumer and producer goods, Taiwan and South Korea needed to be incorporated into an Asian trading bloc which could then gain access to European and other Asian markets. Gabriel Kolko and Bruce Cumings argue that the structure of the political economy in the US was important and shaped this policy orientation.[5] What has become equally clear during the course of this study is that the political economy in Britain had an equally important, but strikingly different, influence on British policy towards China.

IMPERIALISM REVIVED: BRITISH POLICY

Throughout the period British government policy continued to work within the liberal framework established by recognition. On the political side, British governments sought to establish relations with the PRC,

to admit China to the UN and to involve China in a political settlement to diffuse international cold war tensions in the Far East. On the
economic side, British governments wanted to encourage trade with
China and to maintain, if possible, foreign direct investments in China.
They were also determined to retain Hong Kong. There were differences between the Labour and Conservative governments; the desire
for a *modus vivendi* with China was more coherently expressed during
the Labour government while the Conservative government could not
decide how to reconcile such a *modus vivendi* with its commitment to
a non-communist Taiwan. However, Labour and Conservative governments were forced to retreat from these aims over the course of the
1950s. Britain introduced and maintained an economic embargo on trade
with China, did not try to break the diplomatic impasse over the issue
of political relations and accepted Taiwan as the 'second China'. During the first stage of the Korean War, between June and October 1950,
the British government worked for China's admission to the UN, strongly
resisted American pressure for economic controls on trade with China
and tried to formulate a solution which defused tensions over Taiwan
by establishing the framework for its return to China. Once China had
intervened in the Korean War, the emphasis of British policy shifted.
Between 1951 and 1953, British governments acquiesced in US initiatives to prevent China's admission to the UN, to tighten controls on
strategic exports and to increase military pressure on China. Britain
also accepted that Taiwan should not be returned to the communists;
the Labour Party argued the island should be declared independent
while the Conservative administration was willing to accept Chinese
Nationalist control.

   This retreat was the result of a number of factors. The British government reconsidered policy because the CPG refused to establish political relations with Britain, destroyed British investments in China, tied
itself to the Soviet Union and fought the West in Korea. With British
prestige slighted, the government became reluctant to 'chase' the Chinese for trade, diplomatic relations and peace. The influence of these
factors, however, was ephemeral. Britain's retreat from its internationalist stance during the Korean War can only be explained with reference to Anglo-American relations. Once the US had made a firm
commitment to Taiwan, British governments faced a trade-off: they
could either retreat from a liberal policy on China and ensure work-
able relations with the US, or could pursue a liberal policy towards
China at the cost of good Anglo-American relations. Given that Anglo-

American relations were the bedrock on which British foreign relations were based, the first option was the only realistic one open to policy-makers. In the 1950s the US allowed Britain to shelter from the full force of the liberal international order by providing the British economy with dollars and underpinning, both politically and economically, the British empire, including Hong Kong. The retention of empire gave Britain safe markets, non-dollar areas of supply for raw materials, support for the pound (because Sterling Area balances were held in London), and Great Power status. Whether a breach over policy towards China in this period would have seriously jeopardised Anglo-American relations is uncertain. US State Departments, under Acheson and even Dean Rusk, were deeply committed to American support for Britain. But within administrations, in Congress and in the public arena, there were a range of opinions on Communist China and the value of US support for Europe. Indeed there were many who were more committed to US aid for Taiwan than to Britain. Ultimately British governments neither wanted to damage relations with the US nor fuel an internal public debate in America about the value of the Atlantic alliance. It was only in the early months of 1951 that the Labour Party, riven by factional and ideological divides, came close to entering an Atlantic abyss.

The trade-off between policy towards China and Anglo-American relations poses the obvious question: why did British governments pursue and continue to adhere to a liberal policy towards China? Two influences arose in the period which had some influence on British thinking. Firstly, it could be argued that the government was reluctant to lose 'face' by reversing policy on China, a recurring theme in many British Foreign Office documents. But considerations of prestige are multi-faceted: surely the government lost more 'face' by opposing the Americans. Secondly, British policy-makers believed that adhering to a *modus vivendi* could be used as a vehicle to moderate American policy towards China. The British Foreign Office did believe its 'wise head' could reign in the young American diplomatic blood. But as previous chapters have shown, Britain was not a strong influence on American policy-making. In 1950, if the priority for Britain was to prevent a Sino-American conflict in the Far East, then British policy failed. From then on, Britain influenced the direction of US policy, but the power of restraint was extremely limited. Moreover, these two factors were not just misconceived influences on British government policy-making but also minor ones. This brings us back to some of the factors which explain the British decision to recognise China in 1950.[6]

Throughout the period British governments maintained that their policy was the best approach for engendering Sino-Soviet tensions, thus weakening the communist world. However, developments between 1950 and 1954 altered Foreign Office views on the Sino-Soviet relationship. During the Korean War, the British Foreign Office accepted that Sino-Soviet relations were close and unlikely to be influenced by the West. Hopes for Titoism in China had been misconceived; even in the event of a Sino-Soviet split, the PRC would not have aligned with the West. Moreover, if this was the aim, British governments may have been better off abandoning attempts to develop political and economic relations with China and instead siding with the Americans. The Chinese would not have reached rapprochement with the West if the US remained hostile. Equally, while this is not the place to assess the differing British and American approaches to China – in any case a rather subjective enterprise – it could be argued that American attempts to isolate the PRC and make communist rule as difficult as possible were more effective in the long term in causing China's split with Moscow. Clearly talk of playing off one power against another was a way of legitimising policy along the corridors of Whitehall rather than an explanation for British policy.

A number of political influences continued to act as a block on a more vigorous British containment policy in the Far East. In Britain there remained a political consensus, between the left-wing of the Labour Party, left-wing groups and pacifist organisations, in favour of a liberal policy towards China. These groups lobbied for trade with China, China's admission into the UN and the return of Taiwan to China. Their zeal was intensified by a belief that British and American policies towards China might precipitate a third world war, and their influence on British public opinion and government thinking was at its strongest immediately after China's intervention in Korea. It remained throughout a thoughtful thorn in the side of policy decision-makers.[7] More importantly, Asian opinion was still, despite the evident orthodoxy of the communist regime in China, strongly in favour of China's acceptance into the world community and vehemently objected to blatant American hostility towards China. By divorcing containment from a *modus vivendi*, Britain would have alienated Asian nations, and thus damaged its relationship with the Asian Commonwealth, which British governments perceived to be vital to maintain Britain's economic and political interests in the Far East.

British business interests were the most powerful lobbying influence over policy towards China. The business lobby was divided. It contained British manufacturing firms, represented by bodies such as Chambers of Commerce and the FBI, and other British-based trading organisations such as the '48 Group of traders', the London Export Corporation, the British Council for the Promotion of International Trade, and the China Association, which represented mercantile firms in the Far East and British multinationals with interests in China.[8] All these business lobby groups agreed with the basic strategy adopted by the government towards China: they wanted China integrated into the world economy and did not question the retention of empire in the Far East. The relationship between the British state and businesses with interests in China was highly complex. Some government policies worked directly against the interests of businesses. The government failed to support British businesses either financially or politically in their struggle to withdraw from China, imposed an economic embargo on the PRC, did not encourage British firms to attend the Moscow or Peking conferences and did not set up a Sino-British trade mission in Peking. Clearly the government was not a pawn in the hands of businessmen. And thus it would be wrong to conclude that business interests shaped government policy or that the state represented particular class interests. First and foremost the British state was acting in its own interests, which it perceived to be the maintenance of a global role for Britain, an institutional response that was clearly a legacy of Britain's hegemonic position in the world economy pre-1914.[9]

British governments assumed that trade with China and the retention of Hong Kong were in the best interests of the British economy and thus British industry. However, in the case of policy towards China, these state goals benefited certain mercantile interests more than industrial ones.[10]

Hong Kong's status as a British colony both determined British government policy towards China and ensured a symbiotic relationship between the British state and British mercantile interests. Two developments over the course of 1950–54 made Britain's retention of Hong Kong possible: the CPG's acceptance of British control and an American realisation that a capitalist outpost in China was useful and should be supported. The British government wanted Hong Kong for numerous reasons. Firstly, it was cheap to run; the overheads of an indefensible and undemocratic state were low and the colony's economy was self-sufficient in dollars. Secondly, it was perceived to be useful for the British economy. Hong Kong's sterling balances were part of the Sterling Area balances held in London thought integral for maintaining the value of the pound, while, as an entrepôt centre for British and international business, it generated invisible earnings.[11] Finally, it symbolised Britain's continued political influence in the Far East. The government's decision to retain Hong Kong directly benefited British mercantile concerns, which could overcome the loss of their business interests in China by relocating to Hong Kong. Equally, Hong Kong's economy, and thus British rule, was not viable without capital from overseas and access to world markets: it needed British businessmen. In Hong Kong they could operate under a British legal system which guaranteed their property rights, where they could avoid punitive taxation and employ abundant, flexible and cheap labour which was not under a tight union grip. From their base in the colony they could continue to service China's trade with the outside world. Moreover, British businessmen could also re-establish links with Chinese industrialists, who had emigrated from the mainland and who now needed capital for new ventures and merchants with a wide range of international contacts to market their products. British merchants hence survived the political, social and economic upheavals ongoing in China, just as they had done in previous revolutionary epochs.[12] In many ways, the existence of a British territory in China explains British and Chinese attitudes towards political and economic relations in this period. Ultimately Hong Kong made Sino-British relations necessary but difficult.

Appendix

Table A1   British Foreign Resident Community in China, 1899–1951

Year	British Population in China
1899	5 562
1913	8 966
1930	13 915
1934	13 344
1945	5 000
1951	1 700

Sources: for figures 1899–1945, S. Endicott, *Diplomacy and Enterprise: Britain's China Policy, 1933–1937*, Manchester 1975, tables and charts no.1; for figures 1945–51, CAB129(CP50)/45; memorandum by Secretary of State for Foreign Affairs, 3 May 1951.

Table A2   Commodity Composition of British Imports from China, 1946–54 (£) (with % in brackets)

	A	B	C	Total Imports
1946	208 820 (7.7)	2 326 518 (86)	157 638 (5.8)	2 696 823
1947	1 047 531 (14.6)	5 784 729 (80.6)	314 065 (4.3)	7 172 090
1948	3 550 268 (43)	4 445 428 (54)	180 920 (2.2)	8 201 085
1949	2 262 560 (62.5)	1 269 858 (35)	146 053 (4)	3 622 320
1950	7 111 341 (68.8)	2 208 324 (21)	1 004 298 (9.7)	10 324 328
1951	3 397 782 (44.3)	3 211 888 (41.8)	1 059 965 (13.8)	7 669 804
1952	2 022 739 (67)	657 451 (21.8)	331 533 (11)	3 011 897
1953	4 641 991 (45.4)	4 921 591 (48.1)	658 451 (6.4)	10 222 182
1954	3 139 626 (35)	4 447 910 (49.6)	1 371 148 (15.3)	8 958 694

Breakdown of classes: Class A Food, beverages and tobacco
Class B Raw materials and basic materials
Class C Manufactured goods

Source: *Annual Statement of the Trade of the UK with Commonwealth Countries and Foreign Countries*, vol. 1, London 1946–54.

Appendix

Table A3 Commodity Composition of British Exports to China, 1946–54 (£) (with % in brackets)

	A	B	C	Total Exports
1946	135 496	87 960	7 577 793	7 827 079
	(1.7)	(1.1)	(96.8)	
1947	29 526	32 862	12 684 876	12 777 090
	(0.2)	(0.25)	(99.2)	
1948	38 350	57 131	8 527 523	8 649 844
	(0.44)	(0.66)	(98.5)	
1949	12 915	128 419	2 107 228	2 257 077
	(0.57)	(5.6)	(93.3)	
1950	5 053	7 311	3 574 825	3 587 189
	(0.14)	(0.2)	(99.6)	
1951	624	386 971	2 888 624	2 676 319
	(0.02)	(14.4)	(85.5)	
1952	551	771 272	3 768 863	4 541 249
	(0.01)	(16.9)	(82.9)	
1953	21 196	3 586 906	2 533 270	6 161 377
	(0.34)	(58.2)	(41.1)	
1954	22 175	3 587 669	3 206 257	6 825 913
	(0.32)	(52.5)	(46.9)	

Source: *Annual Statement of the Trade of the UK with Commonwealth Countries and Foreign Countries*, vol. 1, London 1946–54.

Table A4 Commodity Composition of British Imports from Hong Kong, 1946–54 (£) (with % in brackets)

	A	B	C	Total Imports
1946	7 485	197 192	166 876	392 337
	(1.9)	(50.2)	(42.5)	
1947	239 300	1 592 290	196 639	2 088 387
	(11.4)	(76.2)	(9.4)	
1948	759 235	3 638 541	1 046 199	5 510 467
	(13.7)	(66)	(18.9)	
1949	933 786	8 010 827	1 211 493	10 265 175
	(9.0)	(78)	(11.8)	
1950	667 120	5 571 303	5 753 895	12 059 441
	(5.53)	(46.1)	(47.1)	
1951	1 016 551	5 360 678	7 783 370	14 237 298
	(7.1)	(37.6)	(54.3)	
1952	565 655	2 462 758	2 937 748	6 121 614
	(9.2)	(40)	(47.9)	
1953	540 093	3 148 671	4 298 253	8 186 627
	(6.5)	(38.4)	(52.5)	
1954	1 043 678	1 579 597	8 774 083	10 957 273
	(9)	(14.4)	(80)	

Source: *Annual Statement of the Trade of the UK with Commonwealth Countries and Foreign Countries*, vol. 1, London 1946–54.

Table A5 Commodity Composition of British Exports to Hong Kong, 1946–54 (£) (with % in brackets)

	A	B	C	Total Exports
1946	856 711 (14.3)	40 246 (0.67)	4 892 575 (83.1)	5 989 526
1947	1 608 979 (12.6)	23 019 (0.18)	10 964 102 (86)	12 742 797
1948	2 257 673 (10.9)	40 189 (0.19)	18 114 943 (88)	20 575 326
1949	2 332 730 (8.3)	81 725 (0.2)	25 272 033 (90.5)	27 907 388
1950	2 244 934 (8.0)	174 727 (0.62)	25 136 776 (90.5)	27 761 824
1951	3 156 638 (8.75)	2 003 619 (5.5)	30 316 655 (84)	36 056 665
1952	2 261 792 (7.7)	1 520 427 (5.2)	24 726 165 (85)	29 043 278
1953	2 298 805 (8.4)	1 375 418 (5)	23 064 003 (84.4)	27 297 481
1954	2 240 118 (9.3)	895 189 (3.7)	26 391 396 (84.7)	24 074 510

Source: Annual Statement of the Trade of the UK with Commonwealth Countries and Foreign Countries, vol. 1, London 1946–54.

Table A6 Commodity Composition of China's Imports and Exports, 1950–54 (total imports/exports = 100)

	Exports			Imports	
	A	B	C	I	II
1950	9.3	33.2	57.5	83.4	16.6
1951	14.0	31.4	54.6	81.3	18.7
1952	17.9	22.8	59.3	89.4	10.6
1953	18.4	25.9	55.7	92.1	7.9
1954	24.0	27.7	48.3	92.3	7.7

Exports
A **Industrial and Mineral Products:** including metals and mineral products, machinery and instruments, chemicals, western medicine, chinaware, chemical fibres and chemical fibre products.
B **Processed Farm and Sideline Products:** including processed grain and edible oil food, textiles, native and animal products and handicrafts.
C **Farm and Sideline Products:** including grain, cotton, edible oil, eggs, livestock and poultry, aquatic products, vegetables and dried fruits, raw lacquer and crude Chinese drugs.

Imports
   I Means of Production.
  II Means of Subsistence.

Source: *Statistical Yearbook of China 1981*, compiled by State Statistical Bureau, PRC (English Edition), Hong Kong 1981.

Table A7 Commodity Structure of Chinese Trade with the Soviet Union, 1950–54 (% of total imports from USSR)

	1950	1951	1952	1953
Imports				
Total US $ million	389.0	478.0	554.0	759.0
Comp Plant	0.2	6.8	7.2	12.3
Other Mach.	10.4	16.1	21.0	13.9
Ferrous Metals	5.2	10.4	12.0	11.6
Non-ferrous Metals	0.8	3.5	2.8	2.9
Petrol. & Prods.	2.9	8.1	5.8	5.9
Chem. Prods	1.8	3.3	1.8	1.1
Other	78.7	51.8	49.4	52.3
Exports				
Total US $ million	191.0	331.0	414.0	475.0
Comp Plant	47.1	32.9	44.0	44.4
Other Mach.	8.9	9.1	9.4	12.2
Ferrous Metals		1.1	3.5	3.6
Chem. Prods	10.7	13.8	17.7	21.3
Other	33.3	–	25.4	18.5

Source: Feng-hwa Mah, *The Foreign Trade of Mainland China*, Edinburgh 1972, pp. 197–8.

Notes

INTRODUCTION

1. Imperialism here is defined as including both formal imperialism (political control of territory overseas) and informal imperialism (economic dominance over foreign economies). The latter is a disputed notion; in practice it is difficult to assess who has economic control and, as a result, the use of this term has often been based on political and personal interpretation. It is used within this study because Chinese communist ideology embraced both concepts.

2. See P.J. Cain and A.G. Hopkins, *British Imperialism: Innovation and Expansion, 1688–1914*, London 1993 and P.J. Cain and A.G. Hopkins, *British Imperialism: Crisis and Deconstruction, 1914–1990*, London 1993. On the dualism within British capitalism between mercantile and industrial capital see also the various articles by Perry Anderson and Tom Nairn in the *New Left Review* since 1964, and in particularly Perry Anderson, 'The Figures of Descent', *New Left Review*, no. 161, Jan./Feb. 1987, pp. 20–78. This line has been heavily criticised. See especially, Alex Callinicos, 'Exception or Symptom: The British Crisis and the World System', *New Left Review*, no. 169, May/June 1988, pp. 97–108 and David Nicholls, 'Fractions of Capital: The Aristocracy, the City and Industry in the Development of Modern British Capitalism', *Social History*, vol. 13, 1988, pp. 71–83.

3. The impact of empire on the British economy is extremely difficult to unravel. The most recent work by Catherine Schenk disputes that the retention of empire was a massive drain on the British economy. She argues that the Sterling Area balances did not destabilise the pound; that investment in the empire did not deprive British industry of funds; and that 'soft' imperial markets did not undermine the competitiveness of British industry. See Catherine Schenk, *Britain and the Sterling Area: From Devaluation to Convertibility in the 1950s*, London 1994. But there is a general consensus that the British state was overcommitted post-1945 and that this placed a strain on the British economy. For the most polemical accounts see Correlli Barnett, *The Audit of War: The Illusion and Reality of Britain as a Great Nation*, London 1986 and Malcolm Chalmers, *Paying for Defence: Military Spending and British Decline*, London 1985. See also Geoffrey Ingham, *Capitalism Divided? The City and Industry in British Social Development*, London 1984. For the dominance of non-industrial wealth and its influence on elite formation see W.D. Rubinstein, *Men of Property: The Very Wealthy in Britain since the Industrial Revolution*, London 1981.

4. James T.H. Tang, *Britain's Encounter with Revolutionary China, 1949–54*, London 1992 and Wenguang Shao, *China, Britain and Businessmen: Political and Commercial Relations, 1949–57*, London 1991. And also

Brian Porter, *Britain and the Rise of Communist China: A Study of British Attitudes 1949–1954*, London 1975 and Robert Boardman, *Britain and the People's Republic of China 1949–1974*, London 1976.

5. See Ritchie Ovendale, 'Britain, the United States, and the Recognition of Communist China', *Historical Journal*, vol. 26, no. 1, 1983, pp. 139–58; David Wolf, 'To Secure a Convenience: Britain's Recognition of Communist China', *Journal of Contemporary History*, vol. 18, no. 2, April 1983, pp. 299–326 and Zhong-ping Feng, *The British Government's China Policy*, Keele 1994.

6. Also quoted in Tang, 1992, p. 32 and Wolf, 1983, p. 27.

7. See Aron Shai, *Britain and China 1941–47: Imperial Momentum*, Oxford 1984.

8. Disagreements within the British government were not over the nature of policy but over the timing of recognition. There were reservations within the Colonial Office and the Foreign Office about the impact early recognition would have on anti-communist movements in South East Asia, in particular the Bao Dai regime in Vietnam. Further difficulties with the US and with the 'white' Commonwealth caused Bevin to delay a move until after the December Commonwealth conference in Colombo and then to switch recognition from the end of December 1949 to January 1950. See Ovendale, 1983, pp. 150–3. The Treasury, the Colonial Office and the Board of Trade expressed reservations during 1949.

9. For a discussion of this aspect of British policy see Ovendale, 1983, pp. 144–5.

10. CAB129(CP49)/214; memorandum by Bevin, 24 Oct. 1949.

11. For the importance of empire and commonwealth in the formation of British external policy in the 1940s see John Kent, *British Imperial Strategy and the Origins of the Cold War, 1944–49*, London 1993.

12. Tang, 1992, p. 46. Porter argues that, after the capture of the *Amethyst*, public opinion turned against recognition, but thereafter became increasingly in favour. Porter, 1975, p. 26.

13. For British policy towards China in the 1930s see Stephen Endicott, *Diplomacy and Enterprise: British China Policy, 1933–1937*, Manchester 1975. Endicott argues that the Treasury, under Neville Chamberlain, was the most important agent for formulating policy towards China in the 1930s. Chamberlain wanted to adopt a policy of appeasement towards Japan and pacify the Chinese Nationalists with a sterling loan, which would reinvigorate the Chinese economy and increase Sino-British trade. Business interests had a persuasive influence on the formulation of this policy. Endicott argues this was misconceived; it neither cultivated Chinese good-will nor successfully contained Japanese expansion and completely misunderstood the level of antagonism between China and Japan.

14. CAB129(CP49)/214; memorandum by Bevin, 24 Oct. 1949.

15. BT11/3510; memorandum by export promotion department, 21 Nov. 1947. This total included British trade with Hong Kong, much of which then went into China.

16. Also discussed by Tang, 1992, p. 49. Wolf disputes the influence of the business lobby; he argues that 'the century old myth of a lucrative China market remained alive at Whitehall on its own merits'. Wolf, 1983, p. 82.

17. Manchester Chamber of Commerce, *Monthly Reports*, vol. LXI, 1950, p. xxvii.
18. CHAS/C/2; circular, 'Present Position of British Traders in China', 17 Aug. 1949.
19. *Hansard, Commons*, vol. 475, col. 2073; speech by Eden, 24 May 1950.
20. There are severe problems in estimating the exact figure for British investments in China. The China Association estimated the sum at £300 million, the figure for 1935; the China Year Book for 1936 estimates the figure at £240 million (5.9 per cent of total British foreign direct investment). However, Board of Trade and Treasury estimates, based on a survey of 40 British firms in 1947, put the figure at £124 million; and the Economic and Industrial Planning Staff of the Foreign Office puts the figure at £110 million in 1947. See BT11/3390. A true estimate is difficult to arrive at due to the problem of assessing wartime depreciation and because figures for mercantile companies, especially those in shipping, are unavailable. This legacy compares to total new global UK external investment in 1946–51 of £1635 million. See Schenk, 1994, p. 107.
21. The viability of these assets had also been undermined by the Treasury's refusal to allow the export of capital, required in the 1940s to facilitate recovery from the destruction and depreciation of capital stock caused by the war. See BT11/3390; letter from S.D. Wale (Treasury) to A.E. Welch (BT), 11 July 1946.
22. CAB129(CP50)/214; memorandum by Ernest Bevin, 24 Oct. 1949.
23. See Schenk, 1994.
24. See Table 7.4 in Chapter 7. The corresponding figures for 1913 are 0.7 per cent (exports) and 0.08 per cent (imports); and for 1922, 0.76 per cent (exports) and 0.06 per cent (imports).
25. CAB129(CP49)248; memorandum by Bevin, 12 Dec. 1949. British diplomatic representatives in the Far East expressed reservations about recognition. Malcolm MacDonald, the British commissioner-general in Asia, and Sir Franklin Gimson, the governor of Singapore, argued British recognition would provide a moral boost for communism by implying Britain wanted to follow a policy of appeasement towards China. See Ovendale, 1983, p. 149. After the Chinese refused to establish relations with Britain in 1950, the Malayan authorities revived the debate regarding the establishment of Chinese communist consuls and successfully persuaded the Labour government to resist Chinese requests for diplomatic representation in Malaya. See FO371/83550/2; telegram from FO to Singapore, 6 April 1950.
26. See James T.T. Tang, 'From Empire Defence to Imperial Retreat: Britain's Postwar China Policy and the Decolonisation of Hong Kong', *Modern Asian Studies*, vol. 28, no. 2, 1994, pp. 317–37.
27. Hong Kong's deficit with China was not huge in the early 1950s because the West was embargoing China. However, subsequently, given that Hong Kong was reliant on imported foodstuffs and raw materials, the annual deficit became substantial, totalling approximately $15 million by 1957 and £64 million by 1971. (See Tables 7.1 and 7.2 in Chapter 7.)

CHAPTER 1: HISTORY REVISITED

1. In contrast, the Soviet bloc countries and states such as India, Sweden and Denmark established full diplomatic relations.
2. Whether a positive Chinese response would have resulted in recognition by a large number of nations is unlikely. Australia and New Zealand were opposed to early recognition; they did not want to jeopardise a US commitment to a Pacific security pact. The Canadians, more sympathetic to the British line, required 'some further event'. China's recognition of Ho Chi Minh, the Viet Minh's leader, instead of Emperor Bao Dai, the head of the pro-French government in control of South Vietnam, precluded French recognition. See FO371/83013/20; FO record of talks with Robert Menzies, Australian Prime Minister, and Percy Spender, 12 March 1950: FO371/88415; letter from Terence Shone to Gladwyn Jebb, 13 April 1950: FO371/88418/74; telegram from UKHC New Zealand, 13 June 1950: FO800/462/264; record of meeting between Bevin and R. Schuman, 7 March 1950.
3. For a full text of Mao Tse-tung's proclamation, see Michael Y.M. Kau and John K. Leung, eds, *The Writings of Mao Zedong: 1949–1976: Vol. 1, September 1949 – December 1955*, New York and London 1986, pp. 10–11. John Gittings argues this was a conciliatory and moderate tone which was 'never put to the test'. John Gittings, *The World and China, 1922–1972*, London 1974, p. 166.
4. FO371/83288/319; telegram from Peking to FO, 9 May 1950. Note also Zhong-ping Feng, *The British Government's China Policy*, Keele 1994, pp. 139–45. Harold Hinton isolates three reasons why the Chinese did not establish relations with Britain: Britain's possession of Hong Kong, Britain's retention of a consulate in Taiwan and Britain's 'rather negative policy' towards the Chinese community in Malaya. H. Hinton, *China's Turbulent Quest: An Analysis of China's Foreign Policy Since 1949*, New York 1972, p. 271.
5. FO371/83288/319; telegram from Peking to FO, 9 May 1950.
6. FO371/88502; *Kwangming Daily*, 17 Jan. 1950 (in a telegram from Nanking to FO, 21 Jan. 1950).
7. *FRUS1950*(2), pp. 200–1; Edmund O. Clubb (Peiping) to Dean Acheson, 20 Jan. 1950.
8. Quoted in Beverly Hooper, *China Stands Up: Ending the Western Presence 1948–1950*, Sydney and London 1986, p. 170.
9. See Michael M. Sheng, 'Chinese Communist Policy towards the US and the Myth of the "Lost Chance", 1945–1950', *Modern Asian Studies*, vol. 28, no. 3, 1994, pp. 475–502 and Chen Jian, *China's Road to the Korean War: The Making of the Sino-American Confrontation*, New York 1994, pp. 33–64. See also Michael Sheng, 'America's Lost Chance in China? A Reappraisal of Chinese Communist Policy towards the United States before 1945', *Australian Journal of Chinese Affairs*, no. 29, Jan. 1993, pp. 135–61.
10. FO371/83314/47; telegram from Moscow to FO, 15 Feb. 1950. For a summary of Foreign Office comment on these agreements see P. Lowe, *The Origins of the Korean War*, London 1986, pp. 119–21.

11. Sergei N. Goncharov, John W. Lewis and Xue Litai, *Uncertain Partners: Stalin, Mao, and the Korean War*, Stanford, Calif. 1993, p. 102.
12. Steven Levine, 'Perception and Ideology in Chinese Foreign Policy', in Thomas W. Robinson and David Shambaugh, eds, *Chinese Foreign Policy: Theory and Practice*, Oxford 1994, pp. 30–46.
13. Lucien W. Pye, 'How China's Nationalism was Shanghaied', *Australian Journal of Chinese Affairs*, Jan. 1993, pp. 107–33.
14. Levine, in Robinson and Shambaugh, 1994, p. 44.
15. FO371/83285/255; *Shih Chieh Chih Shih*, 13 Jan. 1950 (in telegram from Nanking to FO, 31 Jan. 1950).
16. Mao Tse-tung, *Selected Works of Mao Tsetung*, vol. IV, Peking 1961, p. 371.
17. FO371/83285/255; telegram from Nanking to FO, 31 Jan. 1950.
18. C.P. Fitzgerald, *The Birth of Communist China*, London 1964, p. 213.
19. Zhou Enlai, *Selected Works*, vol. II, Beijing 1989, p. 96. Also quoted in James Tuck-Hong Tang, *Britain's Encounter with Revolutionary China, 1949–54*, London 1992, p. 29 and in Chen Xiaolu, 'China's Policy towards the United States, 1949–1955', in H. Harding and Yuan Ming, eds, *Sino-American Relations, 1945–1955: A Joint Reassessment of a Critical Decade*, US 1989, pp. 185–7.
20. A line accepted by Qiang Zhai in, *The Dragon, the Lion and the Eagle: Chinese-British-American Relations, 1949–1958*, Kent, Ohio 1994, pp. 12–13.
21. Mao Tse-tung, 1961, vol. V, p. 27.
22. Kau and Leung, 1986; telegram to 'Five-man Independent Group' of the British Labour Party in the House of Commons, 12 Oct. 1949, p. 16 and telegram to the Britain–China Conference in London, 30 Nov. 1949, p. 43. (The Britain–China Friendship Association was established as a result of this conference.) Michael Lindsay admitted that Chinese perceptions of the outside world 'were often fantastic', grossly exaggerating the importance of communist parties abroad. M. Lindsay, 'China: Report of a Visit', *International Affairs*, vol. 26, no. 1, Jan. 1950, p. 28.
23. Kau and Leung, 1986; telegram to the Communist Party of Great Britain, 24 Sep. 1950, p. 134.
24. Goncharov, Lewis and Xue, 1993, pp. 80 and 125–6.
25. *Hansard, Commons*, vol. 475, col. 2083; speech by Bevin, 24 May 1950.
26. CAB129(CP50)/73; memorandum by Bevin, 20 April 1950 and FO800/462/259; record of conversation with René Massigli (French ambassador in London), 2 March 1950.
27. CAB129(CP50)/73; memorandum by Bevin, 20 April 1950. Noted in C. Alcock, 'Britain and the Korean War', unpublished Manchester University PhD Thesis 1986, p. 17.
28. FO371/83344/30; record of meeting between Foreign Office and China Association, 11 March 1950. Also quoted in Peter Lowe, 'Hopes Frustrated: The Impact of the Korean War upon Britain's Relations with Communist China, 1950–53', in T.G. Fraser and K. Jeffery, eds, *Men, Women and War: Historical Studies XVIII* (Papers read before the XXth Irish Conference of Historians), Dublin 1993, p. 213.
29. CAB129(CP50)/73; memorandum by Bevin, 20 April 1950.

30. Ibid.
31. A number of groups were pressing for a more responsive British line towards China in the months before the Korean War. The British–China Friendship Association was viewed as left-wing and merely seeking to undermine the Labour government's policy in the Far East. See FO371/83305/7; letter from J. Dribbon (secretary) to K. Younger, 6 July 1950 and minute by Franklin, 20 July 1950. The China Campaign Committee, founded in 1937, was a more mainstream organisation and met Younger in June 1950. See Ibid./2; letter from China Campaign Committee to Younger and Ibid./4; record of meeting between the committee and Younger, 5 June 1950. (Chairman Michael Lindsay, a lecturer at University College, Hull, was in China from 1937, worked as the press attaché to the British embassy in Chungking in 1940, visited Yenan in 1944, and was an interpreter with the British Labour Party Mission in September 1954.)
32. FO371/83344/30; record of meeting between Foreign Office and China Association, 11 March 1950.
33. The government argued Britain's consul in Taiwan was only in contact with the provincial rather than the national authorities – implying *de facto* rather than *de jure* recognition of the Chinese Nationalists and that Britain's voting policy in the UN was a diplomatic nuance in line with the UN charter; the British government argued it was better to vote positively once a majority was behind China's admission rather than make a premature vote which might prejudice diplomatic work behind the scenes to admit the Chinese. See FO371/83233/9; minute by P.D. Coates, 11 Jan. 1950 and FO371/83285/228; draft telegram, 7 March 1950.
34. FO371/83285/182; telegram from FO to Nanking, 9 Feb. 1950.
35. *Hansard, Commons*, vol. 475, col. 2129, 24 May 1950 and vol. 473, cols 275–6; speech by R. Crossman, 28 March 1950.
36. FO371/83288/319; minute by William Strang, 16 May 1950.
37. *Hansard, Commons*, vol. 475, col. 2160; speech by Fitzroy Maclean, 24 May 1950.
38. *Hansard, Commons*, vol. 475, col. 2168; speech by W. Fletcher, 24 May 1950.
39. *Hansard, Commons*, vol. 475, cols 2071–3; speech by A. Eden, 24 May 1950.
40. *Hansard, Commons*, vol. 475, col. 2084, 24 May 1950.
41. FO371/83344/30; record of meeting between Foreign Office (Bevin and officials, unspecified) and China Association (W.J. Keswick, J.K. Swire, W.R. Cockburn, E.J. Nathan, D.M. Oppenheim and G.E. Mitchell), 11 March 1950.
42. FO37183288/319; minute by Strang, 9 May 1950.
43. FO371/83279/30; telegram from FO to Tokyo, 11 Feb. 1950.
44. FO371/83289/325; telegram from Peking to FO, 9 May 1950.
45. This situation raised the problem of a Chinese Nationalist veto over the admission of the PRC to the Security Council. This constitutional problem seems to have been resolved by early 1950; Trygve Lie, the Secretary-General of the UN, argued that recognition and representation should not be linked, while Britain and the US (under pressure from London) had reaffirmed that the question was a procedural one, thus not subject to

a Chinese Nationalist veto. For the American position note *FRUS1950*(2), pp. 195–6; Julius Holmes (Minister in the embassy in the UK) to Acheson, 13 Jan. 1950. The Foreign Office was divided on whether the seating of the Chinese Nationalists was a procedural or a substantive question. C.C. Parrott in the UN department argued the Nationalists could use their veto, whereas G.G. Fitzmaurice, the legal secretary to the Foreign Office, argued the question was procedural. FO371/88416/22; minute by Parrott, 24 May 1950. Ibid; minute by Fitzmaurice, 3 June 1950.

46. See Tang Tsou, *America's Failure in China 1941–1950*, Chicago 1963, p. 524.
47. Goncharov, Lewis and Xue, 1993, p. 100.
48. FO371/88507/2; telegram from New York to FO, 3 March 1950.
49. *FRUS1950*(2), pp. 238–43; Ernest Gross to Acheson, 11 March 1950. Acheson made it clear to the US delegation at the UN on a number of occasions that the US would not use its veto on the question of China's admission. *FRUS1950*(2), pp. 186–7; Acheson to Warren R. Austin, 5 Jan. 1950 and Ibid., pp. 202–4; Acheson to Austin, 21 Jan. 1950.
50. FO371/88418; minute by Holmer of tripartite discussions on UN question, 16 May 1950. See also *DBPO*, Series II, vol. II; no. 80, record of second bipartite ministerial meeting held in the Foreign Office, 9 May 1950, pp. 276–81.
51. FO371/88505/77; telegram from New York to FO, 20 March 1950. The French government's position lay between Britain and the US; it admitted that developments endangered the UN, but, having not recognised China, aligned with the US. FO800/462/264; record of meeting between Bevin and R. Schuman, 7 March 1950.
52. See FO371/88418/82; letter from K. Younger to Bevin, 11 May 1950 – quoted in Tang, 1992, p. 134: FO371/88418/79; minute by Younger, 6 June 1950, with comment by Clement Attlee, undated: FO371/88418/82; minute by Dening, 30 May 1950 and minute by R.E. Barclay, 22 June 1950.
53. FO371/88418/79; minute by Younger, 6 June 1950; and letter from Younger to Attlee, 12 June 1950.
54. See FO371/88418/82; letter from Younger to Bevin, 11 May 1950: Ibid.; minute by Dening, 30 May 1950 and minute by Strang, 31 May 1950: FO371/88418/63; telegram from Peking to FO, 31 May 1950.
55. FO371/88503/25; minute by Younger, undated, either Jan. or Feb. 1950.
56. FO371/88502/7; telegram from New York to FO, 17 Jan. 1950. For Rau's suggestion of a tribunal see *FRUS1950*(2), pp. 191–4; Austin to Acheson, 11 Jan. 1950.
57. *The Times*, 19 June 1950.
58. FO371/88418/82; minute by Barclay, 22 June 1950.
59. M.R. Gordon notes that this was not a socialist attitude but more akin to the Tory perception of the League of Nations in the 1930s. M.R. Gordon, *Conflict and Consensus in Labour's Foreign Policy, 1914–1965*, Stanford, Calif. 1969, p. 131.
60. The differing views of the US and the British on the role of the UN reflected a dualism in the UN charter, which made this issue of expulsion especially complex. The charter emphasises the universality of the

organisation in some articles, but Article 4 argues that just peace-loving nations should be members. This was a deliberate ambiguity which provided the UN with two roles: as an executive for collective security and a forum for discussion. In order to be effective in the latter, the UN needs to be universal and yet in order to operate as a peace-keeper, it needs to be able to expel and introduce sanctions against members. Article 6 provides for the expulsion of a member. What the charter did not allow for was aggressive behaviour by a permanent member of the Security Council; it was assumed that this would mean the outbreak of world war and the end of the organisation.

61. Former President Herbert Hoover strongly opposed US policy in Europe and in the Far East and advocated a UN without communist membership. Noted in R.J. Donovan, *Tumultuous Years: The Presidency of Harry S. Truman, 1949–1953*, New York and London 1982, p. 176. For views within the administration see *FRUS1950*(2), pp. 210–14; Gross to Acheson, 27 Jan. 1950. For British perspectives note FO371/88435/4; minute by Holmer, 3 May 1950.

62. *FRUS1950*(2), pp. 220–3; A. Kirk to Acheson, 5 Feb. 1950.

63. FO371/88508/24; minute by Younger, 24 May 1950.

64. See FO371/88418; minute by Ernest Davies, Parliamentary Private Secretary at the Foreign Office, 14 June 1950 and by Hector McNeil, Parliamentary Under-Secretary for Foreign Affairs, 2 June 1950: FO371/88418/86; minute by Pierson Dixon, for the Prime Minister, 15 June 1950: Ibid./87; minute by Dixon, 13 June 1950. The Foreign Office informed the Washington embassy on 15 and 16 June 1950. Ibid.; telegrams from FO to Washington, 15 and 16 June 1950. A Soviet delegate at the UN had also indicated that the Soviet Union wanted to return. See ibid.; minute by Ernest Davies, 14 June 1950.

65. FO371/88418/87; minute by Parrott, 14 June 1950 and minute by P.S. Falla, 14 June 1950.

66. Gaddis argues that the US administration's adherence to a wedge theory stemmed from the ideas of George Kennan. He argues these were evident before Tito's split, and views Marshall Aid as a deliberate attempt to cause tensions between Eastern Europe and the Soviet Union. John Lewis Gaddis, *The Long Peace: Inquiries into the History of the Cold War*, New York 1987, pp. 152–65.

67. Gordon H. Chang, *Friends and Enemies: The US, China, and the Soviet Union 1948–1972*, Stanford, Calif. 1990, pp. 19–20. For a similar position see also Xiang Lanxin, 'The Recognition Controversy: Anglo-American Relations in China, 1949', *Journal of Contemporary History*, vol. 27, April 1992, pp. 319–43.

68. Nancy Bernkopf Tucker, *Patterns in the Dust: Chinese-American Relations and the Recognition Controversy, 1949–1950*, New York 1983, pp. 17 and 176. She believes US businessmen saw opportunities for trade with the PRC and thus advocated recognition, while the administration realised Japan needed trade with China. See also her essay in Douglas Brinkley, ed., *Dean Acheson and the Making of US Foreign Policy*, London 1993, 'China's Place in the Cold War: the Acheson Plan', pp. 109–23. See also Warren I. Cohen, 'Acheson, His Advisers and China,

1949–1950', in Dorothy Borg and Waldo Heinrichs, eds, *Uncertain Years: Chinese-American Relations, 1947–1950*, New York 1980, pp. 13–53.

69. There is no consensus amongst American historians about the exact nature of American policy in this period. Some, notably Tucker and Cohen, have argued that it was not until after the outbreak of the Korean War that the Truman administration ruled out recognition of Communist China. Tucker argues Acheson had a 'moderate, flexible, accommodating stance towards Communist China'. Tucker, in Brinkley, 1993, p. 110.

70. *FRUS1950*(6), pp. 318–21; McConaughy to Acheson, 16 March 1950.

71. DDRS 1977, 283: CIA Report – Review of the World Situation, 18 Jan. 1950.

72. For US policy towards China in the context of the domestic pressures on the American administration see William Stueck, *The Road to Confrontation – American Policy towards China and Korea 1947–1950*, Chapel Hill 1981; Tang Tsou, *America's Failure in China, 1941–1950*, Chicago 1963; Donovan, 1982, pp. 74–88; Dean Acheson, *Present at the Creation: My Years in the State Department*, New York 1969, pp. 355–8; and Tucker, 1983, pp. 143–6.

73. For the close economic and political links between Chinese Nationalists, such as T.V. Soong, K.C. Li, T.K. Tsiang, and the advocates of the roll back in the US administration see Bruce Cumings, *The Origins of the Korean War, Vol. 2: The Roaring of the Cataract, 1947–1950*, Princeton 1990, pp. 106–17.

74. Cumings notes that McCarthy was supplied with documents with which to attack the administration by a range of powerful institutions including SCAP in Tokyo, the CIA and the FBI. Cumings, 1990, pp. 109–10. For the definitive account of 'McCarthyism' see Thomas C. Reeves, *The Life and Times of Joe McCarthy: A Biography*, New York 1982.

75. *Manchester Guardian*, 12 June 1950.

76. Gaddis, 1987, pp. 166–7.

77. See Chang for the various nuances of thought within the State Department in the months before the outbreak of the Korean War. Chang, 1990, pp. 57–9 and 71–4.

78. See *FRUS1950*(1), pp. 234–92. NSC68 had not been officially approved by Truman, who did not finally commit the document as US policy until September 1950.

79. Bruce Cumings, 'Revising Postrevisionism or the Poverty of Theory in Diplomatic History', *Diplomatic History*, vol. 17, no. 4, Fall 1993, p. 565.

80. As Gabriel Kolko acknowledges, the US had not come to terms with the fact that for this task US 'goals inherently outstripped its capabilities' and that this policy meant intervening in highly decentralised agrarian societies which it did not understand and which could not be controlled by American bombs. The US partly came to terms with these contradictions during the Korean War but ultimately it took defeat in the Vietnam war to alter – but not change – the US belief that it could intervene to prevent the fall of such states. See Gabriel Kolko, *Confronting the Third World: United States Foreign Policy 1945–1980*, New York 1988.

81. FO371/83281/72; letter from Oliver Franks, British ambassador in

Washington to Bevin, 7 Jan. 1950 and FO371/83013/10; letter from Franks to FO, 6 March 1950. The British ambassador argued the US had disengaged to deflect attention from British recognition and noted that the reactions of the US public and Republican right to British recognition of China were surprisingly muted.

82. *FRUS1950*(3), p. 1022; Secretary of State to Acting Secretary of State, 9 March 1950.
83. FO371//83286/262; telegram from Washington to FO, 27 March 1950.
84. *FRUS1950*(3), pp. 994–996; US delegation to Acheson, 4 May 1950.
85. FO371/83013/10; minute by Dening, 3 May 1950.
86. CAB129(CP50)/114; cabinet memorandum by Bevin of conversation with Acheson, 19 May 1950.
87. *DBPO*, Series II, vol. II; no. 80, record of second bipartite ministerial meeting held in the Foreign Office, 9 May 1950, pp. 276–81 and *FRUS1950*(3), pp. 994–6; US delegation to Acheson, 4 May 1950.
88. FO371/81615/8; telegram from Washington to FO, 28 March 1950.
89. See Herman Van der Wee, *Prosperity and Upheaval: the World Economy, 1945–1980*, London 1991, pp. 353–8.

CHAPTER 2: THE ORIGINS OF TWO CHINAS

1. Taiwan had been ceded to Japan in 1895 by the Treaty of Shimonoseki, but as a result of Japan's defeat in the Pacific War had, in theory, been returned to China; the Cairo Declaration, 1 December 1943, and the Potsdam Declaration, 26 July 1945, had pledged to return the territory to the Chinese nation after the signing of a Japanese Peace Treaty.
2. See Shu Guang Zhang, *Deterrence and Strategic Culture: Chinese-American Confrontations, 1949–1958*, Ithaca and London 1992, pp. 64–7.
3. Sergei N. Goncharov, John W. Lewis and Xue Litai, *Uncertain Partners: Stalin, Mao, and the Korean War*, Stanford, Calif. 1993, p. 79. Allen Whiting notes that training for an assault on Taiwan was limited and that in May 1950 the Chinese had begun to transfer troops from Lin Piao's 4th Field Army – positioned in the coastal provinces around Taiwan – to the north east. Whiting, *China Crosses the Yalu: The Decision to Enter the Korean War*, New York 1960, p. 64. Monsoon conditions in the area compounded logistical problems; they made an invasion impossible between October and March, while between June and October the frequency of heavy storms made an attack more difficult.
4. Qiang Zhai, *The Dragon, the Lion and the Eagle: Chinese-British-American Relations, 1949–1958*, Kent, Ohio and London 1994, p. 96. For intelligence assessments see FO371/83234/57; Tamsui, report of events, 29 April to 10 May 1950 and *FRUS1950*(6), p. 330; memorandum by Dean Rusk to Dean Acheson, 17 April 1950.
5. FO371/83233/18; report by the Joint Intelligence Bureau, ref. 2/85, 20 Jan. 1950.
6. FO371/83233/22; telegram from Tamsui to FO, 19 Jan. 1950. After Truman's announcement disengaging the US from Taiwan on 5 January 1950, Chinese Nationalist officials began to evacuate their wives and female em-

ployees from the island. Nationalist morale began to recover during February and March 1950, but fell with the capture of Hainan in April 1950.

7. For British government perceptions of the Taiwanese economy see FO371/83354/1; Formosan economic notes, 15 May 1949 to 15 Jan. 1950 and FO371/83233/8; letter from E.T. Biggs to E. Bevin, 29 Dec. 1949.

8. G. Kerr, *Formosa Betrayed*, London 1966, p. 434.

9. See Jon W. Hueber, 'The Abortive Liberation of Taiwan', *China Quarterly*, no. 110, June 1987, p. 267: Whiting, 1960, p. 22 and Shu Guang Zhang, 1992, p. 68.

10. Goncharov, Lewis and Xue, 1993, p. 79 and pp. 99–100.

11. Chou En-lai, 'The Chinese Peoples' Successes', *Communist Review*, Nov. 1950, p. 336.

12. On 11 August, Mao delayed an invasion until 1952. See Goncharov, Lewis and Xue, 1993, p. 158

13. See Whiting, 1960, pp. 54–8 and Hueber, 1987, p. 272.

14. FO371/83375/1; letter from W.P. Montgomery (UK trade commissioner) to E.R. Lingeman (economic adviser in Tokyo), 3 Jan. 1950. The Treasury estimated that 80 per cent of Taiwan's imports passed through Hong Kong. The Treasury and Board of Trade were conscious of the shortage of Hong Kong dollars in Taiwan and wanted the Nationalists informed that sterling was 'every bit as desirable' for trade with Hong Kong. Ibid. letter from Treasury (author unspecified) to N.C.C. Trench (FO), 23 Jan. 1950.

15. The Taiwan question has been extensively debated by American historians. For an account in the context of American policy towards China, see Tang Tsou, *America's Failure in China, 1941–1950*, Chicago 1963. For an understanding of the link between American policy towards Taiwan and Korea see William W. Stueck, *The Road to Confrontation: American Policy towards China and Korea, 1947–1950*, Chapel Hill 1981 and Peter Lowe, *The Origins of the Korean War*, London 1986. For the differing views within the American State Department see W.I. Cohen, 'Acheson, his Advisers and China, 1949–50', in D. Borg and W. Hendricks, eds, *Uncertain Years: Chinese-American Relations, 1947–1950*, New York 1980. For a critical assessment of America's failure to disengage from China see Nancy Tucker, *Patterns in the Dust: Chinese-American Relations and the Recognition Controversy 1949–50*, New York 1983, pp. 184–6.

16. The Nationalists were allowed to pay for military supplies from the US with their own foreign exchange reserves (or from the $125 million dollars of congressional aid to the 'area of China'). The British Foreign Office was concerned that arms shipments to Taiwan would fall into communist hands. Acheson agreed and instructed his administration to reject all Chinese demands for military equipment. *FRUS1950*(6), pp. 316–17; Secretary of State to Secretary of Defense, 7 March 1950.

17. FO371/83233/7; letter from H.A. Graves to P. Scarlett, 11 Jan. 1950.

18. *FRUS1950*(6), pp. 434–8; Acheson to UK embassy, 14 Aug. 1950. In November 1948 and again in the summer of 1949, the Joint Chiefs of Staff had acknowledged that it was not in the interests of the US for Taiwan to fall; they recommended that, short of direct military intervention, the US should act to secure the defence of the island against Chinese

attack. See Lowe, 1986, p. 118. (The Dutch and Spanish had recognised the strategic importance of Taiwan as far back as the sixteenth century. See D. Mendel, *The Politics of Formosan Nationalism,* Berkeley 1970, p. 11.)

19. *FRUS1950*(6), pp. 347–9; memorandum by Fisher Howe to W. Park Armstrong, 31 May 1950.
20. Cumings argues that, by the fall of 1949, the US had the ability to over-throw Chiang and that, in the spring of 1950, Paul H. Nitze (Director of the Policy Planning Staff, Department of State), Phillip Jessup (ambassador at large) and Dean Rusk (Assistant Secretary of State for Far Eastern Affairs) were actively promoting the idea. Rusk has informed Cumings that on the eve of the Korean War elements of the Chinese Nationalist army were ready to move against Chiang, and that Acheson, having been sold the idea by Rusk, was about to take the matter up with Truman. Bruce Cumings, *The Origins of the Korean War, Vol. II: The Roaring of the Cataract 1947–1950*, Princeton 1990, pp. 531–44.
21. Cumings, 1990, p. 525. The British consul in Taiwan reported that 75 tanks had reached Taiwan from the US. FO371/83234/43; telegram from Tamsui to FO, 25 March 1950. The US began to increase military assistance to the Nationalists, utilising the China Aid Act and also Public Law 512 (78th Congress), which allowed the US Navy to supply equipment to the Nationalist government.
22. FO371/83320/7; telegram from Tamsui to FO, 26 May 1950.
23. FO371/83320/9; letter from O. Franks to E. Dening, 7 June 1950; minutes by W. Strang and R. Scott, 10 June 1950.
24. CAB129(CP50)/194; memorandum by Secretary of State, 31 Aug. 1950.
25. Defe4/35/137; minute 3, 25 Aug. 1950. The evidence reaching the British concerning a possible invasion attempt was often contradictory, indicating troop movements to and from the area.
26. See: Defe4/34/121; annex to minute 5, 29 July 1950 and FO371/83298/44; record of meeting between FO (Dening and Pierson Dixon) and CoS.
27. PREM8/1409; letter from J. Nehru to Attlee, 8 July 1950. Nehru instructed the Indian ambassador in China, K. Panikkar, to persuade the PRC not to attack Taiwan during the summer of 1950.
28. FO371/3320/15; minute by Strang (of meeting with French ambassador, M.R. Massigli) and Ibid./22; letter from Sir William Hayter to Dening, 14 Aug. 1950.
29. *DBPO*, Series II, vol. IV; no. 20, Younger to Franks, 14 July 1950, pp. 63–7 and no. 15, Younger to Franks, 8 July 1950, pp. 42–4.
30. CAB129/42(CP50)/194; memorandum by Bevin, 21 Aug. 1950.
31. For a discussion of the Chinese Nationalist repression of the 1947 Taiwanese rebellion see Kerr, 1966, chapters 9–14.
32. Kerr, 1966, pp. 452–5. By the 1950s, the League of Reliberation of Formosa, established in 1948, had split; some leaders such as Hsieh Hsueh-hung and Lin Mu-hsun had aligned with the PRC, while pro-American leaders such as Thomas Liao had set up in Japan. The Formosan Democratic Independence Party was established in February 1950. See Ong Joktik, 'A Formosan's View of The Formosan Independent Movement', in M. Mancall, ed., *Formosa Today,* New York 1964, pp. 165–9. The island's

status could have been decided by a plebiscite of the Taiwanese people, but as the Nationalists retained tight control of the island, a period of UN trusteeship would have had to precede one.

33. United States General Services Administration, *Public Papers of the Presidents of the US: H.S. Truman*, Washington 1965, p. 193.
34. *FRUS1950*(6), pp. 396–8; Acheson to Douglas, 28 July 1950.
35. For an account of his visit to Taiwan and his message to the Veterans, see D. MacArthur, *Reminiscences*, Greenwich, Conn. 1965, pp. 372–452.
36. Whiting, 1960, p. 80.
37. CAB129/42(CP50)/194; memorandum by Bevin, 21 Aug. 1950.
38. *FRUS1950*(6), pp. 534–6; memorandum of conversation between J.M. Allison, Acheson, Dulles, Lucius D. Battle, 25 Oct. 1950.
39. *FRUS1950*(3), pp. 1158–65; minutes of the foreign ministers' conference, Sep. 1950.
40. FO371/83320/18; telegram from Tamsui (naval liaison officer) to FO, 5 Aug. 1950.
41. PREM/1408; letter from Nehru to Attlee, 22 Dec. 1950.
42. PREM8/1200; brief for Washington conference, 2 Dec. 1950.
43. R. MacFarquhar, *Sino-American Relations 1949–71*, New York 1972; doc. 11, p. 91.
44. *The Times*, 11 Dec. 1950.
45. *FRUS1950*(3), pp. 1706–19; minutes of the meeting between Truman and Attlee, 4 Dec. 1950.
46. CAB129/45(CP51)/78; cabinet memorandum, 20 March 1951.
47. FO371/9225/18; letter from R.F. Barclay to D.H.F. Rickett, 9 May 1951.
48. *Hansard, Commons*, vol. 487, cols. 2301–3; 11 Nov. 1951.
49. FO371/92225/23; minute by G.G. Buzzard, May 1951.
50. See *FRUS1950*(6), pp. 413–14; memorandum by Lay, 3 Aug. 1950: ibid., pp. 434–8; Acheson to embassy in China, 14 Aug. 1950 and ibid., pp. 380–1; memorandum by Kennan to Acheson, 17 July 1950.
51. See B. Cumings, 'The Origins and Development of Northeast Asian Political Economy: Industrial Sectors, Product Life Cycles, and Political Consequences', in F. Deyo, ed., *The Political Economy of the New Asian Industrialism*, Ithaca and London 1989. Ho has raised doubts about whether the Japanese legacy was in actual fact a productive industrial structure exploiting Taiwanese comparative advantage, but still acknowledges that the colonial experience transformed various Taiwanese institutions. See S.P.S. Ho, 'Colonialism and Development: Korea, Taiwan, Kwantung', in R.H. Myers and M.R. Petrie, eds, *The Japanese Colonial Empire, 1895–1945*, Princeton 1984.
52. See M. Scott, 'Foreign Trade', in W. Galenson, ed., *Economic Growth and Structural Change in Taiwan: The Post War Experience of the Republic of China*, London 1979, pp. 310–13 and S. Ho, *Economic Development of Taiwan, 1860–1970*, New Haven 1978, p. 115. Taiwan was a small island state and hence trade was of paramount importance; under the Japanese, the export trade had accounted for 44 per cent of GDP, while Taiwanese economic development in the 1960s was primarily export led.
53. See Galenson, 1979, p. 371 and Ho, 1978, p. 112.

54. See E. Landberg, 'Fiscal and Monetary Policies', in Galenson, 1979, p. 268. While recognising the strategic reasoning behind a policy of import substitution, US administrations were anxious to remove import and export controls and wanted to stimulate private industrial investment.
55. See FO371/83237/126; BBC monitor, 30 Aug. 1950 and ibid.; report by naval liaison officer, 1 Aug. 1950.
56. FO371/83239/163; telegram from Tamsui to FO, 9 Nov. 1950.
57. Denis Fred Simon notes that Governor K.C. Wu was a genuine advocate of improved mainlander–Taiwanese relations; his 'retirement' – officially attributed to ill-health – was a setback. Denis Fred Simon, 'External Incorporation and Internal Reform', in E.A. Winckler and S. Greenhalgh eds, *Contending Approaches to the Political Economy of Taiwan*, New York 1988, p. 146. (Kerr points to two attempts on Wu's life in 1953. Kerr, 1966, p. 427.) The Chinese Nationalists only allowed the Taiwanese to participate in the political system if they had returned with them from the mainland.
58. *FRUS1951*(6), pp. 1574–8; memorandum by Merchant to McWilliams, 9 Feb. 1951.
59. For a discussion of the negotiations between Britain and the US on this issue see P. Lowe, 'Great Britain and the Japanese Peace Treaty', in P. Lowe and H. Moeshart, eds, *Western Interactions with Japan: Expansion, Armed Forces and Readjustment, 1859–1956*, Sandgate 1990.
60. FO800/780; record of conversation between Acheson and Eden, 21 Nov. 1951. The British mission in Tokyo informed Eden that 'it is difficult to escape the conclusion that at the time when you were having your conversation with Acheson and Dulles, active pressure was in progress and Yoshida... was either already in the bag or just about to be'. FO371/99403/8; telegram from Tokyo to FO, 16 Jan. 1952.
61. FO371/99404/34; *NCNA*, 22 Jan. 1951, in telegram from Peking to FO, 22 Jan. 1952.
62. See FO371/99260/7; brief by R. Scott, 15 Feb. 1952 and FO371/105177/1; minute by R. Scott, 5 Dec. 1951, with comments by Eden.
63. For Winston Churchill's position on Japan's relationship with Taiwan note FO800/781/4; letter from Churchill to Anthony Eden, 6 Jan. 1952.
64. FO371/105221/6; letter from PM to G. Jebb (New York), 2 May 1953.
65. Defe4/56/113; annex to J.P.(52) brief for Sir W. Elliot, 2 Oct. 1952.
66. FO371/99403/14; minute by R. Scott, 28 Dec. 1951.
67. Karl Lott Rankin, *China Assignment*, Seattle 1964, pp. 69 and 99.
68. DDRS, 1989, 001680; memorandum by General Hoyt S. Vandenberg, (US Air Force, Chief of Staff) 28 March 1952.
69. *FRUS1951*(6), pp. 1521–22; Secretary of State to embassy in the Republic of China, 20 Jan. 1951. Colonel Dick Hayward was training the Nationalists for amphibious operations. The British naval liaison officer in Tamsui, in close contact with his American counterparts, reported that Nationalist claims about extensive raids on the mainland were exaggerated; he had knowledge of only one such attack. FO371/92209/65; general report by naval liaison officer, 14 June to 14 July 1951, 17 July 1951.
70. John L. Gaddis, 'The Unexpected John Foster Dulles: Nuclear Weapons,

Communism and the Russians', in Richard Immerman, ed., *John Foster Dulles and the Diplomacy of the Cold War*, Princeton 1990, pp. 60–7.

71. Nancy Bernkopf Tucker, 'John Foster Dulles and the Taiwan Roots of the "Two Chinas" Policy', in Immerman, 1990, pp. 236–8.
72. *FRUS1952–54*(14), pp. 83–4; telephone conversation between Acheson and Secretary of the Navy, 25 July 1952.
73. *FRUS1951*(6), pp. 1574–8; memorandum by Merchant to McWilliams, 9 Feb. 1951.
74. FO371/105196/9; telegram from FO to Washington, 31 Jan. 1953.
75. FO371/105200/4; minute by E.M. Toplas, 19 Jan. 1953 and FO371/105197/34; telegram from Tamsui to FO, 7 Feb. 1953.
76. FO371/105182; telegram from Washington to FO, 7 March 1953. See also FO371/105196/25; letter from F.S. Tomlinson to R. Scott, 2 Feb. 1953.
77. FO371/105197/81; FO draft on de-neutrality (no author specified), 28 Feb. 1953.
78. FO371/105196/43; minute by R. Scott, 22 Dec. 1952 and FO371/105221/1; letter from J.R. Colville to FO, 8 Jan. 1953. For the American record of a dinner conversation between Dulles, Bernard Baruch, Governor Dewey and Churchill note *FRUS1952–54*(14), p. 126; meeting between Eisenhower and Churchill, 3–8 Jan. 1953.
79. *FRUS1952–54*(14), pp. 184–6; record of meeting between Department of State and JCS, 10 April 1953.
80. Training and equipping Nationalist units would have been expensive and time consuming. See *FRUS1952–54*(14), pp. 118–20; memorandum by Allison, 24 Dec. 1952.
81. See *FRUS1952–54*(14), pp. 307–30; NSC 146/2, 6 Nov. 1953 and DDRS 1988, 000405; NSC report to NSC Planning Board, 27 March 1953.
82. The State Department confirmed that it had advanced warning of the attack but had not encouraged the assault. FO371/105198/112; minute by Biggs, 4 Sep. 1953. Rankin denied any prior knowledge of the attack. FO371/105198/106; telegram from Tamsui to FO, 16 Sep. 1953.
83. LPA; general correspondence file, Formosa, 1953.
84. *Daily Herald*, 31 Jan. 1955.
85. FO371/105179/1; minute by R. Scott, for PM's visit to Washington, 5 Dec. 1952.
86. Kerr, 1966, p. 438.
87. FO371/99264/1; *NCNA*, bulletin 530; statement by Chou, 5 May 1952, in telegram from Peking to FO, 8 May 1952.
88. FO371/92203/264; Chinese News Commentary, Singapore to FO, 11 Oct. 1951.
89. FO371/105210/3; telegram from Peking to FO, 19 Feb. 1953.
90. F0371/105215; *NCNA*, 6 Feb. 1953, in telegram from commissioner-general Singapore to FO, 19 Feb. 1953
91. FO371/105205/4; telegram from Hong Kong Regional Intelligence Office, 26 Jan. 1953.

CHAPTER 3: ROLL BACK NOT RELATIONS

1. See James Tang, *Britain's Encounter with Revolutionary China, 1949–1954*, London 1992, pp. 89–91.
2. FO371/83249/201; telegram from Peking to FO, 29 June 1950.
3. Tang, 1992, pp. 92–5.
4. CHAS/MCP/50/G/67; meeting between E. Dening and J. Keswick, 23 Aug. 1950.
5. FO371/83324/3; UKHC India to FO, 28 June 1950.
6. *DBPO*, Series II, vol. IV; no. 48, Sir G. Jebb (New York) to Younger, 16 Sep. 1950.
7. CAB128(CM50)/55; minute, 4 Sep. 1950.
8. COCOM was established in 1949 to co-ordinate the embargo on the Soviet Union in the aftermath of American pressure on its western allies. The group met infrequently in Paris to discuss the extent and nature of controls. By 1951 there were 15 members including Japan. See F.D. Holzman, *International Trade under Communism – Politics and Economics*, London 1976, p. 136.
9. CAB131/41; working party for the control of strategic exports, 26 July 1950.
10. FO371/83367/83; telegram from Secretary of State for Foreign Affairs to Hong Kong, 25 July 1950. The Americans were using their consulate in Hong Kong to monitor the level of exports moving through the colony into China.
11. CAB128(CM50)/46; cabinet minutes, 17 July 1950.
12. FO371/83367/78; minute by R.M. Hadow, 30 June 1950.
13. FO371/83365/53; draft telegram to Hong Kong, 10 July 1950.
14. FO371/83365/40; FO memorandum, no author specified, 2 July 1950.
15. FO371/83367/61; minute by J.S. Shattock, 13 July 1950.
16. CAB129(CP50)/204; memorandum by Ministry of Defence, 9 Sep. 1950 and FO371/83368/109; letter from H. Gresswell to R.M. Slater, 16 Aug. 1950. Under the auspices of the Joint War Production Committee, a security export working party was set up to consider the question of extending controls on exports to China. The paper presented by this body, on 14 August 1950, argued that there was no case for applying the whole of 'list1B' to the Chinese People's Government but that it was imperative to include some of the goods on this list for political as well as military reasons.
17. CAB129(CP50)204; memorandum by Ministry of Defence, 9 Sep. 1950.
18. FO800/462/373; letter from Bevin to PM, 6 July 1950.
19. *FRUS1950*(6), pp. 640–44; ambassador in the UK (L. Douglas) to Secretary of State, 29 June 1950.
20. FO371/83365/40; FO memorandum: the economic implications of the Korean conflict, no author specified, 2 July 1950.
21. FO371/83364/12; telegram from FO to high commissioners of the Commonwealth, 17 July 1950.
22. FO371/83367/55; telegram from British Joint Staff Mission in Washington to FO, 10 July 1950.
23. CAB128(CM50)/46; minute, 17 July 1950.

24. See Wenguang Shao, *China, Britain and Businessmen: Political and Commercial Relations, 1949–1957*, London 1991, p. 91.
25. FO371/88421/125; minute by C.C. Parrott, 28 June 1950 and minute by Pierson Dixon, 28 June 1950.
26. FO371/88417/22; letter from Parrott to Lasky, 25 June 1950.
27. FO371/88421/130; minute by Dixon, 25 July 1950.
28. CAB128(CM50)/52; cabinet minute, 1 Aug. 1950 and *FRUS1950*(2), p. 245; memorandum by G. Hayden Raynor to G. Perkins, 29 June 1950.
29. CAB128(CM50)/52; cabinet minute, 1 Aug. 1950.
30. CAB128(CM50)/52; minute 2, 1 Aug. 1950 and CAB129(CP50)/195; memorandum by Bevin, 1 Sep. 1950.
31. FO371/88421/131; letter from Bevin to Washington, 29 July 1950.
32. FO371/88425/212; telegram from Peking to FO, 27 Sep. 1950.
33. Zhou Enlai, *Selected Works*, vol. II, Beijing 1989, p. 45.
34. *Daily Worker*, 12 Sep. 1950 in LPPCC 39/32/18.
35. CAB128(CP50)/52; minute, 1 Aug. 1950.
36. FO371/88421/142; telegram from FO to Washington, 1 Aug. 1950. See also *FRUS1950*(2), pp. 259–62; British embassy to State Department, 11 Aug. 1950.
37. *Hansard, Commons*, vol. 478, col. 1383; 24 July 1950.
38. Ibid., col. 1309.
39. LPA; 49th conference report, Margate, 5 Oct. 1950.
40. *The Times*, 1 Sep. 1950 and *Daily Worker*, 29 July 1950 in LPPCC 39/32/18.
41. FO371/88421/125; minute by Parrott, 28 June 1950.
42. *FRUS1950*(2), pp. 251–2; Acheson to Warren Austin, 31 July 1950 and ibid., pp. 262–4; memorandum of conversation by Edmund O. Clubb, of meeting between B.A. Burrows, counsellor embassy Washington, Clubb and Rusk, 14 Aug. 1950.
43. FO371/88423/159; telegram from Washington to FO, 24 Aug. 1950.
44. *FRUS1950*(2), pp. 287–90; position paper prepared by State Department, 14 Sep. 1950.
45. *New York Herald Tribune*, 12 Sep. 1950 in LPPCC 39/32/18.
46. CAB129(CP50)/221; memorandum by Bevin, 6 Oct. 1950.
47. FO371/88423/154; letter from B.A. Burrows to FO, 15 Aug. 1950.
48. FO371/83012; memorandum by Air Chief Marshal Sir J. Slessor, 24 Nov. 1949.
49. Anglo-American discussions on China have been assessed in most works on the Korean War. For the most detailed study see William Stueck, 'The Limits of Influence: British Policy and American Expansion of the War in Korea', *Pacific Historical Review*, vol. 55, no. 1, February 1986.
50. FO371/83296/6; letter from Dening to Burrows, 24 Aug. 1950.
51. PREM8/1405; letter from Acheson to Bevin, 11 July 1950.
52. Ibid.
53. *FRUS1950*(7), pp. 152–3; intelligence estimate prepared by the estimate group office of intelligence research, Department of State, 25 June 1950. Also quoted in Rosemary Foot, *The Wrong War: American Policy and the Dimensions of the Korean Conflict, 1950–1953*, Ithaca 1985, p. 60.
54. John Lewis Gaddis, *The Long Peace: Inquiries into the History of the*

Cold War, New York 1987, pp. 168–9.

55. Bruce Cumings argues that this struggle was a product of the American political economy, whereby two distinct foreign policy strains emerged from the 1930s and remained dominant into the 1950s. The 'roll backers' of the early 1950s were agrarian-based, individualist expansionists, advocating intervention and expansion into new territory. On the other side of the foreign policy spectrum were the industrialists, concerned with corporate expansion and free competition for markets abroad. Bruce Cumings, *The Origins of the Korean War: Vol. 2, The Roaring of the Cataract 1947–1950*, Princeton 1990, pp. 24–32.

56. For a detailed account of the changing balances within the American bureaucracy during the Korean War see Foot, 1985, p. 60.

57. Foot argues that George Kennan wanted to explore the Indian approach but Acheson and Dulles wanted to negotiate from a position of strength. She believes the domestic political environment in the US made any US concession difficult and unlikely. For the early attempts at a peaceful conclusion to the Korean conflict see Rosemary Foot, *A Substitute for Victory: The Politics of Peacemaking at the Korean Armistice Talks*, Ithaca, New York 1990, pp. 21–6.

58. CAB129(CP50)/200; memorandum by Bevin, 30 Aug. 1950.

59. FO371/83008/13; telegram from Tokyo to FO, 28 Sep. 1950. See also FO371/83008/17; telegram from Tokyo to FO, 4 Oct. 1950.

60. See Peter Lowe, 'An Ally and a Recalcitrant General: Great Britain, Douglas MacArthur and the Korean War, 1950–1', *English Historical Review*, vol. 105, no. 416, part 2, July 1990, p. 630.

61. Defe4/34; minute 5, 27 July 1950.

62. The decision to extend the Korean War has been extensively debated by historians. For the decision placed tightly within an ideological and political context see Cumings, 1990, vol. II, pp. 708–56. For a comprehensive account of diplomatic manoeuvres see Peter Lowe, *The Origins of the Korean War*, London 1986, pp. 176–200 and Callum MacDonald, *Korea, The War before Vietnam*, Oxford 1986, pp. 37–55. The best account of the various nuances of opinion within the American administration is Foot, 1985, pp. 55–88.

63. For an account of American assessments of Soviet and Chinese intentions regarding Korea see Foot, 1985, pp. 55–72.

64. CAB128(CM50)/61; minute, 26 Sep. 1950 and ibid./62; cabinet minute, 28 Sep. 1950.

65. Stueck, 1986, p. 78.

66. FO371/83253/276; telegram from Peking to FO, 18 Aug. 1950 and ibid./ 293–4; telegrams from Peking to FO, 14 and 15 Sep. 1950. J. Pollack notes that the Chinese military began to prepare for a conflict at the beginning of August 1950. J. Pollack, 'The Korean War and Sino-American Relations', in Harry Harding and Yuan Ming, eds, *Sino-American Relations, 1945–55: A Joint Reassessment of a Critical Decade*, US 1989, pp. 216–17.

67. FO371/93294/487; telegram from HC India to FO, 21 Sep. 1950.

68. Chiefs of Staff reservations are well documented in Lowe, 1986, pp. 190–1.

69. Stueck, 1986, pp. 84–5.

70. FO371/83253/314; minute by Franklin, 28 Oct. 1950.
71. See FO371/83250/214; telegram from Canton to WO, 30 June 1950: ibid., telegram from GHQFELF to Ministry of Defence, 5 July 1950: ibid. telegram from Machin to WO, 10 July 1950. Much of the information came from Chinese informers, or Chinese Nationalist sympathisers, but British nationals and especially commercial agents in China were an important source. Cumings notes that W.T. Keswick was closely associated with the American Office of Strategic Services (the forerunner of the CIA). See Cumings, 1990, p. 135.
72. FO371/83251/237; minute by Franklin, 29 July 1950.
73. FO371/83249/201; telegram from Peking to FO, 29 June 1950.
74. Ibid.; minute by Franklin, 4 July 1950.
75. Mao Tse-tung, *Selected Works*, vol. V, Peking 1965, pp. 35–6.
76. FO371/83249/201; telegram from Tokyo to FO, 14 July 1950. Information on Soviet air activity originated from the Chinese Nationalist Air Force. The Foreign Office did not dismiss the information, but argued that it was inevitable that the Chinese would need Soviet aid in order to build up their airforce. The US claimed that the Chinese airforce was under complete Soviet domination. Guy Burgess argued such a claim had to be treated with reservation, but others in the Foreign Office believed that this was by no means impossible.
77. FO371/83249/201; telegram from Peking to FO, 29 June 1950.
78. *DBPO*, Series II, vol. 4; no. 19, extract of memorandum by the Foreign Office, 13 July 1950, pp. 52–63.
79. Ibid., no. 59, brief by R. Scott, 28 Sep. 1950, pp. 162–5.
80. Sergei N. Goncharov, John W. Lewis and Xue Litai, *Uncertain Partners: Stalin, Mao, and the Korean War*, Stanford, Calif. 1993, pp. 136–9 and Kathryn Weathersby, 'The Soviet Role in the Early Phase of the Korean War: New Documentary Evidence', *Journal of American-East Asian Relations*, vol. 2, no. 4, 1993, pp. 429–32.
81. Cumings, 1990, p. 355. Cumings argues that Mao realised that if he released a significant number of the Korean volunteer army fighting in China then an invasion of the south would be far more likely. China's ties with North Korea tightened when the Soviets withdrew their military presence; these built upon close political and ideological bonds dating back to the 1930s.
82. *DBPO*, Series II, vol. 4; no. 58, Hutchison to Attlee, 28 Sep. 1950, p. 160.

CHAPTER 4: FEAR AND LOATHING

1. Quoted in George Lichtheim, *Imperialism*, London 1971, p. 96.
2. FO371/92238/193; telegram from Peking to FO, 27 April 1951. A. Whiting argues that this was a calculated Chinese measure aimed at reducing sympathy in China towards the West. A. Whiting, *China Crosses the Yalu*, New York 1960, p. 83. The wave of anti-westernism in China was well documented by the British press, especially by the *Manchester Guardian*. See articles, 7 March 1951 and 11 June 1951.

232 *Notes*

3. FO371/92202/247; Peking monthly report, 29 Aug. 1951.
4. FO371/92237/32; *Shih Chieh Shih Shih*, in *World Culture*, vol. 23. FO371/92378/33; minute by J.O. Lloyd 13 Feb. 1951.
5. For N.V. Roschin's dissatisfaction with the Chinese see FO371/92384/26; telegram from Peking to FO, 27 Sep. 1951. For Panikkar's attitude see FO371/92383/10; telegram from Peking to FO, 4 April 1950.
6. FO371/92200/188; *People's China*, 1 July 1951 (in telegram from Peking to FO, 17 July 1951).
7. FO371/92238/193; telegram from Peking to FO, 27 April 1951.
8. FO371/92234/48; minute by A.E.E. Franklin, 27 Feb. 1951.
9. CAB129(CP50)/267; memorandum by Bevin, 10 Nov. 1950.
10. *DBPO*, Series II, vol. IV; no. 109, Ernest Bevin to Oliver Franks, 15 Jan. 1951, pp. 304–7.
11. FO371/92233/16; telegram from Peking to FO, 2 Feb. 1951.
12. CHAS/C/4; letter from China Association to FO, 12 April 1951.
13. FO371/83255/339; telegram from Machin to FO, 11 Nov. 1950.
14. FO371/83254/348; G.E. Mitchell (Secretary and Vice-Chairman of the China Association) to R. Scott, 29 Nov. 1950.
15. CAB129(CP50)/267; memorandum by Bevin, 10 Nov. 1950.
16. J. Pollack, 'The Korean War and Sino-American Relations', in Harry Harding and Yuan Ming, eds, *Sino-American Relations, 1945–55: A Joint Reassessment of a Critical Decade*, US 1989, pp. 216–17.
17. Sergei N. Goncharov, John W. Lewis and Xue Litai, *Uncertain Partners: Stalin, Mao, and the Korean War*, Stanford, Calif. 1993. pp. 190–1 and Shu Guang Zhang, *Deterrence and Strategic Culture: Chinese-American Confrontations, 1949–1955*, Ithaca and London 1992, p. 98.
18. Bruce Cumings, *The Origins of the Korean War: Vol. II: The Roaring of the Cataract 1947–1950*, Princeton 1990, pp. 350–76 and Qiang Zhai, *The Dragon, the Lion and the Eagle*: *Chinese-British-American Relations, 1949–1958*, Kent, Ohio and London 1994, pp. 65–88.
19. Goncharov, Lewis and Xue, 1993, p. 193.
20. Mao Tse-tung, 1965, vol. V, p. 61.
21. Zhou Enlai, 1989, vol. II, pp. 59–63. Mark Ryan argues that the CCP leadership accepted before intervention that the US might use nuclear weapons against the Chinese mainland. He argues their attitude was a rational assessment based on political and strategic rather than simplistic ideological considerations. Mark A. Ryan, *Chinese Attitudes Towards Nuclear Weapons: China and the US during the Korean War*, New York 1989, pp. 29–32.
22. Shu Guang Zhang, 1992, pp. 89–90.
23. Zhou Enlai, 1989, vol. II, pp. 59–64.
24. PREM1439/332; telegram from FO to Peking 5 Dec. 1950 and Defe4/37/176; minute, 7 Nov. 1950.
25. *FRUS1950*(3), pp. 1761–74; minutes of meeting between President Truman and Prime Minister Attlee, 7 Dec. 1950. Also noted in C. MacDonald, *Korea, The War before Vietnam*, Oxford 1986, pp. 75–6.
26. Instead of offering a formalised buffer zone accompanied and followed by negotiations on wider issues, the initial UN six power resolution, which was introduced on 10 November, merely attempted to reassure

the Chinese that their borders would not be violated. For an account of this subject see P.N. Farrar, 'Britain's Proposal for a Buffer Zone South of the Yalu in November 1950: Was it a Neglected Opportunity to End the Fighting in Korea?', *Journal of Contemporary History*, vol. 18, no. 2, April 1983, pp. 327–51. For a comprehensive account of the ceasefire arrangements see Rosemary Foot, *A Substitute for Victory: The Politics of Peacemaking at the Korea Armistice Talks*, Ithaca, New York 1990.

27. Chou's reply to the Cease-Fire Group proposals of 13 January points to a principal ambiguity in the phrase 'existing international obligation'; this did not, he argued, necessarily refer to the Cairo and Potsdam Declarations but would allow the US to justify the maintenance of their aggressive positions in Korea and in Taiwan. PREM/1405, part 3; text of Chou's reply, 17 Jan. 1950.

28. Christian Alcock, 'Britain and the Korean War, 1950–1953', unpublished Manchester University PhD thesis 1986, pp. 123–4. This stand was taken despite intelligence reports indicating the scale of the Chinese intervention. See FO371/83254/339; telegram from Machin to FO, 10 Nov. 1950; 20 Nov. 1950 and 22 Nov. 1950.

29. FO371/9219/2; telegram from New York to FO, 28 Dec. 1950. PREM/1405; telegram from Washington to FO, 10 Jan. 1951. *FRUS1950*(3), pp. 1706–19; minutes of meeting between President Truman and Prime Minister Attlee, 4 Dec. 1950.

30. CAB128(CM50)/71; minute, 6 Nov. 1950.

31. Defe4/38; CoS confidential annex on implications of Chinese intervention, 30 Nov. 1950.

32. FO371/9233/3; minute by R. Scott, 30 Dec. 1950. See also FO371/83019/13; minute by Pierson Dixon, 8 Dec. 1950.

33. FO800/517; memorandum by Bevin, 12 Jan. 1951, drawn up in consultation with Strang, Makins and Dixon. Also quoted in A. Bullock, *Ernest Bevin: Foreign Secretary, 1945–51*, London 1983, p. 816.

34. PREM8/1439; telegram from Bevin to PM (Washington), 12 Dec. 1950.

35. *FRUS1951*(7), pp. 39–40; Secretary of State to embassy UK, message from President, 9 Jan. 1951.

36. Dean Acheson, *Present at the Creation*, New York 1969. Acheson acknowledges that Attlee's discursive technique was skilled; he admits that the Prime Minister often 'led the President well on to the flypaper'. The problem with analysing the conference is in estimating the British aim; if it was consultation with the US over atomic usage, then Britain received a verbal but not a written promise (this satisfied the Prime Minister, but not the Chiefs of Staff); if it was to help to undermine the concept of a 'limited war' then Britain succeeded; if it was to persuade the US to negotiate, then it went some way to delaying the aggression resolution. The main impact of the conference was on British domestic opinion see K.O. Morgan, *The People's Peace: British History 1945–1990*, Oxford 1990, p. 87. For a detailed discussion of the conference see Alcock, 1986, pp. 141–86.

37. These were by no means empty threats. The President had ordered nuclear capacity to be sent to the Far East. The use of nuclear weapons remained under active consideration throughout the next six months and

Cumings argues the US came closest to using them after MacArthur had been relieved of his far eastern command and while the Chinese were launching their spring offensive. Cumings, 1990, p. 750. Ryan is more sceptical over whether the Truman administration was close to using nuclear weapons; he argues reports by the State Department and Joint Chiefs of Staff deemed nuclear attacks on China inappropriate because there were few suitable targets and because of the impact on world opinion. Ryan, 1989, pp. 33–8.

38. *FRUS1951*(7), pp. 427–31; letter from Herbert Morrison to Acheson, 10 May 1951. *FRUS1951*(7), pp. 412–14; Walter S. Gifford to Secretary of State, 3 May 1951. The dismissal of General MacArthur went some way to reducing British opposition to this concession. The Chiefs of Staff doubted whether the Chinese would launch such an attack.

39. PREM/1405; telegram from FO to Washington, 30 Aug. 1951.

40. PREM8/1200; record of the meeting between Truman and Attlee, annex 2, 5 Dec. 1950.

41. DDRS 1989, 000991; NSC48/5, 17 May 1951.

42. DDRS 1983, 001338; National Intelligence Estimate, undated, 1951.

43. *FRUS1951*(7), Part 2, pp. 1503–6; CIA memorandum, 11 Jan. 1951. This report emphasised that there were 700 000 actively resisting the communist regime in south China, of which 300 000 were directly linked to the Nationalist regime on Taiwan. A Special Intelligence Estimate, of 22 May, put the figure at 600 000, with 300 000 under Nationalist control; it argued that with covert US logistical support this group could be a core of resistance in China, perhaps providing a bridgehead for the return of Chiang Kai-shek or Nationalist forces under an alternative leader. (No source provided for this intelligence, but presumingly Nationalist.)

44. Ibid., pp. 1476–1503; memorandum of conversation prepared in the Department of State, 6–7 Jan. 1951.

45. Ibid., pp. 1510–14; National Intelligence Estimate, 17 Jan. 1951 – National Intelligence Estimates involved contributions by the intelligence organisations, the Department of State, the Army, the Navy and the Airforce. See DDRS 1989, 000991; NSC48/5, 17 May 1951.

46. *FRUS1950*(7), pp. 1671–2; editorial note. This strategy was accepted by J.P. Davies, who argued that the 'Korean issue' provided the best opportunity to foster friction between the Soviet Union and the Chinese. *FRUS1950*(7), pp. 1607–8; memorandum by J.P. Davies, 24 March 1951. Paul Nitze, of the Policy Planning Staff, agreed that the long-term policy of the US had to be the encouragement of internal revolt, with an ultimate objective to establish a new regime. See *FRUS1951*(1), pp. 79–94; Draft paper prepared by the Policy Planning Staff, 26 June 1951.

47. FO371/92194/57; minute by Buzzard, 28 Feb. 1951.

48. For an account of MacArthur's dismissal see Robert Donovan, *Tumultuous Years: The Presidency of Harry S. Truman, 1949–1953*, New York 1982, pp. 340–54. For the British reaction see Peter Lowe, 'An Ally and a Recalcitrant General: Great Britain, Douglas MacArthur and the Korean War, 1950–1', *English Historical Review*, vol. 105, no. 416, part 2, July 1990, pp. 624–54.

49. PREM/1405; telegram from Oliver Franks, Washington to FO, 21 Jan. 1951.

50. FO371/92233/8; telegram from Peking to FO, 23 Jan. 1951. Tang argues the resolution 'cast a long shadow on Anglo-Chinese relations'. James Tang, *Britain's Encounter with Revolutionary China, 1949–54*, London 1992, p. 107.
51. *FRUS1951*(7), pp. 98–100; memorandum of telephone conversation by Lucius D. Battle, Special Assistant to the Secretary of State, 18 Jan. 1951.
52. CAB128(CM51)/5; minute, 22 Jan. 1950.
53. PREM/1405; minute no. 2 of Prime Ministers' meeting, 8 Jan. 1951.
54. FO371/92067/2; minute by Dixon, 2 Jan. 1951.
55. *FRUS1951*(7), pp. 98–100; memorandum of telephone conversation by Battle, 18 Jan. 1951.
56. Donovan, 1982, pp. 321–2.
57. See particularly a speech by Tom Driberg in *Hansard, Commons*, vol. 481, cols 1382–91; 30 Nov. 1950.
58. LPA; general correspondence files, Korea, January 1951. It is noticeable that 43 positive replies out of a total of 64 came from constituencies which had not returned a Labour member. Many of these constituencies, especially in the south, tended to be more radical because they had no chance of obtaining power.
59. M.R. Gordon, *Conflict and Consensus: Labour's Foreign Policy, 1914–1965*, Stanford, Calif. 1969, p. 230.
60. *The Times*, 3 Feb. 1951. Letter from N. Bower and H. Carter of the Peace with China Council to *The Times*. FO371/92238/174; minute by J.S. Shattock, 17 April 1951.
61. Brian Porter, *Britain and the Rise of Communist China: A Study of British Attitudes 1949–1954*, London 1975, pp. 106–8.
62. CAB128(CM50)8; minute by Minister of State, 25 Jan. 1951. See also Alcock for a detailed account; Alcock, 1986, pp. 208–26. Younger acknowledges that the initial decision was taken 'against what everyone thought Ernie would have done'; Younger's diary; quoted in Bullock, 1983, pp. 826–7.
63. *New Statesman*, 3 Feb. 1951.
64. LPA; International sub-committee of NEC, 12 Feb. 1951 and 9 April 1951.
65. Gordon argues that while Bevan was driven by personal ambition he was also a 'self-confessed ideologue' and hence desired to defend a socialist domestic and foreign policy. Gordon, 1969, pp. 232–46.
66. Quoted in Bullock, 1983, p. 826.
67. *The Economist*, 12 May 1951; *Daily Telegraph*, 3 Feb. 1951.
68. *Manchester Guardian*, 1 Feb. 1951; *The Times*, 1 Feb. 1951.
69. *The Observer*, 4 Feb. 1951.
70. *Manchester Guardian*, 1 Feb. 1951.
71. FO371/92234/25; telegram from FO to New York, 10 Feb. 1951 and FO371/92236/103; telegram from FO to New York, 6 April 1951.
72. FO371/92234/33; minute by Shattock, 15 Feb. 1951.
73. FO371/92234/25; telegram from New York to FO, 12 Feb. 1951.
74. FO371/92236/107; telegram from New York to FO, 17 April 1951. Jebb reports that the State Department was anxious to have some move towards

sanctions before MacArthur's statement to Congress on 19 April 1951. By the spring of 1950, the American public were in a vengeful mood: a government poll suggested that one-third would support a general war against the China, while the majority believed that the US should bomb Manchuria. See Rosemary Foot, *The Wrong War: American Policy and the Dimensions of the Korean Conflict, 1950–1953*, Ithaca, N.Y. 1985, p. 139.

75. FO371/95594; minute by Dixon, 10 March 1951. It was a prominent issue at a National Peace Council meeting on 8 January 1951. See FO371/92233/17; letter from D. Smith to Bevin, 9 Jan. 1951. This was a line taken by a number of local constituency Labour parties; for example, the Denton Labour Party sent a memorandum to Bevin advocating admission. FO371/92235/69; minute by Trench, 13 March 1951.
76. Ibid.; letter from Bevin to Franks, 14 Feb. 1951.
77. FO371/95594; minute by G.G. Fitzmaurice, second legal adviser, 16 March 1951.
78. FO371/95594; minute by Dixon, 16 March 1951.
79. Ibid.; minute by R. Scott, 1 March 1951.
80. FO371/95594; letter from Acheson to Bevin, 26 Feb. 1951. L. Merchant was most 'disappointed with the British attitude'. *FRUS1951*(2), pp. 227–8; memorandum of conversation by Special Assistant to the Bureau of Far East Affairs (R. Bacon), 14 Feb. 1951.
81. *FRUS1951*(2), pp. 246–7; British embassy to Department of State, 10 May 1951.
82. CAB134/291/7; Far East (Official) Committee, memorandum; Working Party on Economic Sanctions against China, 5 Feb. 1951.
83. *The Economist*, 17 March 1951.
84. CHAS/C/4; letter from Lever to Mitchell, 2 Nov. 1950.
85. *DBPO*, Series II, vol. IV; no. 83, Bevin to Franks, 1 Dec. 1950, pp. 225–7.
86. FO371/92276/112; Working Party report on Exports to China (EPC 50), note by the Minister of Defence, 21 Dec. 1951.
87. *FRUS1951*(7), pp. 1874–6; memorandum by Officer in charge of General Assembly in Office of UN Political and Security Affairs (David Popper), 9 Jan. 1951.
88. The State Department disliked the amendment but could not veto it because it was a rider on an important military appropriation bill. For details of the administration's response to this development and for Truman's position note, *Public Papers of the Presidents of the US: H.S. Truman, 1950–53*, Washington 1965, pp. 316–20.
89. FO371/92272/2; telegram from Washington (Ormond, Ministry of Transport) to FO (W. Harpham), 7 Dec. 1950.
90. FO371/92277/131; minute by Trench, 28 Feb. 1951.
91. FO371/92272/2; minute by W.S. Laver (FO), of meeting between CO, BT, Ministry of Supply, Ministry of Transport and Ministry of Defence, 16 Jan. 1951.
92. FO371/92276/117; minute by Trench, 22 Feb. 1951.
93. FO371/92276/111; telegram from FO to Washington, 1 March 1951.
94. FO371/92278/152; letter from K.W.D. Strong to S.E.V. Luke, 17 April

1951. The US Joint Intelligence Bureau was especially vigilant in its reporting of smuggling. The British government argued that it was exaggerating the problem and countered American claims by pointing to smuggling from Japan to China.

95. CAB128(CM51)/34; minute 2, Review of Strategic Exports to China. Malaya exported 120 tons to Tsingtao and 495 tons to Tientsin in the first half of January 1951. A major weakness of the Chinese advance was their lack of motorised equipment and motorised spares; with the import of truck tyres prohibited, rubber was an essential raw material import.

96. FO371/92277/140; meeting between the FO, CO and the Chiefs of Staff; comment by R. Scott, date not specified, 1951. For a detailed examination of British controls see Wenguang Shao, *China, Britain and Businessmen: Political and Commercial Relations, 1949–57*, London 1991, pp. 93–8.

97. FO371/92238/152; telegram from New York to FO, 10 May 1951. The resolution was adopted on 17 May, with 45 votes for the resolution, 9 abstentions (Ecuador, Egypt, India, Indonesia, Pakistan, Sweden, Syria, Afghanistan, Burma) and the Soviet bloc not participating in the voting.

98. FO371/92238/185; *Peking Daily*, 25 May 1951, in telegram from Peking to FO, 25 May 1951. The Chinese Vice-Minister of Foreign Affairs privately indicated his dissatisfaction with Britain's voting policy on 22 May to the Indian ambassador, Panikkar. Ibid., telegram from Peking to FO, 22 May 1951.

99. The possible imposition of a naval blockade was formalised in a Joint Chiefs of Staff paper, 12 January 1951. Foot, 1985, p. 119.

100. *FRUS1951*(7), pp. 1907–11; memorandum (James Lay to NSC) – Report by the Economic Co-ordinating Administration, Feb. 1951. A number of intelligence reports indicated that it was only by restricting equipment to the railway network that an embargo could cause significant bottlenecks in China.

101. *FRUS1951*(7), pp. 1600–4; Acheson to US mission, 14 April 1951. In order to co-ordinate 'special China lists' the western nations established CHINCOM (China Co-ordinating Committee) in September 1952. See J. Wilczynski, *The Economics and Politics of East – West Trade: A Study Between Developed Market Economies and Centrally Planned Economies in a Changing World*, London 1969, p. 272.

102. FO371/92201/211; telegram from Peking to FO, 14 July 1951.

103. FO371/95500/152; minute by R. Scott, 9 July 1951.

104. FO371/92284/308; Mitchell to Homewood (BT), 7 Aug. 1951.

105. FO371/95600/159; minute by J.O. Lloyd, 4 Aug. 1951.

106. *FRUS1951*(7), pp. 889–91; position paper for US delegate to Washington meeting, Sep. 1951.

107. Ibid., pp. 893–9; meeting US/UK foreign ministers, 11 Sep. 1951 and FO37192285/332; minute by Shattock, 27 Sep. 1951.

108. FO371/92202/225; R. Scott to Jebb, 14 Aug. 1951.

CHAPTER 5: EMPIRE RETAINED

1. Quoted in G.B. Endacott, *A History of Hong Kong*, London 1958, p. 10.
2. In 1842, in the aftermath of the first Opium War, China ceded Hong Kong to Britain. In 1860 the districts of Kowloon and Stonecutters Island were secured; in 1898 the New Territories, a much larger area of mainland China, was leased to Britain.
3. In 1943 the US and Britain agreed to abrogate extra-territorial rights in China and, while Britain refused to concede sovereignty over Hong Kong or include the New Territories in the treaty, Britain's hold on Hong Kong post-war remained uncertain. See K.C. Chan, 'Abrogation of British Extra-territoriality in China, 1942–43: A study of Anglo-American-Chinese Relations', *Modern Asia Studies*, vol. 11, no. 11, 1977, pp. 257–91. For Anglo-American-Chinese discussions about the status of Hong Kong see Chan Lau Kit-Ching, 'The Hong Kong Question during the Pacific War (1941–45)', *Journal of Imperial and Commonwealth History*, vol. 11, no. 1, Oct. 1973, pp. 56–79.
4. In November 1944 Attlee confirmed that Hong Kong was included in W.S. Churchill's declaration that he would not preside over the liquidation of the British Empire. FO371/46251/2119; official report, 9 Dec. 1944. During the war, the Colonial Office set up a small planning unit and a more extensive committee under N.L. Smith to consider the return to Hong Kong. CAB96/8; Far Eastern Subcommittee, 11 Jan. 1945
5. A. Bullock, *Ernest Bevin: Foreign Secretary 1945–51*, London 1983, p. 673. For a more detailed account of government discussions in 1949 note Zhong-ping Feng, *The British Government's China Policy*, Keele 1994, pp. 117–22.
6. FO371/8398/38; Ministry of Defence to GHQ, 4 Oct. 1950. *DBPO*, Series II, vol. IV; no. 61, Ministry of Defence to B.D.C.C. (Singapore), 4 Oct. 1950, pp. 167–9. A.N. Porter and A.J. Stockwell, eds, *British Imperial Policy and Decolonisation, 1938–64, Vol. 2, 1951–64*, London 1989, no. 14, The Defence Programme: Report by the Chiefs of Staff, 31 October 1952, CAB 131/12, pp. 180–5.
7. Quoted in B. Porter, *The Lion's Share: A Short History of British Imperialism 1850–1970*, London 1967, p. 311.
8. See Mark Curtis, *The Ambiguities of Power: British Foreign Policy Since 1945*, London 1995, pp. 12–13.
9. On average Hong Kong received 2.1 per cent of British exports to the commonwealth and Irish Republic.
10. CO1030/284; letter from A. Grantham to Secretary of State for Colonial Affairs, 2 Aug. 1955.
11. P.J. Cain and A.G. Hopkins, *British Imperialism: Crisis and Deconstruction, 1914–1990*, London 1993, pp. 275–81. They argue that this financial consideration was fundamental to the renewed British commitment to empire. Schenk argues that the sterling balances were not a source of instability to the pound because they were not on the whole very liquid liabilities. She argues that 'their liquidity ... varied considerably depending on how the assets were accumulated and who controlled their spending'. As a large and growing proportion were in government re-

serves and hence less likely to be drawn on, they were more stable than first thought. Catherine R. Schenk, *Britain and the Sterling Area: From Devaluation to Convertibility in the 1950s*, London 1994, pp. 25 and 35.

12. Schenk, 1994, pp. 50–3.
13. Catherine R. Schenk, 'Closing the Hong Kong Gap: The Hong Kong Free Dollar Market in the 1950s', *Economic History Review*, vol. 47, no. 2, May 1994, pp. 343–5.
14. Ibid., p. 345.
15. CO1030/392; minute by W.G. Hullard (BT), 29 May 1949. The Treasury was subsequently concerned about guaranteeing Hong Kong government borrowing for capital projects. Hong Kong's reserves were 150 per cent of the colony's annual expenditure, indicating how cheap the colony was to run. Schenk, 'Closing the Hong Kong Gap', p. 350.
16. Quoted in James T.T. Tang, 'From Empire Defence to Imperial Retreat: Britain's Postwar China Policy and the Decolonisation of Hong Kong', *Modern Asian Studies*, vol. 28, no. 2, 1994, p. 328.
17. *The Economist*, 12 May 1951. Wenguang Shao, *China, Britain and Businessmen: Political and Commercial Relations 1949–57*, London 1991, p. 7.
18. FO371/53637/11480; letter from G.W. Swire to G.V. Kitson, Under-Secretary at the Far Eastern Department, 18 May 1945.
19. H.H. Frank King, *The Hong Kong Bank in the Period of Development and Nationalism, 1941–1984: From Regional Bank to Multinational Group*, vol. IV of *The History of the Hong Kong and Shanghai Banking Corporation*, Cambridge 1991, p. 396.
20. In 1950, 20 per cent of Hong Kong's trade was with China; and the mainland provided essential food and water supplies.
21. For the failure of the CCP to take command of economic and social organisations in the colony see CO537/6075/54504; monthly report of the Special Branch, Hong Kong, June, July, Aug. and Nov. 1950.
22. Shao, 1991, p. 32.
23. FO371/83264/108; telegram from E. Dening to FO, 3 Nov. 1950.
24. FO371/83260/25; minute by G. Burgess, report on communist activity in Hong Kong for the six months ending Dec. 1949, 21 March 1950.
25. CO537/6032/53508/34; letter from Bevin to C.H. Johnston, 18 Feb. 1950.
26. CO537/6045/6; telegram from Hong Kong to CO, 11 April 1950 and FO371/83261/43; telegram from Hong Kong to FO, 5 May 1950.
27. CO967/51; speech by Arthur Creech Jones, Colonial Secretary, at a luncheon in honour of the Hong Kong Delegation to the British industrial fair, 15 May 1950.
28. CO537/5389; circular despatch by Creech Jones, 18 Feb. 1950.
29. FO371/83260/25; minute by Burgess, report on communist activity in Hong Kong for the six months ending Dec. 1949, 21 March 1950.
30. FO371/99244; telegram from Hong Kong to FO, 7 Feb. 1952.
31. C. MacDonald, *Britain and the Korean War*, Oxford 1990, p. 22.
32. FO371/83397/17; telegram from GHQ to Defence, 10 July 1950 and *DBPO*, Series II, vol. IV; no. 97.(i), Air Vice-Marshall Bouchier (Tokyo) to Ministry of Defence, 24 Dec. 1950.
33. CO537/6075; monthly report by Special Branch of Hong Kong Police,

Oct. 1950. The Chinese Nationalists were active in Hong Kong, but during 1950 Taiwan did not liaise closely with units in the colony. These units were in contact with Nationalist guerrilla forces in south China. CO537/6075; monthly report by Special Branch of Hong Kong Police, Aug. 1950. Steve Tsang argues the Triad group '14 K', established by General Kot Siu-wong, was a real threat to security in Hong Kong. Steve Tsang, *Democracy Shelved: Great Britain, China and Attempts at Constitutional Reform*, Hong Kong and Oxford 1988, p. 137.

34. FO371/83297/15; paper by Commander in Chief of Far East Land Forces, Hong Kong, 11 April 1950.
35. CO537/6032/53508; cabinet minute, 7 Feb. 1950. The Hong Kong and Kowloon Trade Union Congress comprised about 100 unions and was dominant in the waterfront trades; the communist Federation of Trade Unions controlled between 30 and 40 unions.
36. CO537/53508; letter from A. Grantham to J.J. Paskin (CO), 6 Aug. 1950.
37. CO537/53508; minute by J.H. Watson, assistant head of information research department, 8 Feb. 1950.
38. FO371/83260/5; telegram from Hong Kong to Secretary of State for the Colonies, A. Creech Jones, 31 Jan. 1950. Police broke up a rally, estimated by Hong Kong authorities as involving 3–5000 people. FO371/832261/36; telegram from Hong Kong to FO, 31 March 1950.
39. Tsang notes that two unofficial members of the Legislative Council, M.K. Lo and P.S. Cassidy, were directors of the Tramways Co. Tsang, 1988, pp. 126–7.
40. FO371/8322261/36; telegram from Hong Kong to FO, 31 March 1950. CO537/6075/54504; monthly reports of Special Branch, Hong Kong, June, July and August 1950.
41. Tsang, 1988, p. 129.
42. FO371/83264/107; minute by Trench, 2 Jan. 1951.
43. FO371/83263/81; report on communist activity in Hong Kong, author unknown, 21 July 1950.
44. FO371/83241/26: weekly Hong Kong intelligence appreciation, 29 June 1950; and Ibid./48; 29 Nov.
45. CO537/6075/54504; monthly report by Special Branch of Hong Kong Police, Aug. 1950.
46. Tsang, 1988, pp. 133–4.
47. CO537/6075/54504; monthly report by Special Branch of Hong Kong Police, Aug. 1950.
48. FO371/83262/45; telegram from Hong Kong to FO, 8 May 1950.
49. See FO371/83514/33: minute by P.D. Coates, undated, April 1950; telegram from Peking to FO, 28 March 1950: FO371/83262/45; telegram from FO to Hong Kong, 8 June 1950. FO371/92371/6; telegram from Peking to FO, 4 Jan. 1951: FO371/83516/68; telegram from Hong Kong to FO, 17 June 1950. See also E. Luard, *Britain and China*, London 1962, pp. 194–5.
50. FO371/83264/107; telegram from Hong Kong to FO, 23 Dec. 1950; and minute by Trench, 2 Jan. 1951.
51. FO371/99243/7; telegram from Hong Kong to FO, 16 Jan. 1952. The CCP initiated an attempt to take control of the local film industry in the summer of 1950.

52. FO371/99502/10; telegram from Hong Kong to FO, 8 April 1952. See also *The Times*, 6 May 1952.
53. FO371/99302/32: minute by R. Scott; minute by Lord Reading; minute by Eden, 3 June 1952.
54. N.J. Miners, 'Plans for Constitutional Reform in Hong Kong, 1946–52', *China Quarterly*, no. 107, Sept. 1986, p. 463. There were three unofficial Chinese members of the Legislative Council and three on the Urban Council, but these were appointed by the governor acting on advice from the Colonial Office (two unofficial on the Legislative Council were preselected, one by the Justices of the Peace, and one by the Hong Kong Chamber of Commerce). The only concession to democratisation was the two unofficial members elected by those qualified to be on the list of jurors.
55. It was proposed that administrative functions would be gradually handed over to the Municipal Council, elected on a fully representative basis, to all who were permanent residents in Hong Kong. The council would be financially autonomous, raising revenue from a rating system. FO371/53634/6982; memorandum by Hong Kong Planning Unit, 26 June 1945.
56. Tsang, 1988, p. 187.
57. Tsang, 1988, pp. 108–9 and 152–65. There had also been a significant shift in the attitude of the unofficials on the Legislative Council who had become more reluctant to introduce reform; between 1949 and 1952 they had forwarded, supported by Grantham, an alternative proposal for a large unofficial majority in the Legislative Council, which had moved away from the 1946 Young Plan for introducing elections to a new Municipal Council. Grantham opposed any reform, but believed this scheme would appease demands for reform while maintaining colonial power.
58. *The Economist*, 17 March 1951.
59. See CO1030/284; Report of Industrial Development in Hong Kong, 1955: BT11/4139; Trade with China, 1955 and BT11/4465; Hong Kong Economic Survey, 1950–51.
60. The US eased controls in 1951 and in 1952 allowing the export of certain goods if Hong Kong could guarantee that such exports were not reexported to China. Previously, in July 1950, the government requisitioned all oil stocks in Hong Kong. Hong Kong argued, with some justification given the attitude of US officials in Japan, that the Americans were trying to make Hong Kong unviable. See FO371/8339720; telegram from Hong Kong to FO, 24 July 1950.
61. FO371/99243; letter from Paskin to R. Scott, 9 Jan. 1952.
62. FO371/83302/7; minute by G.G. Fitzmaurice, (second legal adviser), 17 Feb. 1950.
63. CAB129(CP50)/6; memorandum by the Secretary of State for the Colonies and by the Minister of State, 3 April 1950. The Soviet ambassador in China, N.V. Roschin, argued there had been a real prospect of progress in the negotiations with the Chinese until a stalemate descended upon this case in the Hong Kong court. FO371/83290/367; telegram from Peking to FO, 24 May 1950.
64. Alexander Grantham recalls that 'Big Bull Donovan' personally, and forcefully, demanded the return of the aircraft. Alexander Grantham, *Via Ports: From Hong Kong to Hong Kong*, Hong Kong 1965, p. 162.

65. Bruce Cumings, *The Origins of the Korean War, Vol. 2: The Roaring of the Cataract 1947–1950*, Princeton 1990, p. 164.
66. CAB129 (CP50)/74; memorandum by the Secretary of State for Colonies, 21 April 1950.
67. *The Times*, 9 Oct. 1952 and *Daily Telegraph*, 14 Oct. 1952. Shao indicates that after the privy council decision of 28 July 1952, armed police raided Kai Tak airport to arrest employees and seize the assets of the two companies. Shao, 1991, p. 79.
68. FO371/922756/105; Information Office British embassy Washington, memorandum on Hong Kong's trade with China.
69. *FRUS1951*(7), pp. 1899–1902; memorandum by W. Thorp (Assistant Secretary of State for Economic Affairs) to G. Mathews (Deputy Under-Secretary of State), 9 Feb. 1951. See also FO371/92275/68; telegram from Washington to FO, 2 Feb. 1951: FO371/92282/291; meeting of Senate Foreign Relations Committee, US embassy, 11 July 1951; Prime Minister, Foreign Secretary, Minister of Defence, President Board of Trade all present.
70. *DBPO*, Series II, vol. IV; no. 100, extracts from the conclusion of a meeting of the cabinet held at 10 Downing Street on Tuesday, 2 Jan. 1951, pp. 278–81 and ibid.; no. 109; Bevin to Sir O. Franks, 15 Jan. 1951, pp. 304–7.
71. FO800/781/11; conversation between Dean Acheson and Eden, 22 Feb. 1952 and *FRUS1952–54* (12), p. 96–7; minutes of bipartite foreign ministers' meeting, 26 May 1952.
72. Martin Gilbert, *Never Despair: W.S. Churchill, Vol. VIII 1945–65*, London 1988, p. 583.
73. *FRUS1950* (6), pp. 556–63; minutes of the 39th Meeting of the United States delegation to the UN General Assembly, 14 Nov. 1950.
74. DDRS, 00009/6A, 1981; State Department Papers for Winston Churchill/Eisenhower talks, 5 Jan. 1952.
75. *FRUS1951*(7), pp. 1936–7; memorandum by the Deputy Assistant Secretary of State for East Asia (James Bonbright) and Rusk to Acheson, 21 March 1951. This assessment was supported by a report by the CIA. See *FRUS1951*(7), pp. 1995–9; memorandum by the Director of the CIA to W. Park Armstrong, Special Assistant for Intelligence to Acheson, 27 June 1951.
76. DDRS, 002929, 1987; White House Document, Operation Co-ordinating Board, 1 Dec. 1953. On 26 June 1950, Truman, commenting on moves to resist North Korean aggression, declared that he wanted 'everyone in on this including Hong Kong'. *FRUS1950* (7), pp. 178–83; memorandum of conversation by Ambassador at Large, P.C. Jessup, 26 June 1950.
77. *FRUS1952–54*(14), pp. 142–3; pt.1; memorandum of conversation by Assistant Secretary of State for Far Eastern Affairs (J. Allison) with Admiral Radford.
78. *FRUS1952–54* (12), part 1, pp. 339–40; memorandum by the Secretary of State for European Affairs (Merchant), 8 Sep. 1953 and *FRUS1951*(7), pt.1, pp. 1949–50; Marshall to Acheson, 9 April 1951.
79. *FRUS1952–54*(12), part 1, pp. 242–56; report by the staff planners to the military representative to the ANZUS council, 25 Nov. 1952 and

FRUS1952–54(12), part 1, pp. 303–6; report of Conference from the principal military authority representing Australia, France, New Zealand, UK and US in South East Asia, held at Pearl Harbor, 6 April 1953.

80. S.E. Ambrose, *The President, Vol. 2, 1952–1969*, London 1984, p. 182.
81. Defe4/60//27; minute 4, 24 Feb. 1953.
82. Defe5/43/647; commander of British Forces in the Far East, 31 Dec. 1952.
83. DDRS, 00009/6A, 1981; State Department Papers for Winston Churchill/Eisenhower talks, 5 Jan. 1952. The US decided to step up intelligence work in 1951 and, despite reports from Hong Kong and from K. Rankin, US ambassador in Taiwan, that a 'Third Force' was not viable, continued to promote such a movement in the colony. See *FRUS1951*(7), pp. 1764–8; memorandum by Deputy Director of the Office of Chinese Affairs (Perkins) to the Deputy Assistant to the Secretary of State for Far Eastern Affairs (Merchant), 1 Aug. 1951 and *FRUS1951* (7), pp. 1778–85; Rankin to Rusk, 13 Aug. 1951.
84. FO371/83560/12; telegram from Hong Kong to CO, 23 Nov. 1950. In June 1950 there were 67 US officials in Hong Kong and by September 1952 this had increased to 96.
85. FO371/92385/9: minute by J. Lloyd, 5 Oct. 1951; minute by R. Scott, 5 Oct. 1951.
86. FO371/92212; letter from R. Scott to Paskin, 9 Jan. 1952. The IRD supported the Foreign Office position. See FO371/99379/10; minute by P.S. Falla, 26 Sep. 1952.
87. FO371/99244/53; letter from Johnston to L. Lamb, 16 May 1952. Fechteler also noted that the 'Chinese Communists themselves are not anxious [for] Hong Kong to fall'. See *FRUS1952–54*(12), pp. 22–34; memorandum of the substance of discussion at a Department of Defense–JCS meeting, 16 Jan. 1952.
88. CO537/6075/54504; monthly report of the Special Branch, Hong Kong, Nov. 1950.
89. FO371/92372/36; *Lien Hon Pao*, Canton, 28 Jan. 1951; *Nan Fang Jih Pao*, 10 Feb. 1951 and FO371/99244/56; *Nan Fang Jih Pao*, 15 April 1952, in telegram from Canton to FO, 21 April 1952.
90. See FO371/99230/5; political summary, Peking 29 Jan. 1952; ibid./18; political summary, 8 May to 27 May 1952: FO371/99244; telegram from Peking to FO, 11 May 1952: FO371/99244/65; telegram from Peking to FO, 20 May 1952.
91. See FO371/99257/19; *NCNA*, 17 Jan. 1952 (in Singapore analysis of the Chinese press, 17–23 Jan. 1952).
92. FO371/99230/9; political summary, Peking 22 Feb. 1952.
93. FO371/99244/64; *NCNA*, 13 May 1952. See also FO371/99257/19; *NCNA*, 19 Jan. 1952 (in Singapore analysis of the Chinese press, 17–23 Jan. 1952): FO371/99257/19: *NCNA*, 7 Feb. 1952: Peking Radio, 2 Feb. 1952 (in Singapore analysis of the Chinese press, 7–13 Feb. 1952): FO371/99243; *NCNA*, 11 Feb. 1952.
94. Tsang, 1988, pp. 175–7.
95. James Tang, *Britain's Encounter with Revolutionary China, 1949–54*, London 1992, p. 186.

96. Tsang, 1988, p. 134.
97. Sergei N. Goncharov, John W. Lewis and Xue Litai, *Uncertain Partners: Stalin, Mao, and the Korean War*, Stanford, Calif. 1993, p. 100.
98. Peking Radio announcement; quoted in Luard, 1962, p. 186.
99. Noted in the *Daily Telegraph*, 22 Nov. 1952; *The Times*, 22 Nov. 1952; Shao, 1991, pp. 79–83. Chang Han-fu argued that this was an unfriendly act against China. The *Daily Worker*, 9 Oct. 1952.
100. Shao, 1991, p. 22. The PRC did not formally declare Hong Kong and Macao to be Chinese territories until 1963, when they argued both territories should be restored by peaceful negotiation.
101. Tang, 1992, p. 186 and Shao, 1991, p. 22.
102. Harry Hinton, *China's Turbulent Quest: An Analysis of China's Foreign Policy Since 1949*, New York and London 1972, p. 273 and C.P. Fitzgerald, *Revolution in China*, London 1952, p. 236.
103. H. Trevelyan, *World's Apart: China 1953–5, Soviet Union 1962–5*, London 1971, p. 60. In 1953, for example, the Chinese agreed to legitimise the position of the Queens Messenger Service in China in return for freedom of access in Hong Kong for a Chinese courier service.
104. See H.C. Hinton, *Communist China in World Politics*, London 1986, p. 24. John Darwin argues that Hong Kong's status remained unchanged for three reasons: the New Territories were leased territory, British and Chinese politicians recognised that China would not tolerate an enhancement of the colony's internal status and the colony was economically significant for China. J. Darwin, *Britain and De-colonisation: The Retreat from Empire in the Post War World*, London 1988, p. 310.
105. FO371/83397/20; telegram from Hong Kong to FO, 24 July 1950. Remittances from Hong Kong to the mainland were also substantial. See Hinton, 1972, p. 273.
106. Alexander Eckstein, *Communist China's Economic Growth and Foreign Trade: Implications for U.S. Policy*, New York 1966, p. 161.
107. Fitzgerald argued that China was less hostile towards Britain as compared to the US 'largely' because of the 'mutual benefits of trade and the common value of Hong Kong to both countries'. Fitzgerald, 1952, p. 218.

CHAPTER 6: END OF INFORMAL EMPIRE

1. See T.N. Thompson, 'China's Nationalisation of Foreign Firms: The Politics of Hostage Capitalism, 1949–57', Baltimore, Mass., unpublished dissertation 1979; Wenguang Shao, *China, Britain and Businessmen: Political and Commercial Relations*, Oxford 1991; and Aron Shai, 'Imperialism Imprisoned. The Closure of British Firms in the People's Republic of China', *English Historical Review*, vol. 104, no. 410. January 1989, pp. 88–109. For a more detailed examination of the plight of an individual business see chapter 9 in Frank H.H. King, *The Hong Kong Bank in the Period of Development and Nationalism, 1941–1984: From Regional Bank to Multinational Group*, vol. IV of *The History of the Hong Kong and Shanghai Banking Corporation*, Cambridge 1991.

2. For an introductory account of British business in China see Jürgen Osterhammel, 'British Business in China, 1860s–1950s', in R.P.T. Davenport-Hines and Geoffrey Jones, eds, *British Business in Asia since 1860*, Cambridge 1989, pp. 189–227. Davenport-Hines argues that because of the complex nature of ownership, it is difficult to label companies British. See also P.J. Cain and A.G. Hopkins, *British Imperialism: Innovation and Expansion, 1688–1914*, London 1993, pp. 422–47 and P.J. Cain and A.G. Hopkins, *British Imperialism: Crisis and Deconstruction, 1914–1990*, London 1993, pp. 235–60.

3. See introduction footnote 18.

4. BT11/3390; Board of Trade survey of British companies in China 1947.

5. Osterhammel, in Davenport-Hines and Jones, 1988, pp. 201–9. British investments benefited from the growth of Shanghai in the inter-war years which increased the value of real estate and allowed firms to move into public utility provision, including gas, water and tramways. Shipping companies maintained their dominant position in the China market.

6. Jürgen Osterhammel, 'Imperialism in Transition: British Business and the Chinese authorities, 1931–37', *China Quarterly*, no. 98, June 1984, pp. 260–87.

7. CAB129/(CP49)/248; memorandum by Bevin, 12 Dec. 1949. This argument reflected the views of experts on Chinese communism in the Foreign Office. See FO371/83341/2; minute by Guy Burgess, 6 Jan. 1950.

8. Stuart Schram, *The Political Thought of Mao Zedong*, New York 1969, p. 202. Schram argues Mao's thought was not strictly original here, but because of China's semi-colonial status the Chinese leader stressed, to a far greater extent, the longevity of the bourgeoisie's role in the Chinese revolution. Schram, 1969, p. 68. See also Carl Riskin, *China's Political Economy: The Quest for Development since 1949*, Oxford 1987, p. 40.

9. Quoted in Schram, 1969, p. 229.

10. Note Cheng Chu-yuan, *Communist China's Economy, 1949–1962: Structural Changes and Crisis*, South Orange, N.J. 1963.

11. Zhou Enlai, *Selected Works*, vol. II, Beijing 1989, p. 22. Chen Yun reaffirmed that private capitalists had a role in the Chinese economy. Chen Yun, 'The Economic Situation and Problems concerning Readjustment of Industry, Commerce and Taxation', in *New China's Economic Achievements, 1949–52*, compiled by China Committee for the Promotion of International Trade, Peking 1952, pp. 61–79.

12. Peter Schran argues that the economic policies of the CPG derived from the Yenan period and hence were not satisfactory to meet China's economic problems. Peter Schran, 'On the Yenan Origins of Current Economic Policies', in Dwight H. Perkins, ed., *China's Modern Economy in Historical Perspective*, Stanford, Calif. 1975, p. 297.

13. Zhou Enlai, 1989, vol. II, p. 21.

14. Beverly Hooper, *China Stands Up: Ending the Western Presence 1948–1950*, Sydney and London 1985, p. 66.

15. Shao, 1991, p. 50. Whether this bureau was set up to consider joint Sino-Soviet as well as joint Sino-Western enterprises is unclear from Shao's evidence.

16. Hooper, 1985, p. 59.

17. Suzanne Pepper, *Civil War in China: The Political Struggle, 1945–1949*, Berkeley, La. 1978, pp. 350–1.
18. See Shai, 1989, pp. 88–96 for a detailed account.
19. FO371/833532/40; letter from British Chamber of Commerce, Shanghai, to Esler Dening, 15 Oct. 1950.
20. Willy Kraus, *Private Business in China, Revival between Ideology and Pragmatism*, London 1989, p. 54. See also Osterhammel, 1984, pp. 269–70.
21. See Shao, 1991, p. 37.
22. For a breakdown of taxation changes in June 1950 see Po Yi-po, 'On the Question of Tax Readjustment', in *New China's Economic Achievements, 1949–52*.
23. FO371/83353/240; letter from British Chamber of Commerce, Shanghai, to Dening, FO, 15 Oct. 1950.
24. FO371/83345/40; memorandum by the British Chamber of Commerce, Shanghai, March 1950, enclosed in a letter from British Chamber of Commerce to China Association, 1 April 1950.
25. CHAS/C; letter from China Association to FO, 26 April 1951.
26. King, 1991, p. 383.
27. See CHAS/MCP/50/G/29; China Association minute and circular, 4 April 1950: FO371/83346/76; British Chamber of Commerce to China Association, 27 April 1950 and FO371/83345; telegram from FO to Shanghai, 6 April 1950. (Report of meeting with a delegation of British firms, including British-American Tobacco, Lever Bros., Calico Printers, Patons.) The British Chamber of Commerce may have proposed withdrawal to force government action, but their position also reflects the extent of their disillusionment.
28. CHAS/MCP/53/46; China Association Bulletin, 26 March 1950.
29. Mao Tse-tung, *Selected Works*, vol. V, Peking 1977, p. 34. The Chinese unified the exchange rate in July 1950, facilitating trade for private Chinese and to a lesser extent foreign businessmen.
30. CHAS/MCP/50/G; letter from H.J. Collar (ICI) to G.E. Mitchell (Secretary and Vice-Chairman of the China Association), 13 July 1950.
31. FO371/92262/66; aide memorandum from Shanghai Chamber of Commerce to FO, 26 April 1951 and FO371/92262/74; telegram from Shanghai Chamber of Commerce to the China Association, 11 June 1951.
32. Mao Tse-tung, 1977, vol. V, p. 65.
33. F.C. Teiwes, 'The Establishment and Consolidation of the New Regime', in R. MacFarquar and J.K. Fairbank, eds, *The Cambridge History of China: The People's Republic, Part 1, The Emergence of Revolutionary China, 1949–65*, Cambridge 1987, p. 90.
34. K.G. Lieberthal, in his intuitive study of the consolidation of communist rule in Tientsin, argues that the various campaigns inaugurated by the CPG galvanised the young and the new industries, but, more generally, failed to transform the basic value system of the urban Chinese and made the populace increasingly disillusioned with the regime; forcing subsequent mass mobilisation campaigns to be more dogmatic and intense. K.G. Lieberthal, *Revolution and Tradition in Tientsin, 1949–52*, Stanford 1980, pp. 180–90.
35. FO371/99282/27; telegram from Shanghai to FO, 25 Feb. 1952.

36. CHAS/MCP/70/M/4; China Association Bulletin, 20 Feb. 1952.
37. King, 1991, p. 377.
38. FO371/99282; copy of letter from Collar to the home directors of ICI, 25 Feb. 1952.
39. FO371/99284/81; telegram from Peking to FO, 28 March 1952.
40. FO371/83344/30; minute by J.S. Shattock, 13 March 1950. Shipping companies such as Williamson, George Grimble and Sons, and insurance companies such as Lambert Bros. and Lloyds, who were suffering losses because of the blockade, were also lobbying the government on this issue.
41. The British Chiefs of Staff agreed intervention to end the blockade of the Chinese east coast was feasible and in a letter to William Strang, Permanent Under-Secretary of State at the Foreign Office, Admiral Sir Rhoderick McGrigor, the First Sea Lord, requested action against Nationalist ships. Defe4/29/27; minute 5, 15 Feb. 1950 and CAB134/289/1; minutes of meeting, with Dening in the chair, 27 Feb. 1950. The Far Eastern (Official) Committee of the cabinet discussed this question frequently and in depth. The Foreign Office rejected military action because of its consequences on Anglo-American relations and tried instead to persuade the US to pressurise the Chinese Nationalists.
42. FO371/83344/30; record of meeting between Foreign Office (Bevin and officials, unspecified) and China Association (W.J. Keswick, J.K. Swire, W.R. Cockburn, E.J. Nathan, D.M. Oppenheim and G.E. Mitchell), 11 March 1950.
43. FO371/83345/52; letter from China Association to FO, 11 April 1950. Shao, 1991, p. 119. James Tang, *Britain's Encounter with Revolutionary China, 1949–54*, London 1992, p. 149.
44. FO371/99282/34; letter from Tony Keswick to R. Scott, 10 March 1952.
45. FO371/99290/236; telegram from Shanghai to FO, 16 June 1952.
46. FO371/99283/63; letter from Mitchell to Eden, 19 March 1952 and FO371/99283/35; telegram from Peking to FO, 11 March 1952. The Hong Kong and the Shanghai Bank was against remittance control.
47. FO371/83348/135; telegram from FO to Peking, 26 May 1950 and CAB129(CP52)/107; memorandum by Eden, 8 April 1952.
48. FO371/83345/31; telegram from Peking to FO, 22 March 1950.
49. FO371/83345/45; minute by Dening, 3 March 1950.
50. CAB129(CP50)/73; memorandum by Bevin, 20 April 1950.
51. CHAS/MCP/50/G; minutes of meeting between Tony Keswick (Chairman of China Association) and Bevin, 17 March 1950.
52. FO371/83345/52; telegram from Peking to FO, undated April 1950.
53. FO371/99287/169; draft paper for cabinet, by J.K. Drinkall, 29 May 1952.
54. CAB128/(CM50)17/24; cabinet minute, 25 May 1950. Also quoted in Tang, 1992, p. 153 and Shai, 1989, p. 90. The government informed British merchants in March and August of 1950. See FO371/83345/56; minute by Shattock, 27 March 1950, of meeting with China Association, 16 March 1950 and FO371/83350/206; minute by Dening (of meeting with British merchants), 23 Aug. 1950.
55. *Hansard, Commons*, vol. 475, col. 2073; speech by Eden, 24 May 1950.
56. FO800/780; meeting between the British government and the China Association, 7 April 1952.

57. FO371/83345/39; minute of meeting between Treasury, FO and BT, 30 March 1950.
58. FO371/99289/229; letter from D.R. Serpell (Treasury) to Johnston (FO), 18 June 1952.
59. FO371/99287/169; telegram from Hong Kong to FO, 13 March 1952.
60. FO371/99289/228; letter from J.B. Sidebotham (CO) to C. Johnston (FO), 14 June 1952.

CHAPTER 7: A MOST UNFAVOURED TRADING NATION

1. Manchester Chamber of Commerce, *Monthly Record*, vol. LXIV, 1953, p. 1.
2. Feng-hwa Mah notes that Chinese exchange rates distort the true pattern of Chinese trade somewhat because the yuan was over-valued against the dollar and the official yuan-dollar rate was inconsistent with the ruble-yuan and with the ruble-dollar rate. Chinese figures thus underestimate the level of Sino-Western trade and overestimate China's trade with the communist bloc. See Feng-hwa Mah, *The Foreign Trade of Mainland China*, Edinburgh 1972, p. 16.
3. British exports to Hong Kong averaged 1.1 per cent of total British exports, compared to 0.7 per cent in 1913 and 0.76 per cent in 1922.
4. If there was any long-term economic trend it was for a reduction in China's trade with the West and a rise in intra-regional trade with the rest of East Asia, a process also curtailed in this period by the cold war.
5. For a breakdown of the pre-1978 Chinese trading system see Nicholas Lardy, *Foreign Trade and Economic Reform in China, 1978–1990*, Cambridge 1992, chapter 2. He notes that with the exception of a few individual products the state made financial losses on exports, but profits on imported goods offset losses on exports.
6. It should be noted that much of China's textile industry had been destroyed during the war and clothing entrepreneurs had fled to other Asian bases and especially Hong Kong where they kick-started industrialisation.
7. Zhou Enlai, *Selected Works*, vol. II, Beijing 1989, p. 20.
8. Suzanne Pepper, *Civil War in China: The Political Struggle, 1945–49*, Berkeley, Los Angeles 1978, pp. 372–3. This was a pattern of trade also pursued by the Soviet bloc at this time. See J. Wilczynski, *The Economics and Politics of East-West Trade: A Study Between Developed Market Economies and Centrally Planned Economies in a Changing World*, London 1969, p. 61.
9. See Chen Jian, *China's Road to the Korean War: The Making of the Sino-American Confrontation*, New York 1994, pp. 33–64.
10. *First Five Year Plan for Development of the National Economy of the People's Republic of China in 1953–57*, Peking 1956, p. 162.
11. See Sergei N. Goncharov, John W. Lewis and Xue Litai, *Uncertain Partners: Stalin, Mao, and the Korean War*, Stanford, Calif. 1993, doc. 21, p. 240.
12. Yeh Chi-chuang, 'Three Years of China's Foreign Trade', in *New China's Economic Achievements, 1949–52*, compiled by China Committee for the Promotion of International Trade, Peking 1952, p. 242.

13. FO371/99292/317; *Ta Kung Pao*, 20 July 1952.
14. *Hansard, Commons*, vol. 501, col. 269; speech by Harold Davies (Labour, Stafford, Leek), 20 May 1952.
15. FO371/99303/2; minute by Marquis Reading (Parliamentary Under-Secretary of State at the FO) 15 Aug. 1952.
16. A conclusion also reached by James Tang, *Britain's Encounter with Revolutionary China, 1949–54*, London 1992, p. 158 and Wenguang Shao, *China, Britain and Businessmen: Political and Commercial Relations, 1949–57*, London 1991, p. 128.
17. Goncharov, Lewis and Xue, 1993, p. 245.
18. Zhou Enlai, 1989, vol. II, p. 21.
19. See FO371/92289; telegram from Prague to FO, 26 June 1951: FO371/92291; BBC monitor report, 23 Jan. 1951: FO371/92295; telegram from Warsaw to FO, 6 Feb. 1951: FO371/105259/4; telegram from Moscow to FO, 26 March 1952.
20. *The Economist*, 5 Sep. 1953. Trade was essential for the East European satellites because being small relatively self-contained states they were reliant on outside supplies.
21. Alexander Eckstein, *Communist China's Economic Growth and Foreign Trade: Implications for U.S. Policy*, New York 1966, pp. 139–41. Moreover, by not joining the Council of Mutual Economic Assistance the Chinese could sell primary goods to the highest bidder.
22. FO371/105259/13; *NCNA*, 15 Sep. 1952.
23. Eckstein, 1966, pp. 154–6.
24. See Carl Riskin, *China's Political Economy: The Quest for Development since 1949*, Oxford 1987, pp. 73–4 and Frank King, *A Concise Economic History of Modern China, 1840–61*, Hong Kong 1969, p. 179.
25. Eckstein, 1966, p. 161.
26. Goncharov, Lewis and Xue, 1993, pp. 125–6.
27. For CPG policy towards the national minorities see T. Heberer, *China and its National Minorities*, New York 1989 and J.T. Dreyer, *China's Forty Millions: Minority Nationalities and National Integration in the Peoples' Republic of China*, Cambridge, Mass. 1976.
28. *The Observer*, 13 April 1952 in LPPCC; 118/1/1.
29. *The Times*, 16 June 1952 and *Manchester Guardian*, 6 June 1953.
30. *The Economist*, 20 Dec. 1952 and 7 March 1953.
31. *Hansard, Commons*, vol. 518, col. 466; question by D. Donnelly, 22 July 1953 and *Hansard, Commons*, vol. 501, cols 932–3; speech by Silverman, 26 May 1950.
32. *Hansard, Commons*, vol. 518. col. 233, 21 July 1953.
33. LPA; NEC, international sub-committee, 17 Feb. 1953.
34. FO371/99318/14; *Peking Daily*, 11 April 1952 (enclosed in telegram from Peking to FO, 17 April 1950). Noted also in Shao, 1991, p. 154.
35. Lord Boyd-Orr was the first director of the UN Food and Agriculture Organisation, 1945–48; his pessimistic predictions about future world food shortages may explain his advocacy of trade with China.
36. FO371/105248/4; paper by British Chamber for the Promotion of International Trade, undated Jan. or Feb. 1953.
37. *The Economist*, 26 July 1952. *The Economist* saw these developments as

positive but were sceptical as regards Soviet and Chinese communist motives.
38. CHAS/A/11; China Association Annual Report, 1 March 1953 to 31 March 1954. Australian trade did not increase substantially until the early 1960s, as the Australian economy began to reorient away from the Sterling Area towards Asia.
39. *The Economist*, 7 March 1953 and 7 Feb. 1953.
40. FO371/105262/47; letter from G.E. Mitchell (China Association) to J. Mckenzie (FO), 21 April 1953.
41. FO371/99318; letter from John Keswick to Tony Keswick, 8 April 1952.
42. FO371/99320/98; letter from R. Radcliffe Steel, Lambert Bros., to Under-Secretary of State, 3 Oct. 1952.
43. FO371/105262/47; letter from G.E. Mitchell (China Association) to J. Mckenzie (FO), 21 April 1953.
44. Manchester Chamber of Commerce, *Monthly Record*, vol. LXIV, 1953, p. 1.
45. FO371/99292; minutes of meeting between FO and China Association, 25 July 1952. H.J. Collar reported that a source in Shanghai had evidence suggesting the Chinese were not enthusiastic about trading through Berlin. (R. Scott, Lord Reading and C.H. Johnston represented the Foreign Office, Collar, Gray, R. Heyworth (Lever) and W.R. Cockburn (Chartered Bank of Australia, India and China) represented the China Association.)
46. CAB129(CP50)/81; memorandum by the President of the Board of Trade, 2 March 1953.
47. *Hansard, Commons*, vol. 501, col. 268; speech by Anthony Eden, 20 May 1952.
48. PREM/11/233; letter from W.S. Churchill to Eden, 28 April 1952 and CAB129/CP(53)/37; cabinet paper by Eden, 3 Feb. 1953.
49. FO371/105261/10; letter from E.A. Cohen (BT) to Norman Kipping (FBI), 10 Feb. 1953.
50. See FO371/10561/3; minute by J. Snodgrass, 10 Jan. 1953: Tang, 1992, p. 163: PREM11/233; Eden to Churchill, 25 April.
51. FO371/105261/10; letter from E.A. Cohen (BT) to Norman Kipping (FBI), 10 Feb. 1953.
52. See P.J. Cain and A.G. Hopkins, *British Imperialism: Crisis and Deconstruction, 1914–1990*, London 1993.
53. FO371/99291/280; telegram from Shanghai to FO, 19 July 1952.
54. CHAS/C/4; letter from China Association to Johnston (FO), 9 July 1952.
55. FO371/99297/431; note from China Association to FO, 17 Dec. 1952.
56. FO371/99318/44; minute by A.E. Percival (BT) of meeting with four British delegates who attended the conference, 4 April 1952.
57. *The Economist*, 7 March 1953.
58. *The Economist*, 7 March 1953.
59. FO371/99321/114; S.H. Levine (BT) to Johnston, 4 Dec. 1952.
60. CAB128(CM53)/60; discussion of cabinet memorandum by Board of Trade, CAB129(CP53)/294; 22 Oct. 1953.
61. For COCOM discussions regarding the imposition of economic sanctions against China see chapters 3, 4 and 8.
62. CAB129(CP53)/81; memorandum by the President of the Board of Trade, 2 March 1953.

63. *Hansard, Commons*, vol. 518, col. 2609; reply by H. Strauss, Parliamentary Secretary to the Board of Trade, to parliamentary question by Swingler, 27 Oct. 1953.
64. FO371/105180; letter from Peter Thorneycroft to Eden, 27 Nov. 1957.
65. BT11/4494; letter from C.J. Homewood to G.E. Mitchell, 29 Jan. 1952.
66. F.D. Holzman argues that from 1953 the Soviet Union no longer benefited economically from the separation of East and West, and that because Eastern Europe had historically relied to a far greater extent on trade with the West, there was a residual demand in the Eastern European economies for economic contact with the West. J. Wilczynski agrees that economic pressures within the Soviet Union were the spur. He notes that the imposition of economic embargoes by the West and autarkic policies in the Soviet bloc had reduced the level of East–West trade from 2.6 per cent of world trade in 1948 to 1.3 per cent in 1953. But he also argues that it was western controls that had forced the Soviet bloc to adopt autarkic policies in the first place. See F.D. Holzman, *International Trade under Communism – Politics and Economics*, London 1976, pp. 137–8 and Wilczynski, 1969, pp. 52, 285.
67. FO371/99321/105; minute by R. Scott, 27 Oct. 1952 (with comments by Eden).
68. FO371/105211/11; minute by P. Wilkinson, 10 Dec. 1953.
69. FO371/99320/88; letter from Johnston to L. Lamb, 26 Sep. 1952.
70. FO371/99320/91; minute by Johnston, 4 Sep. 1952.
71. FO371/99321/102; letter from F.S. Tomlinson to Johnston, 22 Oct. 1952.
72. CHAS/C/2; statement of policy by FO and BT, 11 Nov. 1953.

CHAPTER 8: STALEMATE AND RESTRAINT

1. PREM11/301; letter from W. Churchill to S. Lloyd, 26 Aug. 1952. Also quoted in M. Dockrill, 'The Foreign Office, Anglo-American Relations and the Korean Truce Negotiations, July 1951 – July 1953', p. 102, in J. Cotton and I. Neary, eds, *The Korean War in History*, Manchester 1989; and in P. Lowe, 'The Significance of the Korean War in Anglo-American Relations, 1950–1953', p. 5,. in J. Young and M. Dockrill, eds, *British Foreign Policy*, 1945–56, London 1989.
2. Clement Attlee, 'Britain and America: Common Aims, Different Opinions', *Foreign Affairs*, vol. 32, no. 2, Jan. 1954.
3. FO800/782/84; letter from Eden to PM, 1 Sep. 1951.
4. M. Gilbert, *Never Despair, W.S. Churchill, Vol. VIII, 1945–65*, London 1988, pp. 680 and 918.
5. *Hansard, Commons*, vol. 503, cols 285–6, 1 July 1952.
6. James Tang, *Britain's Encounter with Revolutionary China, 1949–1954*, London 1992, p. 113.
7. FO371/99260/9; minute by R. Scott, 25 Jan. 1952. Also quoted in Tang, 1992, p. 114.
8. FO371/99260/9; letter from Lionel Lamb to R. Scott, 11 Jan. 1952.
9. FO371/105179/1; minute by R. Scott, 5 Dec. 1952 and FO371/99217; minute by R. Scott, 17 May 1952. Scott had a difficult relationship with

Eden, who accused him of trying to dictate British policy in the Far East. Tensions between the two men come across in the oral interview Scott gave to Anthony Seldon in 1980, in the Robert Scott Papers (ACC8181/18).

10. FO371/99235; letter from Lamb to R. Scott, 17 April 1952. Teiwes agrees that these campaigns successfully undermined the basis of social relations in China, replacing ties of family, school and work place with state control. F.C. Teiwes, 'Establishment and Control of the New Regime', p. 90, in R. MacFarquhar and J.K. Fairbank, eds, *The Cambridge History of China: Vol. 14, The People's Republic, Part 1, The Emergence of Revolutionary China, 1949–65*, Cambridge 1987. Lieberthal, analysing developments in Tientsin, disagrees with this assessment, arguing that the campaigns, while radically changing the attitudes of a minority, did not seriously affect the social relationships of the majority. K.G. Lieberthal, *Revolution and Tradition in Tientsin*, 1949–52, Stanford, Calif. 1980, pp. 189–90.

11. FO371/99234/49; telegram from Peking to FO, 19 Feb. 1952.

12. FO371/105194/67; BDCC (Far East) to FO (record of conversation with Lamb), 19 Aug. 1953.

13. FO371/92238/142; telegram from Peking to FO, 30 Oct. 1952.

14. FO371/99234; letter from R. Scott to A. Grantham, 13 March 1953.

15. FO371/992681/5; letter from R. Scott to F.S. Tomlinson, 21 March 1952.

16. FO371/92265/33; FO memorandum by Pierson Dixon, 27 Aug. 1952.

17. FO371/105193/54; letter from Lamb to Churchill, 16 June 1953.

18. FO371/99230/26; political summary (Peking), 13–28 Aug. 1952 and telegram from Peking to FO, 29 Aug. 1952.

19. FO800/780; telegram from Paris to FO, 9 Nov. 1951.

20. FO371/99267/68; draft intel by R. Scott, 9 Oct. 1952.

21. FO371/105182/6; brief by R. Scott, on the Prime Minister's visit to Washington, 25 Feb. 1953. Also noted in C. MacDonald, *Korea, the War before Vietnam*, Oxford 1986, p. 158.

22. FO371/99268/15; letter from R. Scott to Tomlinson, 21 March 1952.

23. FO371/99265/8; minute by C.H. Johnston, 22 Feb. 1952. This assessment was supported by evidence that the Soviet Union had not supplied Mark II/28 bombers to China, only light to medium bombers; this suggested that they were concerned only that the Chinese would precipitate a war against the US. FO371/99228/2; minute by Toplas, 21 Oct. 1952; J.I.C.(52) 57, 4 Sep. 1952. Peking argued Chinese statements were more likely to be an attempt to improve morale amongst the Chinese people rather than a means of inducing a greater commitment by the Soviet Union to the Far East. FO371/99265/22; telegram from Peking to FO, 2 Feb. 1952.

24. Rosemary Foot, *The Wrong War: American Policy and the Dimensions of the Korean Conflict, 1950–1953*, Ithaca 1985, pp. 198, 224 and 232. Foot notes that the mere existence of the Sino-Soviet Treaty acted as a restraint on the US strategy for ending the war.

25. CAB128(CM52)/202; 18 June 1952.

26. For the best account of the strain of rearmament see Alex Cairncross, *Years of Recovery: British Economic Policy, 1945–51*, London 1985.

27. Sidney Pollard, *The Development of the British Economy*, London 1992, pp. 354–6.
28. FO371/99218; letter from R. Scott to Tomlinson, 18 April 1952.
29. FO371/99267; minute by R. Scott, 9 Sep. 1952.
30. FO371/99268/11; letter from Tomlinson to G. Jebb, 23 April 1952.
31. Clement Attlee, 'Britain and America: Common Aims, Different Opinions', *Foreign Affairs*, vol. 32, no. 2, Jan. 1954.
32. *Hansard, Commons*, vol. 514, col. 2089; speech by A. Benn, 28 April 1953.
33. LPA, international sub-committee of the NEC, 17 Feb. 1953. The Labour Party established the British Labour-Asian Friendship Association in 1953 for developing contacts with socialist parties in Asia. It was set up as a way of preventing Labour Party members joining the British-China Friendship Association and the National Peace Council, which were perceived as communist front organisations.
34. Michael Foot, *Aneurin Bevan: A Biography*, London 1962, pp. 305 and 404.
35. *News Chronicle*, 18 Aug. 1952 in LPPCC 118/1/1.
36. *The Times*, 18 Sep. 1952. See also *Manchester Guardian*, 10 Aug. 1952 and *The Times*, 6 Aug. 1952. All in LPPCC 118/1/1.
37. *Manchester Guardian*, 24 Jan. 1952 and *The Times*, 29 Jan. 1952.
38. Rosemary Foot, *A Substitute for Victory: The Politics of Peacemaking at the Korean Armistice Talks*, Ithaca 1990, p. 133. Foot argues that the allies perceived negotiating opportunities where the US saw none.
39. Dockrill, 1989, p. 102.
40. See *FRUS1952–54*(14), part 1, pp. 175–80; NSC study, April 1953; DDRS 1981 96A; State Department Paper for Churchill/Eisenhower talks 1952, undated; *FRUS1952–54*(14), part 2, pp. 1383–9; NSC118/2, 20 Dec. 1951.
41. FO371/99268/15; letter from R. Scott to Tomlinson, 21 March 1952.
42. FO371/99220; minute by R. Scott, 28 Dec. 1952.
43. FO371/105179/1; minute by R. Scott, 5 Dec. 1952.
44. FO371/105179/1; minute by R. Scott, with comments by Eden, 5 Dec. 1952.
45. Defe4/19/210; agenda for the tripartite meeting on South East Asia, 4 Dec. 1951.
46. J. Colville, *The Fringes of Power – Downing Street Diaries, 1939–1955*, London 1980, p. 658.
47. DDRS 1986, 000954, minutes of Truman/Churchill talks, 8 Jan. 1952. B. Bernstein notes that Churchill admitted to Acheson that he thought that from a military point of view an armistice would be a mistake, hence implying that the US could and should seize the opportunity of a breakdown in the armistice talks to punish China. B. Bernstein, 'The Struggle over the Korean Armistice: Prisoners of Repatriation?', in B. Cumings, ed., *Child of Conflict: The Korean-American Relationship, 1943–53*, Seattle and London 1983, pp. 288–9.
48. *Hansard, Commons*, vol. 503, cols 271 and 285–6; speech by Churchill, 1 July 1952.
49. FO371/95612/5; letter from Franks to M.P. Mason (UN department), 12 Oct. 1951.

50. FO800/781/4; letter from Churchill to Eden, 6 Jan. 1952.
51. *FRUS1952–54*(3), pp. 625–6; Acheson to mission at the UN, 8 Sep. 1952.
52. *FRUS1951*(2), pp. 279–80; minutes of meeting between Acheson and Eden (Paris), 4 Nov. 1951 and FO371/95602/97; minute by Eden, 6 Nov. 1951. The French agreed with the British that this American proposal should be opposed; R. Schuman branded the idea as 'objectionable'.
53. FO371/95603/211; minute by Dixon, 5 Nov. 1951.
54. FO371/107032; letter from Jebb to Churchill, 15 June 1953.
55. FO371/950602/99; minute by R. Scott, 7 Nov. 1951.
56. *FRUS1951*(2), pp. 280–1; memorandum by A. Fisher and D. Sandifer (advisers to US delegation) (Deputy Assistant Secretary of State for UN Affairs) to Secretary of State, 5 Nov. 1951.
57. *New York Times*, 18 March 1953, in LPPCC 39/32/19.
58. FO371/107032; letter from Jebb to Churchill, 15 June 1953. Steven Ambrose in his biography of Eisenhower confirms that the President desired such a change. S.E. Ambrose, *Eisenhower – The President, Vol. II, 1952–1969*, London 1984, p. 99.
59. *FRUS1952–54*(3), p. 652–3; memorandum by R. Bacon, 25 May, 1953.
60. The US and UK had attempted to persuade the Ceylon government to adopt more stringent controls on their rubber exports to China, but had failed to change its attitude. PREM11/120; letter from General H.L. Ismay to PM, 19 March, 1952.
61. CAB128(CM52)/9; minute 4, 29 Oct. 1952.
62. FO371/99312/51; letter from Ministry of Transport (B.R. Dickerson) to FO, 11 Sep. 1952. The Ministry of Transport argued that Britain would be faced by retaliation if they introduced such measures. Shao agrees that controls were in practice untenable and ineffective, mainly because the controls introduced by other nations were less strict, hence allowing British ships to carry prohibited goods from these destinations. Wenguang Shao, *China, Britain and Businessmen: Political and Commercial Relations, 1949–57*, London 1991, p. 102.
63. FO371/99310/2; telegram from Hong Kong to FO, 28 Dec. 1951.
64. *FRUS1952–54*(14), part 1, pp. 19–20; Acheson to Eden, 14 March 1952.
65. *FRUS1952–54*(14), part 1, p. 104; President to Acheson, 18 Sep. 1952 and ibid., pp. 109–11; Acheson to President, 25 Sep. 1952. Acheson informed Truman that he was confusing the annual and the monthly figures for Hong Kong's trade with China and that a similar allegation had embarrassed the State Department in the winter of 1951–52.
66. FO371/105248/52; telegram from Washington to FO, 1 May 1953.
67. *FRUS1952–54* (14), part 1, pp. 2–3; Acheson to Eden, Jan. 8, 1952.
68. FO371/105248/6; letter from Tomlinson to J.S. Shattock, 19 Feb. 1952.
69. FO800/781/4; letter from Churchill to Eden, 6 Jan. 1952: FO800/781/22; letter from Eden to Lord Leathers, 7 March 1952.
70. FO371/105248/24; telegram from Saigon to FO, March 1953. The US embassy in Saigon asserted that a British ship had transported steel pipes to Tientsin.
71. CAB128(CM53)/16; minute 4, 3 March 1953.
72. FO371/10248A/6; letter from Tomlinson to Shattock, 19 Feb. 1953.
73. FO371/105250/113; telegram from Hong Kong to FO, 14 June 1952. In

July 1951 the *Perico* had been requisitioned by the Chinese communists and forced to transport 467 Chinese troops while the *Miramir* had
been seized by the Nationalists and at the end of November 1951 had
fallen into communist hands.

74. In this respect a nation-wide broadcast by Oliver Franks on 18 May
defending the British position was successful, illustrating that the American
administration could have done more to publicly undermine McCarthy's
anti-communist diatribe. See B. Porter, *Britain and the Rise of Communist China: A Study of British Attitudes, 1945–54*, London 1975, p. 120.
Eisenhower's policy for dealing with McCarthy was to ignore the Senator and wait for his influence to wane. Ambrose, 1984, p. 57.

75. FO371/105250/122; letter from R. Makins to FO, 1 July 1953.

76. See Mark Ryan, *Chinese Attitudes to Nuclear Weapons: China and the
United States during the Korean War*, New York 1989, p. 54; Foot,
1985, pp. 176–7; MacDonald, 1990, p. 62; and Alcock, 1986, p. 312.
The statement was not to be publicised until the aftermath of an armistice for Korea, but in the first few months of 1953 the US, partly for
domestic political reasons but mainly because they believed Chinese knowledge of the threat would hasten an armistice, leaked details to the press.

77. Foot, 1985, p. 176.

78. Ryan, 1989, p. 56.

79. Foot, 1985, pp. 205–11.

80. Defe4/56/113; annex: 'Possible deterrents to further Chinese aggression
in South East Asia', Sep. 1952. Defe5/504; memorandum by Admiralty,
10 Sep. 1952. Defe5/515; note by secretary on co-ordinated allied military action in the Far East, 15 Sep. 1952.

81. FO371/99268/15; letter from R. Scott to Tomlinson, 21 March 1952.

82. For details see MacDonald, 1986, pp. 109–10, 158 and 169 and Alcock,
1986, p. 349.

83. Bernstein, 1983, p. 290.

84. *FRUS1952–54*(14), part 1, pp. 59–63; special estimate: 'Probable effects
of various possible courses of action with respect to Communist China',
5 June 1952 and DDRS 1984; CIA Report, 9 March 1953.

85. Eisenhower believed greater use of the deterrent effect of nuclear weapons could reduce military expenditure and allow American troops to retreat from the Asian mainland, whilst Dulles's support for the incorporation
of nuclear weapons into America's strategic planning for the Far East
complemented his ideas on massive retaliation.

86. Ryan concludes that it cannot be proved for certain that the American
threat to use nuclear weapons against Korea and China was not simply
bravado but reaffirmation by the administration, in October 1953 and
January 1954, that nuclear weapons could and should be used if the
Chinese broke an armistice tends to suggest that Eisenhower was prepared to use such weapons. Ryan, 1989, p. 66.

87. Dwight Eisenhower, *Mandate for Change: The White House Years, 1953–
56*, London 1963, p. 180. Ryan agrees that the President thought rifts
could be 'repaired'. Ryan, 1989, p. 59.

88. P. Boyle, in John Young, ed., *Foreign Policy of Churchill's Peacetime
Administration, 1951–55*, Leicester 1988, p. 35.

89. See Bernstein, 1983, p. 303.
90. See Foot, 1985, p. 218.
91. Zhou Enlai, 'Our Foreign Policy and our Tasks', 30 April 1952 (Address to meeting of China's diplomatic envoys to foreign countries, Zhou Enlai), in *Selected Works*, vol. II, Beijing 1989, pp. 94–102.
92. *Daily Worker*, 9 Oct. 1952, in LPPCC 118/1/38.
93. FO371/99260; *NCNA*, 16 Jan. 1952 and FO371/105210/2; *NCNA*, 1 July 1952.
94. FO371/99257/29; *NCNA*, 17 Jan. 1952.
95. FO371/99260/6; *Peking Daily*, 4 Feb. 1952 (in telegram from Peking to FO, 9 Feb. 1952) and in Zhou Enlai, 1989, pp. 94–107.
96. Zhou Enlai, 1989, pp. 94–102.
97. FO371/99404/34; *NCNA*, 22 Jan. 1952, in telegram from Peking to FO, 22 Jan. 1952.
98. Ibid.
99. FO371/99260; *NCNA*, 16 Jan. 1952.
100. FO371/105192/4; telegram from Peking to FO, 6 Feb. 1953 and Ibid.; *NCNA*, 11 Feb. 1952.
101. Foot, 1990, p. 198. (Foot reverses her early view as expressed in *The Wrong War*, that nuclear diplomacy affected the Chinese position.) Ryan makes a clear distinction between Chinese communist concern over the affect of nuclear weapons on China, as evidenced in their civil defence programme, and their determination not to be 'bludgeoned out of the Korean War'. Ryan, 1989, p. 169.

CHAPTER 9: RAPPROCHEMENT DENIED

1. H. Trevelyan, *World's Apart: China 1953–55, Soviet Union 1962–65*, London 1971, p. 51.
2. FO371/105225/29; letter from Trevelyan to Allen, 27 Aug. 1953. In September, the British ambassador in Switzerland was invited to a function at the Chinese embassy in Berne. FO371/105225/30; letter from Trevelyan to Allen, 28 Aug. 1953.
3. FO105225/30; letter from Trevelyan to Allen, 28 Aug. 1953.
4. FO371/105225/31; letter from Allen to Trevelyan, 30 Sep. 1953. Also noted in James Tang, *Britain's Encounter with Revolutionary China, 1949–54*, London 1992, p. 119.
5. FO371/105225/21; telegram from FO to Peking, 19 Aug. 1953.
6. FO371/105225/21; minute by Lord Reading (Parliamentary Under-Secretary), 18 Aug. 1953.
7. FO371/105225/41; minute by C. Crowe, 25 Nov. 1953 and ibid./29; minute by Wilkinson, 27 Aug. 1953.
8. FO371/105228; letter from Crowe to Peking, Sep. 1953.
9. FO371/105227/2; *NCNA*, 9 Oct. 1953.
10. For China's post-Korean War foreign policy line see Mineo Nakajima, 'Foreign Relations: From the Korean War to the Bandung Line', in R. MacFarquhar and J.K. Fairbank, eds, *Cambridge History of China, Vol. 14, The People's Republic, Part 1, The Emergence of Revolutionary China,*

1949–65, Cambridge 1987, pp. 280–4; Zhai Qiang, 'China and the Geneva Conference of 1954', *China Quarterly*, no. 129, March 1992, p. 107; Jia Qingquo, 'Searching for Peaceful Co-existence and Territorial Integrity', in H. Harding and Yuan Ming, eds, *Sino-American Relations: A Joint Reassessment of a Critical Decade*, Wilmington, Del. 1989, p. 269; Kuo-Kang Shao, 'Zhou Enlai's Diplomacy and the Neutrality of Indochina, 1945–5', *China Quarterly*, no. 107, Sept. 1986, p. 486.

11. Zhou Enlai, 1989, vol. II, pp. 114–27.

12. Shu Guang Zhang, *Deterrence and Strategic Culture: Chinese-American Confrontations, 1949–1958*, Ithaca and London 1992, pp. 178–86 and 190–4.

13. FO800/784/94 and FO371/105180/21; letter from Eden to PM, 25 Nov. 1953.

14. M. Gilbert, *Never Despair, Winston. S. Churchill, Vol. VIII, 1945–65*, London 1988, p. 1015.

15. *Hansard, Commons*, vol. 517, col. 2247; 16 July 1953.

16. FO800/784/94 and FO371/105180/21; letter from Eden to PM, 25 Nov. 1953.

17. CAB129(CP53)64/330; memorandum by Eden, 24 Nov. 1953.

18. H.W. Brands, 'The Dwight D. Eisenhower Administration, Syngman Rhee, and the "Other" Geneva Conference of 1954', *Pacific Historical Review*, vol. LVI, no. 1, Feb. 1987, p. 61.

19. CAB128(CM50)/44; minute 4, 21 July 1953.

20. CAB128(CM50)/44; minute 4, July 1953.

21. *FRUS1952–54*(15), p. 1616; memorandum of discussion, NSC 171, 19 Nov. 1953 and Mark Ryan, *Chinese Attitudes towards Nuclear Weapons: China and the US during the Korean War*, New York and London 1989, p. 67.

22. See R. Pruessen, 'John Foster Dulles and the Predictions of Power', in R.I. Immerman, ed., *John Foster Dulles and the Diplomacy of the Cold War*, Princeton 1990, pp. 25–6 and Ryan, 1989, p. 69.

23. According to Anthony Short, the administration 'fudged' the question of intervention in order to dissuade the French from withdrawing and to deter the Chinese from intervening. A. Short, *The Origins of the Vietnam War*, London 1989, pp. 133 and 108. Herring argues that Dulles was less bellicose than was previously thought; his 'United Action' plan advocated multilateral intervention and he proposed harassing tactics, rather than strikes against the Chinese mainland. G.C. Herring,' "A Good Stout Effort": John Foster Dulles and the Indochina Crisis, 1954–1955', in Immerman, 1990, pp. 216–17.

24. See Ryan, 1989, p. 71 and Herring, in Immerman, 1990, p. 216.

25. John Lewis Gaddis, *The Long Peace: Inquiries into the History of the Cold War*, New York 1987, pp. 127–8.

26. Defe4/66/132; minute 4, 24 Nov. 1953.

27. Defe5/548; memorandum, 4 Nov. 1953 and Defe4/66/132; minute 4, 24 Nov. 1953.

28. See J. Colville, *The Fringes of Power – Downing Street Diaries 1939–1955*, London 1985, p. 684; Ryan, 1989, p. 69; and Gordan H. Chang, *Friends and Enemies: The US, China, and the Soviet Union, 1948–1972*, Stanford, Calif. 1990, p. 96.

29. *FRUS1952–54*(5), pp. 1817–18; Second Restricted Tripartite Meeting, 7 Dec. 1953. See also Chang, 1990, p. 96. For an assessment of the Bermuda conference see John Young, 'Churchill, the Russians and the Western Alliance: The Three Power Conference at Bermuda, December 1953', *English Historical Review*, vol. CI, no. 401, Oct. 1986.

30. Warner, 'The Settlement of the Indochina War', in John Young, ed., *Foreign Policy of Churchill's Peacetime Administration, 1951–55*, Leicester 1988, pp. 235–40. Harold Hinton notes that the French were using the threat of US military strikes against China to prevent Chinese overt intervention in Indochina. Harold Hinton, *Communist China in World Politics*, London 1966, p. 244.

31. FO800/785; letter from Eden to PM, 19 Jan. 1954.

32. Tang, 1992, p. 145.

33. CAB128(CM50)/51; minute 4, 8 Sep. 1953.

34. FO800/785; letter from Eden to PM, 19 Jan. 1954.

35. FO371/107032/6; letter from R. Makins to Salisbury, 31 Aug. 1953.

36. *Hansard, Commons*, vol. 522, col. 610, 17 Dec. 1953. For others who raised the issue see *Hansard, Commons*, vol. 517, cols 2247–8; question by W. Wyatt (Labour, Birmingham, Aston), 16 July 1953. Ibid., vol. 518, col. 2417; questions by William Hamilton (Labour, Fife, West) and Stephen Swingler (Labour, Newcastle-under-Lyme), 26 Oct. 1953.

37. *Hansard, Commons*, vol. 518, col. 498, 22 July 1953.

38. *Daily Telegraph*, 21 Aug. 1953; *Daily Herald*, 19 Aug. 1953; *Manchester Guardian*, 7 Sep. 1953; *The Times*, 29 Sep. 1953. All these in LPPCC 118/1/2.

39. FO371/105211/10; letter from J. Colville to C.A.E. Shuckburgh, undated, Aug. 1953.

40. *FRUS1952–54*(3), p. 685; position paper prepared in Department of State for US delegation to the resumed 8th Session of the UN, 6 Aug. 1953. In June 1953, Dulles rejected an idea that the problem of the admission of China be divided into two questions, with the unseating of the Nationalists and the seating of the communists being dealt with separately.

41. *The Times*, 13 Sep. 1953.

42. CAB129(CP50)62/247(53); memorandum by the Lord President of the Council, 4 Sep. 1953.

43. *FRUS1952–54*(3), p. 716; memorandum by Secretary of State regarding a conference with British ambassador, Makins, 5 Jan. 1954. There was a suggestion by Cabot Lodge in March 1954 that, if need be, the US should gain Britain's acceptance of the American position on a seat for China in the UN by agreeing to relax UN economic sanctions against China. Dulles, not wanting to tie his hands, or relax any element of the American hardline approach to China, rejected this proposal and instead adopted an uncompromising attitude. ibid., pp. 720–3; memorandum by Lodge to Secretary of State, 30 March 1954 and ibid., pp. 728–30; Secretary of State to Lodge, 10 April 1954.

44. FO371/105211/11; minute by Wilkinson, 10 Dec. 1953.

45. Gilbert, 1988, p. 918.

46. PREM11/418; minutes of meeting between Eden and Dulles, 7 Dec. 1953. This issue was raised by Stan Awbery (Labour, Bristol, Central) in the

House of Commons. See *Hansard, Commons*, vol. 517, col. 2038, 15 July 1953.

47. PREM11/425; minutes of tripartite meeting between the American, British and French foreign ministers, 13 July 1953 and FO371/105211/10; Minister of State brief on UN question, undated, Aug. 1953.
48. Wenguang Shao, *China, Britain and Businessmen: Political and Commercial Relations, 1949–57*, London 1991, p. 107.
49. FO371/105253/164; letter from G. Brigstocke to G.G. Kesby (CO), 10 Sep. 1953 and ibid./175; telegram from Washington to FO, 25 Nov. 1953. The Foreign Office informed Washington that McCarthy's figures were erroneous because he had chosen the three lowest months of 1952 for a comparison with the figures for 1953. A bareboat chartered ship did not have a resident crew and nor was end use stipulated in the contract.
50. FO371/105252/160; minute by Addis, 4 Aug. 1953 and minute by Lord Reading, 5 Aug. 1953.
51. *FRUS1952–54*(14), pp. 265–77; memorandum of discussion at the 169th meeting of NSC, 5 Nov. 1953.
52. Tucker, 'Cold War Contacts: America and China, 1952–1956', in Harding and Yuan Ming, 1989, p. 243.
53. *FRUS1952–54*(14), p. 265–77; memorandum of discussion at the 169th meeting of NSC, 5 Nov. 1953.
54. *FRUS1952–54*(14), pp. 238–9; the Secretary of State to Certain Diplomatic and Consular Offices, 29 July 1953 and PREM11/425; minutes of tripartite meeting between the American, British and French foreign ministers, 13 July 1953.
55. FO371/105211/11; minutes by UK delegation to the Bermuda Conference between the US, Britain and France, 8 Dec. 1953.
56. *FRUS1952–54*(14), pp. 265–77; memorandum of discussion at the 169th meeting of the NSC, 5 Nov. 1953.
57. Tucker, in Harding and Yuan Ming, eds, 1989, p. 244.
58. Eisenhower took action against McCarthy in July 1953 only after the Senator had threatened to subpoena CIA officer William P. Bundy; Eisenhower would not let McCarthy investigate the CIA. See Thomas C. Reeves, *The Life and Times of Joe McCarthy: A Biography*, New York 1982, pp. 436, 438–9, 475, and 502–6.
59. *Manchester Guardian*, 7 Sep. 1953.
60. Henry Brands, Jr, 'The Dwight D. Eisenhower Administration, Syngman Rhee, and the "Other" Geneva Conference of 1954', *Pacific Historical Review*, vol. LVI, no. 1, 1987, p. 67.
61. FO371/105194/81; minute by Wilkinson, 6 October 1953.
62. Tucker, in Immerman, 1990, p. 255.
63. Gaddis, 1987, p. 179 and Tucker, in Harding and Yuan Ming, eds, 1989, p. 245.
64. PREM11/418; minutes of meeting between Eden and Dulles, 7 Dec. 1953 and Pruessen, in Immerman, 1990, p. 28.
65. Tucker, in Immerman, 1990, pp. 237–8.
66. *Manchester Guardian*, 14 Jan. 1954.
67. FO371/105211/11; minutes by UK delegation to Bermuda conference between the US, Britain and France, 8 Dec. 1953.

68. See J.W. Dower, *War Without Mercy: Race and Power in the Pacific War*, London 1986.
69. Warren Cohen argues that Dulles was trying to 'isolate, encircle, and bring about the collapse of the Peking government'. W.I. Cohen, *America's Response to China: An Interpretative History of Sino-American Relations*, New York 1971, p. 215. The establishment of the South East Asian Treaty Organisation, at the Manila Conference of 6–8 September 1954, is indicative of American attempts to build up a defence structure to act as a deterrent to communist aggression in Asia.
70. *FRUS1952–54*(15), p. 1170; draft statement of Policy proposed by NSC for NSC 154, 15 June, 1953.
71. *FRUS1952–54*(15), pp. 1341–4; statement of NSC, 154, 7 July 1953 and ibid., (14), pp. 278–307; NSC 166/1, 6 Nov. 1953; see also Short, 1989, p. 123.
72. *FRUS1952–54*(15), p. 1170; draft statement of policy proposed by the NSC, 15 June 1953.
73. *FRUS1952–54*(15), pp. 1174–7; NSC staff study, 15 June 1953.
74. *FRUS1952–54*(14), pp. 278–307; NSC166/1, 6 Nov. 1953.
75. *FRUS1952–54*(15), pp. 1174–7; NSC staff study, 15 June 1953.
76. Tucker, in Harding and Yuan Ming, 1989, p. 256.
77. *FRUS1952–54*(14), pp. 175–9; study prepared by the Staff of NSC (annex to NSC 148), 6 April 1953. Quoted in Gaddis, 1987, p. 178, and in Chang, 1990, p. 92.
78. Chang, 1990, p. 91.
79. Gaddis, 1987, p. 178.

CONCLUSION

1. For China's historically derived desire to control relations with the West see William Kirby and Madelyn Ross in Thomas W. Robinson and David Shambaugh, eds, *Chinese Foreign Policy: Theory and Practice*, Oxford 1994. For the role of ideology on Chinese foreign policy see Levine and Shambaugh in Robinson and Shambaugh, eds, 1994.
2. For the best insight into the relationship between the Chinese and Soviet leaderships see Sergei N Goncharov, John W. Lewis and Xue Litai, *Uncertain Partners: Stalin, Mao, and the Korean War*, Stanford, Calif. 1993.
3. See Rosemary Foot, *The Wrong War: American Policy and the Dimensions of the Korean Conflict, 1950–1953*, Ithaca, N.Y. 1985; Nancy Tucker in Harry Harding and Yuan Ming, eds, *Sino-American Relations, 1945–55: A Joint Reassessment of a Critical Decade*, US 1989; Gordon H. Chang, *Friends and Enemies: The US, China, and the Soviet Union 1948–1972*, Stanford, Calif. 1990; John Lewis Gaddis, *The Long Peace: Inquiries into the History of the Cold War*, New York 1987.
4. For the change in US policy towards Japanese recovery see Shigeto Tsuru, *Japan's Capitalism: Creative Defeat and Beyond*, Cambridge 1993, pp. 37–41 and for the importance of Japan in American strategic thinking see various works by Gabriel Kolko including *Confronting the Third World: United States Foreign Policy 1945–1980*, New York 1988, p. 32.

5. See Gabriel Kolko, *The Roots of American Foreign Policy: An Analysis of Power and Purpose*, Boston 1969 and Bruce Cumings, *The Origins of the Korean War, Vol. II: The Roaring of the Cataract 1947–1950*, Princeton 1990, pp. 3–35.

6. D.C. Wolf, 'To Secure a Convenience: Britain's Recognition of Communist China', *Journal of Contemporary History*, vol. 18, no. 2, April 1983, pp. 299–326; Ritchie Ovendale, 'Britain, the United States, and the Recognition of Communist China', *Historical Journal*, vol. 26, no. 1, 1983, pp. 139–58; and Zhong-ping Feng, *The British Government's China Policy*, Keele 1994.

7. For a broader study of the impact of left-wing opinion on colonial policy see Stephen Howe, *Anticolonialism in British Politics: The Left and the End of Empire, 1918–1964*, Oxford 1994.

8. For differences between businessmen see also Wenguang Shao, *China, Britain and Businessmen: Political and Commercial Relations, 1949–57*, London 1991.

9. See Geoffrey Ingham, *Capitalism Divided? The City and Industry in British Social Development*, London 1984.

10. Industrial interests in Britain did not start to question this liberal policy until the late 1950s when China turned to autarkic development in the shape of the Great Leap Forward and, more especially, when an industrialising Hong Kong began to export manufactures to Britain.

11. See P.J. Cain and A.G. Hopkins, *British Imperialism: Crisis and Deconstruction, 1914–1990*, London 1993.

12. For an account of how the most infamous British agency house struggled to survive in the Far East see Edward LeFevour, *Western Enterprise in Late Ch'ing China: A Selective Survey of Jardine Matheson & Company's Operations, 1842–1895*, Cambridge, Mass. 1968.

Bibliography

UNPUBLISHED MATERIALS

British Board of Trade Records: BT5 & BT11
British Cabinet Office Records: CAB128, CAB129, CAB131, CAB134
British Colonial Office Records: CO537, CO1023, CO937, CO968
British Foreign Office Records: FO371, FO115, FO953, FO800
British Prime Ministers Office Records: PREM 8, PREM 11
British Chiefs of Staff/Joint Planning Staff Records: Defe4, Defe5, Defe6
British Treasury Records: T236, T237, T220
China Association Papers (SOAS, University of London): CHAS: MCP; S/A;S/C
Labour Party Records (National Museum of Labour History, Manchester): Minutes of Parliamentary Labour Party 1950–54; General Correspondence Files: China 1953–62; Korea, 1950–51; NEC Minutes 1950–54; Annual Conference Reports 1950–54
Sir Robert Scott Papers (National Library of Scotland, Edinburgh)

NEWSPAPERS AND JOURNALS

Daily Express
Daily Herald
Daily Mail
Daily Mirror
Daily Telegraph
Daily Worker
The Economist
Evening Standard
Manchester Evening News
Manchester Guardian
New Herald Tribune
New Statesman
New York Times
News Chronicle
Observer
Reynolds News
Sunday Times
The Times

OFFICIAL PUBLICATIONS

British

Yasamee, H.J. and K.A. Hamilton, eds, *Documents on British Policy Overseas, Series II, Vol. IV: Korea, June 1950–April 1951*, London 1991
Bullen, R. and M.E. Pelly, eds, *Documents on British Policy Overseas, Series II, Vol. II: The London Conferences: Anglo-American Relations and Cold War Strategy*, January–June 1950, London 1987
House of Commons Debates (Hansard), Fifth Series, 1950–54, London 1949–53
House of Lords Debates (Hansard), Fifth Series, 1950–53, London 1949–53
Manchester Chamber of Commerce, Monthly Reports, vols 158–65, 1950–54
Annual Statement of the Trade of the UK with Commonwealth Countries and Foreign Countries, vol. 1, London 1946–54

US

Declassified Documents Reference System. Retrospective Collection. Collections, Virginia 1975–90
Foreign Relations of the United States, Conferences at Cairo and Teheran, 1943
Foreign Relations of the United States, Conferences at Malta and Yalta, 1945
Foreign Relations of the United States, The Conference of Berlin (The Potsdam Conference), 1945
Foreign Relations of the United States, 1945, Vol. VI: British Commonwealth and the Far East
Foreign Relations of the United States, 1946, Vol. VIII: The Far East
Foreign Relations of the United States, 1947, Vol. VI: The Far East
Foreign Relations of the United States, 1948, Vol. VI: The Far East and Australasia
Foreign Relations of the United States, 1949, Vol. VIII: The Far East and Australasia (2 parts)
Foreign Relations of the United States, 1949, Vol. IX: The Far East: China
Foreign Relations of the United States, 1950, Vol. II: The United Nations; the Western Hemisphere
Foreign Relations of the United States, 1950, Vol. III: Western Europe
Foreign Relations of the United States, 1950, Vol. VI: East Asia and the Pacific
Foreign Relations of the United States, 1950, Vol. VII: Korea
Foreign Relations of the United States, 1951, Vol. II: The United Nations; the Western Hemisphere
Foreign Relations of the United States, 1951, Vol. VI: Asia and the Pacific
Foreign Relations of the United States, 1951, Vol. VII: Korea and China (2 parts)
Foreign Relations of the United States, 1952–54, Vol. V: Western European Security
Foreign Relations of the United States, 1952–54, Vol. XV: Korea (2 parts)
Joint Economic Committee of the US Congress, An Economic Profile of Mainland China, New York and Washington 1968

United States General Services Administration, Public Papers of the Presidents of the US: H.S. Truman, 1950–53, 3 vols, Washington 1965
United States General Services Administration, Public Papers of the Presidents of the US: D. Eisenhower, 1953, Washington 1960

Chinese

First Five Year Plan for Development of the National Economy of the People's Republic in 1953–57, Peking 1956
Miscellany of Mao Tse-tung's Thought, (1949–68) Parts 1 & 2, Joint Publications Research Service, Arlington, Vancouver 1974
New China's Economic Achievements, 1949–52, compiled by China Committee for the Promotion of International Trade, Peking 1952
Selected Works of Mao Tse-tung: Vols I–III, Peking 1965; *Vol. IV*, Peking 1969; *Vol. V*, Peking 1977
Selected Military Writings of Mao Tse-tung, Peking, second edition, 1967
Selected Works of Zhou Enlai: Vol. I, Beijing 1981; *Vol. II*, Beijing 1989
Hinton, Harold, *The People's Republic of China, 1949–1979: A Documentary Survey*, 5 vols, Wilmington, Del. 1980
Statistical Year Book of China 1981 (English edition), compiled by the State Statistical Bureau, PRC, Hong Kong 1982
Ten Great Years: Statistics of the Economic and Cultural Achievements of the People's Republic of China, compiled by the State Statistical Bureau, PRC, reprint, Washington 1974
Kau, Michael Y.M., and John K. Leung, eds, *The Writings of Mao Zedong, 1949–76, Vol. I, September 1949 – December 1955*, New York and London 1986

Others

Cordier, Andrew W. and W. Foote, eds, *Public Papers of the Secretary-General of the United Nations, Vol. 1: Trygve Lie, 1946–53*, New York 1969

MEMOIRS AND DIARIES

Acheson, Dean, *Present at the Creation: My Years in the State Department*, New York 1969
Attlee, Clement, *As it Happened*, London 1954
Bohlen, C.E., *Witness to History, 1929–1969*, New York 1973
Colville, John, *The Fringes of Power: Downing Street Diaries, 1939–1955*, London 1980
Dalton, Hugh, *Memoirs, 1946–1960: High Tide and After*, London 1962
―― *Political Diary, 1918–40: 1945–60*, Ben Pimlott, ed., London 1986
Eden, Anthony, *Full Circle: The Memories of Sir A. Eden*, London 1960
Eisenhower, Dwight, *The White House Years, 1953–56: Mandate for Change, Memoirs, Vol. II*, London 1963
Gaitskell, Hugh, *The Diary of Hugh Gaitskell 1945–1956*, Philip M. Williams, ed., London 1983

Gladwyn, Lord, *The Memoirs of Lord Gladwyn*, London 1972
Grantham, Alexander, *Via Ports: From Hong Kong to Hong Kong*, Hong Kong 1965
Kelly, Sir David, *The Ruling Few*, London 1952
Kennan, George F., *Memoirs, Vol. I, 1925–1950*, Boston 1967
Khruschev, Nikita, *Khruschev Remembers*, Edward Crankshaw, ed., Strobe Talbott, trans., Boston 1970
—— *Khruschev Remembers: The Last Testament*, Strobe Talbott, ed. and trans., Boston 1974
MacArthur, Douglas, *Reminiscences*, Greenwich, Conn. 1965
Morrison, Herbert, *An Autobiography*, London 1960
Panikkar, K.M., *In Two Chinas: Memoirs of a Diplomat*, London 1955
Rankin, Karl Lott, *China Assignment*, Seattle 1964
Shuckburgh, E., *Descent to Suez: Diaries 1951–56*, selected for publication by J. Charmley, London 1986
Strang, Lord, *Home and Abroad*, London 1956
Trevelyan, Humphrey, *World's Apart: China 1953–5; Soviet Union 1962–5*, London 1971
Truman, Harry S., *Memoirs: Vol. I: Years of Trial and Hope 1946–1953*, New York 1956
Urquhart, Brian, *A Life in Peace and War*, London 1987

OTHER PUBLICATIONS

Alcock, Christian, 'Britain and the Korean War, 1950–1953', Manchester University unpublished PhD Thesis 1986
Ambrose, Steven, *Rise to Globalism: American Foreign Policy since 1938*, New York 1983
—— with R.I. Immerman, *Ike's Spies: Eisenhower and the Espionage Establishment*, New York 1981
—— *Eisenhower: The President, Vol. 2, 1952–69*, London 1984
Anderson, Perry, 'The Figures of Descent', *New Left Review*, no. 161, January/Febuary 1987, pp. 20–78
Attlee, Clement, 'Britain and America: Common Aims, Different Opinions', *Foreign Affairs*, vol. 32, no. 2, January 1954, pp. 190–202
Barnett, Correlli, *The Audit of War: The Illusion and Reality of Britain as a Great Nation*, London 1986
Beloff, Max, 'Soviet Policy in China', *International Affairs*, vol. 27, no. 3, July 1951, pp. 285–96
Bevan, Aneurin, 'Britain and America at Loggerheads', *Foreign Affairs*, vol. 36, no. 1, October 1957, pp. 66–8
Bianco, Lucien, *Origins of the Chinese Revolution, 1915–1949*, Stanford, Calif. 1967
Blum, William, *The CIA: A Forgotten History. US Global Intervention since World War II*, London 1986
Boardman, Robert, *Britain and the People's Republic of China 1949–1974*, London 1976
—— and A.J.R. Groom, eds, *The Management of Britain's External Relations*, London 1973

Borg, Dorothy, and Waldo Heinrichs, eds, *Uncertain Years: Chinese-American Relations, 1947–1950*, New York 1980

Boyle, Peter G., ed., *The Churchill-Eisenhower Correspondence 1953–1955*, Chapel Hill 1990

Brands, Henry W. Jr., 'The Dwight D. Eisenhower Administration, Syngman Rhee and the "Other" Geneva Conference of 1954', *Pacific Historical Review*, vol. LVI, no. 1, 1987, pp. 59–87

Briggs, Phillip J., 'Congress and the Cold War: US China Policy, 1955', *China Quarterly*, no. 85, March 1981, pp. 86–96

Brinkley, Douglas, ed., *Dean Acheson and the Making of US Foreign Policy*, London 1993

Buckley, Roger, *Occupation Diplomacy: Britain, the United States and Japan, 1945–52*, Cambridge 1982

—— *US–Japanese Alliance Diplomacy 1945–1990*, Cambridge 1992

Bullock, Allan, *Ernest Bevin: Foreign Secretary*, London 1983

Cairncross, Alex, *Years of Recovery: British Economic Policy, 1945–51*, London 1985

Callinicos, Alex, 'Exception or Symptom: The British Crisis and the World System', *New Left Review*, no. 169, May/June 1988, pp. 97–108

Camilleri, Joseph, *Chinese Foreign Policy: The Maoist Era and its Aftermath*, Oxford 1980

Carlton, David, *Anthony Eden*, London 1986

Catron, Gary, 'Hong Kong and Chinese Foreign Policy, 1955–1960', *China Quarterly*, no. 51, July/September 1972, pp. 405–25

Cain, P.J. and A.G. Hopkins, *British Imperialism: Innovation and Expansion, 1688–1914*, London 1993

—— *British Imperialism: Crisis and Deconstruction, 1914–1990*, London 1993

Chalmers, Malcolm, *Paying for Defence: Military Spending and British Decline*, London 1985

Chan Lau kit-Ching, 'Hong Kong during the Pacific War', *Journal of Imperial and Commonwealth History*, vol. 2, no. 1, October 1973, pp. 56–79

—— 'Abrogation of British Extraterritoriality in China 1942–43. A Study of Anglo-American-Chinese Relations', *Modern Asian Studies*, vol. 11, no. 2, 1977, pp. 257–91

Chang, C.M., 'Communism and Nationalism in China', *Foreign Affairs*, vol. 28, no. 4, July 1950, pp. 548–65

Chang, Gordon H., *Friends and Enemies: The US, China, and the Soviet Union 1948–1972*, Stanford, Calif. 1990

Chang, Jung, *Wild Swans: Three Daughters of China*, Glasgow 1991

Chang, K.N., *The Inflationary Spiral: The Experience in China, 1939–1950*, Cambridge, Mass. 1958

Chen, Nai-Ruenn and Walter Galenson, *The Chinese Economy under Communism*, Chicago 1969

Cheng Chu-yuan, *Communist China's Economy, 1949–1962: Structural Changes and Crisis*, South Orange, N.J. 1963

Chiu, H., ed., *China and the Question of Taiwan: Documents and Analysis*, New York 1973

Chou En-lai, 'The Chinese Peoples' Successes', *Communist Review*, November 1950, pp. 335–44

Chou, S.H., *The Chinese Inflation 1937–1949*, New York 1963

Cohen, Warren I., *Dean Rusk*, New Jersey 1980

—— *America's Response to China: An Interpretative History of Sino-American Relations*, New York 1971

—— and Akira Iriye, eds, *The Great Powers in East Asia, 1953–1960*, New York 1990

Collar, H.J., 'British Commercial Relations with China', *International Affairs*, vol. 29, no. 4, October 1953, pp. 418–28

Cotton, James and Ian Neary, eds, *The Korean War in History*, Manchester 1989

Cumings, Bruce, *The Origins of the Korean War, Vol. I: Liberation and Emergence of Separate Regimes, 1945–1947*, Princeton 1981

—— *The Origins of the Korean War, Vol. II: The Roaring of the Cataract 1947–1950*, Princeton 1990

—— ed., *Child of Conflict: Korean-American Relations 1943–1953*, Seattle and London 1983

—— '"Revising Postrevisionism" or the Poverty of Theory in Diplomatic History', *Diplomatic History*, vol. 17, no. 4, Fall 1993, pp. 539–70

Curtis, Mark, *The Ambiguities of Power: British Foreign Policy since 1945*, London and New Jersey 1995

Danchev, Alex, *Oliver Franks: Founding Father*, Oxford 1993

Darwin, J., *Britain and De-colonisation: The Retreat from Empire in the Postwar World*, London 1988

Davenport-Hines, R.P.T., and Geoffrey Jones, eds, *British Business in Asia since 1860*, Cambridge 1989

Davis, Lance E., and R.A. Huttenback, *Mammon and the Pursuit of Empire*, Cambridge 1987

Deighton, Anne, ed., *Britain and the First Cold War*, London 1990

Deyo, F., ed., *The Political Economy of the New Asian Industrialism*, Ithaca and London 1989

Dicks, Anthony, 'Treaty, Grant, Usage or Sufferance? Some Legal Aspects of the Status of Hong Kong', *China Quarterly*, no. 95, September 1983, pp. 427–56

Dockrill, Michael, and John Young, eds, *British Foreign Policy, 1945–56*, London 1989

—— *The Cold War, 1945–1963*, London 1988

—— 'The Foreign Office, Anglo-American Relations and the Korean War, June 1950–June 1951', *International Affairs*, vol. 62, no. 3, 1986, pp. 459–76

Domes, Jurgen, and Yu-ming Shaw, *Hong Kong: A Chinese and International Concern*, London 1988

Donovan, Robert J., *Tumultuous Years: The Presidency of Harry S .Truman, 1949–1953*, New York and London 1982

Dower, J.W., *War Without Mercy: Race and Power in the Pacific War*, London 1986

Dreyer, J.T., *China's Forty Millions: Minority Nationalities and National Integration in the People's Republic of China*, Cambridge, Mass. 1976

Eastman, Lloyd, *Seeds of Destruction: North China in War and Revolution, 1937–1949*, Stanford, Calif. 1984

Eden, Anthony, 'Britain in World Strategy', *Foreign Affairs*, vol. 29, no. 3, April 1951, pp. 341–50

Eckstein, Alexander, *Communist China's Economic Growth in Foreign Trade: Implications for US Policy*, New York 1966

Endacott, G.B., *Hong Kong Eclipse*, Oxford 1978

—— *A History of Hong Kong*, Hong Kong 1958

Endicott, Steven. L., *Diplomacy and Enterprise: British China Policy 1933–1937*, Manchester and British Columbia 1975

Fairbank, John K. and Albert Feurwerker, eds, *The Cambridge History of China, Vol. 13 'Republican China 1912–1949', Part 2*, Cambridge 1986

—— *The United States and China*, Cambridge, Mass. 1971

—— A.M. Craig and E.O. Reischauer, *East Asia: The Modern Transformation*, Boston 1965

—— 'The Problem of Revolutionary Asia', *Foreign Affairs*, vol. 29, no. 1, October 1950, pp. 101–14

Farrar, Peter N., 'Britain's Proposal for a Buffer Zone South of the Yalu in November 1950: Was it a Neglected Opportunity to End the Fighting in Korea?', *Journal of Contemporary History*, vol. 18, no. 2, April 1983, pp. 327–51

Feng, Zhong-ping, *The British Government's China Policy*, Keele 1994

Fletcher, R.J., 'British Propaganda since World War II: A Case Study', *Media, Culture and Society*, no. 4, 1982, pp. 97–109

Frankel, J., *British Foreign Policy 1945–73*, London 1975

Feis, Herbert., *From Trust of Terror: The Onset of the Cold War 1947–1950*, London 1970

—— *The China Tangle: The American Effort in China from Pearl Harbour to the Marshall Mission*, New York 1953

Fitzgerald, C.P., *The Birth of Communist China*, London 1964

—— *Revolution in China*, London 1952

Foot, Michael, *Aneurin Bevan, Vol. II*, London 1973

Foot, Rosemary, *The Wrong War: American Policy and the Dimensions of the Korean Conflict, 1950–1953*, Ithaca, New York 1985

—— *A Substitute for Victory: The Politics of Peacemaking at the Korean Armistice Talks*, Ithaca, New York 1990

Fung, S., *The Diplomacy of Imperial Retreat: Britain's South China Policy, 1924–1931*, Hong Kong 1991

Gaddis, John L., *The United States and the Origins of the Cold War, 1941–1947*, Oxford and New York 1972

—— *The Long Peace: Inquiries into the History of the Cold War*, New York 1987

Gaitskell, Hugh, 'The Search for Anglo-American Policy', *Foreign Affairs*, vol. 32, no. 4, July 1954, pp. 563–76

Galenson, Walter, ed., *Economic Growth and Structural Change in Taiwan: The Postwar Experience of the Republic of China*, London and New York 1979

Gardner, R.N., *Sterling–Dollar Diplomacy: The Origins and the Prospects of Our International Economic Order*, New York 1969

Garth, Bryant G., ed., *China's Changing Role in the World Economy*, New York 1975

Garver, John W., *Chinese-Soviet Relations, 1937–1945: The Diplomacy of Chinese Nationalism*, New York and Oxford 1988

Gilbert, Martin, *Never Despair: W.S. Churchill, Vol. VIII 1945–65*, London 1988

Gittings, John, *China Changes Face: The Road from Revolution 1949–1989*, Oxford 1989

—— *Survey of the Sino-Soviet Dispute: A Commentary and Extracts from the Recent Polemics 1963–1967*, London 1968

—— *The World and China, 1922–1972*, London 1974

Goncharov, Sergei N., John W. Lewis and Xue Litai, *Uncertain Partners: Stalin, Mao, and the Korean War*, Stanford, Calif. 1993

Gordon, Leonard, 'American Planning for Taiwan, 1942–45', *Pacific Historical Review*, vol. 37, 1968, pp. 201–47

Gordon, M.R., *Conflict and Consensus: Labour's Foreign Policy, 1914–1965*, Stanford, Calif. 1969

Gorst, A., L. Johnman and W. Scott Lucas, eds, *Contemporary British History, 1931–61: Politics and the Limits of Policy*, London 1991

Gowing, Margaret, *Independence and Deterrence: Britain and Atomic Energy 1945–52*, London 1974

Gray, Jack, *Rebellions and Revolutions: China from the 1800s to the 1980s*, Oxford 1990

Gross, Ernest A., 'Revising the Charter: Is it possible, Is it Wise?', *Foreign Affairs*, vol. 32, no. 2, January 1954, pp. 203–17

Gull, E., *British Economic Interests in the Far East*, London 1943

Gupta, P.S., *Imperialism and the British Labour Movement, 1914– 64*, London 1975

Harding, Harry and Yuan Ming, eds, *Sino-American Relations, 1945–55: A Joint Reassessment of a Critical Decade*, US 1989

Harris, Kenneth, *Attlee*, London 1982

Heberer, T., *China and its National Minorities*, New York 1989

Hao, Yufan and Zhai Zihai, 'China's Decision to Enter the Korean War: History Revisited', *China Quarterly*, no. 121, March 1990, pp. 94–116

Hennessy, Peter, *Never Again: Britain, 1945–51*, London 1992

Hinton, Harold, *China's Turbulent Quest: An Analysis of China's Foreign Policy Since 1949*, New York and London 1972

—— *Communist China in World Politics*, London 1966

Ho, Samuel P.S., *Economic Development of Taiwan 1860–1970*, New Haven 1978

Hollander, A.N., ed., *Contagious Conflict: The Impact of American Dissent on European Life*, Leiden 1973

Holzman, F.D., *International Trade under Communism – Politics and Economics*, London 1976

Hook, Brian, 'The Government of Hong Kong: Change with Tradition', *China Quarterly*, no. 95, September 1983, pp. 491–512

Hooper, Beverley, *China Stands Up: Ending the Western Presence 1948–1950*, Sydney and London 1986

Hoopes, Townsend, *The Devil and John Foster Dulles*, Boston 1973

Hou Chi-ming, *Foreign Investment and Economic Development in China, 1840–1937*, Cambridge, Mass. 1965

Houn, F.W., 'The Principles and Operational Code of Communist China's International Conduct', *Journal of Asian Studies*, vol. 27, no. 1, 1967, pp. 21–40

Howe, Christopher, 'Growth, Public Policy and Hong Kong's Economic Relations with China', *China Quarterly*, no. 95, September 1983, pp. 512–34

Howe, Stephen, *Anticolonialism in British Politics: The Left and the End of Empire, 1918–1964*, Oxford 1994

Hsu, Immanuel C.Y., *The Rise of Modern China*, New York and Oxford 1983

Hueber, Jon W., 'The Abortive Liberation of Taiwan', *China Quarterly*, no. 110, June 1987, pp. 256–75

Hughes, Emrys, *Sydney Silverman: Rebel in Parliament*, London 1969

Hungdah Chiu, ed., *China and the Question of Taiwan*, New York 1973

Immerman, Richard, ed., *John Foster Dulles and the Diplomacy of the Cold War*, Princeton 1990

Ingham, Geoffrey, *Capitalism Divided? The City and Industry in British Social Development*, London 1984

Iriye, Akira and Nagai Yonosuke, eds, *The Origins of the Cold War in Asia*, New York 1977

—— and W.I. Cohen, eds, *The United States and Japan in the Post War World*, Kentucky 1989

James, Robert Rhodes, *Anthony Eden*, London 1986

Jebb, Sir Gladwyn, 'The Free World and the United Nations', *Foreign Affairs*, vol. 31, no. 3, April 1953, pp. 382–91

Jian, Chen, *China's Road to the Korean War: The Making of the Sino-American Confrontation*, New York 1994

Johnson, Chalmers H., *Peasant Nationalism and Communist Power: The Emergence of Revolutionary China, 1937–1945*, Stanford, Calif. 1962

Kennedy, Paul, *The Realities Behind Diplomacy: Background Influence on British External Policy, 1865–1980*, London 1981

Kent, John, *British Imperial Strategy and the Origins of the Cold War, 1944–49*, London 1993

Kerr, George, *Formosa Betrayed*, Boston and London 1965

King, Frank, *A Concise Economic History of Modern China, 1840–1961*, Hong Kong 1969

—— *The Hong Kong Bank in the Period of Development and Nationalism, 1941–1984: From Regional Bank to Multinational Group*, vol. IV of *The History of the Hong Kong and Shanghai Banking Corporation*, Cambridge 1991

Koen, R.J., ed., *The China Lobby in American Politics*, New York 1971

Kolko, Joyce and Gabriel Kolko, *The Limits of Power: The World and US Foreign Power, 1945–1954*, New York 1972

Kolko, Gabriel, *The Roots of American Foreign Policy: An Analysis of Power and Purpose*, Boston 1969

—— *Confronting the Third World: United States Foreign Policy 1945–1980*, New York 1988

Kraus, Willy, *Private Business in China, Revival between Ideology and Pragmatism*, London 1989

Lall, Arthur, *How Communist China Negotiates*, New York 1968

Lardy, Nicholas, *Foreign Trade and Economic Reform in China, 1978–1990*, Cambridge 1992

LeFevour, Edward, *Western Enterprise in Late Ch'ing China: A Selective Survey of Jardine Matheson & Company's Operations, 1842–1895*, Cambridge, Mass. 1968
Levy, Richard, 'New Light on Mao: His Views on the Soviet Union's Political Economy', *China Quarterly*, no. 6, March 1975, pp. 95–118
Lichtheim, George, *Imperialism*, London 1971
Lieberthal, Kenneth G., *Revolution and Tradition in Tientsin, 1949–52*, Stanford, Calif. 1980
Lindbeck, John M., ed., *China: Management of a Revolutionary Society*, Washington 1971
Lindsay, Michael, *China and the Cold War: A Study in International Politics*, London and New York 1955
—— 'China: Report of a Visit', *International Affairs*, vol. 26, no. 1, January 1950, pp. 22–31
LittleJohn, Justin, 'China and Communism', *International Affairs*, vol. 17, no. 2, April 1951, pp. 137–51
Long, Simon, *Taiwan: China's Last Frontier*, London 1991
Louis, William Roger and Hedley Bull, eds, *The Special Relationship: Anglo-American Relations since 1945*, Oxford 1986
Lowe, Peter, *The Origins of the Korean War*, London 1986
—— *Britain and the Far East: A Survey, 1819 to the Present*, London 1981
—— and H. Moeshart, eds, *Western Interactions with Japan: Expansion, the Armed Forces and Readjustment 1859–1956*, Sandgate 1990
—— 'An Ally and a Recalcitrant General: Great Britain, Douglas MacArthur and the Korean War, 1950–1', *English Historical Review*, vol. 105, no. 416, part 2, July 1990, pp. 624–54
Luard, Evan, *Britain and China*, London 1962
—— *A History of the United Nations, 1945–55*, London 1982
—— *The United Nations: How it Worked and What it Does*, London 1979
MacDonald, Callum, *Britain and the Korean War*, Oxford 1990
—— *Korea, The War before Vietnam*, London 1986
MacFarquhar, R., *Sino-American Relations 1949–71*, Trowbridge 1972
—— and John K Fairbank, eds, *The Cambridge History of China, Vol. 14; The People's Republic, Part 1, The Emergence of Revolutionary China, 1949–65*, Cambridge 1987
Mah, Feng-hwa, *The Foreign Trade of Mainland China*, Edinburgh 1972
Mancall, Mark, ed., *Formosa Today*, New York 1964
Meisner, Maurice, *Mao's China and After: A History of the People's Republic*, New York 1977
Mendel, D., *The Politics of Formosan Nationalism*, Berkeley, Calif. 1970
Miners, N.J., *The Government and Politics of Hong Kong*, Hong Kong 1978
—— 'Plans for Constitutional Reform in Hong Kong 1946–52', *China Quarterly*, no. 107, September 1986, pp. 463–83
Morgan, Kenneth O., *The People's Peace: British History 1945–1990*, Oxford 1990
—— *Labour in Power, 1945–51*, Oxford 1984
Myers, R.H. and M.R. Petrie, eds, *The Japanese Colonial Empire, 1895–1945*, Princeton 1984
Nicholls, David, 'Fractions of Capital: The Aristocracy, the City and Industry

in the Development of Modern British Capitalism', *Social History*, vol. 13, 1988, pp 71–83

Norman, John., 'MacArthur's Blockade Proposals against Red China', *Pacific Historical Review*, vol. 26, 1957, pp. 161–217

Northedge, F.S., *Descent from Power: British Foreign Policy 1945–1973*, London 1974

Osterhammel, Jürgen, 'Imperialism in Transition: British Business and the Chinese Authorities, 1931–37', *China Quarterly*, no. 98, June 1984, pp. 260–87

Ovendale, Ritchie, *The English Speaking Alliance: Britain, the United States, the Dominions and the Cold War 1945–51*, London 1985

—— ed., *The Foreign Policy of the British Labour Government, 1945–51*, Leicester 1984

—— 'Britain, the United States, and the Recognition of Communist China', *Historical Journal*, vol. 26, no. 1, 1983, pp. 139–58

Pelling, Henry, *The Labour Governments, 1945–51*, London 1985

Pepper, Suzanne, *Civil War in China: The Political Struggle, 1945–49*, Berkeley, La. 1978

Perkins, Dwight H., ed., *China's Modern Economy in Historical Perspective*, Stanford, Calif. 1975

Pimlott, Ben, *Harold Wilson*, London 1992

Pollard, Sidney, *The Development of the British Economy, 1914–90*, London 1992

Porter, A.N. and A.J. Stockwell, eds, *British Imperial Policy and Decolonisation, 1938–64, Vol. 2, 1951–64*, London 1989

Porter, Bernard, *The Lion's Share: A Short History of British Imperialism 1850–1970*, London 1967

Porter, Brian, *Britain and the Rise of Communist China: A Study of British Attitudes 1945–1954*, London 1975

Pye, Lucien W., 'How China's Nationalism was Shanghaied', *Australian Journal of Chinese Affairs*, January 1993, pp. 107–33

Reeves, Thomas C., *The Life and Times of Joe McCarthy*, New York 1982

Riskin, Carl, *China's Political Economy: The Quest for Development since 1949*, Oxford 1987

Robinson, Thomas W. and David Shambaugh, eds, *Chinese Foreign Policy: Theory and Practice*, Oxford 1994

Rubenstein, W.D., *Men of Property: The Very Wealthy in Britain since the Industrial Revolution*, London 1981

Ryan, Mark A., *Chinese Attitudes Towards Nuclear Weapons: China and the US during the Korean War*, New York and London 1989

Schaller, Michael, *The US Crusade in China*, New York 1979

—— *The US and China in the 20th Century*, New York 1979

—— *The American Occupation of Japan: The Origins of the Cold War in Asia*, Oxford 1985

Schenk, Catherine R., *Britain and the Sterling Area: From Devaluation to Convertibility in the 1950s*, London 1994

Schram, Stuart, *Political Thought of Mao Zedong*, New York 1969

Scott, Ian, *Political Change and the Crisis of Legitimacy in Hong Kong*, Honolulu 1989

Seldon, Anthony, *Churchill's Indian Summer: The Conservative Government 1951–55*, London 1981

Shai, Aron, *Britain and China 1941–47: Imperial Momentum*, Oxford 1984
—— 'Imperialism Imprisoned. The Closure of British Firms in the People's Republic of China', *English Historical Review*, vol. 104, no. 410, January 1989, pp. 88–109
Shao, Kuo-kang, 'Zhou Enlai's Diplomacy and the Neutralisation of Indochina 1954–5', *China Quarterly*, no. 107, September 1986, pp. 483–505
Shao, Wenguang, *China, Britain and Businessmen: Political and Commercial Relations, 1949–57*, London 1991
Sheng, Michael, 'America's Lost Chance in China? A Reappraisal of Chinese Communist Policy towards the United States before 1945', *Australian Journal of Chinese Affairs*, no. 29, January 1993, pp. 135–61
—— 'Chinese Communist Policy towards the US and the Myth of the "Lost Chance", 1945–1950', *Modern Asian Studies*, vol. 28, no. 3, 1994, pp. 475–502
Shichor, Yitzhak, *The Middle East in China's Foreign Policy 1949–1977*, Cambridge 1979
Shigeto Tsuru, *Japan's Capitalism: Creative Defeat and Beyond*, Cambridge 1993
Short, Anthony, *The Communist Insurrection in Malaya, 1948–1956*, London 1977
—— *The Origins of the Vietnam War*, London 1989
Shu Guang Zhang, *Deterrence and Strategic Culture: Chinese-American Confrontations, 1949–1958*, Ithaca and London 1992
Singh, Anita Inder, *The Limits of British Influence: South Asia and Anglo-American Relationship, 1947–56*, London and New York 1993
Snow, Edgar, *Red Star Over China*, New York 1961
Steele, A.T., *The American People and China*, New York 1966
Stone, I.F., *The Hidden History of the Korean War*, New York 1969
Strange, Susan, *Sterling and British Policy: A Political Study of an International Currency in Decline*, London 1971
Stueck, William, *The Road to Confrontation: American Policy toward China and Korea 1947–1950*, Chapel Hill 1981
—— 'The Limits of Influence: British Policy and American Expansion of the War in Korea', *Pacific Historical Review*, vol. 55, no. 1, February 1986
—— 'Cold War Revisionism and the Origins of the Korean Conflict', *Pacific Historical Review*, vol. 42, no. 4, November 1974, pp. 537–60
Tang, James Tuck-Hong, *Britain's Encounter with Revolutionary China, 1949–54*, London 1992
Tang, James T.T., 'From Empire Defence to Imperial Retreat: Britain's Postwar China Policy and the Decolonization of Hong Kong', *Modern Asian Studies*, vol. 28, no. 2, 1994, pp. 317–37
Tang Tsou, *America's Failure in China 1941–1950*, Chicago 1963
Tashjean, John, E., 'Review Article: The Sino-Soviet Split: Borkenaus's Predictive Analysis 1952', *China Quarterly*, no. 94, June 1983, pp. 342–62
Thompson, T.N., 'China's Nationalisation of Foreign Firms: the Politics of Hostage Capitalism, 1949–57', Baltimore, Mass., unpublished dissertation 1979
Tsang, Steve, *Democracy Shelved: Great Britain, China and Attempts at Constitutional Reform*, Hong Kong and Oxford 1988
Tucker, Nancy Bernkopf, *Patterns in the Dust: Chinese-American Relations and the Recognition Controversy, 1949–1950*, New York 1983

Van der Wee, Herman, *Prosperity and Upheaval: The World Economy, 1945–1980*, London 1991

Waller, Michael, *The Language of Communism: A Commentary*, London 1972

Wallerstein, Immanuel, *Historical Capitalism*, London 1983

Wang Gungwu, *China and the World since 1949: The Impact of Independence, Modernity and Revolution*, New York 1977

Warner, Geoffrey, 'The Korean War', *International Affairs*, vol. 56, no. 1, January 1980, pp. 98–107

Watt, D.C., *Succeeding John Bull, America in Britain's Place 1900–1975: A Study of the Anglo-Politics in the Context of British and American Foreign Policy-Making in the Twentieth Century*, Cambridge 1984

Weathersby, Kathryn, 'The Soviet Role in the Early Phase of the Korean War: New Documentary Evidence', *Journal of American-East Asian Relations*, vol. 2, no. 4, 1993, pp. 429–32

Weiler, Peter, *Ernest Bevin*, Manchester 1993

Wesley-Smith, P., *Unequal Treaty, 1898–1997: China, Great Britain and Hong Kong's New Territories*, Oxford 1980

Whiting, Allen S., *China Crosses the Yalu: The Decision to Enter the Korean War*, New York 1960

Wilczynski, J., *The Economics and Politics of East–West Trade: A Study Between Developed Market Economies and Centrally Planned Economies in a Changing World*, London 1969

Wilson, David. A., 'China, Thailand and the Spirit of Bandung (part 1)', *China Quarterly*, no. 30, June 1967, pp. 149–70

Wilson, Dick, *A Quarter of Mankind: An Anatomy of China Today*, London 1966

—— *Mao: The People's Emperor*, London 1979

—— *Chou: The Story of Zhou EnLai 1898–1976*, London 1984

Winckler, Edwin A. and Susan Greenhalgh, eds, *Contending Approaches to the Political Economy of Taiwan*, New York 1988

Wolf, D.C., 'To Secure a Convenience: Britain's Recognition of Communist China', *Journal of Contemporary History*, vol. 18, no. 2, April 1983, pp. 299–326

Xiang, Lanxin, 'The Recognition Controversy: Anglo-American Relations in China, 1949', *Journal of Contemporary History*, vol. 27, April 1992, pp. 319–43

Yahuda, Michael, *China's Role in World Affairs*, London 1978

—— 'Review Article: The Study of China's Foreign Relations', *China Quarterly*, no. 67, September 1976, pp. 611–22

Young, A.N., *China and the Helping Hand, 1937–45*, Cambridge, Mass. 1963

Young, John, ed., *Foreign Policy of Churchill's Peacetime Administration, 1951–55*, Leicester 1988

—— *The Longman Companion to Cold War and Detente 1941–91*, London and New York 1993

—— 'Churchill, the Russians and the Western Alliance: The Three Power Conference at Bermuda, December 1953', *English Historical Review*, vol. 101, no. 401, October 1986, pp. 889–913

Younger, Kenneth, 'Public Opinion and British Foreign Policy', *International Affairs*, vol. 40, no. 1, January 1964, pp. 22–33

Yu-ming Shau, 'John Leighton Stuart and US-Chinese Communist Rapprochement in 1949. Was There Another "Lost Chance in China"', *China Quarterly*, no. 89, March 1982, pp. 74–97

Yun-yuan Yang, 'Controversies over Tibet: China versus India 1947–1949', *China Quarterly*, no. 111, September 1987, pp. 407–21

Zagoria, Donald S, *The Sino-Soviet Conflict, 1956–1961*, New York 1964

Zhai, Qiang, 'China and the Geneva Conference of 1954', *China Quarterly*, no. 129, March 1992, pp. 103–20

—— *The Dragon, the Lion and the Eagle, Chinese-British-American Relations, 1949–1958*, Kent, Ohio and London 1994

Index